THE NEW FIELD BOOK OF
NATURE ACTIVITIES
AND HOBBIES

THE NEW FIELD BOOK OF

Nature Activities
and Hobbies

WILLIAM HILLCOURT

*With 300 drawings and diagrams
and 90 photographs*

Special Project Index of 500 Activities

G. P. PUTNAM'S SONS   NEW YORK

Published simultaneously in Canada
by Longmans, Green & Company, Toronto

Revised edition of
Field Book of Nature Activities and Conservation

Fourth Impression

SBN: 399-20080-0

Library of Congress Catalog
Card Number: 78–96211

PRINTED IN THE UNITED STATES OF AMERICA

CONTENTS

PART I

GENERAL ACTIVITIES AND HCBBIES

PART II

SPECIFIC ACTIVITIES AND HOBBIES

To GRACE

and all others

who share her

curiosity, wonder, and love

of nature

CHAPTER 1

Your Personal Pursuits in Nature

NATURE has a way of speaking to all of us, of calling us out under the open sky to listen to her "various language." To the born scientist, her call is a challenge to know and to probe. To woodsmen and campers, she is a friend providing materials to use in woodcraft. To those among us who think beyond the immediate present, she is a rich environmental heritage to protect for generations to come. To each of us, she suggests things to do in the outdoors.

There is no end to the possibilities that nature presents to you! The way you accept her message and act upon it depends on yourself: your background, your temperament, your ambition.

Your interest in nature may cause you to undertake an occasional short-term nature activity in a certain field, or it may involve you in a whole string of activities in a wide variety of areas.

Sooner or later one or more of these activities may catch your wholehearted imagination and cause you to pursue them further. What started as a simple activity, perhaps casually indulged in, may then turn into a long-term nature hobby with lifelong implications and fulfillment. Such a hobby may center in a single phase of animal or plant life—birds, for instance, or mammals, or insects; flowers, ferns, or trees—or in one of the earth sciences. Or it may take in all the phases of an ecological environment—field or meadow, marsh or swamp, desert or forest, mountain or lake or ocean.

ON CHOOSING YOUR PURSUIT—The golden rule for your personal pursuit is this: *Pick a nature activity or hobby that will give you enjoyment and satisfaction.* Start out in a spirit of adventure, and make up your mind to have a good time.

There is a nature pursuit for *every taste.*

There are simple things you can do alone, complex activities that require the cooperation of many people. Nature gives you a chance for artistic or literary self-expression, for easy, leisure-time recreation or intensive study. Your early friendly familiarity with nature may become a thorough scientific knowledge that will enable you to add to our understanding of wildlife. The beauty and order of nature may open your mind to the Guiding Force behind it all.

There is a nature activity to fit *every age*.

If you are young, there is a vigorous life before you in the out-of-doors, exploring the unknown, bringing home with you the results of your excursions. Your interest in nature may possibly lead you into your life's work.

If you are an adult, a nature activity will help you get more out of life. Most people hurry through life only half alive. They have no ears to hear the songs of the birds, no eyes to see a nodding flower. They lead lives of "quiet desperation" engulfed in a thousand worries. Their tension might be broken by a vigil under the open sky, by watching the quiet, enduring things in nature.

If you have reached your prime or perhaps have entered into "senior citizenship," there are still many years of nature fun ahead of you. An interest, an absorbing hobby, is your best life insurance. Throw yourself into a nature activity to "stay alive after sixty-five," mentally as well as physically.

There is a nature hobby for *every pocketbook*.

Many nature activities require no equipment and no expense. On the other hand, if you have the money, spend it on whatever supplies you feel you need to get the most out of your favorite interest.

ON SETTING OUT— *You* require enjoyment and satisfaction from your nature activity. What does *it* require of you, in turn?

It requires *curiosity*—a mind that is open to the What? When? Where? Why? and How? of nature. Without wonder, your nature pursuit is meaningless.

It requires *keenness of observation*. You must learn to observe things not just with your eyes, but also with your ears, your nose, your palate, your fingers. All your senses come into play, including that important sixth sense, common sense, which makes it possible for you to comprehend, to figure out the meaning of what you have observed with the other five.

It requires *patience*. You cannot hurry things in nature. It takes time for the seasons to roll around, for flowers to open and trees to grow. It takes time and vigilance to follow the lives of birds and mammals and insects.

It requires *honest effort*. Your ultimate satisfaction will depend to a great extent on the effort you have made, the neatness and finish of your workmanship.

If you live up to these requirements, your rewards will be great. Your eyes will be opened to the marvels of nature, your life will be filled with rich experiences—and you will have a wonderful time!

FIELD TRIPS

The one nature activity, above all others, is the *field trip*. It is in nature that you learn nature—not by hearsay, but by actual experience and your own observations.

If you like to walk, nature walking will add a new meaning to your outdoor excursions. If walking is not as yet in your blood, take yourself out in the open whenever an opportunity presents itself. You will soon catch the bug and enjoy your outdoor hours.

Equipment for Field Trips

CLOTHING—Any sturdy outdoor clothing will do. Dress to suit the weather. Bring along a sweater or other warm covering for cool mornings and evenings, a raincoat for rainy days.

Proper footwear is of special importance. If you are accustomed to low-cut shoes, use them. Some outdoorsmen prefer 8-inch- to 10-inch-high boots. The important thing is that they be old acquaintances. New shoes may cause blisters. Break them in before you use them on a field trip.

STUDY EQUIPMENT—**Field Book**—For identification purposes, bring along a field book on the subject in which you are particularly interested—whether birds, mammals, insects, trees. The titles of recommended books will be found in each of the chapters of Part II of this book.

Notebook—In one of your pockets, carry a notebook and a pencil. Keep a record of each of your field trips—date, place, weather—and of the things you see.

Pocketknife—For almost all field trips, you will want to bring a strong pocketknife. Best model is probably the popular Scout knife with its small and large blades and variety of tools.

Special equipment—Specialized field trips require special equipment—binoculars for bird watching, insect net, plant press, and so on. Such equipment is dealt with in detail in chapters throughout the book.

TRAVEL EQUIPMENT—**Compass**—For extensive field trips, always carry a compass. With a knowledge of its use and a mental picture of the general lay of the land you are traversing, you should have no difficulty finding your way (see page 284).

Map—If the territory in which you are traveling is new to you, also bring along a topographic map, or if a printed map is not available, a sketch map containing the main features of the landscape—roads and trails, rivers and lakes, hills and ridges (see page 283).

First-aid items—Be prepared to take care of cuts and scratches with a minimum of first-aid items—a few adhesive bandages, a small piece of soap for washing a wound. Take mosquito repellent along in areas where you expect to run into insect pests.

Carrying equipment—If your equipment is rather extensive, tote it in a side bag (musette bag) on a strap over one shoulder, or in a small knapsack on your back.

EATS—For an all-day field trip, carry one or more pocket meals. Sandwiches may be your most logical choice. Or you may develop your own field ration of chocolate bits, raisins, nuts.

A canteen of drinking water will prove a blessing if you aren't certain of finding potable water in the field.

Where? And When?

WHERE?—Nature, like charity, begins at home. From there, you can expand your horizons in all directions.

Your backyard—The distance of your field trip is immaterial. Many famed naturalists—Jean Henri Fabre, Gregor Mendel, and others—never went beyond their own immediate environment. In your own backyard or your garden there may be the ingredients for a lifetime's study of insects and plants, birds, and small mammals.

Specific areas—The investigation and natural history survey of a local park, a campsite, the school grounds may be of great value to yourself and to others. The next step is to get out into the whole wide environment that is your year-in year-out living arena to find out about its plantlife-wildlife communities—its ecological systems or ecosystems (from Greek *oikos*, home or living place)—its fields and woods, marshes and swamps, streams, lakes, or ocean shore. You may want to spend your time in one specific part of this environment—like Henry David Thoreau at Walden Pond—or make your whole parish or county your theater of operation—like Gilbert White in his Selborne.

Your nature travels—With modern transportation, you have a chance to travel to faraway places. By automobile or train, ship or plane, the whole country and our whole world can become your field. You can travel to a certain spot of unusual features—like John Muir into California redwood territory—or circumnavigate the globe in search of knowledge, following in the wake of the *Beagle* that carried Charles Darwin around the world.

WHEN?—**Time of year**—If you are interested in a certain field of nature, you must watch the time of the year. If all of nature is your oyster, there is no closed season for your activities.

SPRING is ushered in by the chorus of peepers. It is the time of awakening life—of early flowers and bursting buds, of returning birds, of nest building and young animals.

During SUMMER, the long drowsy days hum with the song of the cicada in green trees and wind over flowering meadows. When twilight falls, animals roam through woods and over fields, katydids tune up their fiddles, and fireflies flash in the darkness.

FALL brings a brilliant display of dying leaves and a vast array of autumn flowers. Bird visitors leave for the south; there is the honking at night of high-flying wedges of wild geese. It is a season of seeds and fruits, of nature getting ready for its winter sleep.

Many people interested in nature prefer their activities to be solitary and to concentrate on individual pursuits.

In WINTER the trees stand like dark silhouettes against the sky. In the north, snow covers the ground, its smooth surface broken only by the hieroglyphics of tracks of animals and birds. Plants are at rest, ready to be called back to active life when the lengthening days return.

Time of day—Unless you are a professional naturalist or a retired businessman, you will have to fit your nature activities into your daily work schedule, giving them whatever time you can manage. The best way—and probably the only way—of finding that time is by careful planning. Set aside some minutes in the morning, and some hours on definite evenings during the week. Plan to use certain weekend hours for field trips or intensive work at home.

DAWN—If your main interests are in the fields of bird and animal life, early morning, around dawn, is your best time of day. Those are the hours when the bird chorus is at its loudest, and when most mammals are abroad.

For many other nature activities, it pays to be an early riser. The air is bracing, the smell of the good earth stimulating. There is a feeling of expectancy all around you, as if all nature were waiting for the coming of the new day. Then the first rosy blush in the eastern sky, fading stars overhead, and finally a golden sun above a far horizon. You haven't experienced nature at her best until you know the magic of the dawn.

EVENING AND NIGHT—From early twilight to full darkness is your next best time of day for studying the life of wild animals.

You hear the rustle of their footfalls among dry leaves. You can watch them as they come to their watering places. As darkness falls, bats sweep overhead and night-flying insects appear; brilliant-hued moths are attracted to your sugaring places. And high above you, the constellations of the season form their ageless patterns.

DAYTIME—The height of day is your best time if your nature interests involve flowers and trees, insects and water life. For nature photography, sunlight is preferable to any of its weak imitations.

Field Techniques

The field techniques for specific phases of nature are described in the chapters of Part II of this book. In all cases, a few simple rules apply:

Be methodical.—Decide in advance what you want to do and what you expect to accomplish. Your earliest field trips may be reconnaissance expeditions to learn the lay of the land and to discover its wildlife communities. When this job has been done, be specific: Lay out a plan of action for each field trip, and bring along the necessary equipment and note-taking material.

Be leisurely.—You are not out to break records but to discover and observe. You can do this only if you take your time. Get to your starting point quickly, then slow down. Get into the habit of walking Indian style—gliding, rather than striding, with a smooth rhythmic movement of the whole body, arms hanging loosely at your sides.

Be quiet.—Avoid unnecessary noise—talking, stepping on dry twigs, or crunching gravel. You will be quietest if you travel alone. There are times when that is the only way you can gain your objective. But you will probably enjoy your field experience more if you have with you a congenial companion—a good friend, a sweetheart, or your life partner. Bring such a companion, if you like, but be certain that he or she shares your nature interest and knows when to speak and, more important, when to fall quiet. Four eyes are better than two, but four feet make more noise than two. A companion gabbing at the wrong time may mean the difference between seeing the bird or animal you came for and missing it altogether.

Be alert.—Walk with all senses keen. Scan the landscape around you, from your immediate surroundings to the farthest distance. Stop completely from time to time to listen, moving your head around to find out from what direction sounds come.

Be inquisitive.—The way to find things is to look for them. A movement in the underbrush—was it an animal? Investigate. A bird flies up suddenly—from its nest? Locate it. A flat rock on the ground—what life does it hide? Turn it over. A purple flower among the black-eyed susans—which is it? Find out.

RECORDING YOUR FINDINGS
Nature Notes

The moment you set out on a nature activity, start your nature notes. Get into the habit of jotting down your observations and your thoughts about nature. They will prove of special value if the nature activity should eventually turn into a nature hobby.

You may think such notes unimportant. Well, perhaps they are, but maybe not. Some of our richest treasures in the whole field of nature have come from men who observed and made a record of their observations—men like Gilbert White, Henry David Thoreau, John Muir, William Henry Hudson, John Burroughs, Jean Henri Fabre, Richard Jefferies, and in our own day, Donald Culross Peattie and Edwin W. Teale. They were unknowns at first, but their work has added immeasurably to our understanding of nature.

NOTEBOOKS—Many types of notebooks have been used in the past; countless others will be used in the future. Pick the kind that fits your own idea and style.

Many naturalists use a small, pocket-sized booklet, 3 by 5 inches or slightly larger, for their entries, transferring them afterward into larger books. Others like the loose-leaf method. They write their observations of each phenomenon on a single page, afterward taking out the sheets and filing them according to subjects.

For special research, it often pays to have pages made up with headings and columns that make it easy to insert the findings. Such pages may be mimeographed, photo-offset, or printed at a very reasonable price.

NOTE TAKING—The most important point in your note taking is that you *write down what you see*. The literary style matters little as long as your notes are correct, exact, and clear. Several approaches are feasible.

Records—Keep a record of each field trip you take—of date, route, destination, weather, fauna and flora observed. Such records supply the minimum data for your work.

Lists—Get into the habit of listing the specimens you see of any specific field of nature in which you are particularly interested—whether birds or other animals, flowers or trees. You can do this in your notebook or in the margin of the field guide you are using, next to the description of the specimens.

Logs—Expand your field trip records to include detailed accounts of what you see. Add sketches, maps of territory covered, photographs.

Diaries—Many naturalists have kept copious diaries of their comings and goings, their observations and musings. Try it. It may prove the method that suits you best.

Observations—The most important notes you can make are the detailed descriptions of observations of the activities and behavior of wildlife. Although much is known about birds, mammals, reptiles, insects, and so on, much is still obscure. Your own exact observations may cast a new light on natural phenomena and may become accepted facts when corroborated by the findings of other naturalists.

Nature Writing

Poets of all ages, from King Solomon through Shakespeare to the present day, have extolled the beauty of nature. Imaginative fiction writers have written tales about all kinds of animals. Nonfiction writers have told of their experiences in nature.

If you combine a deep interest in nature with a serious ambition to become a writer, you will find in nature a never-ending source of inspiration and subject matter. Before taking up nature writing, you will find it to your advantage to study what has been done in the past and what is being published today.

Juvenile Nature Writing—Thousands of titles of nature books for children are published every year. A great number of them depend on a single, simple idea. Many others base their appeal mainly on elaborate and often beautiful artwork.

Some writers of juvenile nature books take after Aesop in his *Fables* and use animals for heroes and villains; others follow in the footsteps of Hans Christian Andersen, who used plants for characters in some of his lesser-known *Fairy Tales*. Still others simply relate what they have seen in nature. All three approaches seem to have a great attraction for children of all ages.

Adult Nature Writing—In nature writing for adults, there has been a great shift in taste over recent years. A few decades ago, adult best sellers in the nature field were such books as Ernest Thompson Seton's *Wild Animals I Have Known*, Rudyard Kipling's *Jungle Books*, and Jack London's *The Call of the Wild*. In these books the animals felt and acted and spoke like human beings.

In today's nature writing this anthropomorphic approach (from Greek *anthrop + morphos*, of human form) is generally frowned on. Readers like their nature stories straight and prefer the nonfiction tale describing the relationship between animals and human beings, such as Joy Adamson's *Born Free* (about a lioness), Sterling North's *Rascal* (a raccoon), Gavin Maxwell's *Ring of Bright Water* (an otter).

Nature Sketching

Your nature notes will be greatly enhanced if you are able to accompany them with simple sketches.

If you have already done life drawing, the step to nature drawing is comparatively simple. If drawing is a new venture for you, get hold of a good book on nature sketching, obtain the help of a local artist, and go to work. You may never become a John Audubon or a Roger Tory Peterson, a Livingston Bull or a Georgia O'Keeffe—but you can try!

In drawing mammals, use a square or a rectangle as your basic pattern. The egg is the starting pattern in bird drawing. When drawing a tree, draw it the way it grows: trunk first, major branches, small branches, leaf masses.

BOOKS ON ANIMAL SKETCHING—Ken Hultgren, *Art of Animal Drawing*. New York, McGraw-Hill Book Co.

Jack Haum, *How to Draw Animals*. New York, Grosset and Dunlap.

Arthur Zaidenberg, *Drawing Wild Animals*. (New York, World Publishing Company.) *How to Draw Birds, Fish & Reptiles. How to Draw Butterflies, Bees & Beetles. How to Draw Flowers, Fruit & Vegetables*. New York, all, Abelard-Schuman.

Victor Perard, *Drawing Animals. Drawing Flowers. Drawing Trees*. New York, Pitman Publishing Corporation.

To a great extent, nature drawing—any drawing, for that matter—is a question of courage. Observe, then put on paper what you see, to the best of your ability. Draw without hesitation; make long, confident lines. Try to catch the feeling of your subject. Don't aim for details in the beginning; beginners see too many of them and try to get them all in. To prevent this common fault, close your eyes to narrow slits, and look out from under the lids. In this way details are blurred, and you see your subject as masses of light and shadow.

It is, of course, not possible here to go very deeply into the techniques of nature sketching, but a few hints may prove helpful:

Birds—Think of the egg from which the bird came. The general body shape of the adult bird is almost the same. Begin your sketch by suggesting this egg-shape—rounded or lengthened, depending on the bird you are sketching. Add head, tail, legs. Then indicate the feathers—not individual feathers, but feather masses. The feathers are not scattered over a bird, but are arranged in a well-defined pattern.

Animals—Practice side views until you can do them readily, then try other views. For side views of long-legged animals—deer, elk, moose—start with a square. One top corner is the shoulder, the other the rump; one bottom corner is the forefoot, the other the hind foot. Draw in two circles, one to indicate the ribs, the other the hindquarters. Connect them, and you have the general basis for your drawing. For side views of short-legged animals begin with a rectangle or a parallelogram of the proper proportions, add the two circles, and go on from there.

In drawing an animal in motion, remember that the four legs move independently of one another. Study the action of walking and running animals until you get the rhythm right.

Fish—Probably the easiest creatures to draw. First the long arc of the back, then the usually flatter arc of the belly. Fins and tail—finally the details of gills and head.

Insects—Insects are generally sketched from the top. Keep in mind that insects, like most other creatures, are bilaterally symmetrical: One side of the body is a mirror picture of the other. This suggests your procedure: Draw one half of the body, then copy this for the other half.

Flowers—The advantage in drawing flowers is that they keep their pose. You can study them from all angles and arrange them for best effects. Flower sketching calls for a certain daintiness in execution to catch the personality of your models. Draw the flower heads first, then add the leaves to complete your composition.

Trees—Draw a tree the way it grows—trunk first, then sweep up into the branches. Catch the outline that shows its individuality—whether slender, vase-shaped, or whatever it happens to be. Finally, the foliage. Keep in mind that large branches govern the arrangement of the leaves, each major branch has its own leaf mass. The trick is to show these leaf masses in their various planes, with highlights and shadows. A tree's foliage is never still; try to get the sensation of restlessness into your sketches by using fast-moving, vivacious lines.

NATURE PHOTOGRAPHY

The camera is taking a place of ever increasing importance in all nature work. Nature photographs are giving us a deeper understanding of all phases of wildlife and of the problems involved in conserving our natural resources for future generations.

Nature photography has all the thrills of the hunt, but leaves the game—whether small or large—for others to enjoy.

BOOKS ON NATURE PHOTOGRAPHY—Edna Bennett, *Nature Photography*. Philadelphia, Chilton Book Company.

Russ Kine, *Complete Book of Nature Photography*. Cranbury, N.J., A. S. Barnes & Company.

David Linton, *Photographing Nature*. New York, Doubleday & Company.

Percy Morris, *Nature Photography Round the Year*. New York, Appleton-Century-Crofts.

Your Approach to Nature Photography

Why photograph?—Before you set out on nature photography, make up your mind in regard to the results you expect to achieve. The selection of equipment depends on your decision.

Are you interested mainly in a personal record of your nature pursuits? Almost any camera will do—from the cheapest snapshot camera to the most expensive miniature camera.

Do you want to use your photographs as the basis for a scientific study? No snapshot camera will serve the purpose, but a medium-priced camera may, depending on your requirements.

Do you expect to show your photographs to a larger audience than your immediate family, and possibly use them for educational work? In that case, you need to investigate the idea of taking color slides or movies.

Do you hope to have nature photography assist you in earning money for the further pursuit of your nature hobbies? Is it your ambition to see your nature photographs occupy honored positions in national exhibitions? Then buy the kind of equipment that will produce clear, crisp enlargements of professional quality, and learn to use it to the limit of its capacity.

MARKETS FOR NATURE PHOTOGRAPHY—The nature magazines listed on page 29 are in the market for suitable photographs.
Photographic section, *The Writer's Market*. Writer's Digest, Cincinnati, Ohio.

ANNUAL SALONS OF NATURE PHOTOGRAPHS—Among others: Buffalo Museum of Science, Buffalo, New York. Kentucky Society of Natural History, University of Louisville, Louisville, Kentucky. Natural History Society of Maryland, Baltimore Museum of Art, Baltimore, Maryland. Chicago Natural History Museum, Chicago, Illinois. Cranbrook Institute of Science, Bloomfield Hills, Michigan. Write for particulars.

What do you intend to photograph?—Every season of the year presents a multitude of opportunities for outstanding nature photography.

You may like the idea of becoming a free lancer in all of nature, photographing whatever comes your way of special interest and human appeal. On the other hand, there may be a specific subject in which you want to specialize.

Your decision in this respect also will have a direct bearing on the equipment you need to purchase. You will readily realize that the equipment required for ultra close-up insect photographs will have to be somewhat different from the kind that you can get along with in photographing tree silhouettes.

The most profitable procedure, therefore, before you buy your equipment, is to check the general suggestions presented in the following pages, and to add to them the recommendations contained in the chapter of this book that treats the subject you want to cover.

¶ *Tip*—Think both black-and-white and color. This may mean two cameras or a camera with interchangeable film magazines.

Working with others—Instead of learning nature photography solely "by guess and by golly," learn from the experience of others as well.

Very possibly, a photographic club already exists in your locality. Find out from your photographic dealer how to join it.

SOCIETY—Photographic Society of America, Nature Division. Headquarters: 2005 Walnut Street, Philadelphia, Pennsylvania 19103. Periodical: *PSA Journal*.

If your specialty is motion pictures, join a club or society that deals with your subject. Get the added benefit of direct advice from the technicians of the national headquarters of this association.

SOCIETY—Photographic Society of America, Motion Picture Division. (For address, see above.)

Stills

Stills in black-and-white and color transparencies have the greatest variety of uses, from general study material and corroboration of observations made in the field to printed reproductions and visual aids.

CAMERAS AND LENSES—Cameras—whether for general purposes or for nature work—may be considered in four main categories:

Fixed-focus cameras—Inexpensive, fixed-focus, snapshot cameras —box and folding types—have only limited use in nature photography. They can be used "as is" mainly for taking record shots of general landscape features, geological formations, trees, and other large subjects.

The fixed focus of these cameras ensures sharpness within the focusing range from infinity to 3 or 4 feet. The camera needs only to be set for proper exposure. In adjustable cameras this is done by adjusting lens opening and shutter speed to fit the light conditions. No adjustments are necessary when you use an automatic camera of the Instamatic type. In this a built-in photoelectric cell does the job.

By slipping a close-up lens over the fixed-focus camera's regular lens, you can get closer to an object and in this way get a larger image on the film. Close-up lenses come in different strengths, or powers, such as $1+$, $2+$, and $3+$. The higher the number, the closer you can get to the subject. By combining the $2+$ and the $3+$ close-up lenses, you arrive at a $5+$ close-up lens which, with one of the better snapshot cameras, permits you to photograph a field $4\frac{3}{4}$ inches square from a distance of $7\frac{1}{2}$ inches.

When using these close-up lenses, you must do the focusing by measuring distances and fields according to tables that accompany the lenses.

BOOK—*How to Make Good Pictures.* Eastman Kodak Company, Rochester, New York 14650.

Reflex cameras—Single-lens reflex—In a single-lens reflex camera —Pentax, Leicaflex, Contaflex, Kodak Retina Reflex—you look through a hood at a ground glass onto which an image of the object as seen by the camera is reflected from a mirror, right side up. You focus the object on ground glass to the desired depth of field and compose the picture to suit your fancy. As you press the shutter release, the reflex mirror flips out of the way, and the film is exposed.

A number of high-grade single-lens reflex cameras have built-in electronic light meters that indicate the amount of light that enters through the lens, and make exact exposures possible.

The "standard" lens with the usual focal length of 50 mm is interchangeable with wide-angle lenses (28 and 35 mm focal lengths) that can be used for close-up photography, and with telephoto lenses of 85 (or 90), 105, 135, 200, 280 (or 300), 400, 600, 800, and 1000 mm focal lengths that bring distant objects close and enlarge close-up objects.

¶ *Tip*—Instead of carrying several telephoto lenses, you may decide on a single zoom lens that embraces the focal lengths of the more commonly used telephoto lenses.

For close-ups to full size (1:1 ratio), and for extreme close-ups (macrophotography: defined as photography, using the camera lens in a 15:1 ratio), you have the choice of bellows attachments and extension tubes—metal tubes of varying lengths that screw in between lens and camera body. These tubes can be used singly or in combination.

¶ *Tip*—Some manufacturers of single-lens reflex cameras offer "macro lenses" by which it is possible to photograph an object directly to life size (1:1) without accessories.

Single-lens reflex cameras have speeds to $^1/_{1000}$ second. The small cameras use 35-mm film and produce 1-by-1½-inch black-and-white negatives or color transparencies. The small negatives make enlarged prints necessary. The transparencies, in 2-by-2-inch slide mounts, can be projected to large size.

The larger-size Hasselblad camera uses roll film to give 2¼-by-2¼-inch negatives or 2-by-2-inch superslides.

BOOK—Bates, *Single Lens Reflex Manual*. Hastings-on-Hudson, New York, Morgan & Morgan.

Twin-lens reflex cameras—In a twin-lens reflex camera—Rolleiflex, Exacta 66, Mamiyaflex type—the upper lens forms an image of the object, reversed from right to left, for focusing on a ground glass. The lower lens exposes the film. The two lenses, about 2 or more inches apart, cover the same area except when focusing is done at short distances.

In most twin-lens reflex cameras, lenses are not interchangeable. This, of course, precludes the use of telephoto lenses.

For close-ups, photographed closer than 3 feet, built-in synchronized parallax correction and close-up lenses are required.

Twin-lens reflex cameras, with speeds up to $^1/_{1000}$ second, use roll films for making 2¼-by-2¼-inch negatives.

BOOK—Pearlman, *Rollei Manual*. Hastings-on-Hudson, New York, Morgan & Morgan.

Range-finder cameras—The range-finder miniature cameras—Leica, Contax, Kodak Retina type—are, as the name implies, compact and easy to carry. For general purposes, you focus this kind of camera through its coupled range finder. For more exact composition and determination of depth of field, you can use the camera in conjunction with a reflex housing that provides knife-sharp focusing on ground glass.

For long-distance shots, the "standard" lens can be replaced, as in single-lens reflex cameras, with telephoto lenses of varying lengths.

For close-ups and extreme close-ups, bellows and extension tubes are available.

Range-finder miniature cameras have speeds up to $^1/_{1000}$ second. They use 35-mm film, black-and-white and color.

BOOK—Willard D. Morgan, *Leica Manual*. Hastings-on-Hudson, New York, Morgan & Morgan.

View cameras—Press and professional—The view cameras—Graphic, Linhof press, and professional view types—have a ground-

Single-lens reflex camera (below) is versatile for nature.

Honeywell Pentax Spotmatic

Range-finder camera (below) set the 35 mm trend in photography.

Leica M4

Professional View camera makes large-size negatives possible.

Calumet 4 x 5 View Camera

Kodak Instamatic 814

Fixed-focus camera is suitable when used with close-up lenses.

Rolleiflex T-L-R

Twin-lens reflex camera will provide 2¼- by 2¼-inch negatives.

View camera—Press (below).

Crown Graphic 4 x 5

glass back on which the image of the object appears, upside down. When the object is focused, the ground glass is replaced with a film holder, and the exposure is made.

View cameras are provided with swinging and tilting, rising and shifting features. The swing-back is used to control perspective and parallelism, and to rectify distortions, such as those that occur in photographing trees which, taken from a low angle with the ordinary camera, would look as if they were falling backwards. The tilting lens brings the object into sharp focus. Raising and lowering and shifting the front sideways simplify the job of composition.

For long-distance shots, the view camera can be provided with telephoto lenses.

By using the normal lens and extending the double bellows, you can take a full-size shot (1:1 ratio) of a small object. The magnifying power of the lens can be increased in some of these cameras with the help of extension tubes and spacers.

View cameras have speeds up to $1/1000$ second. They use $2^1/_4$-by-$3^1/_4$-, $3^1/_4$-by-$4^1/_4$- or 4-by-5-inch or even larger cut film or film packs. Because of the large negatives, contact prints rather than the far more expensive enlargements will usually do.

BOOK—*Camera Techniques for Professional Photographers*. Eastman Kodak Company, Rochester, New York 14650.

OTHER EQUIPMENT—Tripod—For most nature photography, you need a steady tripod. Pick a telescoping model that will make it possible for you to set it at a low height, as well as at 5 feet. A tilting head or a ball-and-socket joint greatly simplifies its use.

Light meter—A light meter is indispensable—unless your camera has a built-in meter. You may be able to get along without it for average outdoor photography by using the exposure guides that come with the various films. But you will need it for close-ups and color photography.

Flash equipment—For daylight photography in poor light and for night photography, you may want to obtain flash equipment. For best results, purchase the flash equipment—electronic or flashbulb—specifically designed for your camera.

FILMS—Your selection of films depends on your objects and the light conditions under which they are to be photographed.

Black-and-white films—*Color sensitivity—*In the early days of photography, negative material was *orthochromatic*—sensitive to all colors except red. The result was that a deep blue sky photographed pure white, and orange flowers solid black. By adding dyes to the emulsion, film manufacturers have succeeded in developing *panchromatic* films that are sensitive to all colors and correctly express the relative brilliance of colors in nature.

Although some orthocromatic films are still available for certain types of photography, practically all nature photography depends upon panchromatic films to render true tonal values in black-and-white negatives.

¶ *Tips*—An outdoor shot can often be enhanced by the use of a *filter*. A medium-yellow filter (No. 8–K2) will darken a sky background to obtain cloud effects, lighten green foliage, and brighten red and yellow objects. A deep-yellow filter (No. 15–G) will darken the sky even more, reduce distant haze, and improve the texture of sunlit outdoor objects; it is indispensable for use with telephoto lenses. A red filter (No. 25–A) will lighten anything red, darken green foliage, and render a blue sky nearly black. A yellow-green filter (No. 11–X1) will provide a correct tonal rendition of multicolored objects, such as flowers and butterflies.

Speed—Film speeds are indicated by ASA numbers (named for American Standards Association). The higher the ASA number, the faster the film.

Stationary objects can be photographed to best advantage with a slow film—ASA 32. Such a film gives an extremely fine-grained negative suitable for great enlargement.

Fast-moving objects and objects photographed under poor light conditions require a faster film—ASA 125 or faster.

Color—Color slides are strong competitors of movies for visual instruction and entertainment. With advanced printing processes, color transparencies have also become of high importance in magazine and book illustration. The vast majority of color photographs for projection and reproduction is made with 35-mm cameras. Color film is available for larger-size cameras as well, in rolls and sheet form.

Color films, produced by various manufacturers, come under many different names with many different speeds: ASA 25, 50, 64, 100, 200, 400. Pick the film whose color values and speed best serve your purpose.

Some of these films come in two types: Daylight Type for use outdoors or with blue flash, Tungsten Type for use under artificial light.

¶ *Tip*—Use a skylight filter (No. 1A) to reduce the bluishness in shots of distant landscapes and in photographs taken in open shade or on a heavily overcast day. A polarizing screen will darken a clear blue sky, emphasize the color of foliage, and cut down unwanted reflections.

Nature Movies

Taking nature movies is considerably more difficult than shooting nature stills. It takes far more planning, more skill in approaching wildlife, and imagination in editing the scenes into a unified whole. But the result is often breathtaking, especially when the film is shot in color.

Before starting on movies, decide on your aims. Is your main purpose to produce shots that will please your family and friends, or is it your hope to reach a larger audience?

In the first case, movies on a film width of 8 mm will do. They can be successfully projected in your living room.

But if you want to show your efforts before a large audience, you will have to use 16-mm film for a larger projection image.

If you intend to make talkies rather than silent films, consider this point carefully before purchasing your camera and include sound equipment in your budget.

BOOK—*How to Make Good Movies*. Eastman Kodak Company, Rochester, New York 14650.

8-MM CAMERAS AND LENSES—Some 8-mm cameras use 25-foot rolls of 16-mm-wide film which, after exposure, is split into 8-mm to a length of 50 feet. Others take cartridges of 50 feet "super 8" film that has an image area 52 percent larger than the regular 8-mm—therefore projects bigger, brighter, and sharper pictures.

The more modern 8-mm cameras have built-in electronic light meters that completely eliminate the guesswork of correct exposure. Most of them shoot at a pre-set speed of 18 frames per second (fps): $1/40$ second to each frame. Some permit slow motion at 32 fps.

Fixed-focus cameras—Fixed-focus 8-mm cameras belong in the "snapshot" class. They usually come with 13-mm ($\frac{1}{2}$-inch) focal-length lenses, fixed at 15 feet. In bright sunlight, this setting will give you sharp focus from infinity to about $3\frac{1}{2}$ feet.

For close-ups, fixed-focus cameras can be provided with close-up lenses. These are available in three powers: $1+$, $2+$, and $3+$. The $3+$ close-up lens makes it possible to get within $12\frac{3}{4}$ inches of the object.

Zoom-lens cameras—Certain types of 8-mm cameras come with zoom lenses. These take the place of a battery of lenses to provide wide-angle, normal, and telephoto shots. When using a zoom lens, you look through the viewfinder, adjust the lens to frame the object, then shoot.

A few of these zoom-lens cameras permit you to focus to within 1 inch of the object, for a filming field of 24 mm by 18 mm—macrophotography without extra lenses, bellows, or extension tubes.

16-MM CAMERAS AND LENSES—In the better kind of 16-mm movie cameras—Cine Kodak Special, Bolex, B & H type—the "standard" lens of 25 mm (1 inch) can be replaced with any of several telephoto lenses—50, 63, 75, 86, 100 (102), 120, 150 (152), and others.

In some cameras these interchangeable lenses are fitted directly into a standard mount; others come with turret mounts for quick changes from one of three lenses to another. Zoom lenses are also available.

The best 16-mm cameras can be set at varying film speeds of 24, 32, 48, and even 64 frames per second. Cameras with single-frame control make possible time-lapse photography in which the opening of a tree bud or a flower can be photographed to take only a few seconds.

Professional types of 16-mm cameras come with through-the-lens reflex viewing, constant-speed electric motor, and film rewind to permit double exposure, superimposition, and other special effects.

8- mm movie camera of the "instamatic" type uses super 8 film cartridges. It is suitable for general nature photography and, with special lenses, will permit distant shots as well as close-ups.

Kodak Instamatic M30

8- mm movie camera of a more sophisticated nature —and consequently more expensive—has zoom lens for shooting long and medium shots and for taking close-ups within one inch of the subject.

Bolex 155 Super

Kodak K-100

16- mm movie camera is the preferred camera for shooting movies to be shown to large audiences. Some 16 mm cameras are easy to use, others have features that require great skill in using to advantage.

Bolex H-16 Rex 5

16- mm movie camera for semiprofessional use may have turret mounts with a large selection of lenses, full-speed range, extra long-run film magazine, and battery packs that can be recharged.

OTHER EQUIPMENT—Tripod—A few moviemakers get along without a tripod—their movies show it! There are occasions when you have to shoot without one, but for perfect shots, you do need a tripod. Get a model with sturdy, telescoping legs and with a tilting and panoraming head—not that you will ever want to panoram, but so that you will be able to swing the camera easily into position.

Light meter—By all means get a light meter, unless the camera has its own built-in electronic meter. Although the exposure guides packed with each roll or magazine of motion picture film are adequate for ordinary amateur shots, they do not have the answer for all the exposure problems you will run up against in nature photography. The meter has.

FILMS—Black-and-white films for movies, ranging from speeds of ASA 50 to 160, are still on the market, but the comparatively low cost of color films has turned almost all amateurs to color.

Color films come in two types: Daylight Type for outdoor shooting and Type A for shooting in artificial light. They range in speeds: ASA 25, 40, 50, 100, and 200.

¶ *Tip—*If it is necessary for you to shift repeatedly from outdoor to indoor shots, use Type A or Tungsten Type throughout, with conversion filter (No. 85) when shooting in the open.

YOUR NATURE COLLECTION

A nature collection is far more than a conglomeration of inanimate objects. It is a record of your nature activities, supplementing your nature notes, sketches, and photographs. In addition, each item is a reminder of interesting hours spent in the field, and also, often, of pleasant moments passed at home preparing the specimen for inclusion in your collection.

You will want to be proud of your nature collection. You will be if it is well developed and well kept. A great portion of this *Field Book* is devoted to the methods involved in making collections. If you follow the suggestions, you will have a collection of professional quality.

Equipment and Supplies

Each type of collecting requires its own type of equipment. You will get most out of your hobby if you make the equipment yourself. You will find detailed suggestions for doing so in the chapter of this book dealing with your nature specialty.

Certain equipment and supplies cannot be made at home. Some of these may be improvised from materials found in neighborhood shops. The rest may be purchased from biological and scientific supply houses.

For local supply houses, check the yellow pages of your telephone book or get the information from a local biology teacher. When writing to supply houses with mail order distribution for information or catalogs, specify your subject and indicate the items in which you are interested.

SUPPLY HOUSES—Ward's Natural Science Establishment, Inc., P.O. Box 1712, Rochester, New York 14603; P.O. Box 1749, Monterey, California 93940.

General Biological Supply House, Inc. (Turtox Products), 8200 South Hoyne Avenue, Chicago, Illinois 60620.

Central Scientific Company (Cenco), 2600 Kostnew Avenue, Chicago, Illinois 60623.

Cambosco Scientific Company, 342 Western Avenue, Boston, Massachusetts 02135.

Carolina Biological Supply Company, Burlington, North Carolina 27215; Gladstone, Oregon 97027.

Connecticut Valley Biological Supply Company, Valley Road, Southampton, Massachusetts 01073.

J. R. Schettle Biologicals, P.O. Box 184, Stillwater, Minnesota 55082.

Your Nature Workshop

If it is at all possible, set aside a separate room in your home for a nature workshop. The great advantage in doing this is that you can leave whatever project you are working on spread out on table and desk without worrying about having it disturbed.

WORKSHOP EQUIPMENT—**Worktable**—Whether you can manage a separate nature shop or must use a corner of the living room, the main feature of your layout will be your worktable. Select one of a size to fit the job you are doing. It can be comparatively small if you specialize in insects, but you need plenty of elbow room for preparing a herbarium. For some jobs, you will be most comfortable seated; for other work, you will find standing more efficient. Pick your table height accordingly.

Cabinet—A cabinet for equipment and supplies is the next requirement. Provide it with a lock if any of your supplies contain poisons, such as the cyanide jars used in insect collecting.

Storage—Storage facilities should be developed to suit your specific needs. For some collections, cabinets with shelves are suitable. For others, drawers are preferable. Design your storage units to a standard pattern so that more can be added as needed. Make doors and drawers as airtight as possible to exclude insect pests.

Bookshelf—And then, of course, you need a bookshelf for your technical books, notebooks, and scientific periodicals.

HELPS IN YOUR NATURE PURSUITS

"No man is an iland, intire of it selfe . . ." You do not stand alone. The work of naturalists before you is available to you, and many institutions and associations are ready to welcome you and help you.

Your Nature Library

BOOKS—There are nature books by the thousands. Choose those that will be of greatest value in your work.

Your minimum needs—To get a satisfactory experience out of any phase of nature, you need *two good books* in that field: a book that will give you a basic knowledge of your specialty, and a field book for the identification of specimens.

Throughout the following chapters, titles of such books are given. An earnest attempt has been made to include only titles that are in print.

Other books—You would hardly stop with two books. From that small start, your nature library will grow by leaps and bounds as your interest increases.

In most instances, your first two books will contain bibilographies that will lead you on to others.

Check with your local library and find out what books it has in the field in which you are interested. Some of those books may appeal to you so much that you will want to own them. If they are still in print, you can purchase them through your regular bookstore. If they are out of print, a secondhand bookstore or a "book hunter" may be able to locate them for you.

At the same time, keep your eyes open for new books in the book columns of your newspaper and in the book section of nature periodicals.

PAMPHLETS—Our federal government publishes a great number of pamphlets on wildlife and plant life of interest to naturalists throughout the country.

PAMPHLET CATALOGS—Write to Superintendent of Documents, U.S. Government Printing Office, Washington, D.C. 20402, and request price lists of government publications: PL21, *Fish and Wildlife*; PL41, *Insects*; PL44, *Plants*; PL43, *Forestry*; PL15, *Geology*; PL48, *Weather, Astronomy, and Meteorology*. From these price lists, order the pamphlets you desire.

In addition to the federal government, your own state has probably published pamphlets on your local fauna and flora and mineral resources, and on problems connected with their protection and management.

Write to the agencies involved for a list of their publications, and send for those that relate to your interests.

ADDRESSES—State Department of Conservation, your state capital.
State Fish and Game Commission, your state capital.
State Museum, your state capital.
State Agricultural Extension Service, your state agricultural college.

PERIODICALS—In addition to the specialized bulletins of scientific associations, a number of excellent nature periodicals aimed at a wider audience are published regularly. They pick their subjects from the whole wide field of nature and are profusely illustrated, mostly with photographs.

Besides providing you with enjoyable reading and excellent pictures, each of these magazines will help you to keep up with new discoveries, new methods of studying nature, and new books.

PERIODICALS—*Natural History* (adults) and *Junior Natural History* (juvenile). American Museum of Natural History, Central Park West at Eighty-seventh Street, New York, New York 10024.

Audubon Magazine. National Audubon Society, 1130 Fifth Avenue, New York, New York 10028.

Nature and Science. Natural History Press, Garden City, New York 11531.

Outdoors Illustrated. Audubon Society of Canada, 177 Jarvis Street, Toronto 2, Ontario, Canada.

Hobbies. Buffalo Museum of Science. Humboldt Park, Buffalo, New York 14205.

National Wildlife (adult) and *Ranger Rick's Nature Magazine* (juvenile). National Wildlife Federation, 1412 Sixteenth Street, NW, Washington, D.C. 20036.

The Scientific Monthly. American Association for the Advancement of Science, 1515 Massachusetts Avenue, NW, Washington, D.C. 20005.

Occasional nature articles: *National Geographic* magazine, National Geographic Society, 1145 Seventeenth Street, Washington, D.C. 20036.

Persons and Institutions

PERSONS—There is almost certainly somebody in your "neck of the woods" already interested in the same or a similar type of nature activity as the one on which you are concentrating. Trouble is that most such people go about their work in a quiet manner, and it is hard to find out who they are.

Consult your nearby high school biology teacher or college biology professor. In all probability, they will know of nature-interested people within the community and can suggest how you may meet them.

INSTITUTIONS AND OFFICES—In addition to locating individual naturalists, find out what local institutions and offices deal with subjects related to your nature interest, such as:

Natural history museum or college nature exhibit—zoological garden — aquarium — botanical garden — observatory — state or national park or sanctuary—state or federal forester, fish, game, or wildlife representatives—agricultural county agent.

Make the acquaintance of curators, wardens, or agents. They will gladly give you their technical assistance.

Nature Associations

Your luckiest break will be a chance to join a local nature club or branch of a national nature association. The great advantage in belonging to such groups is the opportunity to get together with like-minded people for indoor meetings with talks and discussions, and, more important, for field trips under expert guidance. The best known association is probably the National Audubon Society. While its main specialty is bird study, it deals with all other phases of nature as well. It sponsors adult and junior groups in numerous cities and towns throughout the country.

GENERAL NATURE ASSOCIATIONS—National Audubon Society. Headquarters: 1130 Fifth Avenue, New York, New York 10028. Periodical: *Audubon*.

American Nature Study Society. Headquarters: 35 North University Circle, Deland, Florida 32720. Periodical: *Natural History*.

SPECIALIZED ASSOCIATIONS—The names and addresses of associations and clubs that specialize in certain subjects will be found in the chapters describing these subjects.

Many of these associations are members of the American Association for the Advancement of Science. In joining this association, you will meet scientists and amateurs with whom you can discuss your nature hobby.

ASSOCIATION—American Association for the Advancement of Science. Headquarters: 1515 Massachusetts Avenue, NW, Washington, D.C. 20005. Periodicals: *Science* (weekly) and *Science Education News* (quarterly).

Nature Camps and Schools

If you can possibly manage to do so, plan to spend some time—a couple of weeks or more—with other naturalists, in pursuit of your nature interests.

There are a number of nature camps in various sections of the country, with two-week periods of intensive work—among them the Audubon nature camps in Maine, Connecticut, Wisconsin, and Wyoming.

REFERENCE—For information on the Audubon nature camps, write to National Audubon Society, 1130 Fifth Avenue, New York, New York 10028.

Many universities, teachers' colleges, and biological laboratories provide graduate and undergraduate courses in various fields of nature. Several of these courses are open to the general public. Some of the institutions make their facilities available to people who wish to do independent study and special research.

-A. B. Comstock, *Handbook of Nature Study*. Ithaca, New
 Comstock Publishing Associates.
aret M. Hutchinson, *Children as Naturalists*. New York,
Macmillan Company.

CALS—*The Science Teacher* and *Science and Children*. Official
zines of the National Science Teachers' Association, 1201
nth Street, NW, Washington, D.C. 20036.
can *Biology Teacher*. Official magazine of the National
iation of Biology Teachers, 1420 N Street, NW, Washington,
20005.

DULTS: *Experiences and Exchange*—Almost every adult has
erest in nature. In a few, it finds ready expression. In others,
e hidden in the back of their minds, waiting to be called to
Still others are too shy, or too sophisticated, ever to admi
est; yet they may become strongly stirred in close contac
are.
mplest means of getting adults interested in nature i
shared experiences and the exchange of ideas. A walk wit
imate friends through the woods at twilight, a campin
n, a fishing trip, the showing of a nature movie—any
y be the kind of experience that may send an adult into
ature hobby.

Nature Clubs

m in nature leadership is to get people interested in natu
succeed in establishing a general interest in many,
erest in a few. It may prove worth your while to give
nterested more of your time, even to the point of help
t themselves organized into a nature club, for the purp
deeper into their particular fields.

ke up the club?—Whether the club consists of youngs
s, keep in mind that the club belongs to its members.
ling to sponsor it, and you may be of great help in get
der way, but the moment it is started, it is important
ber accept a definite responsibility in the club an
to carry it out.
lly best to start a club with relatively few members,
e number as others want to join.

constitution—To get everything off in a busines
end some time during the first meetings develop
for the club. It need not be elaborate. Its main pu
stablish rules for membership and decide on the ai
e suggested form on page 35 may prove suitable:

of the club—With the club established, the memb

rder of business is to lay out the program of the c
may be fulfilled. If it is a project on which all me

CHAPTER 2

Getting Others Interested in Nature

A S YOUR own interest in nature deepens, you may want to awaken in others the same curiosity, wonder, and love that you feel. If you are a parent, or a youth leader, or a scientist, it may be your desire to do so. As a teacher or camp counselor, it may be your responsibility.

NATURE LEADERSHIP

Your success as a nature leader will depend on your personality, your understanding, and your approach.

YOUR PERSONALITY—You can't make others enthusiastic about nature unless you are genuinely enthusiastic yourself. A bubbling, contagious enthusiasm is your best ally for catching the interest of others—not the artificial slap-on-the-back kind, but the kind that is the result of a deep love for nature in all her forms. The sincerity of your enthusiasm will be evident to all who come in contact with you; they will soon catch some of it themselves.

But enthusiasm is not enough. You need a certain amount of leadership ability to go with it. Almost any person who knows where he is going can become a leader. It is a matter of having a program that you believe in, and the ability to present it simply and sincerely.

YOUR UNDERSTANDING—It is of great help if you have a good general understanding of nature—not necessarily the deep insight of an expert, but rather the knowledge of the interested amateur. You need not be a walking encyclopedia. On the contrary, it will prove of far greater importance to the people with whom you deal if you can get them to seek out the information for themselves, in field books and pamphlets, rather than have the answer pat for them the moment they ask you. There is no question which of the attitudes is better when, for example, a youngster brings you a wiggling snake and you have the choice between, "Well, well, what have we here? Let's see if we can find out what it is!" and "That's a garter snake! Next!"

One of your big objectives is to inspire others to become self-active,

31

self-observant, and self-reliant. But that requires far more than an understanding of subject matter. It requires an understanding of the people you are attempting to lead—a realization that any one of them is as important as anyone else. Remember that each has his own interests and is trying to pursue them to the best of his ability, gropingly perhaps, and needing a helping hand.

If you can make each person feel your sincere interest in him, you will have little difficulty in inspiring him to do his best toward broadening his own knowledge and toward advancing the work of the group.

YOUR APPROACH—Your relationship to the people you are to lead will determine your approach.

FOR THE PARENT: *Example and Exposure*—The best way for a parent to instill a nature interest in a child is to keep his or her own interest in nature before the child, as an ever-present example. What the child sees he will try to imitate. Through imitation comes understanding and the desire for repetition. The repeated action may then eventually become a habit that will follow the child through adolescence into adulthood.

If you are interested in birds, what would be more normal than to let your children help you as you go about feeding birds in winter, help you put up birdhouses in the spring, go with you to look for them in field and forest all summer long, watch with you the flocks that gather for southward flight in the fall?

You will succeed most easily if your own nature interest is a natural part of your life, if you cannot help observing the things that happen around you, and if you have a deep-rooted love for all living things. Your children will early begin to feel and share that love and will eagerly follow your leadership in nature activities if you keep their nature pursuits on a happy, enjoyable basis.

FOR THE YOUTH LEADER AND CAMP COUNSELOR: *Exploits and Excitement*—In dealing with Scouts, campers, and other young people, your main problem is to catch them long enough to influence them. At best, you have them for a hike a month and a few weeks in camp. They come with their own ideas of what they want to do. To many of them, nature is "sissy stuff." You must prove to them that it is virile and vital. This cannot be done by setting aside a morning or an afternoon period for "Nature." It must be done by correlating nature with the rest of the program, making use of opportunities as they come along, creating experiences—infiltration, if you like.

Hiking along some twilight hour, you may happen upon a deer. A quiet warning silences the group. "How close can we get to it?" There's a thrill to stalking a deer through dew-laden grass. There may be a beaver dam somewhere near camp; an evening's vigil watching the colony at work will never be forgotten. Climbing for a squirrel's nest, diving for samples of life from the lake bottom, gliding silently in a canoe close to a kingfisher's perch, getting up before the break of dawn to listen to the bird chorus—there's excitement and challenge to each of these exploits.

Excitement in the beginning to the few, per reach them all. You want them all in on the f the others? By *souvenirs* brought home f gnawed branches, a live snake, a praying animal skull. By publicizing the unusual c camp or meeting room. By creating *nature tr* By short *nature reports* around the coun uninitiated feel the mysterious fraternity tha nature enthusiasts, and making them eager

You can catch youth through a great described in the following chapters. The tr activity at the right time, keeping at it a shifting to another before the interest wa there—it takes time and effort and patienc walk woodsmanlike through nature, aw around him.

REFERENCES—William Gould Vinal, *Na Guidance for the Outdoors.* New York William Hillcourt, *Boy Scout Handboo* North Brunswick, New Jersey. William Hillcourt, and others, *Fieldbo* Scouts of America, North Brunswick, Marie E. Gaudette, *Leader's Nature* U.S.A., New York, New York.

FOR THE TEACHER: *Excursions and E*ₓ nature study to a science teacher mea blackboard outlines are gone forever— longer a matter of cramming a certain nu of the students, but rather of arousing desire in pupils to find out about nature according to his or her own interest an

Whenever possible, study nature in n on excursions as often as you can a techniques described on page 36, varyi suit the age of the participants. For an the pupils, figuratively speaking, and nature projects (see page 40) that may individually. For a group of young ch nature games (page 41).

Much of the schoolwork must, of four walls of the schoolroom. The indoors in the form of experiments— about things. Projects started outd continued indoors—collections, terr students or small teams may be en bring in their nature finds, and rep From the great number of projects c a series of activities may be schedule year.

Constitution of the

....
(NAME)
Nature Club

ARTICLE I—NAME
The name of this club shall be ....

ARTICLE II—PURPOSE
The purpose of this club shall be as follows:
Sect. 1. To foster and keep alive an interest in ....
Sect. 2. To increase our knowledge in the special field of ....
Sect. 3. ....

ARTICLE III—MEMBERSHIP, DUES
Sect. 1. Membership in this club shall be open to ....
Sect. 2. Dues shall be $......... (monthly) (yearly), payable ....

ARTICLE IV—OFFICERS
Sect. 1. The officers of this club shall consist of President, Vice-president, Secretary, Treasurer, and ....
Sect. 2. The officers shall be elected by ballot and majority vote, for a term of ....
Sect. 3. The duties of the officers shall be as follows: ....

ARTICLE V—MEETINGS
Sect. 1. Regular meetings shall be held on .... day, ... month.
Sect. 2. The order of business at regular meetings shall be as follows: roll call—reading of the minutes—unfinished business—committee reports—new business—main program feature—project work—announcements—adjournment.
Sect. 3. Special meetings may be called by ....
Sect. 4. The annual meeting of this club shall be held on ....

ARTICLE VI—AMENDMENTS
Sect. 1. This constitution may be amended by vote of two-thirds of the members.

can get busy, well and good. If the project divides itself into a number of phases, form as many separate committees as necessary, each committee responsible for the work in one of the phases. The committee chairmen together may make up a "steering committee" that will keep the project as a whole moving along smoothly.

"Action" is the key word to success in a nature club. You will have no luck keeping a club alive on business discussions and talks. Members join a nature club for outdoor activities, not for indoor gabfests. If you are a sponsor of a club for youngsters, help them stay on the active line with field trips and projects. If you are working with adults, make your voice heard and do your part to make your nature club a club of the out-of-doors.

GUIDE BOOKS—Science Clubs of America, *Sponsor Handbook*. Science Service, 1719 N Street, NW, Washington, D.C. 20036.
Audubon Study Program—Guide for Adult Leaders. National Audubon Society, 1130 Fifth Avenue, New York, New York, 10028.

Cooperating with Existing Agencies

Instead of starting a separate nature club, you may be inclined to make your abilities available to established youth organizations that include nature pursuits as part of their regular program. They will most certainly welcome your services.

Look in your telephone book or check with a local schoolteacher to find out what groups of boys or girls are found in your vicinity. Then make the necessary contacts and discuss the type of activities that may be developed.

In some instances your help may be needed in direct work with the youngsters. In other cases, you may be of even greater assistance in training their leaders in a dynamic nature program—not just for camp, but for year-round use.

ADDRESSES—*Boys*—Boy Scouts of America, North Brunswick, New Jersey 08902.
Boys' Clubs of America, 771 First Avenue, New York, New York 10017.
YMCA, YMHA—see local directory.
Girls—Girl Scouts of the U.S.A., 830 Third Avenue, New York, New York 10022.
Camp Fire Girls, 65 Worth Street, New York, New York 10013.
YWCA, YWHA—see local directory.
Boys and Girls—4-H Club, Federal Extension Service, U.S. Department of Agriculture, Washington, D.C. 20250.

FIELD TRIPS

The field trip is your best means of imparting to others a love for nature, of showing them the multitudes of ecological systems that exist, of helping them understand the interrelationship between all living things, of teaching them to observe and to know nature.

Whether you are undertaking a field trip for a group of adults, a school class, nature club, or Scout troop, it is important to plan it well in advance, to use an effective field technique, and to provide for a follow-up to evaluate the results.

Planning the Field Trip

The preparation for a field trip of a small group of five to eight people will take less planning than for a larger group, and each of the participants will get more out of the experience. The larger group requires stronger leadership and closer supervision. For greatest effectiveness, it is generally advisable to divide a large group into subgroups, each with a well-liked student leader, along the lines of the patrol method used in Scouting.

WHAT?—Before you set out, arouse the interest of the participants and make them clearly aware of what you expect to accomplish. The What? may be the discovering of the main plantlife-wildlife communities along the route, learning the ecological or economic aspects of the environment, looking for birds and animals, flowers, and trees, exploring a specific destination, collecting specimens. Unless there is a definite reason for going, known to all, some will look upon a field trip as a picnic, others will come along "for the ride," and the results will be meager.

WHERE?—The Where? should be picked to provide maximum opportunity for the investigations that are the aim of the trip. Some of the students may be able to make specific recommendations, or a map may show the possibilities. It pays for the leader to make a personal reconnaissance hike over the route, in advance of the field trip, to make certain that it suits the purpose. If you are not too familiar with the subjects that may open up on the trip, you may want to ask a specialist to come along.

WHEN?—Set the *date* in conference with the participants. Determine the *time for starting*, and figure out from the length of the route the approximate *time for the return*.

HOW?—Get *permission* in advance from owners of property you may want to cross. In the case of youngsters, get parents' permissions, and for schoolchildren, the permission of principal and superintendent as well.

Figure out what *equipment* to take and make some of the participants responsible for bringing it along.

Each person will bring his or her own *luncheon* if the trip extends for the whole day. Bring water in *canteens* if you do not expect to pass places where safe drinking water is available.

Take a small amount of *first-aid supplies*—mostly Band-Aids. Teach the participants what poison ivy looks like and warn them against touching it or brushing against it.

Arrange for *transportation* to a suitable starting point—by private cars, public carriers, or chartered bus.

Field Trip Techniques

Each type of field work has its own techniques: Bird hiking requires one method, animal study another, investigating pond life still another. Detailed techniques are described in the chapters that follow. Certain procedures apply to all kinds of group field trips:

Follow the leader while traveling.—The leader sets the pace and the directions; the participants follow closely behind. In that way they have a chance to see what the leader sees, and can assemble quickly.

Obey signals.—To get close to wildlife on a field trip, you must proceed in silence. This is not feasible for most groups, and not necessary all the time. Instead, establish a simple system of silent signals: hand held up for "silence," hand swung in circle for "gather round," hand pushed up repeatedly from shoulder height for "come here."

Practice good outdoor manners.—Stay on the trail; keep it narrow. Obey "no trespass" signs. Leave no debris for others to pick up. If a luncheon fire is built, make POSITIVE it is out before leaving.

> Let no one say—and say it to your shame—
> That all was beauty here until you came.

Don't pour in; draw out!—Encourage the participants to learn by observing and questioning. Don't attempt to lecture on the trail. When the occasion suggests and the trail opens up sufficiently, gather the group in horseshoe formation, and discuss what you have seen. Ask questions; give as many of the participants as possible a chance to tell what they have noticed. When a question is asked, don't snap out the answer; ask another question of the whole group: "Does anyone know the answer?" If it is finally up to you to provide the answer, give it, if you know it. If you don't, be frank about it: "I don't know. Let's find out." The field book in your knapsack will probably have the information.

Work from base.—From time to time, stop to establish a base. Give everyone a chance for independent roaming and exploration. Set a time limit when all are to be back at the base. Before continuing, have the participants report on things of interest they may have seen on their roaming.

Take it easy.—Take a short rest occasionally. Make the lunch hour a time for happy relaxation; for a young group, throw in a few nature games.

Follow-up After Field Trip

Discuss experiences.—After a field trip, arrange a discussion of the shared experiences: "What did we accomplish?" "Did we reach our aim?" "Where do we go from here?" Again, make use of questioning to draw out each participant.

Collect results.—Encourage the making of reports of the field trip as a whole and of specific observations. Have the reports accompanied by drawings, map sketches, photographs, if possible.

Prepare collections.—If specimens have been collected, have the group prepare them properly.

Send thank-you notes.—Mail out notes as promptly as possible to thank the people who may have helped to make the experience a success.

NATURE PROJECTS

A nature project is a nature activity with a specified, tangible result. "Make an insect collection" is a nature activity which can last as long as life itself. "Make a collection of 100 local insects" is a limited-time project within the ability of any interested person.

The right kind of projects will keep the nature interests of a club, a camp, a class, or a youth group alive and humming.

A well-run field trip has a great appeal to young people. Their interests revolve around the What? and the Where?

To adults, a field trip has added meaning. Beyond learning what is what, they want to know the How? and the Why?

Selecting the Project

To help you in proposing and developing nature projects for any season of the year and any type of group work, a special Project Index accompanies the regular index of this *Field Book*, starting on page 379. The information necessary for carrying out the projects is contained in this volume.

The projects vary in difficulty from the pressing of plants and the making of an aquarium to the taking of a bird-nesting census and the planting of a community forest. Some of the projects can be handled effectively by a single person or by a buddy team; other projects require the cooperation of large groups and a certain amount of equipment and expenditure. Still other projects are combinations of a number of procedures.

Presenting the Project

In a nature club, a project may be proposed "from the floor" or suggested by an officer or a committee. In a school or youth group, a project should be presented, listing its possibilities to make the group enthusiastic about attempting it. For greatest effectiveness, the main part of the planning for any project should be done by the members of the group. The work connected with it should be self-imposed, not assigned. Only then will the project have its full significance and provide its maximum training potential.

Carrying Out the Project

The individual project needs little organization. Group projects must be handled differently. The following methods suggest the approaches to two types of group projects—one, an easy one, the other more complex:

"*Let's make a simple camp museum.*" What shall it contain? Quick discussion among camp members, then specific suggestions put down on cards: Make up an exhibit of five kinds of soil; collect and exhibit ten insects; make a display of six common rocks; make four plaster casts of animal tracks; plant six different tree seedlings in cans and identify them; make a rearing cage and inhabit it with six caterpillars; collect ten twigs and mount them for display; make a terrarium; find five shells—and so on. "Who will do what?" Campers, singly or as buddies, volunteer, and the cards are distributed. A time limit is set for the completion of the project—an hour or an hour and a half. A moment later the campers are on their way. You wind up with the nucleus of a camp museum that can be further developed.

"*Let's make a tree survey of our school ground.*" What is involved? Map sketching—who will do it? Locating the trees and taking their measurements—who? Identifying the specimens—who are our experts? Someone to take photographs of the more important trees, someone for sketching, someone for leaf printing, someone for wood samples. Volunteers and still more volunteers!

When a project is finished, it should be "tied up" neatly, and those working on it credited with its successful completion. If feasible, develop a report of the accomplishment for future use by the group.

NATURE GAMES

All work and no play . . . In working with young people, remember that even the most eager nature student needs moments of relaxation. The wise nature leader intersperses periods of study with periods of games. Sometimes games of a purely recreational nature are in order. Most of the time you can use games that will add to the nature experience of the player.

BOOKS OF NATURE GAMES—Virginia W. Musselman, *Learning About Nature Through Games*. Harrisburg, Pennsylvania, Stackpole Books.
Sylvia Cassell, *Nature Games and Activities*. New York, Harper & Row Publishers.

The games that follow are designed mostly for young people, but many of them can be used with older groups as well. Even nature experts will enjoy matching themselves against Nature Questions, Nature Art Gallery, I Know Me, Who Am I? and other games.

Outdoor Games

Nature far-and-near—Make a list of twenty or thirty items to be found along the route, with a score for each—such as "Bird's nest, 10 points—Live snake, 15 points—Monarch butterfly, 5 points—Frog, 10 points—Animal track, 5 points—Flying crow, 5 points." First player to observe one of the items and report to the leader scores.

Listen!—On a sign from the leader, players remain perfectly still for three minutes, listening and writing down the sounds they hear: Bird songs, insect "songs," tree rustles, and so on. Player with the most complete list wins.

Nature hunt—Leader announces an item to be collected. First player to bring it in scores 5 points. Continue as long as desired.

Nature memory hunt—Teams study for two minutes a display of thirty nature specimens—leaves, flowers, shells, insects, etc.—trying to memorize them. They then set out to duplicate the exhibit. Team scores 5 points for each item collected, loses 5 points for each thing collected that was not in the original exhibit.

Leaf hunt—Teams are given ten minutes to gather only *one* leaf from each of as many different trees as they can find. When brought in, the leaves are arranged on the ground, and slips of paper with names are placed next to them. Team with the most leaves correctly identified wins.

Leaf matching—Start as for LEAF HUNT. Instead of labeling, proceed as follows: One team holds up a leaf, identifies it, scores 5 points. First other team to hold up similar leaf scores 10 points, other teams that have leaf score 5 points each. Team first to identify holds up next leaf, and so on. If a team identifies incorrectly the leaf it holds up, it scores nothing, but the team first to correct the mistake scores 10 points extra.

Unnatural nature—In a small area, "doctor up" a number of plants—tie oak leaves on a tulip tree, pine cones on spruce, black-eyed susan on thistle, and so on. Send out teams to discover these freaks. Team bringing back report of greatest number of oddities within certain time limit wins. Score extra if the team identifies both the original plant and the unnatural addition.

Tree tagging—Give each team twenty pieces of 1-inch gauze bandage, 12 inches long, with numbers from 1 to 20 written on them, in a different color for each team. Object is to tie gauze bandages on as many different trees as possible, within 100 feet of starting point. One team member keeps a list of trees tagged. Team tagging the most trees correctly within the time limit wins.

Nature scavenger hunt—Give each team the sealed letter: "Our Indian chief has not slept for twenty nights. The witch doctor of our tribe has promised to cure him with his famous sleeping brew, but he needs your help. Bring him the following ingredients within one hour from the moment you read this: ten dandelion seeds—two bird feathers—four dead flies—bit of rabbit fluff—ten white pine needles—live frog or toad—two caterpillars . . . (and so on, around twenty items)." Team bringing in the largest number of items within the time limit wins.

Nature treasure hunt—Each team gets a sealed envelope. On signal, the envelopes are opened. Inside is a card reading: "Go to tallest hemlock you see from this point." At hemlock is sign: "Follow direction of largest branch to patch of cattails at water's edge." Here is another message: "Follow shore toward setting sun to second alder." A number of arrows scratched in the ground lead from the alder to a large boulder; in a crevice is a message: "To oak." There is a solitary oak out in the field—must be it. And so on, until the last message: "Look under dead pine." Here the winning team finds the treasure: Candy, peanuts, or what-have-you.

Quiet Games for Indoors or Out

Who am I?—Prepare a set of file cards with the name of a bird, a tree, etc., on each. Pin name card on the back of each player without letting the player know what name he has. Players circulate and ask one another questions that can be answered by "yes" or "no" or "don't know." Only three questions may be asked of one person. Each player learning his identity within a time limit scores.

Nature Kim's game—Teams gather around a table covered with a cloth. Cloth is lifted for one minute to reveal about twenty to thirty nature items. Teams go into a huddle and attempt to make a complete list of items. Team with the largest number wins.

Museum—Arrange a number of specimens on a table or the ground. Each specimen has a number on a file card. Players write down the numbers and names of items they recognize. When the time is up, the player with the most correct identifications wins.

Girl Scouts and Camp Fire Girls, Boy Scouts and Cub Scouts pick up much nature knowledge through games.

Nature art gallery—Fasten twenty or more pictures, without names, of birds, or trees, or flowers, etc., on the wall. Number the pictures. Players move around with pencils and numbered sheets, and try to identify the pictures. They write down the names on their sheets and turn in the sheets at a certain time limit. Player with the most correct names after the time limit wins.

This and that—Obtain pictures of animals and of animal tracks, of birds and of birds' nests, of trees and of tree leaves—or, even better, animal pictures and track casts, bird pictures and feathers, tree pictures and winter twigs—and so on. Place the items on display, with each item numbered. Object is for the players to write down numbers of matching pairs.

Identification—Each team has a field book on the subject in question. Leader shows a not-too-common specimen of tree, flower, insect, and so on. First team to identify it correctly from the field book wins.

Scrambled names—Give to each team a list of fifteen or more scrambled names of birds, or trees, or flowers, etc., such as: "1. MOSITETU 2. NIDRALAC 3. CUJON 4. PODOWKRECE." First team to bring in correct unscrambled list wins: "1. TITMOUSE 2. CARDINAL 3. JUNCO 4. WOODPECKER."

True or false—Leader reads a list of statements, some of them true, others false. Such as: "Poison ivy is not an ivy, all bats are blind, toads cause warts, deer chew cuds, ants have no wings, all animals have hair, spiders are insects . . ." First player to yell correctly "True" or "False" scores.

Nature questions—Similar to the familiar party game Twenty Questions—but not necessarily restricted to twenty questions: Leader assumes the identity of a tree, a bird, an animal, or whatever, without revealing the name. He answers with "yes" or "no" questions put to him by the players trying to find out what he is, such as: "Are you a plant?" "No." "Are you an animal with four legs?" "No." "With wings?" "Yes." "Are you a large bird?" "No." And so on. May be played as team game: Each team interrogates a separate leader. All leaders have the same identity. First team to get the name wins.

I know me—Leader reads a series of graded statements leading toward the identity of some specimen—bird, tree, etc. Player first to yell the name scores according to the number of the statement, from 8 points to 1, as for instance: "8. I am one of the tallest trees in the forest in Northeast America. 7. My leaves drop in the fall. 6. My wood is soft, white. 5. My bark is light gray, furrowed. 4. My trunk is straight, like a column. 3. My fruits fall apart into many pieces. 2. My leaves look as if the tips were cut off with scissors. 1. My flowers resemble a well-known garden flower. I am the TULIP TREE."

NATURE TRAILS

It is not always that you or some other leader is available to take a group of nature enthusiasts on a trip through the wilds. In working toward the creation of a nature trail, you solve this problem by providing absentee leadership. The thought behind this is to give a person a chance to take a self-guided walk over a clearly defined path, marked with occasional signs that tell the story of the more important natural-history features along the way.

The spirit of the nature trail was well expressed by Dr. Frank E. Lutz—who may be considered the father of the modern application of this idea—at the entrance to one of his early trails:

"A friend somewhat versed in Natural History is taking a walk with you and calling your attention to interesting things."

The best location for a nature trail is a park, a camp, a grove adjacent to the school grounds. Get permission from the proper authorities for laying out the trail, and get the help of others for doing the work.

General rules—Follow these rules in establishing a nature trail:

1. *Keep the trail narrow.*
2. *Keep it natural.*—Don't destroy, tear up, fake.
3. *Keep it woodsy.*—Office labels and baggage tags do not belong in nature.
4. *Keep it simple.*—Don't attempt to say too much about too many subjects. Give facts; whimsy will be misunderstood. Present some of the facts in a humorous vein.
5. *Keep it protected.*—No ax scars, no nails. Make it a sample of good conservation.
6. *Keep it growing.*—Add to it and change it with the seasons.
7. *Keep it beautiful.*

REFERENCE—Byron L. Ashbaugh, *Trail Planning and Layout*. New York, National Audubon Society.

Training Trail

The training trail is a general trail intended to create an interest in all phases of nature.

LAYING OUT THE TRAIL—If your trail is to be a success, the entrance to it should be readily accessible. The trail should not be too long—half a mile or so is a good distance—and it should return to a spot close to the starting point or end at a suitable destination announced at the entrance.

The trail should run through as many types of wildlife communities as possible. To do this, it will probably have to be rather rambling. For this reason, it will seldom be feasible to make use of established paths—a new trail has to be created.

Before laying out the trail, walk back and forth, cross-country, through the location. Get a clear picture of the spots that should be incorporated in the trail and decide on their sequence. Then take a walk along the trail-to-be with a helpful companion: a ball of twine. Tie an end to a tree at the starting point, then unwind the twine to mark the trail. After you mark the trail in this manner, you can distribute groups of helpers all along the trail for the clearing job.

Use only hand sickles, hand axes, and pruning saws for clearing. Make your co-workers aware that the rule "*Keep the trail narrow*" means "Keep it so narrow that it must be followed single file."

MARKERS—The cheapest way to mark a nature trail is with paraffin-dipped linen tags or file cards. Such marking is apt to make the trail "cheap" in more ways than one. Better to use markers that suggest more permanency and fit into the spirit of the woods. Place them about twenty steps apart, or just so far that you can sight the next one.

TYPES—Plain markers—Plain markers may be made of wood or sheet tin or aluminum.

For *wooden markers*, cut pieces of ¼-inch outdoor plywood or masonite, 5 by 7 inches or larger. Or use ½-inch boards, 6 inches wide or wider. Cover the markers with a primer, then paint them with one or two coats of outdoor flat paint, or high-quality enamel, in whatever color you prefer.

Screw to rustic poles pointed at one end.

¶ *Tip*—Excellent for wood markers—and usually free—are slabs and ends of orange crates and apple boxes. Or use the slats from old venetian blinds.

For *metal markers*, cut sheet tin, or better, sheet aluminum into suitable pieces. Prime them with a primer specifically made for priming metal, to ensure firm bonding. Then cover that with two coats of outdoor paint or enamel.

Nail to posts or make two pairs of holes in each marker by which the markers can be wired to the posts.

Insertion markers—Instead of making plain markers of sheet tin, you may turn the top and bottom over so that removable *cardboard markers* can be inserted. Prime and paint as above, then prepare cardboard inserts.

Cut the cardboard to size, and write the legend on it by pen or large-type typewriter. Cover the cardboard front and back with two coats of top-quality exterior varnish.

¶ *Tip*—For added attractiveness, use poster cardboard in several colors—one color for flowers, another for trees, and so on.

Lifting markers—People like to touch things, and the lifting marker gives them the chance.

This can be the ordinary wood marker, with another piece of wood of the same size hinged to it at the top. The front piece is lifted to reveal the legend of the marker. Or the front might have a question that is answered by the legend of the marker.

Or use plain sheet-tin markers. Make two nail holes in them near the top edge, and hang them by wires in the holes of perforated metal straps fastened around the tree trunks.

Swinging markers—Bend a piece of strap iron into a U. Cut a wood marker to fit in the U and suspend it by two nails through holes bored in the uprights of the U-frame. Part of the legend is on the front; the rest can be read only by swinging the marker over.

LETTERING—Oil paint—The markers can be lettered with diluted oil paint or artists' colors in a color to contrast with the color of the markers. Use a fine, pointed brush. Cover the marker with a coat of varnish when the lettering is completely dry.

India ink—Lettering with pen and India ink does a quicker job than painting. Use a speedball pen: No. B-5 for light lines, No. B-2 or B-3 for heavier lines.

To prevent the ink from running when applied over paint, abrase the surface lightly by rubbing it down with fine steel wool. Varnish the surface when the ink is dry.

WORDING—The wording on the markers should be short and catchy—more than names, lots of information in a small "nugget"—with no pretentious scientific approach. The way to get the proper wording is to write it on the spot. As Lutz expresses it: "Desk-written labels are apt to be desky." A classic example is the chatty:

This lead-pencil tree—Red Cedar—is the favorite wood for making pencils. It is also used for cedar chests. Smell it.

as against the "desk" label:

Red Cedar, *Juniperus virginiana*,
Northeastern United States.

The labels can be straight IDENTIFICATION:

W-H-I-T-E Pine—five letters to the name, five needles to the cluster.

Bark like alligator skin? It's Dogwood.

Leaflets three—let it be! Poison ivy.

Markers for nature trails may be made from metal or wood: simple (top), or designed to be lifted or swung (bottom).

They may suggest USES:

Staghorn Sumac—fruits for refreshing drinks.

Early pioneers used the hardwood of Dogwood for skewers or "dags"—hence its name.

American Hornbeam wood is as tough as the "muscular" branches suggest!

They may be an invitation to LOOK or to LISTEN:

Along this deer run, Virginia Deer roam down for water.

Silence—would you hear the Thrush
Bell-like in the evening hush.

They may be HUMOROUS:

Happy are Cicadas' lives
For they all have voiceless wives.

Touch me today—I'll itch you tomorrow.

And they can be TEASING, such as this on one side of a swinging label:

Pat yourself on the back IF . . .

and this on the other side:

. . . you noticed the Robin's nest in the Chokecherry tree you just passed.

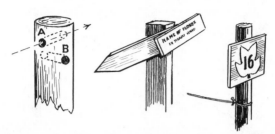

Pointers are useful on the testing trail: log with sighting holes, arrow pointer, marker with string to subject.

POINTERS—A marker can be related more closely to its object by the use of some kind of pointer.

Arrow pointer—Cut one end of a strip of wood into arrow shape and attach the marker to the opposite, blunt end. Fasten to a square post in such a way that the arrow points directly at the object described on the marker.

Peephole pointer—Place a post, three inches or more in diameter, upright in the ground along the trail. Bore one or more holes through the post in such a way that a person looking through them will see the objects described on the markers attached to the post.

String pointer—A string "pointer" is the most obvious way of relating marker and object. Tie a string by one end to the marker, by the other to the subject.

OTHER FEATURES—**Pictures**—Pictures of birds, plants, trees, may be cut out of nature magazines or cheap nature booklets and pasted on some of the markers. Protect the pictures with varnish or outdoor enamel. Or cover them with a piece of clear transparent self-adhesive plastic, such as Con-Tact.

Leaf prints—Tree markers may be provided with oil-paint or ink leaf prints (see pages 273).

Insect cages—Insects may be displayed on their feed plants in transparent cylindrical cages (see page 166–67).

Stump detective—If there is a prominent stump along the trail, put up a Stump Detective sign (see page 264).

Special areas—In a widening of the trail you may demonstrate such things as birdhouses and bird feeders, turtle pens, animal tracking pit, and so on (see Index).

Testing Trails

The testing trail is developed in the usual manner, but instead of giving information, it asks for it. A person wanting to test his nature knowledge enters the trail with a piece of paper and a pencil. As he walks along, he jots down his answers. At the end of the trail he checks their correctness against the right answers, posted on a bulletin board.

NUMBERED TRAIL—The testing trail most easily developed is a numbered trail. In this, a small square marker carrying a number and no other legend is placed next to each specimen to be identified.

QUESTION TRAIL—On this kind of testing trail the markers contain questions based on the legends of the training trail markers: "What is the name of this tree that has bark like alligator skin?" "How many leaflets does poison ivy have to each leaf?" "Is it the female or the male cicada you hear 'singing'?"

NATURE MUSEUMS AND WORKSHOPS

A museum has an important part to play in spreading the nature gospel. Here are displayed the experiences and finds of numerous field trips, arranged in such a way that "he who runs may read"—and may possibly hesitate long enough to pick up some interest in nature. Here are things to arouse the curiosity of the youngster, a place where the advanced naturalist may succeed in instilling in others some of his own enthusiasm.

The large museum is often a place of imposing halls, with quiet onlookers. The small museum should be a living, functioning workshop, with participants sharing in its creation and upkeep.

That word "sharing" is the secret of a successful nature museum. Someone—teacher, camp counselor, youth leader, Scoutmaster, club member, naturalist—must want to share his or her nature enjoyment with others and get students, campers, or people of the community excited about joining in the efforts.

Types of Nature Museums

The most important function of the small nature museum is as a *nature headquarters*—a place where youngsters and adults can come to look at various types of nature exhibits and collections and find out what methods were used in their development, where they can come after a field trip to work on their collections, where they can get help in identifying their specimens, and where they can meet with others to discuss their problems and tell of their successes.

In the *school*, the school science room may be built into such a museum. If no science room is available, a corner in a classroom may do, or an attic room or basement room may be turned into a nature den.

In the *Scout troop* or *club room*, a wall may be set aside for nature displays.

In *camp*, a couple of sturdy tables may be put up and protected by canvas tarps or by a permanent roof. In a larger camp, a rustic shelter or small building may be erected to serve as nature headquarters.

In some communities, nature groups have established *trailside museums* in conjunction with nature trails through parks or community forests.

Private citizens have, in many instances, opened up their *homes* for the purpose of sharing their nature interests with youth groups and nature club members.

The perfect arrangement would involve facilities that are well lighted and provided with shelves and wall space for displays, cabinets or drawers for storage of equipment and supplies, and work-tables large enough to ensure adequate space for group work.

Development and Maintenance

As far as possible, the exhibits should be developed by nature students, and maintained by them. Only in this manner will the museum have its maximum educational effect.

If a nature club is already in existence, it would be logical for such a club to take over the responsibility, electing a curator and assistant curators. In other groups, nature enthusiasts may offer their services.

The curators will develop the general plan for the exhibits, will encourage others to bring in their finds, will help in their arrangement and labeling, and will be responsible for the order and general tidiness of the museum.

REFERENCE—Bryon L. Ashbaugh, *Planning a Nature Center*. National Audubon Society, 1130 Fifth Avenue, New York, New York 10028.

A nature museum should be a growing thing. The *making* of it is more important than the *looking* at it. The exhibits should therefore be worked at, changed, improved upon, in many instances, replaced regularly—partly to keep up with the seasons but, more important, to get other hands to work. Replacement is particularly important where the groups change from time to time, such as in the organizational summer camps and in school.

Museum Exhibits

The size of the museum and the ambition of the curators govern the types of exhibits that can be included. A great number of suitable exhibits are described throughout the pages of this book (see Project Index).

Pictures—Make use of the artistic talent in the group to create an interesting frame for the main exhibits. Bring in original nature sketches, paintings, and photographs, as well as clippings from magazines. Develop nature maps of the surrounding area, showing the location of important trees, animal homes, and so on. Paint posters or even murals.

SOURCES OF INEXPENSIVE PICTURE MATERIAL—Drop a line to Superintendent of Documents, U.S. Government Printing Office, Washington, D.C. 20402 and request Price List of Government Publications: PL81, *Posters and Charts*. This contains a list of display materials available at low cost. For special subjects, request the price lists mentioned on page 28.
U.S. Department of Interior. Fish and Wildlife Service, Washington, D.C. 20025. Request list.

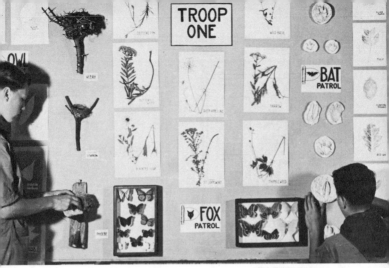

Nature museum in camp or schoolroom should be a living workshop, all participants sharing in creation and upkeep.

National Geographic Society. School Service Department, Washington, D.C. 20036. Request list.
National Audubon Society, 1130 Fifth Avenue, New York, New York 10028. Write for catalog *Audubon Aid to Natural Science.*

Live exhibits—Include only if regular care can be given: aquarium with native fish and water plants, terrariums with plants and amphibians, cages with mammals and snakes, observation beehives, "anthill," rearing cages for insect larvae. Encourage visitors to the museum and users of the workshop to bring in specimens and develop the exhibits. This activity will be described in subsequent chapters of this book.

¶ *Tip*—Loan exhibits of live animals may be available through your state conservation department. Write your state capital.

Nonlive exhibits—Birds' nests, birdhouses, mounted feathers, contents of pellets. Animal-track casts, animal-gnawed things, scat. Snake skins, preserved snakes. Mounted fish. Shells. Insect collections. Pressed flowers, spore prints, leaf prints, wood samples, twig and seed collections. For instructions for making them, see chapters throughout the book.

Models and dioramas—Miniatures of animal homes, wildlife communities, conservation practices. Large models of flower parts, insects, water animals.

How-to-make exhibits—Show-and-do demonstrations—Display of equipment and steps in making nature collections—leaf prints, track casts, and so on (see Project Index).

Record player—With records of bird songs, the calls of frogs and toads, and "songs" of insects.

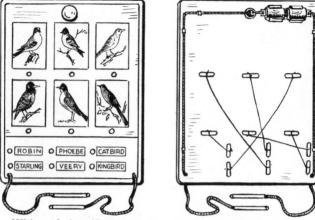

Wiring of electrified chart. For simplicity's sake chart has only six pictures, instead of the usual twenty or more.

Bookshelf—Field books for identification, reference books, nature magazines.

Bulletin board—For questions and answers, clippings, announcements.

In addition to the main exhibits, gadgets that have a special appeal for youngsters may be included:

Electrified chart—In its simplest form, this consists of a large chart with a number of unnamed pictures of animals, birds, plants. The names appear in a special panel at the bottom of the chart. At each picture and each name is a metal knob. Attached to the chart on long wires are two brass rods. When one rod is touched to the knob under a picture, and the other to the correct, corresponding name, a bulb lights up, or a buzzer sounds.

The chart itself may be made of plywood or wallboard. The knobs may be brass paper fasteners or small stove bolts. On the back of the chart, the prongs of the fasteners or the nuts of the bolts are connected in pairs—picture and name—with the bell wire of the extension cord split in half. The wires from the two rods run to two doorbell batteries, or flashlight batteries, and to a buzzer or a flashlight bulb (see wiring diagram, above).

"What is it?" shelf—On a small shelf, have a daily exhibit of an unidentified object found by a student. Or place on the shelf some items to be brought to the students' attention. Special recognition may be given to the first person identifying the object.

PART II

CHAPTER 3

Birds

BIRDS are the most beloved of all living wild creatures. They appeal to young and old alike.

Who does not thrill to the sight of a clutch of downy fledglings in a nest, to the soaring sweep of a bald eagle, to the song of the hermit thrush at dusk, to the flashing beauty of the hummingbird halting on whirring wings before your delphinium?

The flight of birds has been the envy of man through the ages. "Free as a bird in the air . . ." is still considered the ultimate in liberty. It is birds that symbolize happiness, peace, strength.

Poets have written odes in their praise, artists have painted them, scientists have studied them. But you need not be a poet or artist or scientist to enjoy them. A little patience and quick eyes are all that are required.

If you like, you can travel afar looking for birds—into field, marsh, and woodland, and along the seashore. You will see them far out over the expanses of the widest oceans. You will find them nesting in deserts and near mountain summits. Birds and their songs will follow you almost everywhere you go in the great out-of-doors.

And if you don't go, they will come to you. Sit quietly on your front porch some summer morning, and they will congregate on your lawn. Feed them in the winter, and grateful juncos and chickadees, nuthatches and woodpeckers will keep you company. Many valuable observations of bird life have been made through the windowpanes of sickrooms.

You will get a certain amount of casual satisfaction out of seeing a beautiful bird on the wing or of listening to its song. A much greater satisfaction comes to you when the color or shape or sweep of a bird tells you what it is, and when bird songs become as familiar to you as well-loved old tunes.

You reach the peak in your bird-watching career when your observations shed light on some of the mysteries that still abound in our knowledge of birds.

BOOKS ON BIRD LIFE—Arthur A. Allen, *The Book of Bird Life*. New York, D. Van Nostrand Company.

James Fisher and Roger T. Peterson, *World of Birds*. New York, Doubleday & Company.

L. W. Wing, *Natural History of Birds*. New York, Ronald Press.

Birds in Our Lives. $9.00. From Superintendent of Documents, U.S. Government Printing Office, Washington, D.C. 20402.

Roger T. Peterson, *The Birds*. Chicago, Time-Life Books.

Working with Others

You can get much enjoyment out of solitary bird walks. But as your interest in birds mounts, you will want to share your excitement with others. Also, you will want to take advantage of all the help that is available, thus further increasing your own enthusiasm.

Right in your own immediate vicinity, there are bound to be several other people interested in birds, with whom you can discuss your discoveries. They may help you in identification or assist you in solving other problems.

If your city or town has a natural history museum or your zoo an aviary, this may be the place to start your bird study.

Every state and county has amateur bird clubs—branches of the Audubon Society or of an ornithological society. Their members go on bird walks under expert guidance. They meet to hear talks on various phases of bird life, and to watch some of the magnificent films and color slides of birds that are taken in ever-increasing numbers. Many of these local clubs publish their own bulletins or newsletters.

All of these groups are eager to take in new members who are genuinely interested in birds and their conservation. Your local librarian or biology teacher should be able to put you in contact with the nearest group. If not, simply drop a postcard to the National Audubon Society or to one of the ornithological clubs.

When you go traveling, stop in state and national parks and wildlife sanctuaries. In most of these you will find rangers and naturalists who will be glad to assist you in learning about the bird population in these places.

SOCIETIES—National Audubon Society. Headquarters: 1130 Fifth Avenue, New York, New York 10028. Periodical: *Audubon*.

American Ornithologists' Union. Headquarters: Department of Biological Sciences, San Jose State College, San Jose, California 95114. Periodical: *The AOU*.

Wilson Ornithological Society. Mostly Middle West. Headquarters: Museum of Zoology, University of Michigan, Ann Arbor, Michigan 48103. Periodical: *Wilson Bulletin*.

Cooper Ornithological Club. West and California. Headquarters:

Department of Zoology, University of California, Los Angeles, California 90053. Periodical: *Condor*.

Nuttall Ornithological Club. Mostly East. Headquarters: Museum of Comparative Zoology, Harvard University, Cambridge, Massachusetts 02138.

FIELD STUDY OF BIRDS

Equipment for Bird Study

CLOTHING—Since you will be doing your bird watching in the cool of early morning or in the evening, you will need warm clothing. A wool sweater for summer use, and a parka-type coat with an outside layer of wind-resistant material for the cooler seasons of the year will serve you well.

Your clothing should be sturdy and water repellent as well as warm. It has to resist brambles and thorns and withstand all kinds of weather.

Pick a color that blends well with the surroundings. It can be brown, green, blue, or even red. The actual hue is of little importance. It is the tone that counts. A brilliant tone will attract the birds' attention to you and will disclose the slightest motion you make. A subdued tone will make you almost invisible.

Pay special attention to your footwear. Rubbers will protect you in the early morning dew. Use rubber "waders" if you intend to study marshland bird life.

¶ *Tip*—A good insect repellent to smear on exposed skin of face and hands may mean the difference between an enjoyable and a miserable morning walk.

STUDY EQUIPMENT—**Field glasses**—Your eyes may be strong; nevertheless, you will soon feel the need of a pair of field glasses for "pulling" the birds close to you. But there are field glasses and Field Glasses.

OPERA GLASSES—If you have a pair of opera glasses in the house, make use of them in the beginning. They generally magnify two to three times, are easy to carry and easy to handle.

FIELD GLASSES—A common form of field glasses contains a system of lenses that magnify the object four to five times. Higher magnification makes these nonprismatic "Galilean-type" glasses unwieldy because it necessitates greater length, therefore added weight.

PRISM BINOCULARS—Prism binoculars are ideal for bird watching. They consist of a combination of lenses and prisms that make great magnification possible with small size and weight.

Binoculars are expensive. But since they are a lifetime investment, it pays to buy the best and most durable that are available. Before making the purchase, know your needs, and check each of the following points:

Magnification—The magnification, or power, is indicated on the binoculars by the figures $6 \times$, $7 \times$—six times, seven times—and so on.

The figure 6× means that the object, viewed through the binoculars, appears six times as large as it looks to the naked eye. The larger the magnification, the more difficult becomes the use of the glasses: the movement of an unsteady hand is magnified as many times as the object. Many experts prefer 8× or 9× for themselves, but they recommend 6× for their students. You may want to compromise on 7×.

Relative brightness—In full daylight, a high relative brightness is not required, but when the binoculars are to be used in the early morning hours and in the dim light of evening, the extra brightness becomes important. To find the relative brightness of binoculars, first check the diameter of the objective lens—the lens farthest from your eyes. This is usually stamped in millimeters, next to the magnification, such as 7×,35. Divide the diameter by the magnification (in this case, 35 divided by 7). Take the result (5), and square it (25). The relative brightness is 25. Similarly, the relative brightness of 6×,30 is also 25, while the brightness of 8×,30 is 14.1.

"Coated" lenses increase the relative brightness by reducing reflection from the lens surfaces. The coating also improves the contrast of the image thereby making it look sharper.

Field of view—By field of view is meant the diameter of the "picture" you see through the binoculars. A wide field makes it easy to locate your object and keep it in view without moving the glasses. The field should, preferably, be not less than 100 yards wide at a distance of 1,000 yards.

Focusing and alignment—Two types of focusing are in use: *individual focusing* that requires separate focusing of each eyepiece, and *center focusing* by which the focusing of both eyepieces is done simultaneously. Center focusing is the simpler and quicker method, therefore the most popular.

Proper focusing should result in perfect alignment of the two parts of the binoculars so that the two images you see with your two eyes fuse exactly into a single image.

Image quality—When focused, good binoculars will show a sharply defined image from one edge of the lens to the other, with no distortion and no color fringes.

¶ *Tip*—If you use eyeglasses, buy binoculars with adjustable eyecups or with eyecups that can be cut down until the lenses of your glasses almost touch the lenses of the eyepieces.

CARRYING STRAPS—Have your binoculars ready by carrying them on a strap around your neck. Keep the strap as short as easy use permits. The shorter the strap, the less dangling of the binoculars when you walk.

An elastic chest harness, commercially available, will cut down the dangling even more.

Spotting scope—If you are particularly interested in studying waterbirds of lake or seashore, you will find a spotting scope handy. Such scopes are usually set at a magnification of 12 to 30 power.

When using a spotting scope, you will, of course, need a tripod.

Standard prism binocular (right) combines lenses with two Porro prisms. Certain models have electric zoom power that magnifies from 6 to 12 power.

Bausch & Lomb, Inc.: 7 x 35 binocular

Specialty binoculars (below) have a lens-and-prism arrangement making use of three Uppendahl prisms. Result is a reduction of size as well as weight.

E. Leitz, Inc.: Trinovid binocular

Diagrams (center, right) show the path of light beam passing through binoculars provided with Uppendahl prisms and with Porro prisms (far right.)

Bausch & Lomb, Inc.: Balscope Senior

Spotting scope (right) is popular with birdwatchers who specialize in shore birds. It requires the use of a tripod. It can be adapted to telephotography.

Some scopes are sold with a simple attachment that makes it possible to fix them to the window of a car.

Bird books—A good bird book makes it possible for you to identify the birds you see—provided you know how to use it.

In most guides, the birds are arranged by families. It won't take you long to get accustomed to this arrangement. The bird bobbing on the lake's surface "looks like a duck." No doubt it is, so you notice its colors and markings and look it up in the section on "Ducks." A bird feeding on the ground has a short stout bill and a "sparrowlike" build. You refer to the section that covers "Sparrows, finches, etc." Eventually, the classification of a bird and its family becomes almost second nature to you. You are well launched on your career as an expert bird watcher.

BOOKS FOR FIELD IDENTIFICATION—R. T. Peterson, *Field Guide to the Birds. Field Guide to the Western Birds.* New York, Houghton Mifflin Company.

Chandler S. Robbins, Bertel Bruun, and Herbert S. Zim, *Birds of North America: A Guide to Field Identification.* New York, Golden Press.

Leon A. Hausman, *Field Book of Eastern Birds.* New York, G. P. Putnam's Sons.

G. H. Pough, *Audubon Land Bird Guide. Audubon Water Bird Guide. Audubon Western Bird Guide.* New York, Doubleday & Company.

Notebook—No serious bird student is ever without a notebook— a pocket-sized book in which you make notes of the field trips you take, including dates, weather, and locality, and of the birds you see and identify.

Finding Birds

The first indication of the presence of a bird may be its song floating to you through the air. The rustle in dry leaves on the forest floor may tell you of another, motion among the branches in a treetop of still others. Dark silhouettes may soar above you in the sky or move across a sunlit lake.

To find birds, keep your eyes open wherever you are, and scan the whole wide out-of-doors—from sky to ground, the compass round.

WHERE?—Birds may be found almost anywhere.

Here!—The place to begin looking for them is Here—on your own front lawn or in your backyard. Know your own birds well before you start looking in the other fellow's yard.

Wildlife communities—The next step is to become familiar with the wildlife communities in your vicinity—whether grassland or marshes, forests or mountains, deserts or ocean shores—and search out each territory for the bird life in it. By studying birds in relation to their surroundings, you will learn far more about them than by just walking cross-country listing whatever birds you see.

Specific species—Later on, you may want to locate certain species.

Then it is a matter of looking them up in your bird book, finding out in what surroundings they live, and seeking them there.

REFERENCES—Olin S. Pettingill, Jr., *A Guide to Bird Finding East of the Mississippi. A Guide to Bird Finding West of the Mississippi.* New York, Oxford University Press.

Olin S. Pettingill, Jr., ed., *The Birdwatcher's America.* New York, McGraw-Hill Book Company.

WHEN?—Time of year—YEAR ROUND—The number of different birds will fluctuate greatly with the season. Certain birds will be *permanent residents* in your section. In spring, a number of *summer visitors* may arrive from the south. They leave in the fall, to be replaced by *winter visitors* coming down from the north. In spring and fall, *transients* will stop by for a short stay during their migrations. And finally, there are the *accidental visitors* that may drop in, off their usual course.

WINTER—Winter is a good time to begin your bird study. Comparatively few birds are around, and there are no leaves or luxuriant weed growth to obscure them. Then, as spring and summer set in, you add new birds to your list daily, as they arrive.

Now!—But the best time to start is right Now—whether this be winter or summer—provided you don't insist on knowing every bird you see the first time you see it.

Time of day—The early bird catches the worm. The early watcher sees the birds.

DAYBREAK—Birds are active in greatest numbers around daybreak. So check the calendar for the hour of sunrise, and plan to be up and out about an hour earlier. Your best bird-watching time is from early dusk until the sun is four fingers above the horizon.

EVENING—Second best is the evening, from an hour before sunset until dusk turns into darkness.

Weather—The weather conditions will influence the number of birds you see. You will see most on mornings that are cool and clear. When the weather turns rainy and gray, windy and raw, the birds remain in hiding.

Bird Walking

Set the alarm early for a spring or summer bird walk—3 A.M. (four o'clock for Daylight Saving Time). Get up early enough to dress warmly and to eat a bit of breakfast before you set out. There's little enjoyment in a bird walk if you are shivery and hungry. Pick up field glasses, field book, and notebook, and be on your way.

You may like to have a couple of companions along, or even a small group of bird enthusiasts. More than half a dozen is inadvisable unless they are oldtimers in the art of bird walking and know how to walk and act.

"*Go West*"—Greeley's old advice, "Go west, young man, go west," might have been written for early morning bird walkers. By planning your hike, as far as possible, so that you will be going west, you will have the rising sun behind you. Therefore its rays will fall full on the birds in front of you. Instead of seeing them as dark silhouettes, you will be able to observe their colorings.

Walk briskly toward the territory that is the objective of the morning's investigation. When you get there, slow down and move forward softly, with smooth motions.

"Stop . . ."—"Stop, look and listen" is another fitting slogan for bird walkers. Stop often, and scan the surroundings for movements that will betray the presence of a bird. Stop long enough to let birds that may have become alarmed feel secure again and resume their singing. You can then locate them by their song.

When you notice a bird, freeze in your tracks, and bring your field glasses up to your eyes in a long smooth motion. Any sudden, jerky motion is sure to scare the bird. Move closer only when the bird seems to pay no attention to you.

If you want to communicate your findings to your companions, or to get their assurance that your identification is correct, do it in your normal tone of voice, as in ordinary conversation. Some birds pick up the hissing sounds of whispering far more readily than they do the deeper sounds of talking. Leon A. Hausman sums it up very neatly: "When among warblers, talk like a duck." But he adds: "When among ducks, talk like a warbler." Birds with low-pitched calls hear low notes but do not pick up the high-pitched ones.

"Try squeaking"—If your bird is too far away for good observation, you may be able to "squeak" it closer. Purse your lips and place

Squeaking (left) is an effective way of attracting birds. So is the use of the so-called Audubon bird call (right).

them against the back of your hand or against a finger. Then draw in your breath in a long squeaky kiss. Repeat a few moments later. The sound you produce resembles the distress signal of a bird in agony. The inborn curiosity of all birds does the rest.

An even more effective method of drawing a bird closer is an imitation of its song. Your early attempts may be crude, but they should improve with practice (see page 63). You may also use a mechanical device to imitate the sound of birds (see page 64).

"Take notes"—Keep the birds under close watch. Then before

you move on, get out your notebook and jot down your observations.

If the bird was not immediately identified, write down enough notes about it to make identification possible later. The six S's of field identification will suggest the necessary information:

SIZE—Estimate the size as compared with some familiar bird: house wren, 5 inches; house sparrow, 6 inches; robin, 10 inches; blue jay, 12 inches; crow, 20 inches; all measured from tip of bill to end of tail.

SHAPE—Long and slim; short and plump; legs long or short; bill long or short, slender, broad, or conical; tail long or short, squared or forked; head rounded or crested.

SHADINGS—Color and markings; hue, solid or varied; breast, head, wings, tail.

SONG—Harmonious, clear, harsh, shrill, sibilant, buzzy, mechanical, tremulous, etc.

SWEEP—Movements on ground, among branches, while flying: arrowlike flight, erratic, undulating, soaring, skimming, bounding; wingbeats fast, slow.

SURROUNDINGS—Territory where you observed it: woods or open field, marshland, lake, seashore, and so on.

If you come home from your bird walk knowing the birds of your locality a little better, and possibly one of them especially well, your efforts are well paid.

REFERENCES—Henry Hill Collins, *Bird Watchers' Guide*. New York, Golden Press.
Joseph J. Hickey, *A Guide to Bird Watching*. New York, Doubleday & Company.

Bird Songs

When you hear a bird song, locate the singer and identify it. From that moment on, attempt to associate that song with that bird, that bird with that song. Eventually, you will be able to tell a bird by its singing alone.

HELPS FOR IDENTIFYING BIRD SONGS—The only really effective way of identifying a bird by its song is to see the bird so often while it is singing that sight and sound become inseparable. It may take you a number of field trips before you master a song. In the meantime one of the following short cuts may help you:

Recordings—A number of bird songs have been recorded on sound tape and transcribed to records with great fidelity. Listen to repeated playing of these records until your memory retains some of the songs.

RECORDS—Roger T. Peterson, Arthur A. Allen, and Peter Paul Kellogg, *Field Guide to Bird Songs. Field Guide to Western Bird Songs*. Boston, Houghton Mifflin Company.
Cornell University, *Songbirds of America. Birdsongs in Your Garden*. Boston, Houghton Mifflin Company.

Word associations—Your first impression of a bird's singing may be that it is buzzing, chirping, melodious, metallic, raucous, warbling, or what-not. Then, as you listen, the sounds begin to take on a certain coherence. It will help you to remember a bird's song if you can make the sounds spell out familiar words or, better, phrases of related words.

Your bird field book may suggest that the song of the black-throated green warbler sounds like "zee-zee-zoo-zoo-zee." How much easier to remember if you hear it as "Trees, trees, murmuring trees"—or even as "Cheese, cheese, Limburger cheese"—depending upon the poetry in your soul. Check for yourself the olive-sided flycatcher's "whip-whee-wheer" against "Whoops! Three beers!"

It pays to develop your own system, and depend on other people's inventions only when they are as well established as "teacher, teacher, teacher" for the oven bird, "Madgie, Madgie, Madgie, put on your tea-kettle-ettle-ettle" for the song sparrow, and "Old Sam Peabody, Peabody, Peabody" for the white-throated sparrow—or "Oh Sweet Canada, Canada, Canada" if you happen to live north of the border.

Some of these word associations have been so generally accepted that they have become the names of the birds. When a strong and vibrant "whip-poor-will" floats to you on the night air, you know immediately that a whippoorwill is about. Similarly, you will have little difficulty in recognizing killdeer, peewee, bobwhite, chickadee.

Musical notes—If you are musically inclined, you may see a bird song in your mind's eye as a regular piece of music, and jot it down that way. This can be only approximate, since no instrument can faithfully reproduce the songs of birds.

BOOK ON BIRD SONGS—F. Schuyler Mathews, *Field Book of Wild Birds and Their Music*. New York, Dover Publications. Bird songs expressed by means of musical notes.

Symbols—Simpler than musical interpretation is a system of lines and figures representing notes, their length and quality. The pitch of a note may be indicated by the relative position of the sign, its duration by the length of the line that makes up the sign, its quality by the shape of it.

BOOK ON BIRD SONGS—Aretas A. Saunders, *A Guide to Bird Songs*. New York, Doubleday & Company. Bird songs shown by a system of lines.

Sonagrams—By methods developed by Dr. P. P. Kellogg of Cornell University, bird songs can be recorded and reproduced audibly or visually in the form of audiospectograms or "sonagrams." The typical sonagram covers $2\frac{1}{2}$ seconds of song. It shows pitch, quality, phrasing, tempo, lengths, and changes in loudness. With a little practice, you will soon learn to recognize a bird song from its sonagram.

BOOK ON BIRD SONGS—Chandler Robbins, Bertel Brunn, and Herbert S. Zim, *Birds of North America: A Guide to Field Identification*. New York, Golden Press. Includes sonagrams of the songs of most of the species covered.

IMITATING BIRD SONGS—"Let's all sing like the birdies sing . . ." Would be swell if we could! It would be our best means of getting birds close to us for inspection and identification. We can't because we have no syrinx. Nevertheless, with what we have, it is possible to give a fair imitation that will fool the less discriminating birds.

Whistling—Even without being an expert whistler, it should not take you long to learn to imitate the songs of chickadees, orioles, phoebes, and several other birds that have simple call notes. All that is needed is a straight outward or inward whistling through puckered lips.

Lip-tongue whistling—For some bird songs, you need to coordinate lips and tongue. Take the song of the robin, for instance. You can express it fairly well in words: "Cheerily, cheer-up, cheerily, cheer-up." Say those words aloud. Notice how the tip of the tongue flutters behind the upper teeth? Now give a straight whistle. Next, combine this whistle with the flutter of the tongue tip. Finally, get the correct pitch and timing by listening to a real robin. And there you are!

Numerous other bird songs may be imitated in this manner—by combining whistling with steady or quivering lips, with the tongue action used for speaking the approximate sounds. Keep the lips in a tight pucker with a small opening for the high reedy calls. For lower-pitched calls, open up the lips wider, and tighten your cheek muscles to create a sounding box.

Other imitations—For still other calls, you must be able to vibrate the soft palate in the back of your mouth. That's a trick you may master by drawing in your breath along the roof of the mouth. Now combine it with an inward whistle to effect the trill of many bird songs.

By combining quivering lips, fluttering tongue tip, vibrating soft palate, there's hardly a bird song you can't imitate. But it will take plenty of practice before you reach that point.

Use of hands—For imitating the hooting of owls and the mournful moanings of doves and cuckoos, use a sounding box made by cupping

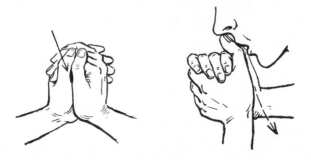

When imitating hollow sounds, make a sounding box of your cupped hands and blow down over thumb knuckles.

your hands together. Wet your lips, place them against the knuckles of your thumbs, and blow down into the hollow between your hands, the way you blow down into a bottle to make it whistle. You can vary the pitch of the sound by wagging your fingers. With a little practice, you can turn your hands into an instrument on which you can produce numerous flutelike birdcall imitations.

Mechanical devices—You can imitate the hammering of a wood-pecker searching for insects in the bark by rubbing the edge of a piece of stiff cardboard or thin plywood over the teeth cut in another piece of the same material.

To honk with geese and gobble with turkeys, cut off the top of a quart-sized plastic bottle down to 3 inches from the bottom. Squeeze the sides of the cup that results into a long oval, then draw a nail file over the edges. Single strokes imitate honking; back-and-forth rubbing gives a fair imitation of turkey gobbling.

The so-called "Audubon birdcall," available in pet shops, is an effective mechanical device for attracting birds. It consists of a small metal tube into which a plug is fitted. By turning the plug at different speeds, the device can be made to give off a wide variety of chirps, trills and other bird notes (see illustration page 60).

Many sporting goods stores carry various devices into which you blow to imitate certain birdcalls, specifically the calls of duck, goose, crow, hawk, and turkey. They are easy to use, even for a novice.

RECORDING BIRD SONGS—With modern tape recording equipment, you can record the songs of the birds of your backyard, garden, or camp.

The most desirable model for bird song recording is a portable, battery-operated tape recorder with AVC (automatic volume control). Pick a model that uses regular, open-tape reels rather than cassettes. It is easy to cut and edit and splice an open tape, but a major undertaking to get at the tape in a cassette.

For a general record, it is just a matter of placing the mike, early on a spring morning, close to the perch from which the male is usually singing, and running a long mike wire to the place where you are hiding with the recorder. When the bird starts singing, switch on the mike and the recorder.

A windscreen around the mike will muffle the whistle of the wind, but it will not prevent the mike from picking up the noises of dogs barking, roosters crowing, airplanes flying overhead, trucks passing on a nearby highway.

¶ *Tip*—The windscreen may be purchased or made from accoustical sponge rubber. Even a ¼-inch-thick slice of a plastic kitchen sponge placed over the mike will do the trick.

REFERENCE—For further information on bird song recording, drop a line to Ornithology Department, Cornell University, Ithaca, New York. Cooperate by sending unusual tapes to the Library of Bird Sounds at the University.

Finding Nests

Finding birds' nests is like playing detective: The untrained sleuth finds his clues by stumbling over them; the trained detective knows where to look for them. You may locate your first few nests by accident, but when you become a skilled bird watcher, your eyes will be drawn almost automatically toward them.

WHERE?—It will help you immeasurably in locating nests if you let your bird field book tell you where to look for them. When you hear a singing towhee, then you will know that there's no sense in looking high in the trees for its nest because towhees build on the ground. Similarly, when you see a Baltimore oriole, you will immediately look up and try to find its hanging nest among the drooping branches of a tall tree high above you.

As in all other bird watching, "Stop, look, and listen" is the key to finding nests—but place the emphasis on the listening. Singing indicates the presence of a male announcing its territorial rights, which, in turn, means a mate and a nest. Locate the singer in your field glasses, watch his actions, look for the female. Follow the two with your eyes until you discover the nest.

REFERENCES—*Audubon Bird Guides* (see page 58) give clear description of nest localities.
Richard Headstrom, *Birds' Nests: A Field Guide. Birds' Nests of the West: A Field Guide.* New York, Doubleday & Company.

Ground nests—Most ground nests are located by flushing the female off her eggs or young by walking zigzag through a field where you suspect a nest. The spot from which the female flies up may not necessarily be where the nest is located. The smarter birds "sneak" along the ground before flying up to draw your attention away from the nest.

¶ *Tip*—In the field, marsh, and meadow, you can make use of a "flushing line"—a 50- or 100-foot-long ¼-inch manila rope or clothesline. With a companion, walk over the ground, with the rope between you in such a way that it drags over the top of the grass.

Low bush nests—Spread some of the branches apart carefully, and peer inside. Or shake or strike gently the outside branches to flush possible birds off their nests. Then study the interior.

Tree nests—Scan the trees systematically with your binoculars, sweeping the field slowly from left to right, along the treetops, then farther down from right to left, still farther down from left to right, from branch tip to branch tip, until the whole location has been carefully studied.

¶ *Tip*—It is easy to ascertain if there are eggs in a nest on the ground or in a low bush, but what about nests in high shrubs and trees? For these, use a pole mirror. This is simply a broomstick or a clip-on mop handle with a hand mirror or shaving mirror attached horizontally, the mirror side down, to the top end. You hold the mirror above the nest and study the mirror image from below.

Cavity nests—Some birds—woodpeckers, owls, flickers, wrens, and nuthatches—nest in cavities in dead trees. Locate a dead tree. Study the base of it for telltale chips that indicate that holes have been expanded into suitable nests. But chips or no chips, scrutinize every dead tree in your binoculars for possible nest holes. Watch the opening until the bird shows itself.

Other nests—Nests of certain birds must be looked for in their own peculiar places: bank swallows by looking in burrows in sandy banks, marsh birds by wading among the reeds in hip boots, barn swallows and phoebes by checking on top of crossbeams in barns and garages, seabirds by following sandy and rocky shorelines, herons, hawks, and eagles by climbing trees with steel climbers attached to your feet, and so on.

CAUTION—Be careful not to disturb the vegetation that shades a nest. Also, do not return too often or go too close to a nest. The human scent you leave may cause one of the bird's enemies to investigate —to the detriment of the bird. Instead, do most of your nest watching from a distance through field glasses.

WHEN?—Birds' nests may be found throughout the year, but they are most easily seen at certain seasons.

FALL AND WINTER—For the beginner, the best time to look for nests is late fall, winter, or early spring, when the leaves are off the trees and therefore do not hide the nests. The trouble is that at that time of the year the nests are empty and therefore of little interest beyond their structure and location.

SPRING AND SUMMER—The perfect time to locate birds' nests is spring and early summer. During nest construction, birds carrying nesting material will give the position of the nest away. Later, after the eggs are incubated, birds carrying food will do the same.

¶ *Tip*—Continue your nest hunting well into the summer—late July or early August. Some birds are late nesters: waxwings and goldfinches, among others. You may also find second broods—or even thirds—of birds you missed earlier.

RECORDING YOUR NEST FINDS—Make a complete census of the nests you find, including such data as:

Nest of...........................(name) Found on...........(date)

On ground? Grass............... Sand............... Rock............

In what bush or tree?.................... Height?....................

Containing.........eggs.........fledglings. Abandoned..............

Make a simple sketch of the area and indicate the nest location so that you can find it again.

Bird Watching

When you begin to bird-watch, you move from the general field of birds to the specific. The difference between bird walking and bird watching may be considered the jump from seeing *birds*, in the plural, to observing *bird*, in the singular. Or if not studying a single bird, at

To do a systematic scanning job, sweep the field of the binoculars from left to right, then from right to left.

least concentrating more definitely on the *intensive* life study of certain species, or on definite problems that await solution. It is no longer a matter of listing birds, but of finding out how birds live. The very word "watching" suggests keen and patient observation. For lasting importance, it should be accompanied by careful and extensive note taking.

BLINDS—While much bird watching can be done with binoculars, much more can be accomplished by using a blind. A blind is simply a structure, put up close to a bird's nest or at a spot where it feeds or bathes, in which you can hide, unobserved by the bird. The blind you want will depend on your needs and your imagination.

Car as blind—If it is possible for you to drive your car reasonably close to the area you want to watch, you have solved your problem in the easiest way possible. After first being scared away by the approach of the car, the birds quickly get accustomed to it when the motor is shut off. You can then observe them with or without binoculars.

Improvised blind—A blind may be of natural materials found on the spot. Push a few sticks in the ground, in the form of a rectangle. Tie crosspieces to them. Then, lean leafy branches or reeds against this crude framework.

¶ *Tip*—A piece of 5-foot chicken wire makes an excellent foundation for a blind made of native materials.

Umbrella blind—The umbrella blind was originally described by Dr. F. M. Chapman. In its simplest form it consists of an old beach

An old beach umbrella makes a good bird blind. Provide it with side curtains, staking them down firmly at bottom.

umbrella camouflaged with green or brownish-green canvas paint. The "handle" is pushed into the ground or tied to a pole driven in at an appropriate spot. A piece of fabric, about 7 feet wide, and slightly longer than the circumference of the umbrella, is attached, as a curtain, along the edge of the umbrella with hooks or safety pins. The bottom edge of the curtain is staked to the ground so that it does not flap.

By using a lightweight cambric, muslin, or percale sheeting dyed leaf green (olive green), you can see out through the fabric while the bird cannot see in. For unobstructed observation, cut slits at suitable places and hold them open with spreaders of thin wood.

Tent blind—Several tent models—particularly those set up with an aluminum frame—are suitable for use as a blind. Even better is a tent specifically designed for the purpose. The easiest blind to transport and to put up is a three-sided tent with one side—the front—vertical.

For this, use two 6-foot lengths and one 9-foot length of 1-inch dowels or bamboo poles. Fasten them together near one end with a tripod lashing or with a long slender bolt with a wing nut. Set up and spread over the tripod a cover made from burlap or tent material, cut and sewn to fit. For entering and leaving, sew a zipper along one edge. For viewing, cut one or more viewing holes in the front side. Sew a piece of netting over each of these holes through which you can see without being seen. Attach tapes at the bottom edges with which to tie the cover to the poles. Or if you like, tack the whole cover onto the tripod for especially easy pitching and striking of the blind.

Framework blind—A tent blind may also be made from a framework of lightweight angle aluminum put together with bolts and wing nuts and covered with burlap or other material. Such a blind can be erected quickly and can be taken apart to occupy little space.

REFERENCE—For detailed instructions for making a framework blind, see booklet *Here's How* (No. 2), Eastman Kodak Company, Rochester, New York 14650.

A frame for a bird blind may be made from one-inch pipe or from dowels or bamboo. Cover with camouflaged burlap.

Box blind—For observation over a long period, you may desire a more permanent structure. Several ornithologists have made use of blinds constructed from walls of waterproof plywood, with small openings at strategical places for observation, and with shelves attached to the inside for equipment—photographic and other.

USING THE BLIND—With the construction of the blind completed, you are ready to place the blind in position for use.

Placing the blind—For certain nest studies, as well as for photography, you will want to be within 5 feet of your bird, or possibly closer. You will have little luck if you should abruptly dump the blind at this distance. You will almost certainly scare the bird away for good.

Instead, put up the blind 30 to 40 feet from the nest. Leave it here for a couple of hours or longer until the bird has become accustomed to this addition to the landscape. Then move it closer by half the distance and leave it again. Work for not more than ten minutes each time, then walk away to permit the bird to return to its nest. At long last, place the blind in its final position. If possible, before you occupy it, leave it here for a number of hours or, better, overnight.

Occupying the blind—For most birds, you can go directly into the blind. They will quickly forget that you are present.

For other birds, a more careful procedure is necessary. Here you may need the help of a companion to act as a decoy. The two of you approach the blind together. You step inside the blind while your friend moves away from it. The bird seems to figure, "Something came; something went; coast is clear," and returns to its nest. Without the decoy, you may have to wait for quite a while before the bird dares come back. When ready to leave, use your friend again to decoy you away.

While in the blind, move as little as possible. Use your observation slots carefully, opening them in slow motion. Keep the interior dark. The darker it is, the harder it is for the bird to notice any movements in the blind.

If you expect to stay in the blind for an extended time, make yourself comfortable. Bring a small collapsible canvas chair to sit on, a sandwich to eat, a canteen of drinkables to refresh you— perhaps even a book to read while you wait for action.

Bird Lists

As you become familiar with more and more birds, you will want to keep track of those you identify. You start listing the birds you see on your walks. Soon, bird listing becomes a sport you play with yourself and with your companions.

Eventually, carefully kept lists may become of scientific importance by throwing light on many things that are not yet clear, such as an abundance of birds at certain times of the year, fluctuation in migration, and so forth.

PERIODICAL—*Audubon Field Notes*—Bimonthly magazine devoted to results of bird watching. National Audubon Society, 1130 Fifth Avenue, New York, New York 10028.

DAILY LISTS—Whenever you take a bird walk, jot down the species you see, and the number of birds of the different species.

Daily field trip card—Instead of writing down the names of the birds each time, you can simplify the matter by using a printed "field trip card" listing the names of birds in your locality. Some of the national bird societies have these available at low cost. A number of local bird clubs print their own.

The filled-in cards can be filed in chronological order or according to locality. Or the information can be transferred to a journal.

Big day list—You may get a kick out of trying to beat your own previous record of number of birds seen. Your best chance comes during the height of the spring migration, in the middle of May. Get up before dawn, and stay out all day. Visit as many different habitats as possible—from wood-edged meadows and open fields to forests and marshes. Return home after evening dusk has fallen.

¶ *Tip—Big Day Walks* often have a strong appeal to clubs and youth groups. On one of these walks, aim for a *Century Run*, where the object is to see a hundred species or more within a day. Organize these walks into tournaments of several teams.

Most-wanted list—Keep a separate list of birds that have been observed in your locality but which you have not yet seen. Be on a special lookout for these birds whenever you go bird walking. You will have an extra thrill whenever you spot one of them.

Christmas bird count—Every year the National Audubon Society sponsors a Christmas Bird Count. The count covers one calendar day during the period, approximately from December 25 to January 2 as announced. Any group interested in birds may organize a count within its own locality.

To prepare for the count, get a topographic map of your area. Draw a circle of 15-mile diameter of the specific territory you want

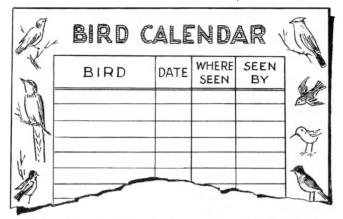

The making of a bird calendar appeals greatly to school children and youth groups. Give credit to the observers.

to cover. Investigate the area in advance and decide on the most effective way of covering it.

A dawn-to-dusk investigation on the day of the count is of greatest significance. If that is not possible, at least seven full hours should be spent in the field.

Write up a report covering location, habitat, time, weather, species, and numbers seen, names of people participating. Mail the report so that it is in the hands of the Audubon Society not later than mid-January. Acceptable reports are published in the spring issue of *Audubon Field Notes*.

Note—Write to *Audubon Field Notes*, National Audubon Society, for full particulars on making the Christmas Bird Count and on preparing the report.

YEAR LISTS—Bird lists become especially valuable when kept on a year-to-year basis.

Yearly records—When you get home from a bird walk, transfer the information from the daily list to a permanent record book, to a loose-leaf notebook, or to separate file cards for each bird. In this way, you build up a list of birds seen the year round.

Two hundred species is a good score if you are located along the American coastline. An inland score of one hundred and fifty is excellent.

RECORD BOOK—H. E. Jaques, *Field Notebook for Studying Birds.* Dubuque, Iowa, William C. Brown Company.

Bird calendars—The dates on which certain birds arrive in the spring will take on special significance to you in making your yearly lists. When do you usually see your first robin? Is spring early or late this year?

With the listing of birds by the calendar, you enter the science of *phenology*—still another case where the "Greeks have a word for it," from *phainein*, to appear, and *logo*, to study: the study of the chronological appearance of things in nature.

¶ *Tip*—The making of *Bird Calendar Charts* appeals to school-children and youth groups. Make a chart with space for the name of the bird, when first seen, where, by whom. If possible, decorate chart with colored Audubon Society pictures or photographs of the birds.

LIFE LISTS—Out of your daily lists and your yearly listings come the names of the birds you have seen throughout your career as a bird watcher.

Keeping a life list—The simplest way of keeping your life list is to use your bird guidebook. Write in it, next to the description of the bird, the date and the place where you first saw it. As the years go by, your bird book will take on life as a permanent reminder of thousands of happy hours spent in the field.

Field Observations

Although great steps have been taken in uncovering the secrets of bird life, today the complete life history is known for comparatively few birds, and there is room for much study of the broad subjects of territory, songs, nesting, migration.

The following list may contain suggestions for phases of bird study that you may want to investigate:

Arrival of migrants—Do males and females arrive together or separately? If separately, which arrives first? Do younger birds arrive before or after the older birds? Relationship between arrival and weather conditions, status of local vegetation and insect life.

Pairing—Are birds paired on arrival, or does pairing take place afterward? Evidences of courtship display observed.

Territory—Do males establish and defend territories (by singing, fighting, pursuit) before or after pairing? How large is the territory? What are its characteristics—forest, field, marsh, edge, or what? Do females assist in territory defense? How? Distinction between breeding and feeding territories? Are both defended?

Singing—How many different types of calls and songs? For what purpose are they used—summoning, scolding, warning, no apparent purpose, etc.? Is singing done in flight, from ground, from nest, from perch? What time of day? Do females sing? At what time of season does singing end?

Nest building—Does male or female build the nest? If both, which does the most work? What time of day is the nest built? Full description of all steps—from selection of spot to final nest, including list of materials used.

Eggs—How soon after nest building are eggs laid? How long before clutch is completed? How many eggs? Do male and female both set? For how long a period does each set? What is the length of the incubation period? How many eggs hatch?

Nestlings—How do parent birds approach the nest with food? How many feeding trips are taken by males, females, during the day? How do nestlings react? What calls have they? How old are nestlings when they leave the nest? Do they leave by themselves, or are they encouraged by parent birds? For how long after leaving are they fed by the parents?

Number of broods—Evidence of second brood? Third brood? Is previous site used for nesting?

Fall migration—Do migrants disappear by couples, small groups, flocks? Do other species join the flock? What maneuvering does the flock perform before leaving? Relationship between departure and weather conditions, status of local vegetation.

Special problems—Testing intelligence and use of senses. Feeding habits. Molting. Deformities, parasites, and diseases. Enemies. Roosting of wintering birds.

REFERENCE—Olin Sewall Pettingill, Jr., *A Laboratory and Field Manual of Ornithology*. Minneapolis, Minnesota, Burgess Publishing Company.

Each issue of the periodicals of the various ornithological societies contains numerous suggestions for investigation and methods to use.

BIRDS AROUND THE HOUSE

Instead of going far afield to watch birds, you may get your main pleasure out of bird watching by attracting them to your home—by having their singing and graceful beauty add charm to your grounds and garden. Your efforts will be comparatively small—whether they involve feeding, nesting helps, or special plantings—but your satisfaction will be great.

REFERENCES—John K. Terres, *Songbirds in Your Garden*. New York, Thomas Y. Crowell Company.

Verne E. Davison, *Attracting Birds: From the Prairies to the Atlantic*. New York, Thomas Y. Crowell Company.

Thomas P. McElroy, *New Handbook of Attracting Birds*. New York, Alfred A. Knopf.

Margaret McKenny, *Birds in the Garden and How to Attract Them*. New York, Grosset & Dunlap.

B. M. Parker, *Birds in Your Back Yard*. New York, Harper & Row Publishers.

W. L. McAtee, *Attracting Birds*. (Catalog No. I 1.72:1/2. Fifteen cents.) From Superintendent of Documents, U.S. Government Printing Office, Washington, D.C. 20402.

Bird Feeding

The feeding you do in summer will be almost completely for your own enjoyment. Many birds will like the idea of an easy handout, even when native food is plentiful.

Done in the winter, the feeding will give you the added satisfaction of knowing that you are helping to conserve bird life, specifically through severe periods of ice and heavy snow. One thing is important: When you have once started winter feeding, be certain to keep it up regularly. You have made the birds depend on you, rather than on their own ingenuity, and it may prove a great hardship for them if you should fail in what, by your own action, has become your duty.

Several small feeders are better than one large one. Whatever your design, put up the feeders close to shelter and quick escape if predators should appear on the scene.

FOODS—The food you serve will depend on the birds you hope to attract. Woodpeckers, nuthatches, and other insect eaters will be attracted by animal or vegetable fats. Sparrows, juncos, cardinals, and finches stick almost exclusively to a diet of seeds, whereas chickadees and titmice prefer variety. Robins, mockingbirds, and cedar waxwings are mostly fruit eaters. Hummingbirds are famous for their preference for flower nectar.

Fats—Suet, fat trimmings from beef and other meats are eagerly accepted by many insect eaters. So are bacon rinds and chopped meat—even bones with a few shreds of meat left on them. Nutmeats are also in demand, especially peanuts, chopped or as peanut butter.

Seeds—There is a great diversity of acceptable seeds. Hemp and millet rank high on the list. They are followed by sunflower seeds, and the seeds of the cucumber family: squash, pumpkin, cantaloupe, watermelon. Then there are the grains: corn (whole, cracked, meal, and hominy), popcorn (popped and ground), whole or rolled oats, barley, wheat. Buckwheat. Kafir corn and other sorghums. Soybeans. Pasture grass seeds.

¶ *Tip*—Screenings from grain mills and sweepings from haymows are sources of inexpensive seed feed.

To provide for varying tastes, use a mixture of seeds; this is better than a single type. Commercial "chicken feed" is a usable mixture. Better still is the so-called wild-bird seeds, mixtures which may be bought by the pound in many grocery stores, and through the National Audubon Society. Most of these wild-bird mixtures contain millet, Kafir corn, cracked peanuts, sunflower seeds.

¶ *Tip*—Add 1 ounce of fine poultry grit or coarse sand to each pound of seed mixture when snow covers the natural supply.

Fruits—Simplest to handle are dried fruits and berries: chopped, dried apples and peaches, raisins and currants. Cut up fresh apples, oranges, bananas.

Miscellaneous—Numerous other foods will be taken by birds: leftover bread, crackers, fatty cakes like doughnuts and pastries, crumbs, bakery scraps, dog meal or crushed dog biscuits, cooked spaghetti or macaroni, table scraps, chopped lettuce, egg shells, ants' "eggs," mealworms.

Nectar—You can make a nectar substitute for summer feeding of hummingbirds by dissolving 1 tablespoon of sugar in 2 tablespoons

Suet feeders come in many forms—from a crocheted bag and a suet stick to a soap tray and pinecones.

of water or by mixing 1 tablespoon of honey with 2 tablespoons of water.

¶ *Tip*—Make a larger supply of nectar in the same 1-to-2 proportion and store it in a plastic squeeze bottle in the refrigerator.

SUET AND FAT FEEDERS—Your feeders can be as simple or as elaborate as you care to make them, as long as they serve their purpose. Pieces of suet, for example, may be tied directly to tree branches with cords, or served up in a number of ways (see illustrations above):

Suet bag—Make a crocheted mesh bag for the suet, or use a plastic mesh bag. Fill with suet. Nail to a post or tie to a branch. The bag will prevent a greedy robber from stealing the whole suet supply in one fell swoop.

Suet sticks—The suet stick is a popular device: Drill a number of holes, 1 inch in diameter, 1½ inches deep, in a small log, about 2 feet long, 2 to 3 inches in diameter. Leave the bark on. Or use a piece of 4 by 4, 18 inches long, instead of the rustic log. Press the suet into the holes.

Suspend the stick by a screw eye in one end, in a piece of wire. Or spike it horizontally to a post.

Suet mixtures—Mixtures of suet and fats with other foods have a great variety of uses.

Mix melted-down suet and fats with bread crumbs, chopped peanuts, and wild-bird seeds, in the proportion of two parts fat to one part dry ingredients. Pour mixture into holes of suet stick. Or pour it into half shells of grapefruit or coconut and hang these up by strings or wire. Or smear it into deep cracks in tree bark. Or pour it over branches of discarded Christmas tree to produce a *bird Christmas tree*. Or pour it into a can from which the mixture can be removed as a *bird cake* when cooled, by dipping it for a moment in hot water.

SEED AND FRUIT FEEDERS—Seed feeders are the most common food dispensers for winter feeding.

Food tray—A food tray or shelf, a foot square or larger, made from 1-inch wood, is about the simplest possible feeding device. Nail a 2-inch rim around the edge to keep the food from being brushed or blown off.

The food tray may be attached to a pole or a tree in a sheltered spot, or placed in front of a window. In the latter case, build it the length of the window and 1 foot wide, and if possible, arrange it so that the food may be replenished from inside the house. Provide it with a glass roof, if this is desired.

Box feeder—For winter feeding, a box feeder is preferable to a tray. In its simplest form, it is a topless wooden box placed on one side so that the opposite side forms a protecting roof over the food. Mount it on a pole or a pivot so that the open front can be turned away from the wind and rain and snow.

¶ *Tip*—If you attach one or two vanes to the box, the wind itself will keep the opening turned in the proper direction (see diagram, page 77).

Feed hopper—A small hopper will simplify the matter of feeding by replenishing the food automatically, by gravity, from a main supply. Commercial hen-house hoppers may be used. You can make your own from wood or construct it by cementing one plastic bottle to a bowl made of another (see drawings, page 77).

An even simpler feed hopper can be made from a large juice can, a pie tin, a pizza tin, and a coat hanger. After opening the can with a juice can opener, cut another couple of holes in the top for pouring

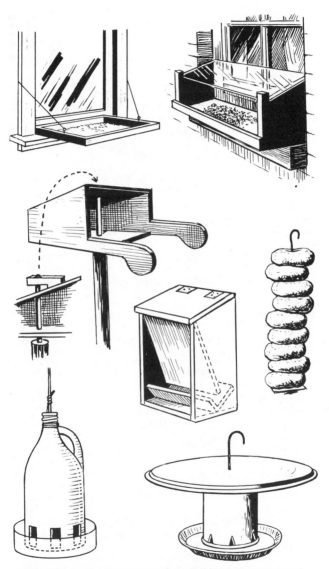

Seed feeders made from wood, cans, plastic bottles. They can be made to swing with the wind (center, left).

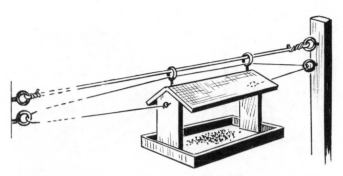

A trolley feeder can be suspended between window and a post in the garden. It moves in screw eyes along a wire.

in the feed, and half a dozen holes in the side of the can along the bottom for the feed to run out. Open up and straighten out the coat hanger, with the exception of the hook. Run the wire down through centered nail holes in the pizza tin, in the top and bottom of can, and in the pie tin. Bend the wire at a 90-degree angle under the pie tin to hold everything in place. Fill with feed and hang over a branch.

¶ *Tip*—The simplest feeder imaginable is a *doughnut feeder*. Open up a coat hanger and straighten out the wire, with the exception of the hook. Bend 2 inches of the opposite end into a similar hook. String the wire with a dozen doughnuts and hang it on a branch or outside a window.

¶ *Tip*—Birds may shy away from your window feeder. To draw them near, make a *trolley feeder*—a roofed tray on a pulley line between the windows and a nearby tree. As the birds get accustomed to coming, draw the feeder closer and closer to the window.

NECTAR FEEDERS—Hummingbirds need a different kind of dispenser for their liquid food.

Hummingbird vials—The sugar "nectar" for hummingbirds (page 74) may be served in tiny vials or small test tubes (size A) or small plastic pill bottles hung by "flower wire" or copper wire among flowers regularly visited. Place them at a height varying from 2 to 5 feet.

¶ *Tip*—For quick attraction, attach a small collar of red crepe paper, cloth, or plastic sheet around the opening of the tube, with a rubber band. Or wrap with waterproof red tape. Or paint with red nailpolish.

Hummingbird feeders—For a larger, self-replenishing supply of nectar you can make a feeder from a pill glass or a small plastic bottle and an unbreakable watch crystal.

Make a number of perforations at the very top edge of the cap, then glue the cap to the center of the watch crystal. Fill the container with nectar and turn it upside down. The nectar will run out slowly into the watch crystal and will stop flowing when at the height of the perforations.

Hang up the feeder by a wire attached with adhesive tape.

If you prefer to purchase a feeder rather than making your own, you will find several models available commercially.

HUMMINGBIRD FEEDERS—Hummingbird Haven, 6818 Apperson Street, Tujunga, California 91042.

Dorbud Products, 7729 Variel Avenue, Canoga Park, California 91304.

Water for Drinking and Bathing

Year round, more individual birds and more species are attracted by water than by food. They all need it for drinking and bathing, and some need it further to produce mud for nest building.

If there is a brook or a lake near your house, the problem is solved. If such is not the case, remedy the situation by making water available—especially during the worst heat of summer and during freezing spells of winter.

The water should be at least $\frac{1}{2}$ inch deep, and not more than 2 inches. The edge and bottom of the container should be rough to provide secure footing. Water should be replenished regularly.

Bird saucer—A flowerpot saucer makes a suitable birdbath. So do pie tins, shallow cake pans, even TV-dinner aluminum dishes. Because of their small size, they need to be filled and cleaned often.

Birdbath—Numerous birdbaths, raised on pedestals, are available commercially. They come in numerous styles and prices, with or without fountains and figures. If you hanker for this type of structure for your formal garden, pick one that fits your surroundings and your pocketbook.

Hummingbird feeder from pill glass with perforated top glued to unbreakable watch crystal (left); from vial (right).

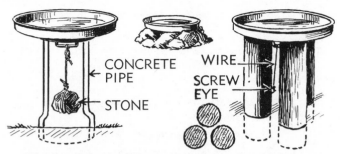

Bird bath from garbage can cover: set on rocks (center), on top of a concrete pipe (left), on three posts (right).

¶ *Tip*—A good substitute may be made from the lid of a garbage can. Paint it with a thin, gravelly cement mixture (1 cup cement, 1 cup fine gravel, 3 cups sand), to give it a rough texture. Mount it on a section of concrete sewer pipe, or on three logs sunk in the ground.

Bird pool—Not all birds like a raised bath; most of them prefer a water supply at ground level. The best location for a bird pool is a spot that is shaded part of the day. Pick it within a few feet of bushes or trees where the birds can perch after a bath to dry themselves.

There is no special difficulty in constructing a bird pool. Scoop out a depression, 3 to 4 feet wide, 5 to 6 feet long, so that the sides slope gently to a depth of 6 inches in the middle. Smooth the inside of your excavation. Line with a sheet of strong, *elastic* plastic, cut about 1½ feet longer and 1½ feet wider than the projected pool. Weigh the edges with stones or bricks. Fill with water. As you do so, the weight of the water will stretch the liner and mold it to the contours of the hole. Trim the liner to within 6 inches of the edge of the pool. Place a line of large flat stones around the edge. Spread a layer of coarse gravel on the bottom of the pool. Add a couple of large stones for birds to stand on.

¶ *Tip*—The sound of dripping and the sight of rippling water have a way of attracting birds' attention. The simplest way of providing this is with a half-gallon plastic bleach bottle. Clean it thoroughly with water, then make a small pin hole on the side of the bottle close to the bottom. Fill it with water while covering the pin hole with a finger. Screw on the cap tightly. Hang the bottle over the pool. Atmospheric pressure keeps the water from running out. Now unscrew the cap slightly—just enough to permit the water to come out in occasional drops.

Nesting Helps

One of the most effective ways of increasing the bird population of your garden or orchard is by providing nesting helps—birdhouses for those species that are willing to have nests prepared for them, building materials for the more independent species.

BIRDHOUSES—The construction of birdhouses is a satisfying handicraft, and watching them as they become occupied, an absorbing pastime.

TYPES—Only about three dozen American bird species regularly make use of birdhouses. Among those, different birds are attracted to different types of houses:

Box houses—Among the better-known species that may move into individual, box-shaped houses are: wrens, chickadees, titmice, nuthatches, bluebirds, flycatchers, flickers, woodpeckers, certain owls (barn, saw-whet, screech), sparrow hawk, wood duck, merganser.

Apartment houses—A colony of purple martins may take over an apartment-house type of structure.

Open shelves—A bracketlike "house" consisting of shelf, back, and roof may be occupied by robin, phoebe, or barn swallow.

¶ *Tip*—A *birdhouse-building contest* can be developed into an exciting activity for a school grade, a Scout troop, or other youth group. Such a contest can be expanded into the development of a "*Bluebird Trail*," building bluebird-size houses to a standard pattern (page 83) and putting them up 400 to 500 feet apart, mounting them 4 to 6 feet off the ground, out in the open, along a fence row or a country lane.

MATERIALS—Scrap wood from packing cases and fruit crates, $\frac{1}{2}$ inch thick and thicker, and slab wood from lumber yards are perfectly suitable for birdhouses.

If you have to buy yard lumber, get so-called 1-inch pine, redwood, or cypress (which is really $\frac{3}{4}$ to $\frac{7}{8}$ inch thick finished), in the commercial widths of 6, 8, or 10 inches ($5\frac{1}{2}$, $7\frac{1}{2}$, and $9\frac{1}{2}$ inches finished, respectively). Or cut the pieces from $\frac{3}{8}$-inch exterior plywood.

Develop your design to make most economical use of your wood.

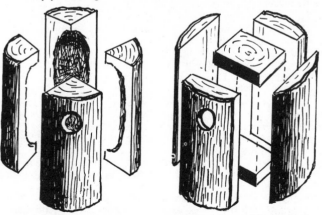

Log birdhouses: log split and hollowed out with ax; log split into slats and provided with square top and bottom.

BIRD HOUSE DIMENSIONS		No. 1	No. 2	No. 3	No. 4
Height of Cavity		8″	8″	10″	16″
Diameter of hole		Wren 1″ Chicka-dee 1⅛″ Titmouse 1¼″	Bluebird 1⅜″ Tree Swallow 1½″ House Finch 2″ Martin 2½″	Flycatcher 2″	Flicker 2½″ Screech Owl 3″ Sparrow Hawk 3″
Center of Hole to Bottom		5″ (Wren 1″-5″)	5″ (Finch and Martin 1″)	7″	12″
Size of Bottom		4″ x 4″	5″ x 5″	6″ x 6″	7″ x 7″

For success in attracting birds, the birdhouses you build must be of a size acceptable to them, as shown in chart.

CONSTRUCTION—As far as design is concerned, you can pretty well follow your own head. You may settle for a square box, with a flat, sloping, or ridged roof. Or you may add to the looks of your birdhouses—although not to their effectiveness—by developing a more complicated pattern.

REFERENCES—*Homes for Birds.* Catalog No. I 1/72:14. Fifteen cents. From Superintendent of Documents, U.S. Government Printing Office, Washington, D.C. 20402.

Walter E. Schutz, *Bird Watching, Housing and Feeding.* Milwaukee, Wisconsin, Bruce Publishing Company.

L. Day Perry and Frank Slepicka, *Bird Houses.* Peoria, Illinois, Charles A. Bennett Company.

Size—Decide on the bird species you want to attract, then build the houses to the floor dimensions and height of cavity that have proved most acceptable to those species (see chart below).

Entrance hole—The diameter of the entrance hole should fit the bird fairly snugly—especially in the case of the smaller birds. It should be large enough to permit the bird to enter easily, but small enough to keep out unwanted birds, such as English sparrows and starlings.

Generally speaking, the entrance hole should be located in the upper third of the front wall, except for martins, which build shallow nests and prefer the entrance not much more than 1½ inches above the bottom.

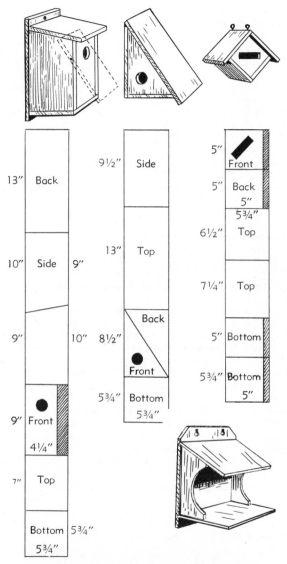

Economical layout of patterns of birdhouses suitable for bluebird (left), finch (center), wren (right). Bottom: shelf for robin or phoebe.

¶ *Tip*—Use an expansive bit for boring the entrance hole. Tip it up slightly toward the inside to keep out the rain.

A perch at the entrance is an unnecessary fixture.

Ventilation and drainage—The entrance hole will usually provide sufficient ventilation. A few holes, $\frac{1}{2}$ inch in diameter, may be bored under the eaves to make the house cooler.

Drill a couple of $\frac{1}{4}$-inch holes in the bottom for drainage and for quicker evaporation of moisture.

Observation—The roof or one side should be hinged or otherwise removable for observation and cleaning. At other times, keep it closed with a screen-door hook.

¶ *Tip*—If you intend to observe from the side, place a removable piece of glass inside the hinged wall to prevent nest or nestlings from falling out when you open up the side.

Finishing—A painted house will last several years longer than a house that is left unpainted.

Paint the outside with a dull green or brown oil paint, or stain it with an oil stain. Leave the inside unpainted.

¶ *Tip*—Put up the houses about one month before the expected occupancy, for weathering and to remove paint odors. Even better, put them up in the fall, but with the entrance hole closed to keep field mice or English sparrows from taking over.

PLACEMENT—The correct location is as important as the right size.

Height above ground—The most effective height above ground varies. It is from 4 to 10 feet for bluebirds and wrens; 5 to 15 feet for tree swallows, chickadees, titmice, and robins; 8 to 20 feet for flickers, woodpeckers, flycatchers, and nuthatches; 15 to 30 feet for owls and sparrow hawks. A house for a wood duck may be put up as high as 20 feet or as low as 4. Mergansers prefer a low location of 3 to 4 feet.

Number of houses—The amount of territory taken over and defended varies with the birds. Put up the houses 30 to 50 feet apart. In most cases, one or two boxes per acre for any one species will prove sufficient. Any more will often remain unoccupied.

CAUTION—Place the birdhouse in partial shade so that it will not be exposed to the broiling sun of midsummer. Protect it from prowling cats by placing a sheet-metal or barbed-wire guard around the post below the house.

CLEANING—After each brood leaves the nest and at the end of the season, take down the birdhouses. Clean out the litter and burn it to kill the mites and insects that generally infest birds' nests. Dust the inside of the houses with pyrethrum, or spray with an insect spray. Then store for the winter and replace it the following spring.

NESTING MATERIALS—Birds not attracted by nesting boxes may instead appreciate a ready supply of materials for nest building.

Types of material—Get together a handful of 6- to 10-inch pieces of string and yarn, hair (horsehair, or hair from your hairbrush or comb), flax, hemp (from a piece of unraveled rope), excelsior, dry sphagnum moss, tufts of cotton. Place in a tree crotch, tie loosely to a branch, or hang in a mesh bag, similar to the suet bag described on page 75.

¶ *Tip*—Include in the material, yarns and strings of various colors. Make an attempt to locate the nests of the birds that have made use of them.

¶ *Tip*—You may be interested in determining whether certain colors are preferred over others. Hang up several bunches of yarn, each bunch of a different color, but with same number of pieces. What color disappears first?

Bird Sanctuaries

Dependable food supply, water, suitable nest locations—add one more thing: protective shelter against elements and enemies (human and otherwise)—and you have all the features of a bird sanctuary.

You can develop your own garden or orchard into a sanctuary for songbirds. If you own fields, you can turn them into sanctuaries for quail, pheasant, and other game birds. You can develop a marsh or a pond on your property into a sanctuary for waterfowl.

But keep in mind that it takes more than casual feeding and occasional protection to make a sanctuary. A long-term view is needed, involving proper management of the area, and the planting of suitable trees, shrubs, vines, and other plants—preferably those that combine food production, nesting sites, and cover.

REFERENCE—Joseph J. Shomon and others, *Wildlife Habitat Improvement*. New York, National Audubon Society.

BIRD PHOTOGRAPHY

Whether you happen to be a student of bird life wanting to make your observations permanent by recording them on photographic film, or an amateur photographer with a newly awakened interest in bird life, you will find bird photography an exciting activity. It will put all your patience and inventiveness to the test, but the results will more than offset your efforts.

REFERENCE—Arthur A. Allen, *Stalking Birds with Color Camera*. Washington, D.C., National Geographic Society.

Stills

EQUIPMENT—**Camera and Lenses**—Camera and lenses depend on your ambition as a bird photographer. Almost any camera can be used for taking pictures of gulls in flight or birds feeding at a window-sill. But if you want to fill your negative or color slide with the bird, you need a camera that can be focused at an object 3 to 4 feet from the lens—either by the camera's own lens or by the added help of a *portrait attachment, extension tubes, or bellows.* With a *telephoto lens,* this distance may be increased several times depending on the lens' focal length.

Tripod—Most bird shots must be taken with the camera on a tripod. A tilting top or a ball-and-socket joint simplifies the task of aiming the camera, particularly in nest photography.

Blind—There is a great advantage to using a blind (see page 67) in bird photography. Hidden within its walls, you can watch the bird closely through the finder of your camera and snap the shutter when the bird shows to best advantage. Also, you can change film and reset the shutter for another shot without scaring the bird away.

Remote shutter release—Working without a blind, you will require a remote shutter release. Several forms are available commercially. You may be able to rig up your own.

The simplest form is an *extra-long cable release* that can be screwed into the release socket of your camera. You can buy such releases up to 12 feet in length through your local camera store.

The *air release* or *pneumatic release* consists of a plunger that fits into the release socket, a length of thin rubber or plastic tubing, and a rubber bulb. The tubing comes in lengths up to 100 feet, but you probably won't need more than 30 to 40 feet. The shutter is tripped when you press the bulb.

SUPPLIES—Burke & James, Inc., 333 West Lake Street, Chicago, Illinois 60606.

The activating part of the *electric release* is a solenoid attached to the shutter release of your camera. The solenoid, in turn, is attached to a long wire leading to your hiding place, a battery, and a switch.

SUPPLIES—Karl Heitz, 979 Third Avenue, New York, New York 10022.

¶ *Tip*—If you know anything about electronics, you may be able to create an electric release from an electric doorbell, some wire, and a 4.5-v battery.

Flash gun—For bird photography, a flashgun is a necessity for supplementing daylight. You must be prepared for all kinds of light conditions, including the deep shade of a hidden nest location and the dimness inside a barn. A high-speed electronic flash, at $1/3000$ second or less, set off when the bird interrupts a light beam, will even make it possible for you to stop the wingbeat of a hummingbird.

CLOSE-UPS—The simplest way to get a close-up of a bird is to observe it carefully and to locate one of the places to which it returns regularly—its perch, its nest, or its feeding ground.

Using a blind—When using a blind for photography, follow the same procedure as for simply watching a bird (pages 69–70). Set up your camera for the kind of shot you want, wait for the bird to settle, then get knife-sharp focus by focusing on its eyes. Shoot when the action is right.

¶ *Tip*—When setting up the blind, check the position of the sun. You don't want to shoot into the sun. The best location for the blind is to the south of the bird's perch or nest.

Birds in flight are shot with telephoto lens on camera with shutter speeds of 1/500 second or faster. A gull shot against a blue sky makes a stunning picture.

Eastman Kodak Company

Nesting birds are best shot from a blind or by remote control. In most cases, it will be necessary to use flash because of the deep shade of usual nesting site.

Eastman Kodak Company

Along-the-way shots are grabbed by having camera ready for shooting when the occasion occurs. Sometimes, feeding may bring mother and brood close to camera.

William Hillcourt

Photographing without blind—If you photograph without the use of a blind, make your preparations as quickly as possible during the absence of the bird. This is particularly important in photographing a nest, since otherwise the eggs may cool before the mother bird has a chance to return.

Set up your camera on its tripod a few feet from the spot where the bird descends, focus it, set the diaphragm and shutter, attach the remote shutter release, then remove yourself to an appropriate distance.

Pick a hiding place from which you have a good view of the spot on which the camera is focused. When the bird reappears, do not snap the picture the very moment it alights. Watch the bird through binoculars. Click the shutter when it strikes an attractive pose.

¶ *Tip*—If you have no remote shutter release, try one of these improvised setups:

If your camera has a shutter lever, tie a fishline to it, then lead the line through a screw eye in a peg driven into the ground below the tripod, and on to your place of concealment. A gentle tug will do the trick. If your camera has a cable-release socket, screw in your regular cable-release and make a simple trigger from a hinge and a few rubber bands, or from a 2½-inch corner iron (see drawing). Attach the gimmick to a separate post so that the camera will remain steady.

The procedure sounds simple, but there's a trick to it. The bird will probably resent the presence of your camera so close to its perch, and stay away. Therefore, first put up your camera at a distance of 30 to 40 feet and let the bird get accustomed to it. Then move it increasingly closer, each time permitting the bird to get so well acquainted with the gadget that the bird approaches the camera without fear.

After taking a shot, wait for the bird to leave on its own. Then step up to the camera to change the film for the next exposure.

Composition and background—In taking a bird shot, you are not just concerned with getting a sharp picture. You want a pleasing one. Therefore, watch your composition and the background.

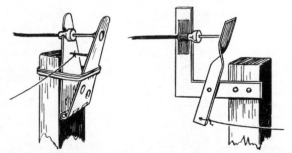

Two simple remote releases for cable release cameras. Attach release to separate support, not to camera tripod.

It is comparatively easy to get a pleasing picture of a bird perched on a branch, taken from a low angle. Similarly, around a feeding station, you have a chance to arrange your props into an attractive composition.

Your main problem is to prevent the background from interfering with the main action.

Aim for a background of an even tone—either the dark of a solid shadow or the light of the sky mellowed with a filter.

If you can't evade a blotchy background of highlights and shadows, soften it by throwing it out of focus. To do this, get your bird into critical focus, then open up the aperture as wide as feasible.

Nest photography—Shots of nests may prove your toughest bird assignment.

A nest is usually located among grass, reeds, or branches that would throw a confused crisscross pattern over your picture. Now don't immediately pull up the grass or tear off the branches. By doing this, you may expose eggs or nestlings to the sun at certain times of day and cause their death. Instead, spread the grass softly apart so that it will have a chance to straighten up again, and tie interfering branches back temporarily while you take your shots.

To look its best, a nest with eggs or young should not be photographed directly from the side or from straight above. A picture taken at an angle of 45 to 60 degrees above the nest will give a far better effect. This is where a tilting top or a swivel head (ball-and-socket joint) on your tripod comes in handy.

¶ *Tip*—In photographing nests high off the ground, lash the tripod to a tree opposite the nest, or use a clamp with toothed jaws, such as a Kodapod, for attaching the camera to a branch.

The diffused light of a hazy or cloudy day is better for nest photography than direct sunlight. Highlights will be less glaring, shadows less black. On a cloudless day, throw a shadow over the nest and its surroundings. Use cardboard, cheesecloth, or photographers' scrim tacked over a wooden frame. If the light is dim, use a flash.

Exposure—Set your shutter speed for the action involved; then open or close your aperture correspondingly.

PERCHING BIRD—On a calm day, exposure up to $1/30$ second. Slight swaying of branches, $1/60$ to $1/100$ second.

SETTING BIRD—$1/30$ to $1/60$ second, depending on the disposition of the bird.

FEEDING—$1/30$ to $1/60$ second.

FLIGHT PICTURES—Photographs of birds in graceful flight have a special appeal.

If you want to be certain of your results, use a high-speed camera, preferably equipped with a telephoto lens. Use a yellow or red filter to darken the sky background if you shoot black-and-white, a sky filter or polarizing filter for color.

Exposures—The speed at which flight photographs should be shot depends upon the bird and the direction of its flight.

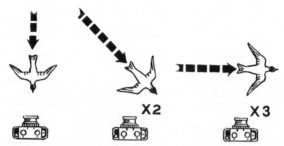

Exposure speed depends on bird's flying direction. Double speed for diagonal flight, triple for crosswise flight.

SLOW FLYERS (birds flying at a speed of less than 30 miles an hour—pelicans, cormorants, ravens, large gulls, herons, soaring turkey vultures, and hawks): Photographed from a distance of 50 feet, flying directly toward the camera, 1/150 second; diagonally toward camera, 1/300 second; crosswise to camera, 1/500 second.

OTHER BIRDS—At a distance of 50 feet, flying directly toward the camera, 1/200 second; diagonally toward camera, 1/500 second; crosswise to camera, 1/1000.

Notice that the speeds are for birds 50 feet away from the camera. For birds at half the distance (25 feet), you need to shoot at twice the speed; for birds at double the distance (100 feet), the speed may be cut in half.

¶ *Tip*—Instead of attempting to focus on an approaching bird, set the camera at an arbitrary distance. Snap your shutter when your range finder or ground glass shows the bird in focus.

Movies

Most of the suggestions for bird stills apply to bird movies as well. A few more suggestions may be of help:

CLOSE-UPS—Nests may be photographed in full sunlight, although the result will prove less pleasing than when scrim is used to diffuse the light over the nest.

A nest in deep shade may be illuminated with light thrown on it by "silvered" cardboard or metal reflectors out in the sun. Or use special, portable electrical lighting designed for movie cameras.

A strong telephoto lens will make it possible for you to obtain certain shots from a distance at which the bird does not mind your presence—either in the open or from the interior of a room or from a parked automobile. Nevertheless, close-ups of adult birds are most effectively taken from a blind, with the camera focused at the perch, nest, or feeding ground.

¶ *Tip*—The sound of the whirring camera motor may scare a bird away. Run the camera empty a number of times until the bird gets accustomed to the sound. Then load and shoot.

FLIGHT PICTURES—For motion pictures of most flying birds, a telephoto lens is a necessity. Close down the aperture as far as is feasible, to ensure the greatest possible depth of focus. In this way, the bird will appear in sharp detail at the varying distance at which you are photographing it.

Occasionally you may want to take a few flight shots at 32 or even 48 frames per second. When these are projected at the usual home speed of 16 frames per second, the bird will be soaring with a more majestic sweep and will remain for a longer time on the screen.

BIRD COLLECTIONS

It is no longer necessary to kill a bird to identify it; with modern binoculars you can name it on the wing. If it does become important for you to study a bird by actually handling it, you will find almost complete sets of study skins in any large natural history museum or university.

The days of dusty stuffed birds are gone; there are other types of bird collections that are of interest. None of them will deplete our bird population.

Bird Nests

Nests are cradles, not homes. They are seldom used a second time. They may be collected as soon as the fledglings have left, and any time during fall and winter.

Collecting—Many nests rest loosely in tree crotches. Lift them out carefully. If you are interested in using the crotch for a display base, cut it off and take it along. In cases where the nest is firmly attached to a branch—vireo, oriole, hummingbird—cut off the branch a few inches toward the tree trunk.

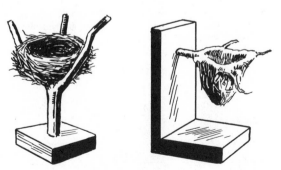

By mounting birds' nests on the branches on which they were found, you get an interesting-looking display.

¶ *Tip*—Carry pruning shears on your bird-nesting expeditions. They will cut the branch in a single snip, and leave the nest intact.

Ground nests are the hardest to collect. They generally come apart when you try to lift them. The only safe way is to slice off the sod on which they are built, and collect both sod and nest.

The simplest way of carrying home a nest is to place it in the middle of a square cloth, bring the corners toward the center, and tie them together hobo fashion.

Make immediate notes of each nest you collect—including the name of the bird, location, how high above ground was the nest, date found, and so on. The nest will, of course, have special significance if you have seen it being built and have followed the life of the inhabitants from eggs to flying fledglings.

Preserving—Recently deserted nests are often infested with mites and insects. Before storing them, dust them with pyrethrum or spray them with insect spray.

To keep the nests fresh-looking, give them a thin coating of clear plastic, sprayed from an aerosol can. This has the further effect of sticking the ingredients together so that the nest does not come apart so easily as it would otherwise.

Nests may be kept in boxes with well-fitting lids. Place a few crystals of paradichlorobenzene or naphthalene with each nest to protect it against insect enemies.

Displaying—You can develop an attractive nest display by fastening the crotches in which the nests were found, or the branches to which they were attached, to wooden bases.

¶ *Tip*—An interesting study, and display, can be made of the items that constitute the nests of a single species. Pull the nests apart, sort out the ingredients, list them.

Eggs

The mania for collecting eggs went out at about the same time that stuffed birds disappeared from the parlor—fortunately. Nevertheless, there's no question that a nest collection looks more intriguing egg-filled than empty. The remedy is to produce a clutch of "reasonable facsimiles" for each nest.

Artificial "eggs"—Find out from a bird book the diameter of the

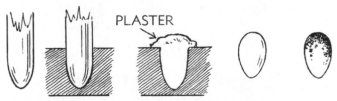

Facsimile eggs are cast from plaster of Paris in a form made by pushing a whittled dowel stick into modeling clay.

 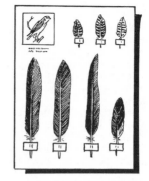

Feathers are mounted on cardboard sheets with pieces of scotch tape. Look for the four main types of feathers.

egg at the widest point, and the length of it. Whittle a dowel stick of the same diameter to an approximate egg "point." Push it as deeply into modeling clay (plasticine) as the egg is long. Make as many holes as there are eggs to the clutch of your particular bird.

Fill each hole with a plaster-of-paris water mixture (see page 120). Let it set for an hour or longer. Sandpaper the blunt end of the plaster "eggs" to proper roundness. Shellac and paint in the natural colors.

REFERENCE—Chester A. Reed, *North American Birds Eggs*. New York, Dover Publications.

Feathers

Feathers are found in greatest numbers during the molting season, from late July to early September. Be on the lookout for the four main types of feathers from each bird: wing flight feathers, tail feathers, coverts, down.

Mounting feathers—Attach the feathers to thin cardboard of a standard size picked by you for your collection. Use household cement or scotch tape.

Several arrangements are possible: by species (all feathers of the same species on the same cardboard), by types of feathers (flight feathers of different birds in one display, tail feathers in another, and so on), or by location (all feathers found in one habitat).

Pellets

The pellets of undigested—and undigestible—food parts regurgitated by owls, hawks, herons, crows, gulls, and some other birds, may be the basis for an interesting collection.

Storing pellets—Pellets may be kept and displayed in individual boxes for the different species or in a larger flat box with partitions.

Mark the boxes to fit your notebook records or keep a label with each pellet.

The simplest way to identify pellets is by their location: under and near nests and roosts of the respective birds. Their shapes and contents are further clues:

OWL: Oval, gray pellets, looking like matted felt, containing hair, *whole* bones, often fairly well-preserved skulls of mice and shrews.

HAWKS: Pear-shaped or round, with hair and *crushed* bones of mice, sometimes feathers.

HERON: Elongated, blackish, almost always with twisted point at end. With hair of mice and rats, but seldom bones—bones are digested by the heron's gastric juices.

CROW: Like miniature horse manure, with remains of beetles, pebbles, and a mixture of plant parts—straw, chaff, or grass seeds.

GULL: Fish bones and remains of various sea animals.

¶ *Tip*—Pick apart a number of pellets from one species. Attempt to reconstruct skeletons of mice and shrews. Cement to cardboard as display of the food habits of species.

Bird Tracks

Along the seashore and lakefront you will often come upon the clearly delineated tracks of some of our wading and swimming birds —the astonishing large imprints of the great blue heron, tracks that show the webbed feet of ducks and gulls, the delicate marks of the least sandpiper.

You can't collect the tracks themselves, but you can make plaster casts of them that will retain all the details of the original tracks. Follow the same procedure as for making casts of animal tracks (pages 120–121).

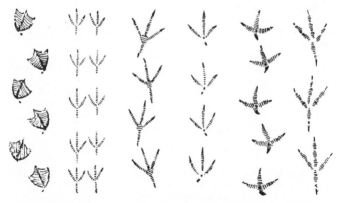

Tracks of some of our common birds. From left: duck, sparrow, heron, pheasant, grouse, crow. Not to scale.

CHAPTER 4

Animals

O F ALL wild creatures, the four-footed, fur-bearing animals—
more exactly called mammals—are probably the most secretive.
They are all around you as you hike over field and through the
woods, but you hardly ever see them. Most of them are asleep in the
daytime, in burrows, caves, or dens. Those that are awake hear your
approach, they smell you—that dangerous human scent—and disappear hurriedly.

Most people get to see very few animals in the wild—an occasional
woodchuck or a gray squirrel in the daytime, a rabbit and deer by
twilight, an opossum or skunk in the headlights of an automobile by
night.

It takes skill and infinite patience to get close enough to animals
to see their actions. But you will be well paid for your efforts.

There is an excitement that cannot be described in watching a
small herd of antelope come down to a desert water hole to drink,
in seeing a mountain goat among its crags and peaks, a grizzly in its
wilderness home, a beaver on its dam.

It is less exciting but more fun, and far easier, to watch pocket mice
filling their cheek pouches with food, to follow the antics of chipmunks among rocks and logs, to sit at night listening to the rustling
overhead as flying squirrels take off from one branch to land on
another—maybe even using your head for a landing field.

Mammals play a great part in nature's scheme. But it is only
recently that we have come to recognize this, and it will be many
years yet before we will have full knowledge of their relationship to
nature's other children, to plants and to man.

Large or small, every mammal has an intriguing appeal to anyone
interested in the out-of-doors. When once you have felt that appeal,
you cannot help but follow it in the future.

BOOKS ON ANIMAL LIFE—Joseph Wood Krutch, ed., *World of Animals.*
New York, Simon & Schuster.

Merle Sery, ed., *Wild Animals of North America.* Washington,
D.C., National Geographic Society.

Ivan Sanderson, *Living Mammals of the World.* New York,
Doubleday & Company.

Richard Carrington, *The Mammals.* Chicago, Ill., Time-Life Books.

Working with Others

Most of your animal activities will have to be solitary occupations. It is hard enough for a single person to get close to wild animals. It is almost impossible for a small group, or for even two people, to get near them without being detected.

However, in some of the activities relating to animals, you will be benefited greatly if you can get other people to share your interest and enthusiasm.

If you happen to be in or near a large town that has a zoo or a natural history museum, contact the curators there who specialize in mammals. In a university town, there may be a zoology or biology professor who can guide you and perhaps put you in contact with others who share your interest. And by all means, get in touch with your home state's game commission or with one of the game wardens of your county.

Through zoological and wildlife societies, you have the chance to find out what other animal students—beginners or experts—are doing.

In addition to all the above, the Fish and Wildlife Service of the U.S. Department of the Interior will assist you with advice and suggestions.

SOCIETIES—American Society of Mammalogists. Headquarters: Zoology Department, Oklahoma State University, Stillwater, Oklahoma 74074. Periodical: *Journal of Mammalogy*.

American Society of Zoologists. Headquarters: Department of Biology, Marquette University, Milwaukee, Wisconsin 53203. Periodical: *American Zoologist*.

Wildlife Society. Headquarters: 3900 Wisconsin Avenue, Washington, D.C. 20016. Periodical: *Journal of Wildlife Management*.

FIELD STUDY OF ANIMALS

Equipment for Animal Study

CLOTHING—If you expect to get close enough to all kinds of animals to study their ways, you must be prepared to cruise through underbrush and hike for miles through the countryside. Most of your roaming will be done in the cool and dew of evening, night, and early morning, when the majority of the animals are active.

Sturdiness, warmth, and water repellency are therefore the main considerations in choosing suitable clothing. The best materials are wool, corduroy, gabardine, with knees and elbows reinforced with patches of soft leather.

¶ *Tip*—Steer clear of canvas (duck). The drum sound of twigs hitting it as you travel through brush will warn animals of your coming.

To the eyes of most animals, what we see as colors appears as various shades of gray. The color of your clothing, therefore, makes little difference. But the tone is important. A great contrast between your clothing and your background—very light against dark shadows, very dark against brilliantly lit sand—attracts attention to your slightest move.

WARNING—Play safe during hunting season by wearing conspicuous red.

Your footwear should suit the territory you intend to cover—hiking shoes, climbing boots, waders for marshland. Many field workers use rubber-footed pacs over woolen socks.

STUDY EQUIPMENT—For seeing more clearly, and for identifying what you see:

Field glasses—Normally, you have to keep at an appropriate distance from the animal you are watching so as not to scare it away. Good binoculars, as described on page 55, will assist you greatly by bringing the animal closer to you.

A high relative brightness is important since so much of your study will have to be done under poor light conditions. Watch out, therefore, in picking binoculars, that you do not purchase magnification at the expense of relative brightness. You will be better off with a 6 × magnification and a relative brightness of 25, than with an 8 × magnification and a brightness of only 14 (see page 56).

Flashlight—A powerful flashlight will make it possible for you to discover and watch certain animals at night. A five-cell flashlight with a focused beam is excellent. A headlight-type flashlight leaves your hands free.

Animal books—Bring your favorite field book.

BOOKS FOR FIELD IDENTIFICATION—H. E. Anthony, *Field Book of North American Mammals*. New York, G. P. Putnam's Sons.

W. H. Burt and R. P. Grossenheider, *Field Guide to the Mammals*. Boston, Houghton Mifflin Company.

E. Lawrence Palmer, *Fieldbook of Mammals*. New York, E. P. Dutton & Company.

Ralph S. Palmer, *Mammal Guide: Mammals of North America, North of Mexico*. New York, Doubleday & Company.

Ann Haven Morgan, *Field Book of Animals in Winter*. New York, G. P. Putnam's Sons.

Notebook—To make complete notes on the animals you see and records of your observation, carry a pocket-sized notebook—loose-leaf, if you prefer.

ORIENTATION EQUIPMENT—Animal study is field work in the truest sense of the word. The pursuit of an animal may often carry you into unknown territory from which you need to find your way out when you have accomplished your mission.

Compass—For extensive field trips, always carry a compass (see page 284). With a knowledge of its use and a mental picture of the general lay of the land you are traversing—gained through past experiences—you should have no difficulty in getting back to your base.

Map—If the territory in which you are traveling is new to you, a compass alone will be of little help. In that case, bring along a topographic map (see page 283). If a printed map is not available, a sketch map containing the main features of the landscape—rivers and lakes, hills and ridges, roads and trails.

¶ *Tip*—For a long wilderness trip, carry a canteen, with water, a small first-aid kit, emergency rations, and matches in a waterproof case.

Finding Animals

Animals are elusive creatures. The best approach to the problem of finding them is to discover their haunts, then come back at the time most opportune for seeing them.

WHERE?—Comb your territory in search of signs of animals.

Animal homes—Be on the lookout for animal homes wherever you go. Check around them for signs of occupancy—fresh tracks, droppings, remains of food, clipped vegetation.

BURROWS in open fields, pasture land, under tree roots, in hillsides, in stream banks will indicate many different animals, depending on size and geographical location: woodchuck, skunk, prairie dog, gopher, fox, coyote, badger, otter, mink, various mice.

MOUNDS and ridges of moles are familiar to everyone. Various mice live in tunnels deserted by moles.

CAVERNS in rocky ledges: porcupine, gray fox, bobcat, bear.

HOLLOW TREES—Raccoons and opossums live in "den trees," flying squirrel and gray squirrel in smaller cavities.

NEST of leaves and twigs: squirrel, wood mouse.

HOUSES—Muskrat in houses of reeds and twigs, beaver in houses of branches and mud.

"FORMS"—Rabbit and hare bed down in depressions in the ground.

"YARDING GROUNDS"—The bedding-down places of deer in dense thickets.

Tracks and runways—Scattered tracks indicate that the animal is around; runways that it lives nearby. Runways vary from the tiny grass tunnels of the meadow mouse, the streamside trails of the muskrat, the crossing place of the mountain lion from one side of a mountain to the other, the path of the coyote to the desert water hole, to the broad lane of deer to the lake shore.

Other signs—SCAT (droppings, dung)—The size, color, and shape of scat identify many different animals (see page 123). Droppings in an attic, cave, or loft may indicate the presence of bats in cracks and crevices overhead.

FEEDING SIGNS—Cut twigs, gnawed bark, peeled saplings, nut shells, chewed cones, remains of bones and feathers. Stored food.

TORN BARK—From deer rubbing its antlers against the tree to remove the "velvet."

¶ *Tip*—Come back again to the same place in late December or in January. You may then find shed antlers.

"Rest trees"—Where porcupines stop for the day when moving from place to place.

"Measuring trees"—Trees with claw marks of bear.

"Scent posts"—Spots where members of the dog family—fox, coyote, wolf—stop to urinate.

"Scratch hills"—Small mounds formed by members of the cat family—bobcat, lynx, mountain lion—covering their urine.

"Otter slide"—Smooth slide down riverbank into the water—playground of otter.

"Bear wallow"—Water hole where bear and other animals roll in the mud.

reference—George F. Mason, *Animal Homes*. New York, William Morrow and Company.

WHEN?—Time of year—Most mammals are active all summer long and, with some exceptions, throughout the winter as well. Many of them slow down when it is cold, spending more of their time sleeping. A few hibernate, going into an almost comalike sleep—mainly bats, woodchuck, eastern chipmunk, ground squirrel, certain mice. The black bear is not a true hibernator, but simply a deep sleeper.

Time of day—Each animal has its own favorite time for moving about, mostly in search of food.

Night—A large number of species are *nocturnal*. They sleep during the day and come out in the dark of night. That is when you hear the bark of the fox, the howl of the coyote, the scampering footfalls of skunk and racoon, the squeal of mice.

Day—Comparatively few animals are *diurnal*. Gray squirrel, ground squirrel, shrew, woodchuck, chipmunk, prairie dog.

Twilight—Many mammals move about during twilight hours. Some of them are *crepuscular:* You have your best chance to observe them in the evening twilight—muskrat and beaver. Others are *matutinal:* You can study them in the morning twilight before daybreak—deer, for instance. Some of these animals may be abroad on overcast days.

Getting Close to Animals

Each kind of animal must be studied in its own special way. Depending on your skill and resourcefulness, you can get close to animals by attempting to attract them to you or by following their tracks and stalking them to their haunts.

ATTRACTING—You can play on the hunger and curiosity of certain animals to attract them to you.

Baiting—Different varieties of bait may draw some animals to a spot where you can study them closely from a window, a tent door, or a blind.

You are familiar with the garbage-can night marauding of skunks and raccoons. Garbage-can ingredients of leftover foods, with a possible further addition of vegetable, fruit, and animal matter—

carrots, corn, apples, raw meat, and fish—will bring in opossums, martens, weasels as well, and may even appeal to a fox.

Rodents of all descriptions go for cereal grains, pelletized rabbit food, nutmeats, and peanut butter. Shrews may be attracted by small pieces of meat.

If you live in deer country, you can attract the deer with salt licks—blocks of rock salt that you can purchase at feed stores. The same idea will have the wholehearted approval of porcupines if they happen to be around.

Commercial scent baits are also useful in attracting animals.

WATCHING NOCTURNAL ANIMALS—Most of the animals that you can attract with bait will be the night-roaming kind. You will hear them at the food, but you will see them only if you light up the scene. Simply play a flashlight on them. Peculiarly enough, this will disturb few nocturnal animals as long as you do it quietly.

If your home is in the country, you may be able to string wire from the house current and turn on a bulb directly over the feeding spot. In camp, use a storage battery or hot-shot battery and an automobile sealed-beam lamp.

¶ *Tip*—Ted S. Pettit suggests the insertion of a rheostat in the wiring so that you can increase the illumination slowly, rather than switching it on suddenly, which may scare the more timid animals away.

Calling—The best-known calling method is possibly the imitation of the bellow of the bull moose in mating season, to draw the cow moose near. Some experts can make this trumpeting sound without apparatus, but most of them use a megaphone made from birch bark—from a *dead* tree, of course. Roll a piece of birch bark, approximately 16 by 20 inches, into a cone, with a front opening about 6 inches in diameter, and a mouthpiece approximately 1 inch wide. While bellowing, point the megaphone up in the air, then toward the ground and up again, to get the proper effect.

Moose may be called by traditional megaphone, deer by blowing over a blade of grass between your fingers.

You can make a reasonable facsimile of the eerie, bleating call of deer with the help of a wide blade of grass. Hold your thumbs sideways. Stretch the grass between them so that it forms a free membrane between first and second knuckles. Bring the thumbs up to your mouth and blow between the knuckles to make the grass vibrate and give off a sharp bleat.

The same blade-of-grass trick, with quickly repeated blows, may sound enough like a fox barking to entice a fox to come closer.

Male elks, and moose as well, may be attracted during the fall mating season by the sound of clashing antlers of two rivals fighting. Hitting brush and trees with a stick may do the trick.

In beaver territory, you can occasionally call beavers with an imitation of their own warning signal of slapping the tail against the surface of the water. Use a canoe paddle or just your hand. Rapping the gunwale of the canoe with a knife handle may work as well.

The squeaking produced by kissing the back of your hand (see page 60) usually works with squirrels. It may also call fox, muskrat, and weasel from their hideouts.

At night you may get answers to an imitation of the yap of a fox, the howl of a coyote, the screech-owl-like whistle of a raccoon. You may draw them nearer, but they will probably keep at a safe distance.

Rabbits, ground squirrels, chipmunks may often be lured close by the sound made by clicking two small stones or two large coins together.

POSTING—Posting is the method of placing yourself in hiding at a strategic spot to which you expect the animal to come, sooner or later. It may be its home, its feeding ground, watering place, or runway. The top requirements for posting are time on your hands and infinite patience.

Be sure that the wind is in your face, and that it blows from the direction from which you think the animal will arrive. Otherwise, you will certainly wait in vain.

Sit down; make yourself comfortable. You can't concentrate on watching if you are in a strained position, worrying about keeping your balance or about a foot that is going to sleep.

Blinds for posting—A blind is often of great advantage in posting. Construct it as you would a bird blind (see page 67). The location of it depends on the animal you are studying. The blind may have to be placed 100 feet or more away from large, keen-sensed or suspicious animals, 30 feet from dens of medium-sized animals, only a few feet from the small unsuspecting kinds.

TRACKING—Tracking is especially important for locating the larger animals—deer, elk, moose, bear—although it will often help you to find the homes of others.

Types of tracks—Shape and size of tracks will tell you what animals made them, their relative position, at what speed the animals traveled.

For tracking purposes, animals fall into four categories:

LONG LEGGERS—Animals with comparatively long legs of about

equal length—members of deer, cat, and dog families, for instance. Tracks are comparatively far apart, generally form a zigzag line. Tracks of hind feet often fall in forefeet tracks.

SHORT-AND-LONG LEGGERS—Rabbits, hares, squirrels, certain mice, with very short forelegs and long hind legs, move in jumps. They usually make paired tracks of hind feet in front of paired tracks of forefeet.

SHORT LEGGERS—Martens, weasels, minks, and otters with long slender bodies and short legs bound along. When the animals are walking, the tracks of their hind feet are made behind tracks of their forefeet. When they are running, their hind feet may fall into the tracks of their forefeet, or even ahead of them.

FATTIES—Animals with thick bodies and comparatively short legs—raccoon, bear, porcupine, beaver, woodchuck, skunk—waddle along flat-footedly. Their tracks usually form two lines, with the imprints close together. When these animals pick up speed, they proceed in short jumps, placing their forefeet and hind feet in paired tracks.

Familiarize yourself with the different tracks so that you will know which animals made them, as you find the tracks in soft ground or snow.

BOOKS ON TRACKS—Ellsworth Jaeger, *Tracks and Trailcraft*. New York, The Macmillan Company.

Olaus Murie, *Field Guide to Animal Tracks*. Boston, Houghton Mifflin Company.

Ernest Thompson Seton, *Animal Tracks and Hunter Signs*. New York, Doubleday & Company.

Tracking techniques—Before you start to follow a track for the purpose of getting close to an animal, be sure it is a fresh track. Otherwise you will have no luck. A fresh track has sharp edges, and no debris has fallen or been blown into it. Tracks show up especially well in sandy soil with little vegetation, in moist riverbanks, and along lake shores. Snow is perfect. It takes a considerable amount of skill to follow tracks on hard bare ground and in dead leaves.

If possible, track against the sun. The shadows in the tracks will make them show up clearly.

Walk at the side of the track you are following, not directly in it. Don't keep your nose in the track. Look up and ahead. It is often easy to see the track for quite a distance. Instead of moving slowly, looking at each imprint, you can move ahead quickly. And incidentally, you may see the animal you are tracking ahead of you.

If you lose the track, try to imagine yourself in the place of the animal: "Where would I go from here?" Then investigate in that direction.

Move forward fast when the tracks show that the animal has been running. Slow down when the tracks slow down. When a deer starts zigzagging, for instance, it is usually a sign that it is looking for a place to bed down. You may be almost on top of it.

When you think you are close to the animal, stop, look, and listen.

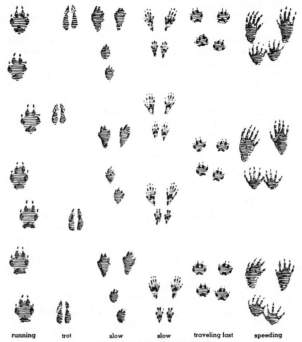

| running | trot | slow | slow | traveling fast | speeding |

Track patterns: long leggers (fox, deer), short and longers (rabbit, squirrel), short leggers (mink), fatties (raccoon).

Do you see it? Then bring up your field glasses slowly to follow its actions.

STALKING—Tracking may locate an animal for you, but you have to resort to stalking (still-hunting) to get near enough to it for close observation.

Animals depend on their keen senses of smell and hearing to protect themselves. Some have sharp eyesight as well; others are nearsighted: They see movement mainly, not details.

If an animal gets your scent or hears you, it may take flight immediately. Therefore, approach it carefully with the wind in your face. If you have discovered it from the wind side without disturbing ir, make a semicircle around it before you proceed closer.

¶ *Tip*—To find the wind direction on a still day, wet a finger in your mouth. Hold it up. The side toward the wind will feel cooler. Or toss leaves in the wind and watch their drift.

Watch where you place your feet. The cracking of a dry twig may sound like a pistol shot. Soft ground, wet forest floor, and light snow are excellent for stalking. Dry leaves and crunchy snow make tough stalking.

If the animal detects you, "freeze" on the spot. It may move about to find out what scared it. If you are motionless, it may look directly at you without noticing you, then quiet down again.

Make good use of all available cover—trees that you can hide behind, stumps, rocks, culverts, hillocks, and mounds.

¶ *Tip*—Here's an old trick for bringing antelopes and some members of the deer family nearer to you. Tie a handkerchief to a stick and wave it slowly back and forth over your hiding place. The animals will approach to find out what's up.

Animal Lists

What animals are there in your territory? As you discover them, start keeping a list of them, adding to this record the observations you may make from time to time.

LIFE LISTS—The simplest way of making a life list is to note down in the margin of your field book—opposite the name of the animal—the date when you first discovered evidence of its presence and the date when you actually saw it for the first time. There is quite a difference between the two. You will almost certainly find evidence of fox, for example (den, scat, food remains), long before you actually see this elusive critter.

The only way in which you can find out what small animals—mice, shrews, and the like—live in your area will be by trapping them (see pages 106–8).

Field Observations

In spite of all the studying of animals that has gone on over the years, our knowledge of life histories and relationships is still amazingly incomplete. Suggestions for field observations are therefore almost limitless.

Home range—How far the animals range, as indicated by their homes, runways, scat, feeding marks, and by observation on marked animals.

Mating—How are mates selected? Courtship; fighting among males? How long do mates stay together?

Young—How many litters a year? How many to a litter? How are young cared for? How long do they remain with the mother?

Disposition and behavior—Skulking, playful, curious, and so on. Reaction to sounds, odors, movements.

Calls—What calls have they? Alarm, challenge, courting, and others.

Tracks—Special study of individual imprints and of imprints in relation to one another. How do distances between imprints change at various speeds? Size of tracks as related to size, sex, age.

¶ *Tip*—Make sketches of tracks. Simplest way is to place a piece of glass or sheet of plastic over the track and draw its outline with crayon or marking pencil. Transfer the outline to paper; rub the crayon lines off the glass and use it again.

Migrations—Any evidence of migration? Where to; where from? Dates of appearance and disappearance.

Hibernation and aestivation—Local animals that hibernate or aestivate. What is the last date of appearance, first date of emerging?

¶ *Tip*—A simple way of discovering the movement of an animal into and out of its burrow is to place a light crisscross layer of fine sticks over the entrances. Visit the place regularly to see if twigs have been displaced.

Eye reflections—The tapetum layer in the retina of the eyes of some animals has the power to reflect the light from a flashlight or headlight, for instance, with a luminous glow. The color of the reflection varies with the animal: red in the case of opossum and bear, orange in deer, green among members of the cat family. What colors are the eye-glow—*chatoyancy*—of other animals?

Special problems—Relationships between animals and their surroundings. Relationships between animals and man—effect of man's activities in lumbering, draining, farming.

WILD ANIMALS IN CAPTIVITY

The ideal place for studying the activities, behavior, and intelligence of animals is, of course, their natural habitat. But wild animals in the field have a way of noncooperating. They simply disappear. For you to find out more about them, it is often necessary to study them in captivity. This is generally a matter of trapping, caging, and keeping your captives healthy as long as the studies last.

In many states, it is unlawful to capture animals outside of the regular hunting season for the different species. Some states require that you take out a special license to hold wild animals captive. So before you decide what animals to keep, find out what your state laws have to say, then follow them scrupulously.

BOOK—Clifford B. Moore, *The Book of Wild Pets*. Newton Center, Massachusetts, Charles Branford Company.

Traps

The traps used by fur trappers are of no use to you. They usually kill or maim. Those for your purpose are referred to as live-catch traps. They are available commercially in many different designs and sizes at rather reasonable prices. Some of them may be had in two forms—regular and collapsible.

SUPPLIES—Havahart, 133 Water Street, Ossining, New York 10562. Mustang Manufacturing Factory, 2225 Lon Ellen, Houston, Texas 77018.

Johnson's, Waverly, Kentucky 42462.

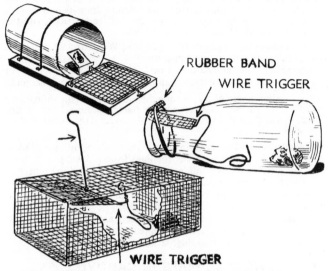

A live trap for a small animals may be produced from a mousetrap and a can, a milk bottle, or a wire mesh.

Instead of buying traps, you can make up your own humane traps.

TRAPS FOR SMALL ANIMALS—Traps for mice, shrews, and other small animals can be made from tin cans, pieces of wire mesh, even from milk bottles.

Snap trap—The snap trap described by Hatt is one of the most effective. It makes use of the traditional mousetrap, a No. 2 tin can, wire, and a piece of $\frac{1}{4}$-inch wire mesh (hardware cloth).

Somewhere along the top edge of the tin can, make a rectangular cut the size and shape of the trap trigger. Wire the can to the base of the trap with the trigger fitting into this cut. Wire a piece of wire mesh, cut to size, over the square loop of the spring. Set the trap the way you would the ordinary mousetrap. When sprung, the wire mesh keeps the animal closed up in the can.

Milk bottle trap—For this trap, suggested by Bailey, cut a piece of wire mesh to a size of 1 by $3\frac{1}{2}$ inches. Bend up 1 inch at one end. Bring the straight end into the milk bottle, and fit the bent part over the edge of the bottle. Hold it in position with a couple of rubber bands around the bottle neck. Make a trigger from an 8-inch piece of No. 16 wire. Bend one end of it into a swanlike neck-head-bill, the other into a double loop, ending in a point. Push the wire-mesh door open and insert the wire so that the bottom of the door rests perilously on the "swan's" bill. When touched, the wire falls over, and the trap snaps shut.

Can trap—Almost any size can—square or round—can be turned into a trap. Cut a swing door from a piece of tin, slightly longer, up and down, than the opening of the can. Hang the door at the top with two wire rings in such a way that the bottom of it fits about an inch inside the can. Set the trap by suspending the door on a "swan's-neck" wire tripper as used in the milk bottle trap, or use the method for a swinging-door trap (see below).

TRAPS FOR MEDIUM-SIZED ANIMALS—The usual trap for medium-sized animals is made in box form, from wood or from wire mesh. Trap sizes vary with sizes of animals: weasels, rats, chipmunk—6 by 6 by 18 inches; mink, squirrel—7 by 7 by 20 inches; rabbit—9 by 9 by 24 inches; woodchuck, raccoon, skunk, opossum—11 by 11 by 36 inches; fox—12 by 12 by 48 inches.

Swinging-door trap—Form a piece of wire mesh into a square tunnel. Close one end with mesh. Fit a piece of tin, as a door, into

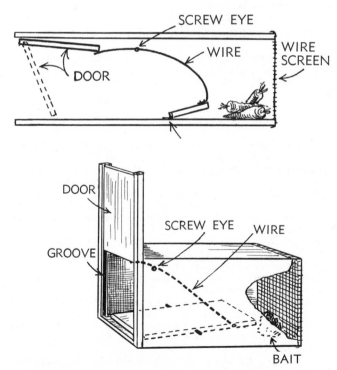

The swinging-door trap (top) and the falling-door trap (bottom) may be made from wood or from wire mesh.

the opposite end. Cut it slightly larger, up and down, than the tunnel opening. Fasten it at the top with two wire rings. Make a nail hole at the bottom of the door. Attach a stiff wire through this hole and run it through the trap roof. At the roof line, make a double bend in the wire that will prevent the door from being raised from the inside. Bend another wire into a trigger with a short and a long arm. Bring it down through the roof. Twist the short end around the long one. Bend the short end to hold up the door. Bend the long end into such a shape that an animal entering the trap will brush against it.

¶ *Tip*—The swinging-door trap can be made equally well from a wooden box. It will attract more animals if the end opposite the door is made of wire mesh.

Falling-door trap—In the falling-door type of trap, the door is raised perpendicularly in two grooved supports over the door opening. When tripped, it falls straight down and closes the trap.

One of the simplest forms of this type of trap makes use of a treadle (see diagram, page 107). When the animal steps on this, the trigger holding up the door is dislodged, and the door falls down.

TRAPS FOR LARGE ANIMALS—Bears are caught in log pens. Deer are taken in specially constructed traps or corrals. Other large animals are captured by highly specialized procedures, ranging from lassoing them to catching them in pit traps. Those are jobs for professionals. Few amateurs will ever have reason or occasion to do them.

Trapping

The trap is only part of it. Next come the steps of setting it where the animals are and baiting it with food they like.

Placing the trap—Investigate your countryside and locate burrows nests, and runways. Place your traps in strategic positions nearby.

In the field, animals often move along low fences, strips of cover. In the woods, they keep close to fallen logs, trunks of trees. Along waterways are places where animals come down to drink. All are good trap locations.

Baiting—Small animals—rodents especially—are attracted by rolled oats, doughnut crumbs, peanut butter, raisins, small pieces of fried bacon—served separately or mixed together.

Larger vegetarians such as muskrat, rabbit, and hare like apples, bananas, carrots, turnips, corn.

Such delicacies as chicken heads and entrails, fish heads, canned sardines may attract skunk and raccoon and, possibly, opossum if the bait has reached a high-odor stage. Skunk may also go for canned cat food with fish base. Mink and weasel may fall for the same kind of baits, or else for chunks of fresh meat.

Red and gray fox may go for fresh-killed chicken or rabbit, even for canned dog food.

The majority of animals like salty things—potato chips, salted peanuts. Dried salted herring and codfish keep well in traps and often prove an effective bait for several kinds of animals.

¶ *Tip*—Throw a few samples of the bait outside the trap entrance as a "come-on."

You can learn only by experience what baits will attract the animals of your locality. Even then, don't be too disappointed if you don't catch the animal your trap is baited for, but possibly an entirely different one. You may have better luck next time.

Transferring the catch—When an animal is caught, slip a sack over the mouth of the trap. Open the trap inside the sack and shake out the animal. Then transfer it from the sack to its cage.

Cages and Cage Health

In deciding on a cage for your captive, you have three important points to consider: size, comfort, and cleanliness.

The size of the cage depends on the size of the animal, its habits, and the study you intend to do. In general, the size should be sufficient to give the animal a chance to get a fair amount of exercise.

COMFORT to most animals means protection against drafts and bad weather, and, especially in outdoor cages, provision for a spot to nestle down to sleep, lined with dry grass, strips of paper toweling, cotton, rope fiber.

CLEANLINESS in small cages may be achieved with a litter of sawdust or shredded paper. It simplifies matters to provide such cages with a floor tray of sheet metal that can be pulled out for cleaning. In medium-sized cages you may want to use a litter of wood shavings, corn husks, excelsior, hay, or straw. In large cages the floor may

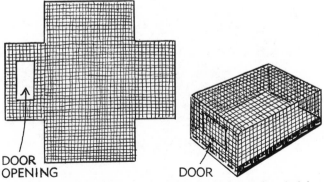

DOOR
OPENING   DOOR

Quarter-inch hardware cloth (wire mesh) is good material for making up simple observation cages for small animals.

consist of a slightly sloping cement surface that can be washed clean with a garden hose.

¶ *Tip*—Practically all wild animals are infested with fleas and other pests. Dust the animals with an insect powder as soon after capture as possible.

INDOOR CAGES—Cages for indoor studies are available from biological supply houses and from many pet shops. They range in floor sizes from 8 by 9 inches to about 2 by 3 feet.

SUPPLIES—Indoor cages: Jewel Aquarium Company, 5005 West Armitage Avenue, Chicago, Illinois 60639.

Small indoor cages—Cages for mice may be made out of $\frac{1}{4}$-inch hardware cloth (wire mesh). For a simple cage, cut a piece of hardware cloth into a top with the four sides attached (see page 109). Bend down the sides, and wire the corner edges together. Staple this structure to the sides of a piece of board. Cut a square hole in one end of the cage, large enough for your hand. Cut a piece of wire mesh to fit as a door over this hole. Hinge it in position with wire rings.

Other types of small cages may be made along the lines of the snake cages suggested on page 139. If your captives are rodents, line the inside with hardware cloth to prevent them from gnawing their way out. If you like, you can install a floor tray to be pulled out for cleaning.

¶ *Tip*—In a small cage intended for rodents, include an exercise wheel. In a cage for larger animals, provide ladders and ramps for exercise.

Jewel Aquarium Company

Well-equipped indoor animal cages have bottle with water supply, exercise wheel, drawer bottom for easy cleaning.

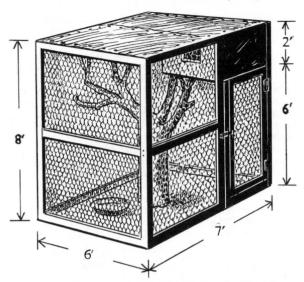

Make an outdoor wire cage to fit your needs. Size shown above is suitable for squirrels, raccoons, and opossums.

Large indoor cages—Make a framework of 1-by-2-inch or 2-by-2-inch wood. Cover with ¼-inch hardware cloth or with ½-inch or 1-inch poultry wire, depending on the size of the animal that is to be kept in the cage. Make a wire door in one side large enough for you to reach in.

OUTDOOR CAGES—There is no end to the sizes and designs of outdoor cages. They may take the form of true cages, completely enclosed, or as screened-in enclosures. They may be directly on the ground or raised with a slightly sloping wood or cement floor. If possible, imitate the natural surroundings of your captives.

Enclosed cages—For squirrels, flying squirrels, raccoons, porcupines, and opossums, make a frame from 2-by-2-inch lumber or rustic poles, at least 4 feet wide, 4 feet long, and 6 feet high. Enclose the top and sides with 1-inch chicken wire. The floor may be of wood, mesh, cement, or the ground itself. In the latter case, the chicken wire should extend 1 to 2 feet below ground level. Cover the top with roofing paper. Place some stout branches inside the cage before you close it up. Make a door on one side for entrance for cleaning and feeding. Fasten a nesting box inside at the top.

Cages for foxes, rabbits, minks, and weasels may be constructed in a similar manner but need not be as high—4 to 5 feet high for foxes, 2 feet for minks. Fasten the nesting box on the outside, at ground level.

Enclosures—For animals which do not usually attempt to escape by climbing, a completely enclosed cage is not necessary. Instead, make a wire enclosure or run.

Chipmunks, ground squirrels, and prairie dogs require a soil floor for making their burrows. Special precautions are necessary to keep them from digging themselves out. Start your construction by digging a hole in the ground the size of the enclosure, to a depth of 2 to 3 feet. Place uprights in the corners for the frame, and line the sides with galvanized chicken wire. Pour in a thin layer of cement—1 inch or so. Throw the dirt back in, and finish the above-ground part of the enclosure. No nesting boxes inside.

For deer, use 8-foot wire fencing stretched between strong posts. Erect an open-front shelter within the enclosure, to protect the animals in inclement weather. The open side should be to the lee side of prevailing winter winds.

If you have a brook running through your grounds, you can make an enclosure for muskrats or beavers. Use wire fencing. Put it up so that it extends 4 feet above ground, 2 feet under ground for beavers, 4 feet for muskrats. Provide a large supply of branches, sticks, and reeds for house construction.

FEEDING—Proper feeding is your main concern for keeping your animals healthy.

What to feed—Check the food habits of your specimens in Anthony's *Field Book of North American Mammals*, and do your best to provide them with the food they eat in their wild state. If that isn't possible, follow Moore's suggestions in *The Book of Wild Pets*, or do some experimenting of your own.

Whatever the feed is, be sure it is fresh. Greens should be young and succulent, meat absolutely fresh. If an animal does not eat all that you give it, remove the remaining food before it spoils.

In addition to food, rodents need sticks to chew on to keep their front teeth at normal length.

Feeding charts—Do your feedings at regular intervals so that the animals learn to expect them. Some animals are interested in only one daily meal, others require frequent feedings.

Keep track of the feedings on a chart attached to the cage of the animal, or in a record book with a page for each specimen. The notes should include the name of the animal, date, time of feeding, kind of food, amount given, amount eaten.

The feeding charts will tell you the foods that appeal to your animals and the amounts they require. The charts will also quickly show you when an animal is "off its feed" and may require special attention.

Water—Have water available at all times. Some animals dirty up their water supply very quickly and need to have it replenished frequently.

Anchor the water container firmly so it can't be tipped over. For a small cage, the water bottle used for hamster cages may be just right.

Taming Animals

Many of your captives will tame easily and will make interesting pets.

The main tricks for taming are food and your personal touch. Use some appealing tidbits for a bribe to get your captives to come close to you and to get accustomed to your presence. They will soon learn that they have nothing to fear from you and will approach you boldly.

Small rodents will quickly get enough confidence to climb right into your hand for a treat of nutmeats.

Chipmunks, squirrels, minks, will take the food from your fingers.

Some of the medium-sized animals may eventually let themselves be picked up and will clamber all over you. This is especially the case if you get them young. Young raccoons, opossums, and skunks make good pets—skunks, though, only if you have no dogs around. These pets often become tame enough to be given the run of the house. When they grow older, they cannot always be depended on. They may become destructive, snappy. That is the time to return them to their cages or, better, to let them loose.

¶ *Tip*—Skunks may be "de-natured" by having their two scent glands removed. It is a simple process, especially if done while the animal is only a month or two months old. The operation may be undertaken by a local veterinarian. This operation does not seem to affect a skunk's health, but of course, it deprives the skunk forever of its natural weapon.

ANIMAL PHOTOGRAPHY

Photographing wild mammals is probably the toughest assignment you can have in the whole field of nature photography. To get close enough to a wild animal in the daytime to "shoot" it, you need all the skills of an expert stalker. To take the shot at night, you need the qualifications of an amateur engineer for rigging up a suitable flash arrangement. To add the larger animals to your collection, you will have to be an inveterate traveler and frequent visitor to national parks and game preserves.

BOOK ON ANIMAL PHOTOGRAPHY—Hugh B. Cott, *Zoological Photography in Practice*. Hastings-on-Hudson, New York, Morgan & Morgan.

Stills

EQUIPMENT—American mammals range in size from the 3-inch-long little shrew to the moose with a shoulder height of 6 feet or more. Some of them approach your camera fearlessly, others must be pursued into the highest, wildest type of mountain territory. It is evident that you must either limit your photographing to animals that fit the scope of your camera, or get equipment that will suit all types.

Camera and lenses—If yours is an ordinary snapshot camera, you may be able to get successful shots of our larger animals, and with portrait attachment and flashgun some of our medium-sized night prowlers.

For more extensive photography, you need a camera with shutter speeds from time to $^1/_{500}$ of a second. You also need a fast lens because much of your work will have to be done under poor light conditions. A telephoto lens is a necessity, not just for that antelope at 200 yards, but also for the white-footed mouse that scampers along almost underfoot.

Tripod—For stationary long-distance photography with telephoto lenses, and for remote control and nighttime flashgun photography, a tripod is indispensable.

Gunstock base—For photographing far-roaming animals, you must be able to move your camera freely and quickly in order to follow the actions of your subject. Here a tripod is of little help. By the time you have set it up, the animal is out of range. Instead, attach your camera to a gunstock base. This makes it possible for you to handle and aim your camera like a gun. Buy it commercially or make your own.

Flashgun—For photographing at night, you have the choice between a separate flashgun, for open-flash shots, and a gun synchronized with your camera.

Shutter release—You may need to buy or rig up a remote shutter release or a trip release, depending on the kind of photography you intend to do (see pages 88 and 116).

Films—For photographing large animals grazing peacefully out in the open sun, you can use slow films—black-and-white or color—and slow exposures—$^1/_{50}$ to $^1/_{100}$ second. Animals on the run may have to be shot at $^1/_{500}$ to stop their action.

Most animals stay in hiding during the day. They prefer cover and twilight. To photograph them under those conditions, you need a supersensitive film and often a wide-open lens.

For flashgun night shots, you can again make use of a wide range of black-and-white and color films.

DAYTIME PHOTOGRAPHY—The most important features in animal photography are knowing where the animals are, and having the skill to get close to them. All the tricks you learned while studying animals in the field will come into play (pages 99 to 104).

Attracting—Many small animals can be brought close to the camera by attracting. Pocket gophers, chipmunks, and squirrels can be led right up to the camera by a trail of bread crumbs or peanuts. Focus on the feeding place.

Posting—If you have discovered the runways or the den of an animal, you can get the animal's picture by posting. Place yourself in a strategic position from which you can watch the approach of the animal. Or put up a blind, as for bird photography, and hide in it. Focus on a likely spot. When the animal gets within range, press the shutter release.

You may have even better success if you place the camera itself in

Large animals are photographed from a safe distance, using a telephoto lens. Have camera ready, set at a suitable distance, opened at proper stop for exposure.

Eastman Kodak Company

Medium animals may take a photograph of themselves at night by flash. In daytime they are most easily shot at or near their dens from a blind or by remote control.

Small animals are generally caught at their feeding places, by setting up camera nearby and shooting by remote control. You can establish spot to suit by baiting.

Boy Scouts of America

position on a tripod close to where the animal will be. Focus the camera, and attach to its shutter a remote-control release—tube and bulb, electrical or homemade gadget (see pages 86 and 88). Retire to a hidden location as far away as the release permits. Then wait.

Stalking—In the case of larger animals, you may have to resort to stalking. This is so, particularly if you have no telephoto lens, since you have to get very close to get a satisfactory picture. With a telephoto lens, you can often get good results shooting from a distance of 100 feet or more.

¶ *Tip*—It takes no stalking skill to photograph animals from an automobile. Nevertheless, you may sometimes succeed in getting within shooting range. Use the opportunity.

In ordinary stalking the main precaution is to approach the animal against the wind. The same holds true, of course, in photographic stalking, but in addition, you have to watch the light. The sun should be at your back or to one side: backlighted models are poor subjects.

¶ *Tip*—Just before shooting, make a squeak with your lips, similar to the sound used for attracting birds (see page 60). The squeak will startle the animal and make it look your way; it may even stop its flight for a moment.

NIGHT PHOTOGRAPHY—Successful night photography depends on reliable flashgun equipment. Use tripods for setting up the camera and flashgun in a likely spot—a runway or a feeding place.

¶ *Tip*—Flashgun should be to the side and slightly above the camera, to give good modeling of the animal. Flashguns attached to the camera will give poor results: An animal looking into the flash when it goes off will seem to have blind eyes because of the eyes' "cat's-eye" reflection.

You can set off the flash yourself by remote control. Or you can have the animal do it by touching a bait or trip string or by stepping on a pressure tripper.

Automatic tripper—An ordinary ten-cent mousetrap can be the

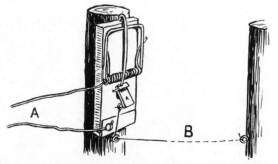

Using mousetrap for automatic tripping: (a) electric wires to solenoid, (b) thread leading across runway or to bait.

Eastman Kodak Company

When an animal steps on the baited pressure tripper, it closes an electrical circuit and takes its own picture.

main item in an electrical tripping gadget—for setting off cameras with electrically operated synchronization, for activating a solenoid coil, for pushing the shutter release of a camera with a synchronized flashgun, or for setting off the flashgun in open-flash photography.

Attach the mousetrap to a small post. Point the post to make it easy to drive it into the ground. Connect one wire from the flashgun or solenoid to the spring of the trap, the other wire to a brass plate or brass screw fastened to the trap's baseboard at such a location that it will be hit by the spring loop (see diagram on page 116). Set up your camera. Then, working *without a bulb in the flashgun*, tie a small loop (slipknot or bowline) in the end of a string and slip the loop loosely over the release of the unset trap. Lead the string through a screw eye on the trap, and on through screw eyes in pegs placed in the ground, either to the feeding place, tying the end of the string to a piece of bait here, or across the runway, tying it to a firm support on the other side.

Go back over the layout, set the trap, place a bulb in the flashgun, open the camera if you are using an open flash, and retire to wait for the flash to be set off. When the flash has occurred, go back to the camera to reset it or close it.

Pressure Tripper—The idea of the pressure tripper is to have the animal step on a pressure plate in a baited area. In so doing, it closes an electrical circuit and takes its picture.

In its simplest form the pressure tripper may consist of two pieces of plywood about 1 foot square. The underside of one and the top side of the other are provided with metal plates from which wires lead to the flashgun. The two metal plates are kept apart by springs between the plywood pieces until pressure is exerted.

SHOTS OF CAPTIVE ANIMALS—It is exceedingly difficult to get good shots in the wild of our smallest animals—mice, shrews, and the like. You will have better luck if you capture them first, then photograph them in a glass-surrounded enclosure against a naturally arranged background, either in the open or indoors, in sunlight or under artificial light. Take these pictures at as fast a speed as the lens and film allow. Use of a flash will permit shorter exposure with a smaller diaphragm, thus giving more depth of focus.

TRACK PHOTOGRAPHS—Photographs of animal tracks in mud or snow can be developed into a unique feature.

Take the shots from an angle of 45 degrees, with a fairly low forenoon or afternoon sun hitting them from the top left, if at all possible. By a queer fluke of the human eye—or mind—tracks lighted in other ways seem to pop up instead of appearing depressed.

¶ *Tip*—For tracks in the snow, take a light-meter reading directly on the snow, then double the indicated exposure for details in the shadows. For black-and-white shots, use a deep-yellow filter to increase the contrast.

To indicate the size of the track, you may want to include a ruler in the shot. Place the ruler next to the track in such a way that it can be cut out of a black-and-white enlargement and can be covered in a slide if you don't want to show it.

Movies

The usual run of animal movies falls into three types: (1) semitame animals in our national parks—bears in Yellowstone, antelopes and elk in Jackson Hole, buffaloes in various game refuges, and so on; (2) more or less tame animal pets—raccoons, skunks, opossums; (3) captive animals, photographed in their cages. The technique for taking such movies is the usual one of long shots, medium shots, and close-ups.

For really wild animals, the suggestions for daylight stills apply. You will need a telephoto lens, a firm support—preferably a gunstock base—ample tracking skill, and a goodly amount of patience.

Some animals may be photographed around their dens or feeding places by setting up the standard-lensed camera and releasing the shutter by remote control—by means of a string run from the release lever through screw eyes attached to small posts in the ground to your hiding place, for instance.

The difficulty with nearby movie taking—as against telephoto shooting—is that the sound of the motor almost invariably scares the animal away. The only way to overcome this is to get the animal accustomed to the sound. To do this, run the camera a number of times without film. When the sound no longer bothers the animal, put the film in the camera and take your scene.

ANIMAL COLLECTIONS

The notion that a naturalist's home should look like a museum, with stuffed animals on shelves and pedestals, has long been outdated.

Although you may eventually want to try your hand at preparing a hunting trophy or mounting a medium-sized animal according to the best traditions of taxidermy, there are many other types of collecting that will help you to increase your knowledge of animals and their ways.

Track Casts

Track casting is one of the best and easiest means of keeping track—literally—of the animals in a certain territory. For this you use the track itself as a mold, filling it with a liquid that hardens as it sets or cools.

To be a true picture of a track, the final cast should be a *positive*; it should show the track as it actually is, a depression. You can't make such a cast directly. You have to go through the step of making a *negative* first—showing the track as a raised hump. This negative can then be used to make the positive.

Negatives are made in the field, positives, usually at home.

If you are satisfied to do what most track collectors do—to stick to negatives—your best material is a good grade of plaster of paris. On the other hand, if you have your mind set on positive casts, you will be better off using paraffin or some other meltable material. The reason is that a number of the tracks you find, especially in soft ground, will be so deeply undercut that you will not be able to separate plaster negative from plaster positive without damaging both. A paraffin negative can be melted out of the plaster positive made in it, in a warm oven.

FINDING TRACKS—Start off by finding a good track. Don't be satisfied with the first track you see. Mark it with a stick, then look around; there may be a better track nearby. If there isn't, you can always return to the first one.

Search for tracks in soil that takes impressions particularly well—in clayish soil after rain or thaw, in the silt along the lake shore. Tracks of small animals are often found in profusion in dried-up drainage ditches.

Prepare the track you have chosen for casting. Dry leaves, weed seeds, and other debris may have fallen into the track after the animal made it. Pick up this litter carefully with your fingers or with forceps, or remove it by blowing through a short length of rubber tubing or by using a rubber bulb. If the ground is very wet, dust some dry plaster of paris into the track to absorb the moisture and to produce a preliminary shell.

¶ *Tip*—In camp, a tracking pit may provide you with an assortment of tracks suitable for casting. On some level spot close to natural cover, spade up an area about 6 feet square. Pull out grass and weeds, remove stones, rake smooth. Dampen the ground enough to make sharp tracks. In the evening, place suitable bait in the middle of the pit (see page 99). Next morning, check to see what visitors you have had during the night.

PLASTER CASTS—THE NEGATIVE—For plaster casts, you need a couple of pounds of plain plaster of paris—patching plaster sets too slowly—a canteen or plastic bottle of water, a mixing bowl, a stick for stirring, strips of cardboard, 1 inch wide and 15 to 18 inches long.

¶ *Tip*—You can use a cup or a tin can for mixing, but a flexible plastic container—such as a plastic bottle with the top cut off—or half a large rubber ball is better. You don't have to wash it out after use. Simply leave the remaining plaster to harden, then crack it off by squeezing.

When you have found a desirable track, make a collar of one of the cardboard strips to fit around it. Hold the two ends of the strip together with a pin or clip. Or make a tear halfway down near one end and a tear halfway up in the other, and lock the two tears together. Press the collar firmly into the ground around the track, deep enough to avoid plaster seepage.

¶ *Tip*—Instead of using cardboard, you can use 1-inch-wide rings cut from a ½-gallon plastic bleach bottle.

Making the cast—Make a rough estimate of the amount of the plaster mixture you will need. Pour about one third of this amount of water into the mixing cup. Sprinkle plaster into the water *without stirring*—let's repeat—*without stirring*—until small "islands" start to form above the surface of the water—the proportion will be approximately 7 (plaster) to 4 (water). Now stir the mixture gently with a stick—this is called spatulating—until it is smooth and even. It should have the consistency of melted ice cream, pancake batter, light molasses—take your pick. If too thin, add a little more plaster. Bang your mixing cup against the ground a few times to get air bubbles to rise and break. Or hit the side of the cup with the mixing stick for the same purpose.

Note—Usual mistake is to make the plaster mixture too thick. It should *flow*, not *drop*!

Pour the plaster mixture slowly into the track, and continue pouring until it fills the collar to about ¾-inch depth above ground level. Smooth the surface with the stick or with a finger.

¶ *Tip*—A pinch of salt added to the plaster mixture speeds up the hardening of the cast (you can ready-mix it into your dry plaster in advance). A little vinegar retards the hardening.

When the track cast has hardened somewhat, you can insert a wire loop in it for hanging, if you like. Also scratch on the back of it the name of the animal, date, and place, with a pencil point or sharpened stick. Add a number, and write in your notebook under that number other pertinent information: whether the track is of the front or hind leg, whether the animal was walking or running, the kind of soil, and so on.

Leave the cast to set for twenty to thirty minutes. Go hunting for other tracks in the meantime and set a cast line the way a trapper sets a trap line. When the plaster has hardened, loosen the earth around it with a stick, and lift up the cast with whatever dirt clings to it. Wrap it in newspaper and bring it home.

When it is completely dry, brush off the dirt with an old toothbrush. Or wash it under a faucet, then dry it again.

Leave the finished cast as it is, or shellac it, or paint it in a color to suggest the kind of soil from which it was taken.

Plaster casts in snow—In the winter you may want to bring home a cast of a track made by an animal in the snow. This can be done fairly easily provided the temperature is below freezing.

In addition to needing the regular materials used in track casting, you will need a plastic squeeze bottle (or rubber bulb) and an atomizer such as is used for spraying a sore throat. Put a small amount of dry plaster into the squeeze bottle, and fill the atomizer with cold water.

After placing a collar around the track, squeeze a dusting of dry plaster into all parts of the track, then spray the track with a mist of water and let it freeze. Repeat until you have formed a firm crust inside the track. Then proceed with making the cast, mixing a bit of snow into the plaster mixture to lower its temperature.

OTHER KINDS OF NEGATIVE CASTS—Paraffin casts—Clear the track of debris and place a cardboard or plastic collar around it as for plaster casting.

Melt paraffin (household wax) in a can over an open fire or, simpler, on a Sterno, Heatab, or gasoline stove. Don't overheat. Pour it slowly into the track. The paraffin cools and hardens quickly. The cast can be removed within a few minutes. Undermine the track, and dig up the cast with its adhering dirt. Wrap it in newspaper. Keep it cool in hot weather. Clean it when you get home.

Sulphur casts—Sulphur—flowers or lumps of sulphur roll—melts into a thin liquid at a temperature slightly above the boiling point for water and cools into a hard but rather brittle cast.

Melt it and use it as in paraffin casting.

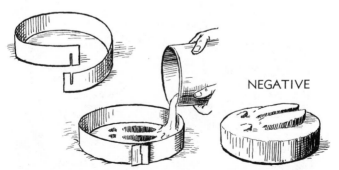

NEGATIVE

To make a negative plaster cast of an animal track, turn cardboard strip into a collar by notching ends together.

PLASTER CASTS—THE POSITIVE—To make a positive plaster cast, use either a negative plaster cast without undercuts or a negative of meltable materials—paraffin or sulphur.

Making the cast—If your plaster negative is suitable, prepare it for positive casting by brushing it with linseed oil, soft soap, melted paraffin, or a mixture of 1 part petroleum jelly diluted with 2 parts kerosene. A paraffin or sulphur negative needs no such preparation.

Cut a 3-inch strip of cardboard. Wrap this as a collar around the negative. Hold it in place with rubber bands.

Mix a batch of plaster-of-paris batter. Pour it into the collar to a height of at least $\frac{1}{2}$ inch above the highest hump of the negative. Put it aside to set completely, for half an hour or more.

Separate the positive from the negative, if necessary by inserting a knife blade between them. If an undercut paraffin negative was used, remove as much of the paraffin as you can, and melt out the rest by placing the cast on a pan in a warm oven.

Leave the track surface intact. Trim down the sides and back smoothly with an old knife, then sandpaper it. Protect the cast by a thin coat of varnish or shellac. For a more naturalistic effect, you can brush the track surface with diluted glue and sprinkle it with sand or dirt. Or you can paint it in an appropriate soil color, using a slightly darker shade in the track indentation.

Animal Traces

Animals leave various traces in addition to footprints, as evidence of their presence. Some of these traces may be incorporated in your collection.

Animal-marked trees—In beaver territory you can find beaver-cut branches of varying thicknesses, showing the marks of strong front teeth. Woodchucks cut off small seedlings by a clear pruning; browsing deer, elk, moose, make fuzzy, uneven cuts. Small gnaw marks running at all angles indicate various mice—pine mouse if

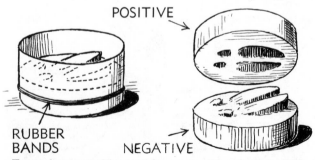

POSITIVE

RUBBER BANDS   NEGATIVE

To produce a positive cast from a negative, fasten a high collar around the greased negative, then pour in plaster.

below the root collar. Complete girdling with well-defined tooth marks indicates the porcupine as culprit.

Other types of markings are the claw scratches of bear, and bark fibers torn loose by rubbing deer antlers.

All such animal-marked tree parts may be trimmed to convenient length and wired to plywood panels for display.

Gnawed nuts and cones—If you come upon a heap of nut shells on an old stump, you can be pretty certain that you are in a squirrel "dining room." If the shells are broken in pieces, the evidence is conclusive.

Two or three holes in a nut indicate a mouse. Look at the tooth marks. After gnawing a small opening, some mice gnaw from the inside out with their lower teeth, keeping the upper teeth steady against the outside of the nut; others gnaw from the outside in with their snouts in the hole. Which do what?

Pine and fir cones with scales carelessly torn off suggest squirrel; smoothly chewed off, mouse.

Scat—Scat or droppings may seem peculiar items for collecting. Nevertheless, they often provide the only readily found evidence of the presence of animals, especially in rocky territory where tracks are not easily seen.

The droppings of *wild vegetarians* are generally found as piles of "beans." The beans of rabbits are coffee-bean size, oval, dark brown; those of hares almost globular. Deer beans are black-glazed, long-oval, uneven, hazelnut size, sometimes flattened at one end and usually pointed at the other.

The scat of *meat eaters* and *omnivores* are dropped in more coherent form. Droppings of mice are tiny, black, spindle-shaped. Scat of weasel, mink, and marten are cylindrical, black, containing feathers, hair, and bone splinters. Otter scat is tarlike, with fish bones and crayfish remains. Fox droppings are finger thick, cylindrical, usually pointed at both ends. They contain a mixture of feathers, hair, bones, beetle wings, and fruit seeds.

If you specialize in "scatology," bear in mind that scat is subject to insect attack. Keep in closed containers with a few crystals of paradichlorobenzene.

REFERENCES—Olaus Murie's *Field Guide to Animal Tracks* contains excellent drawings of scat, claw marks, and gnaw marks, and other animal traces, as well as illustrations of animal homes. So does Ernest Seton's *Animal Tracks and Hunter Signs* (see page 102).

Animal Specimens

Large animals can usually be identified in the field. But it is different with the small animals. We have more than a hundred different species and subspecies of pocket gopher, for instance, many of which can be told apart only by close comparison. Similarly, we have more than seventy different meadow mice, more than sixty shrews, around fifty white-footed mice. Some of these species are confined to certain clearly defined geographical locations, but there may be several kinds in your neighborhood, though in different habitats. The way to ascertain which they are is to trap them, measure them, study their colorings, check their skull shape and teeth arrangement. The skins should then be treated and kept for future reference and study.

STUDY SKINS—A study skin is prepared by carefully removing the skin, impregnating it with a chemical that will protect it against deterioration and insect attacks, stuffing it with cotton, and drying it.

REFERENCES—*Field Collector's Manual.* Smithsonian Institution, Washington, D.C. 20560.

R. M. Anderson, *Methods of Collecting and Preserving Vertebrate Animals.* Bulletin No. 69, National Museum of Canada, Ottawa, Canada.

Taking notes—Before skinning, make up two labels, one for the skin, the other for the skull, with notes on the animal: where found, date, finder. Include the main measurements. Stretch out the animal and take its length from snout to tail tip; take the length of the tail from base to tip and of the hind foot from heel to the point of its longest toenail.

Also place the animal on a piece of white paper and draw an outline of the body, not the fur. This sketch will help you later.

Skinning—Place the animal on its back. Make a slit in the skin from a point just ahead of the vent to the breastbone. Be careful not to puncture the belly cavity. With the fingers, free the skin from the flesh the whole way around the body. Use a knife or scalpel only if the flesh sticks. Have on hand a package of oatmeal. Use the meal generously to absorb blood and other body liquids.

Loosen the skin from one of the hind legs. Pull the leg up, sever it at the knee joint, and scrape the bone between the knee and heel clean of flesh. Treat the other hind leg in the same manner.

Cut carefully around the vent, then loosen the skin around the base of the tail. Pull out the tail bones with the fingers of one hand while holding on to the tail skin at its base with the other.

Grasp the hind legs with one hand and with the other carefully pull the skin off the body, turning it inside out, until you reach the forelegs. Treat them the way you did the hind legs.

The skin usually pulls readily over the neck. Your next trouble spot is at the ears. Cut close to the skull with scalpel or scissors. Do the same when you reach the eye sockets. Be particularly careful here so that you keep the eyelids intact. Cut around the lips, and finally release the skin completely by snipping through the cartilage of the nose.

Keep the skull—or possibly the whole carcass—for further treatment (see page 127).

Scrape off any flesh or fat that remains on the skin. Rub a preservative, such as borax powder, into the skin. Even better is a commercial product specifically designed for the purpose, such as nonpoisonous Calorax, available from taxidermy supply houses.

Sew the lips together with a few stitches of thin thread.

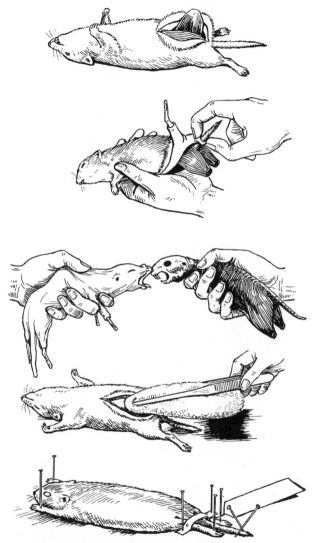

Five steps in preparing study skin (based on suggestions of members of the staff of the Smithsonian Institution). Stuff the prepared skin with cotton. Pin down the stuffed animal to dry in recommended fashion for study skins.

Stuffing—Wrap cotton around the leg bones to approximately the same thickness as the flesh you removed. Then turn the skin right side out.

Stuff the head and body with cotton, using forceps if necessary to put the padding in place. Or better, make a false body by winding cotton around a piece of wire and pushing it into the skin. Use the outline drawing you made before skinning to give the body the correct dimensions. Wrap a small amount of cotton into a tapered spiral around a piece of thin, waxed wire to fit into the tail skin.

Finally, sew up the slit to enclose the filling.

Drying—Place the completed skin on a piece of soft wood, belly down. Pin the front legs straight out to the front, hind legs and tail straight out to the back. Attach the label to the right hind leg. Leave the skin to dry.

MOUNTED SPECIMENS—Any time you like, you can try your hand at taxidermy and turn your study specimen into a more natural-looking mounted specimen.

Or you may start from scratch if you happen to be a hunter yourself or have a hunter friend among your acquaintances.

BOOKS ON TAXIDERMY—Leon L. Pray, *Taxidermy*. New York, The Macmillan Company.

John W. Moyer, *Practical Taxidermy*. New York, Ronald Press Company.

Preparing the skin—For small animals up to the size of a squirrel, you can prepare the skin in the same manner as a study skin.

For larger animals, it pays to salt down the raw pelt thoroughly and send it to a taxidermist for tanning.

Steps in mounting small animals—In general, the steps in mounting a small animal are the following:

Attach the cleaned skull (or a carved replica) to one end of a stiff "backbone" wire about twice as long as the body of the animal. Make a loop in the wire a short distance behind the place where wires from the front legs will meet it, and a double loop at the hip joint.

If the skin is dried up, relax it by moistening the inside with borax solution, then by working it in your hands. Push a wire through each paw, tie it to the leg bone with thread or flower wire. Bring the leg wires through the appropriate loops of the "backbone" wire, then wind them firmly onto this wire. Leave a couple of inches of leg wire below each paw.

Stuff the animal with excelsior (wood wool). Where you can't push it in with your fingers, use forceps. As you go along, squeeze the parts you have stuffed into their natural shape. When the stuffing is completed, sew up the slit in the skin. Set up the animal by pushing the leg wires through holes bored in a wooden base and bending them under.

Mounting large animals—There are many short cuts in the mounting of larger animals. Taxidermists' supply houses furnish head forms or real skulls, excelsior bodies of many sizes and shapes, ear linings, artificial noses and eyes, and stands and bases. Before proceeding, contact one of these supply houses and get their recommendation.

TAXIDERMISTS' SUPPLIES—Penn Taxidermy Supply Company, P.O. Box 156, Hazleton, Pennsylvania 18201.

J. W. Elwood Supply Company, 1202 Harney Street, Omaha, Nebraska 68102.

M. J. Hoffmann Company, 993 Gates Avenue, Brooklyn, New York 11221.

D. M. Wooster Studios, Academy Street, Whitney Point, New York 13862.

Skulls and Skeletons

SKULLS—Thousands of wild animals are run over and killed yearly on our highways. Many, of course, have their heads smashed, but some don't. By being on the lookout, you can obtain skulls of chipmunk, squirrel, rabbit, hare, skunk, opossum, porcupine, raccoon, even coyote and other large animals.

Mice and similar small mammals you can take in traps. You can usually make a deal with local hunters or trappers for other animals that will give you a send-off into the science of *osteology*—from the Greek *osteon*, bone.

Small skulls—The most effective way of preparing small skulls, and the way least likely to damage them, is to let the larvae of a dermestid beetle—*Dermestes maculatus*, hide beetle—do the job for you. These larvae feed on dry animal matter. They will eat off every scrap of flesh, leaving the bones in excellent condition.

Establish a dermestid colony as described on page 170.

Drop the dry skulls to be cleaned into the jar, and let the dermestid beetles and their offspring take over. When the job is done, lift out the cleaned skulls, pick off all beetles and larvae, and drop them back into the jar.

Large skulls—Large skulls can also be cleaned by dermestid larvae. But you will probably not have the patience to wait for this long-drawn-out process, and will decide to do it yourself.

Skin the head first. Be careful, and watch particularly around eye sockets and snout. Then place the skull in a pot of cold water. Add 1 tablespoon sal soda for each 2 quarts of water and bring to a boil. Simmer until the flesh on the back of the head comes off the skull. Cool slowly by pouring cold water into the pot. If the solution is cooled quickly, the tooth enamel may crack.

Now scrape the flesh off with a paring knife. Bring a wire with a flattened, crooked end through the hole at the back of the skull, and break up the brain. Flush out the brain matter and rinse well under a faucet. Then drop the skull into a wide-mouth glass jar filled with diluted ammonia water in the proportion of 4 ounces household ammonia to each quart of water. Cover the jar. Leave undisturbed from two to seven days.

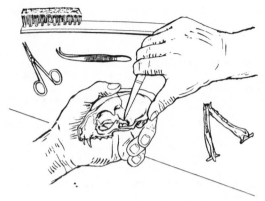

Ward's Natural Science Establishment, Inc.

Do main cleaning of an animal skull with a paring knife. Have other tools handy: scissors, forceps, plater's brush.

Rinse the skull in water and go over it for a final cleaning with the paring knife and a long-handled plater's brush. Then wash it thoroughly.

To remove odors and to bleach it, drop the skull into another wide-mouth jar, cover with full-strength Clorox, and leave overnight. Remove the skull (use rubber gloves!) and wash it. Drain it and dry in the shade.

If the skull appears greasy on drying, it needs degreasing. Place it overnight in some grease-dissolving cleaning fluid—Renuzit, for instance. Then take it out and dry it again in a drafty place.

SKELETONS—A collection of identified skeleton parts will prove of great value to you. It will permit you to recognize the remains of animals found dead in the field, predator kills, materials in scat and in owl pellets.

Small skeletons—For small animal carcasses, make use of the dermestid colony you have established for cleaning skulls. Check daily and remove the skeleton as soon as the dry flesh has been eaten off. (Otherwise the dermestids will continue eating the ligaments that connect the bones.) The result will be a complete skeleton, with all parts intact and fastened together.

Large skeletons—Skeleton parts of a large animal can be prepared in the manner described for large skulls. The preparation of a complete skeleton, on the other hand, is a complicated job.

If you should ever want to undertake the preparation of a large skeleton, it will pay you to seek advice and help from a local expert.

REFERENCES—Pamphlets on *How to Prepare Skeletons* are free from Ward's, General Biological Supply House, Carolina Supply Company. (For addresses, see page 27.)

CHAPTER 5

Snakes, Lizards, and Turtles

MANY people have a morbid fear of snakes. Some get hysterical at the sight of a perfectly harmless garter snake slithering away among the rocks. Others become heroic and go on a St. George rampage to kill the "poisonous critter."

The trouble is that there is possibly more superstition and plain ignorance connected with snakes than with anything else in nature. Rather a pity that false teachings should have created the unreasonable and unreasoned fear of these animals! Anyone willing to cut through the myths and approach the subject rationally, will find snakes highly interesting creatures.

There's no excuse today for people being ignorant of the facts about snakes. On the other hand, you can't really blame our forefathers for their attitude. From early biblical days, the snake had stood as the symbol of all evil. From time immemorial, snakes had been known to have caused the death of people—so why not make it the better part of valor to consider all snakes poisonous and fear all of them? And then there were the folk tales of snakes that bit onto their tails and hoop-rolled downhill after their enemies . . . of snakes that hypnotized their prey with their glassy stare . . . of still others that crept into barns and sucked the cows dry.

The list of snake "facts" that "ain't so" is long. And the list of facts connected with lizards is almost as long—for, after all, isn't the lizard the direct descendant of the fire-spewing dragon of old? The turtle seems to be the only reptile that has come down through the ages with a decent reputation—much of it attributable to Aesop and his fables rather than to scientific investigation.

With all the superstitions regarding reptiles, it is only comparatively recently that we have begun to learn the facts, and we are still far from knowing them all.

BOOKS ON REPTILE LIFE—Clifford H. Pope, *Reptile World*. New York, Alfred A. Knopf.

Raymond L. Ditmars, *Reptiles of North America*, rev. ed. New York, Macmillan Company.

Karl P. Schmidt and Robert F. Inger, *Living Reptiles of the World*. New York, Doubleday & Company.

Archie Carr, *The Reptiles*. Chicago, Illinois, Time-Life Books.

Working with Others

You will have many interesting hours investigating the life and habits of our native reptiles.

Much of this work you can do alone. But you will have more fun and pick up more knowledge if you can work with other people interested in the same hobby.

To get in touch with such people, contact your local school biology teachers. If there is a natural history museum within a reasonable distance, you will find there people specializing in *herpetology*.

Finally, as your interest mounts, you may want to join a national society and in this way keep informed about the latest developments within the field of snake study.

SOCIETIES—American Society of Ichthyologists and Herpetologists. Headquarters: Division of Reptiles, U.S. National Museum, Washington, D.C. 20560. Periodical: *Copeia*.

Herpetologists League. Headquarters: 900 Veteran Avenue, Los Angeles, California 90024. Periodical: *Herpetologica*.

FIELD STUDY OF REPTILES

Identification

In most other phases of nature, the ability to identify a specimen should come as a result of study in the field. In reptile study, it is important to begin with a determined effort to learn to recognize the poisonous snakes of your locality—either for the purpose of avoiding them as you go about studying the harmless snakes or for the purpose of finding them if you intend to concentrate on their study. But don't think of the latter until you have become an experienced herpetologist.

By studying a reptile field book, you will pick up a general knowledge of our poisonous snakes: rattler, copperhead, cottonmouth moccasin, coral snake. A better method is the study of preserved specimens, and, even better, live specimens in captivity. The most effective method is to take your early field trips under the guidance of an experienced snake student.

Equipment for Reptile Study

For general field study of reptiles very little in the way of equipment is needed—unless you get into territory infested with poisonous snakes. Here you will need certain precautionary equipment and specialized tools. If you are reasonably careful, the likelihood of being bitten by a poisonous snake is remote. The best precaution is vigilance. Look where you are stepping; notice where you put your hands.

The statistics in regard to snake bites are exceedingly sketchy. Estimates range from one hundred to two thousand bites each year in the United States. Of the bites reported, it has again been loosely estimated that about 70 percent are on feet or legs (bare feet, low-cut shoes), 25 percent on hands and arms (not watching where hands are placed in climbing rocky ledges; incorrect handling of captured specimens), and 5 percent on head and body (drinking incautiously from spring or stream). Where quick, energetic treatment is applied, a bite only rarely results in death.

CLOTHING—Because most reptile hunting is done in warm weather, wear lightweight clothing. Protect your head against the sun.

The snake-bite reports show the advisability of protecting your legs and hands. When hunting snakes in territory where poisonous species are present, wear high-top boots, or leather puttees, or heavy canvas leggings over regular shoes. For climbing, wear heavy gauntlet-type leather gloves, with cuffs long enough to protect your wrists.

PRECAUTIONARY EQUIPMENT—**Tools**—In rocky country, don't move loose rocks with your hands. Bring along a potato rake or a baling hook such as is used by truckers.

Snake-bite kit—For further protection, carry a snake-bite kit. Small pocket types are available. Each of them contains a thin rubber hose for tying around the limb to arrest the flow of the venom toward the heart, a razor blade for opening up the bite, and a rubber suction cup for sucking out the poison-mixed blood. Learn the function of the kit before the need to use it arises. The method is described in the leaflet that comes with the kit and in the *Field Book of Snakes of the United States and Canada* by Karl P. Schmidt and D. Dwight Davis (New York, G. P. Putnam's Sons).

SNAKE-BITE KITS—Asepto Snake Bite Outfit No. 2006. Beckton, Dickinson & Company, Rutherford, New Jersey.

Compac Snake Bite Kit. Cutler Laboratories, Berkeley, California.

Snake-bite serum—Where extensive explorations through snake-infested territory take you far away from human habitation, it is also advisable to carry Antivenin, a polyvalent serum that, when injected into the bloodstream, counteracts the poisons of rattlesnake, copperhead, and water moccasin. If at all possible, see a physician for the injection.

ANTIVENIN—Antivenin Combination Kit. Wyeth Laboratories, Radner, Pennsylvania 19088, or through your local drug store.

STUDY EQUIPMENT—Depending on the subject you are working on, you may need some or all of the following.

Reptile book—Bring along a field book dealing with your specialty in the reptile field.

BOOKS FOR FIELD IDENTIFICATION—Doris M. Cochran and Coleman J. Goin, *The New Field Book of Reptiles and Amphibians*. New York, G. P. Putnam's Sons.

Roger Conant, *Field Guide to Reptiles and Amphibians* (Eastern North America). Boston, Houghton Mifflin Company.

Robert C. Stebbins, *Field Guide to the Western Reptiles and Amphibians*. Boston, Houghton Mifflin Company.

Herbert S. Zim and Hobart M. Smith, *Reptiles and Amphibians.* New York, Golden Press.

OTHER BOOKS—Clifford H. Pope, *Turtles of the United States and Canada.* New York, Alfred A. Knopf.

Archie Carr, *Handbook of Turtles: The Turtles of the United States, Canada, and Baja California.* Ithaca, New York, Comstock Publishing Associates.

Hobart M. Smith, *Handbook of Lizards.* Ithaca, New York, Comstock Publishing Associates.

Notebook—A pocket-sized book for note taking—possibly a loose-leaf binder with record cards with columns for the information you are seeking.

Measuring equipment—*Balance* for weighing. The simplest type for field work is a spring balance with a hook on which you can hang the bag that holds your captured specimen. *Rule* for measuring—a short pocket rule for small reptiles, a carpenter's rule or metal tape for large snakes.

Flashlight—When looking for reptiles at night, a flashlight strapped to the forehead is superior to the usual hand type.

Catching equipment—You should have no trouble catching turtles by hand—with the exception of some aquatic specimens. For snakes and lizards you will require specialized catching equipment (see page 136).

Finding Reptiles

Snakes

Snakes are elusive creatures. Finding them is mostly a matter of luck—especially in the case of the larger species. Yet, if you know Where and When to look for them, each of your field trips should make it possible for you to chalk up a further score of specimens observed.

WHERE?—The most successful places for finding snakes in large numbers are near their denning areas during the spring awakening. Copperheads and timber rattlers hibernate in crevices among rocks. Ask old villagers. They may be able to tell you of places where these snakes have been known to hibernate year after year. Other snakes hibernate in deserted burrows of woodchucks, prairie dogs, gophers, gopher tortoises, muskrats, rats.

When snakes have left their hibernation places, you will have to hunt farther afield. Keep in mind, then, that all snakes seek a certain amount of coolness and moisture, and therefore they generally go into concealment except when hunting their food. Look for them in appropriate hiding places, or chase them to such places where you may have a chance to trap them. In approaching them, remember that snakes are sensitive to vibrations, but not to sounds. You can talk or even shout without disturbing them, but you have to step lightly.

Look for *small snakes* under loose trees and fallen branches, under bark of decaying trees, and in hollow logs.

¶ *Tip*—Hunt the *small snakes* with a buddy. Even the tiniest snakes can squirm away with incredible speed. Have your buddy lift the stone while you do the grabbing.

For *larger snakes*, investigate piles of dead leaves, heaps of bark slabs around old sawmills, corn or grain shucks left in the field, rock crevices along a creek. Look under pieces of tar paper, tin, and similar debris.

¶ *Tip*—If you live near a farmyard, vacant lot, camp grounds, you may have fair success in attracting certain snakes. Scatter a number of 1-foot squares of tar paper, linoleum, cardboard (waterproofed with paint or shellac), in such a way that they are suspended slightly above the ground, by grass, pebbles, or the like. Visit your "traps" several times a day and investigate which snakes may have been attracted to them.

For *snakes that take to water*, wade carefully upstream looking for them sunning themselves on rocks along the stream's edge or, in the case of certain species, on branches overhanging the stream.

WHEN?—Time of year—Snakes are active in warm weather. Cool temperatures slow them down since their body heat depends on their surroundings. They get sluggish when the temperature drops much below 60 degrees. With the exception of some Southern species, most snakes in the United States go into hibernation when freezing weather approaches—often in balls of intertwining bodies, from a few to a hundred or more. They emerge again in the spring when the surroundings warm up, to scatter far and wide over the countryside.

Obviously, then, the best times of the year for finding snakes are fall when they move toward their hibernation points, and spring when they leave them. Of those two seasons, spring is the better. At that time, the snakes are less wary. Also, spring vegetation provides less concealment than the lush growth of late summer.

Time of day—Weather—On days that are cloudy and cold, you will have little luck. On cool sunshiny days from spring to fall, snakes may be found sunning themselves on rocks and on branches. During hot weather, many of them seek cool shade or hunt among rocks near a brook or river.

A number of species, particularly in desert territories, become nocturnal during the hottest season of the year, sleeping in hiding during the day and hunting in the comparative cool of night. They may be jacklighted. Or look for them crossing roads, by the light of an automobile cruising at slow speed.

Lizards

Lizards are creatures of the sun. For the largest variety of lizards, go south, or better, southwest. You will find a number in other sections of the country, but none in northern New England.

WHERE?—Lizards are usually found in abundance in deserts. You may see them rushing over the surface, popping in and out of rock piles and debris of yucca or joshua trees.

Fields and woodlands hold other lizards, perpetually on the go on warm days hunting for insects and worms. Investigate stone fences, rotting stumps, decaying logs. Strip off the loose bark of southern dead pines and you will almost certainly come upon lizards. And look up from time to time; a lizard may be scurrying up the tree right in front of you.

WHEN?—A bright, sunny summer day is the best time to look for lizards.

When the days turn cloudy and cool, lizards go into hiding. Winter finds them in hibernation.

Turtles

Sandy deserts hold some of our native turtles, but the majority of them have aquatic habits.

WHERE?—While you will come across a few of the turtles in woods and fields—mostly wood and box turtles—you will find far more in and around lakes and streams. On a warm day you may see turtles sunning themselves on every log and rock protruding from the water. Approach them carefully; they have a way of sliding into the water the moment they realize that an enemy is around.

WHEN?—Turtles, like other reptiles, spend their winters in hibernation. They appear on the scene again when spring and warm weather set in.

The best time of the year to look for them is during their nesting season—May and June.

Finding Reptile Eggs

Snake Eggs

Some snakes bear living young—or rather, bring them forth in thin membrane sacs that are ruptured shortly after birth by the snakelet. Other snakes lay elongated creamy-white eggs. Eggs are generally laid in June and July, rarely the first couple of weeks of August. The young emerge from a week to three months later, depending on the species and outside conditions influencing incubation.

Snake eggs may sometimes be located through a search of manure piles, heaps of rotting sawdust, decaying wood pulp in old stumps and logs, occasionally in stone piles. Make careful notes of places where eggs were found, type of soil in which laid, depth below surface, number, arrangement, whether separate or adhering to one another. Measure length and thickness with calipers, if possible, for exact dimensions.

Turtle Eggs

Turtle eggs are globular or slightly elongated, with hard or pliable creamy-white shells. You may be lucky enough to locate a nest of them in sand or soft soil near a lake or stream.

It takes an expert to tell what species laid a particular clutch of eggs. And even experts aren't always certain. The only way you can be sure is to take a few home and hatch them (see page 143).

Reptile Lists

LIFE LISTS—Keep careful records in your notebook of the field trips you take and the reptiles you come across on each of them, including name, habitat, weather conditions.

Carefully made and detailed notes may help to add to our knowledge of reptiles and their habits.

Field Observations

Discovering reptiles in the field and watching their activities can provide you with a lot of interesting experiences. But reptile hunting becomes even more fascinating when you are out to find the solution to a problem you have decided to investigate.

Number of snakes—Common or uncommon in your vicinity? Fluctuation in numbers from year to year.

Growth—By months, by years. When large numbers of snakes are captured, it will be found that they fall into size groups according to age. But tables of "average lengths" are still far from complete.

Weight—Before and after hibernation. What is the weight loss?

Feeding—The stomach contents of a snake that has recently taken a meal can be pushed out without injury to the snake by kneading the snake's body gently below the food "bulge" and slowly pressing the food forward until it is disgorged.

Locomotion—Speed, method of movement. What is the hunting range of the species you are investigating?

Homing instincts—Will a snake or lizard or turtle return if removed a couple of miles from its home ground?

Intelligence, senses—A great number of methods may be invented for testing the intelligence and senses of various reptiles.

In addition to the investigations that you may deliberately plan, good luck or keen observation may give you a chance to contribute to our knowledge of reptiles through chance occurrences. On your hunts, you may happen to come upon some of the life functions that have rarely been observed. It is then a matter of knowing what to look for, how to make complete observation notes, how to sketch or photograph the occasion.

Among such observations may be the following:

Skin shedding of snakes—Note what movements are made to facilitate the shedding, the length of time it takes.

Courtship and mating—Complete description of the actions of male and female.

Egg laying—Nest making of egg-laying species. The actual process of egg laying, how many eggs, length of time required.

Birth of snakelets—In snakes bearing living young.

REPTILES IN CAPTIVITY

Catching Reptiles

The best "instrument" for catching harmless snakes is the hand. A quick reach and a firm hold behind the snake's head will do the trick. The snake may thrash around and let off excrement or a musky-smelling secretion from its anal glands, but if you then support its body with your other hand, it will soon quiet down.

The hand is also the best tool for catching turtles and lizards. In the case of lizards, your hand needs to be extra fast; even at that, you may often wind up with a squirming tail in your hand while the animal itself disappears.

CATCHING EQUIPMENT—Snake sticks—If catching snakes with the bare hands does not appeal to you, use a snake stick.

WARNING—A snake stick should ALWAYS be used for poisonous snakes.

The snake stick, in its simplest form, is a branch 4 to 5 feet long with an L-crotch in the end. Whittle down the side branch that forms the bottom of the L to approximately 2 inches. Pin down the snake by placing this end of the stick over its neck. You can then readily pick up the snake with thumb and forefinger.

A better snake stick may be made by screwing a 2-inch-long, $\frac{1}{2}$-inch-wide angle iron (inside corner plate) to the end of a 4-foot-long broomstick. Or by hammering a $\frac{1}{8}$-inch-thick piece of iron rod, bent at a right angle, into a hole bored in a $\frac{3}{4}$-inch dowel. With this

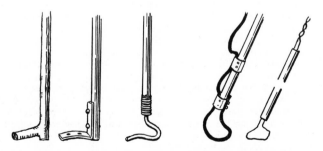

Snake sticks: L-crotch, angle iron, iron rod. Strap stick has strap in metal guides; wire-loop "stick" uses tubing.

type, you can pin down the snake or lift it up by bringing the hook in under its midsection.

If you combine an interest in playing golf with your hobby of studying snakes, you may have on hand an old golf putter that you can file down into a serviceable snake stick.

¶ *Tip*—Some snake experts use a regular insect sweeping net for catching snakes (see page 156–57).

When handling poisonous snakes, use a strap stick. This is a square stick with a leather strap that runs in guides fastened to the stick. The loop is laid over the snake's head around the neck, whereupon it is tightened, holding the snake by the neck in a firm grip.

Western rattlesnake hunters often carry a wire-loop "stick." This consists of a short length of tubing through which is run a long loop of picture wire. It is used in the same way as the loop stick.

Lizard catcher—You can turn a stick or an old fishing rod into a lizard catcher by providing it, at the tip, with a small slip noose made of a short length of horsehair or thin fishline, or of a single copper strand from an electric light cord.

In using the catcher, slowly slip the noose over the lizard's head. A quick jerk, and the noose closes around the animal's neck.

"Noodling" rod—Snapping turtles can be caught during hibernation by "noodling" for them with a piece of $\frac{1}{4}$-inch iron rod, 3 to 4 feet long, with a pointed hook at one end. With the straight end, probe along lake banks, under stumps, in old muskrat holes, until you get the "feel" of a turtle. Turn the rod, and pull out the turtle with the hook in the other end and with your hands.

Turtle traps—Aquatic turtles are often caught in traps. The simplest trap to make is the raft type. This consists of four pine or spruce logs, about 4 inches in diameter and 4 feet long. Notch them, log-cabin style, and nail them together into a rectangular raft. Float this raft and mark the waterline on the logs. Along this line, on the inside of the raft, drive in 16-penny nails at 2-inch intervals, in such a way that they slope slightly downward. Staple or nail a hammock of 1-inch-mesh poultry netting to the underside of the raft.

Float the finished trap in the water. Keep it in place with a stone

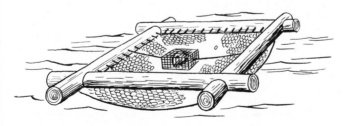

Aquatic turtles can be caught in a floating trap. The turtles slide into it to get the bait and can't get out.

anchor or with a rope attached to a stake. Bait the trap with dead fish or old meat. Turtles attracted by the bait can easily slide over the logs and get inside the trap but can't get out again because of the nails.

¶ *Tip*—By wrapping the bait in wire screening so that it won't be eaten by the first snapper to enter, you can lure a number of turtles into the trap with the same bait.

TRANSPORTING YOUR CATCH—Bags—Have available a number of cloth bags in various sizes for transporting your captives. Unbleached muslin is excellent for making these bags. Flour bags and sugar sacks are satisfactory, with a gunny sack thrown in for large snappers.

Don't depend on a draw string for a snake bag; instead, sew a piece of tape to the outside of the bag, about 1 inch from the top. Fold down the top of the bag after the snake or lizard has been thrown in, then tie it.

Jars—Small reptiles may be transported in glass or plastic screw-top jars. Make nail-hole perforations in the cover to let in air. Make the holes from the inside, so that there will be no sharp points to injure your specimens.

Metal containers—Snake hunters in rattlesnake-infested areas occasionally make use of a minnow bucket (less water, of course) for transporting their poisonous catch.

WARNING—Leaving specimens exposed to the sun in hot weather, even for only a few minutes, may be fatal to them. Keep the bag in the shade. If the snakes have to be carried any distance, put some damp moss or wet leaves with them.

Reptile Cages and Cage Health

Reptiles get along satisfactorily as long as the temperature is right, the ventilation good and without drafts, food adequate, and water and hiding places on hand.

Snakes

SNAKE TERRARIUM—A homemade terrarium case or an old aquarium tank will make an excellent home for one or more small or medium-sized snakes.

Make snakes caught in field or forest at home in a woodland terrarium, desert snakes in a desert terrarium (see pages 242–43). Sink a small dish into one corner of the terrarium and keep it supplied with water.

SNAKE CAGES—In constructing snake cages, you can pretty well suit your own ideas.

TYPES—Many different types are possible—among them those shown on page 139.

Wire-lid cage—The wire-lid cage can be knocked together quickly. It has a glass front held in position by wood strips or moldings, and

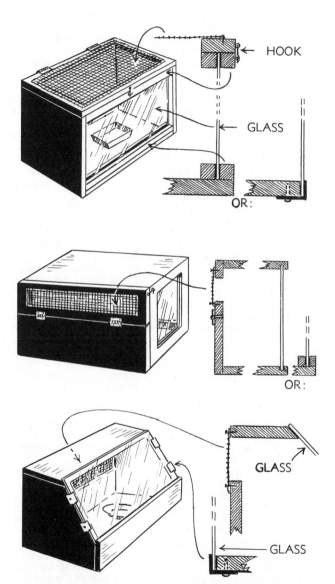

HOOK

GLASS

OR:

OR:

GLASS

GLASS

Reptile cages can be made to many patterns. From top: wire lid cage, battery cage, cage with a slanting front.

a "lid" of wood strips with wire screening tacked to it. The lid fits the outside measurements of the top of the cage and lifts off for feeding and cleaning. Further ventilation is provided through screened holes in the ends of the cage.

Battery cage—The battery cage is made with a solid wooden top. Several cages of this type may be stacked on top of one another, battery style. The top part of the back contains screening for ventilation. It is hinged to swing down. The glass front is held in place by moldings, or set in grooves about $\frac{1}{4}$ inch deep, $\frac{1}{4}$ inch from the front edges of top and bottom.

Slanting front cage—A cage with a slanting glass front has the best possible arrangement for observation. The glass is held in position by pieces of angle irons, such as linoleum moldings.

MAKING THE CAGE—Materials—Scrap wood is suitable for snake cages. A discarded apple box may give you all the wood you need. Or use pieces of commercial 1-inch pine boards.

Regular window wire screening will take care of the ventilation. Use brass, copper, or aluminum screening rather than iron screening; these don't rust. Since some snakes pick up a habit of rubbing their noses against the screening, causing abrasions and infection, keep the size of the screening at an absolute minimum.

Use a piece of glass for front or top to make observation easy.

Size—A general rule of thumb: The cage should be one snake long, half a snake wide, and half a snake high. This rule applies specifically for the smaller species, such as DeKay and ring-necked snakes for which 12 by 6 by 6 inches are suitable. For the larger snakes, 2 feet and over, the proportionate dimensions can be somewhat smaller—about two thirds of a snake long, one third wide, one third high—16 by 8 by 8 inches for 24-inch garter snakes, for instance.

Cages of these sizes will accommodate two to four snakes, if necessary. If you have room for several cages, it is better to have only one snake in each cage. This makes study of individual snakes simpler.

Finishing—Fill cracks and inside corners with patching plaster, plastic wood, regular putty, or a putty made from plaster of paris and shellac. Finish with varnish. It is especially important that the bottom of the cage be waterproof so that it will not absorb moisture from excrements.

Two coats of paint are better than varnish. And why not make your cages colorful? Finish them in a color that suits your taste or use one that will contrast with the color of the snake.

Furnishings—Snakes need to have water available at all times for drinking and bathing. Place the water dish—butter dish or the like—in the middle of the floor. Snakes have a habit of crawling along the sides of their cages and may turn over a dish placed too close to the side. Pick a dish large enough for the snake to coil up in.

A snake also needs a hiding place in its cage. This may be a small board raised on cleats, a piece of bark, a flat stone on top of a few pebbles.

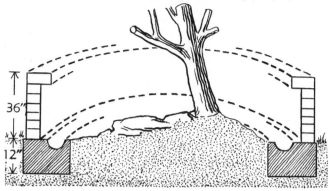

A professional-looking outdoor pit for snakes, lizards, and turtles, with a 36-inch wall on a concrete foundation.

SNAKE PITS—During the warm part of the year, snakes may be kept in an outdoor snake pit. In its simplest form, this is a small piece of ground surrounded by a low wall.

Pick a spot that has both sunlight and shade, at least 6 feet square. Dig a narrow ditch around it, about 8 inches wide, 12 inches deep. Fill with a mixture of cement and crushed rock or small stones. On top of this foundation, build a 3-foot wall of fieldstones, brick, or cement blocks, provided with an overhang toward the pit, of 3 to 6 inches. Coat the inside of the wall with a smooth finish of cement (illustration, see above).

Build up the ground in the middle of the pit into a mound sloping toward the south. Pile up a couple of stone slabs in such a way that they form a hiding place. Put in pieces of logs for decorative effect.

Sink a water basin into the ground or make a cement pool, a couple of feet in diameter, 1 foot deep. A water moat along the inside base of the wall is even better than a pool, and makes it more difficult for the snakes to escape.

¶ *Tip*—A dozen or more snakes may be kept in a snake pit. But be sure that they are about the same size. Do not place king snakes, milk snakes, indigo snakes, and other snake-eating species in the same pit with other snakes.

SNAKE HEALTH—An important condition for keeping your snakes healthy is to pick them healthy in the first place. It doesn't pay to hold on to snakes that are damaged or sick or off their feed.

Snakes newly caught are often infested with tiny mites. Place infested snakes in jars filled with lukewarm water. By morning all mites will have drowned except possibly a few around the eyes. Touch them with a drop of olive oil.

Cuts or abrasions on the body may be brushed with an aqueous antiseptic, such as mercurochrome. Treat infected eyes with boric-acid solution.

Snakes thrive best at a temperature ranging between 65 and 80 degrees Fahrenheit. They suffer if the temperatures vary too greatly.

¶ *Tip*—Snake cages may be kept at an even temperature by hanging an electric light bulb in the cage. Light when more heat is needed.

Keep the cages clean. Clean out excrement as soon as possible, and remove food that has not been eaten.

¶ *Tip*—To simplify the cleaning, cover the bottom of the cages with several layers of newspapers that can be thrown out regularly, or use white pebbles.

Feeding—Snakes live on animal matter only. There is no record of any snake practicing vegetarianism.

The bone structure of mouth and body makes it possible for snakes to swallow whole animals that are larger in diameter than themselves. Living food has greatest appeal to snakes. But most of them can be taught to take dead food, dangled in front of their eyes on a thread, held in forceps or on a thin stick. If the snake does not take the food immediately, leave it in its cage for a few hours.

Remember that snakes do not eat every day. Feed them a fair-sized meal every week or ten days. A fair-sized meal is one that creates a definite bulge, but doesn't necessarily stretch the skin between the scales. During the winter—the regular hibernation season—a meal a month is sufficient. If the snake is in true hibernation, no food is needed.

If your specimens are small, feed them small earthworms, chopped earthworms, chopped meat or fish, larvae and grubs, tiny minnows, small tadpoles, salamanders.

Medium to large snakes will eat earthworms, strips of meat or fish, frogs, toads, "live bait" (minnows or shiners), live or freshly killed mice.

¶ *Tip*—Check in the *Field Book of Snakes* for a list of food usually taken by your captive species.

Keep snakes separate when you are feeding them. Otherwise two of them may catch hold of the same food, with the result that one may swallow the other.

FORCE FEEDING—Force feeding may be necessary if the snake refuses to take food for a couple of weeks. The simplest method is to squirt a mixture of raw egg and milk into its mouth with a rubber syringe. Another method is to impale meat, a skinned mouse or a frog on a thin blunt-pointed stick and push it down the throat.

Force feeding is seldom successful. Instead of trying to keep a native species alive, it is better to turn it loose and find another.

Lizards

LIZARD TERRARIUMS—Lizards get along well in a terrarium—a desert terrarium for desert species (horned "toad," collared lizard, collared swift) and a woodland terrarium for other species (chameleon, fence lizard, blue-tailed skink). Include a couple of hiding places in the furnishings—rocks or strips of bark—and a couple of sticks for climbing.

The lizard terrarium should be kept warm (70 to 80 degrees Fahrenheit) and should receive plenty of sunlight.

Feeding—As far as possible, feed live food: live insects, such as flies, roaches, grasshoppers; mealworms; Enchytra worms, small earthworms. After having kept lizards in captivity for a while, you may succeed in having them take chopped meat if you dangle it in front of them.

Water is necessary. Some lizards drink from a shallow dish, but others need to have water sprayed on the plants of the terrarium once a day so that they can sip the drops.

Turtles

TURTLE CAGES AND PENS—Land turtles will get along well in a snake cage or snake pit, as long as the temperature and food are to their liking. Box turtles may be given the run of the house; they may even hang around in the backyard for years if you let them loose.

TURTLE AQUARIUM—Aquatic turtles need an imitation of their natural habitat. Small specimens may be kept in an aquarium that has a sandy beach or a rock they can climb up on (see page 215).

Larger aquatic specimens are best kept in a combination aquarium-and-pen. You can build it the same way you make a snake pit, erecting a low wall around a small pool (see page 141).

Feeding—Turtles need be fed only a couple of times a week. They take earthworms, slugs, insects, and occasionally lettuce, apples, bananas. Add fish and tadpoles to the diet of aquatic turtles. Some of your captives may learn to take raw hamburger from your fingers.

Hatching Reptile Eggs

If you have had the luck to find a clutch of snake or turtle eggs, by all means try hatching them.

Moisten a paper towel, then wring it out. Place it in a double layer on the bottom of a glass jar. Place the eggs on the paper in a single layer. If they adhere, leave them sticking together or separate them, as you prefer. Cover the eggs with a piece of moistened paper toweling. Place a piece of glass over the container. Keep the "incubator" at room temperature—about 70 degrees.

Be sure that the contents are kept moist but not wet by sprinkling the surface occasionally with water. If the eggs get moldy, take off the glass cover for a while; if they shrink, more moisture is indicated.

Examine the eggs from time to time—say, once a week. When the eggs seem to look swollen and bulgy in spots, examine them more often; hatching is close at hand, and you may have the chance to see snakelets open up their prisons with their "egg teeth." You may even be able to record the event photographically. There will usually be plenty of time to set up a camera; it may take the snakelets several hours to free themselves completely.

Set most of your hatchings free in their natural habitat. Keep only a few for observation in captivity. You will have your hands full feeding them.

PHOTOGRAPHING REPTILES

The peculiar shape that snakes have makes it a tough job to photograph them. The only way to get a good composition is to get the snakes to coil up or to assume a zigzaggy position. Lizards are easier—if you can keep them still. Turtles make the most satisfactory reptile models.

Stills

EQUIPMENT—Camera and Lenses—Any camera that can be focused on a subject within a few feet of the lens will do. In some cases this may require the use of a portrait attachment, extension tube, or bellows.

Tripod—If you can control the movement of your reptile model, a tripod will be a great help. Since most reptile photographs are taken from above at an angle, you will want a tilting top or a ball-and-socket joint on your tripod.

Floodlight—Much of your reptile photography will be done indoors. For this you will need the illumination of one or two floodlights.

INDOORS—The simplest method of photographing a reptile is to snap it in a glass-front cage. Arrange a few props for a pleasing background. Put a single floodlight to give the effect of sunshine. Fill in the shadows with reflected light from the light-colored wall of the cage, or prop up a piece of white cardboard opposite the floodlight. Focus the camera. Watch out for light reflections on the glass of the cage. Finally, arrange the snake and snap the picture.

¶ *Tip*—A poisonous snake should always be photographed within its glass-fronted cage, where you will have it under complete control.

OUTDOORS—An outdoor shot in natural surroundings and with the sun as the light source will give you a better picture than you can get in a studio. Pick a suitable spot and focus your camera on it. Then place your models.

Turtles will give you no problem. But snakes and lizards will. Gently place the snake or lizard in position, and cover it immediately with a black cloth. When your model is quiet, pull the cloth away with one hand as you snap the shutter with the other. Be ready to grab the animal before it disappears.

¶ *Tip*—If you have a helper, have him cup his hands over the snake until it quiets down. Be ready to shoot the moment he takes his hands away.

Snakes are difficult subjects for photography. Cool them to make them sluggish, then pose them and shoot. Poisonous snakes should be photographed in their cages.

Zoological Society of Philadelphia

Lizards are even harder to photograph than snakes, except in their cages. One of the few exceptions is the horned lizard that can be posed and photographed anywhere.

Zoological Society of Philadelphia

Turtles make good photographic models. They can be shot outdoors in natural surroundings or by tabletop photography indoors against natural-looking background.

Isabelle Hunt Conant

Movies

A turtle makes a good movie—if you have the necessary patience. A snake, on the other hand, is a poor actor. It usually slithers off the screen before you have a chance to catch a glimpse of it.

If you do want to shoot movies of a snake in action, take advantage of the fact that reptiles slow down and get sluggish when the temperature drops below 60 degrees. Place the snake in the refrigerator, in a bag, for about half an hour while you set up your equipment. If the actions are still too fast after this cooling-off process, take the movies at 32 frames per second. When the film is projected at the regular 16-frame home-movie speed, the snake's movements will become more deliberate, and it will remain on the screen twice as long.

REPTILE COLLECTIONS

A collection of well-preserved reptiles makes an attractive museum display. The work connected with making it is relatively simple, the materials inexpensive.

PRESERVATION OF REPTILES—Killing reptiles—Reptiles may be killed by injecting a few cubic centimeters of ether or chloroform in or near the heart, with a hypodermic needle. Or wrap the snakes up fairly tightly in a bag and submerge them in the liquid you intend to use for the preserving—alcohol or formalin.

¶ *Tip*—". . . snakes are quite promptly killed if placed in a tight jar with a layer of common moth repellent 'di-chloricide' on the bottom . . ." according to Karl P. Schmidt and D. Dwight Davis.

Preserving—Reptiles may be preserved in 70 percent alcohol (rubbing alcohol) or in 10 percent formalin (1 part commercial

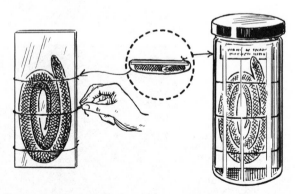

For a neat display, tie the snake to a piece of glass. Place glass upright in a standard biological display jar.

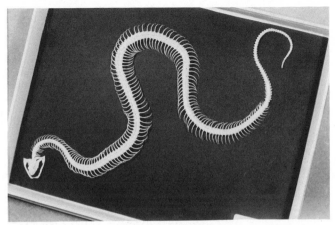

Ward's Natural Science Establishment, Inc.

Only the largest snakes can be skeletonized by hand. For a smaller snake, a dermestid colony will perform the job.

formalin to 3 parts water). Alcohol will keep them soft, whereas formalin will make them rigid and may destroy the color.

¶ *Tip*—To conserve some of the color, try adding 10 percent cane sugar to the formalin.

Before submerging the snakes in the preservative, cut a number of ½-inch slits at intervals of a couple of inches in the stomach wall and in the underside of the tail. This will permit the preserving liquid to penetrate. Or inject the liquid in the body cavity with a hypodermic needle; this is particularly important for turtles. If the extended belly of a snake shows that it is full of food, slit it carefully and remove the food.

A snake should be arranged for preservation underside up, in a flat coil in a glass jar or earthenware container of suitable size. Cover it with preservative for a couple of inches. Put a cover over the container. For the next few days, press it gently each day with a blunt stick until all air bubbles have been removed.

If a snake is especially large, it may not be feasible to preserve it in its entirety. In that case, slit the underside from chin to vent and remove the body, cutting it off an inch or so from the neck and close to the vent, leaving the head and tail attached to the skin. Roll up loosely and place in the preservative.

Mounting—When the snake is partly preserved, it may be coiled up, tail down, in a screw-top glass jar—a domestic jar, such as a mayonnaise or pickle jar, or a standard biological display jar.

A neater display is made by tying the snake in a flat coil to a piece of regular, opal, or opaque black glass. This should have been cut to such size that it will go through the opening of the jar and stand upright in it. Use a strong linen thread and a heavy needle. Bring the thread through the snake, and tie it on the back of the glass plate.

When the snake is properly arranged, pour the final preservative (formalin or alcohol) over it and screw on the top.

Labeling—A label glued to the outside of the jar will fall off sooner or later. Instead, write out a waterproof tag with India ink or crayon and place this inside the jar on the glass plate. The tag should contain the name of the specimen, where found, when, by whom, length and weight, and other pertinent information.

EQUIPMENT—Waterproof Museum Tags. Turtox or Dennison Manufacturing Company.

Higgins' Waterproof Black Drawing Ink. Any artists' or stationery store.

CURING SNAKE SKINS—Snake skins may be cured by a simple salt-and-alum process: Remove the head (preserve it in formalin, if desired). Slit the skin along a line running through the middle of the underside, from the neck to the tip of tail. Remove the body carefully without tearing the skin. If your specimen is a rattlesnake, leave the rattles in place. Spread out the skin, scaly side down, on a smooth board, and "flesh" the inside with a dull knife until all fat and muscle fibers have been removed.

Dissolve $\frac{1}{2}$ pound salt and $\frac{1}{4}$ pound alum (ammonium aluminum sulphate) in 1 quart of hot water. Cool. Submerge the skin in the solution and leave it in it for five days to a week.

Take out the skin, rinse it in water, and blot it partly dry in a cloth

Snake skins can be cured by a simple salt-and-alum process. They are stretched and nailed to board to dry.

or between paper towels. Tack the skin along the edges to a board for drying, flesh side up. When it is almost dry, rub in saddle soap to keep the skin soft. Then dry it thoroughly. A small amount of neat's-foot oil applied to the flesh side after drying will help to keep the skin pliable.

SNAKE SKELETONS—The delicate structure of a snake skeleton makes it difficult to prepare by hand. However, a dermestid colony (see page 170) will do an excellent job of cleaning a small dried snake.

CHAPTER 6

Insects

THERE'S no doubt about it: You have had more intimate contact with insects than with any other members of the animal kingdom —with the exception possibly of the species *Homo sapiens*. Think of the mosquitoes you've squashed, the flies you've swatted, the bugs you've sprayed in your garden, the ants in your picnic food, the moths in your clothes closet, the bees whose honey you've eaten, the butterflies you've admired in their fluttery flight.

Without "good" insects—good to *us*, that is—there would be no human life as we know it. There would be little to eat, no vegetable or animal fibers for clothing, no forests and fields for recreation. On the other hand, if "bad" insects were destroyed, we would be rid of insect-borne diseases, and would save ourselves the billion-dollar losses caused annually by hungry insect enemies devouring our food, ravaging our fields, killing our trees.

We are stuck with insects by the trillions—"for better or for worse." Fortunately, nature herself is keeping the good and the bad in a fairly even balance. As long as she does, we puny humans are safe. If the balance should ever be upset so that the bad win out, the human race would be destroyed more effectively than by a million atom bombs.

There's fascination to insects—not just because of their importance, their colors, their structure. But even more because of some of the wonders of the insect world: the social life of ants and bees, the migration of the monarch butterflies, the carpentry, pottery, paper-making skill of some of the wasps and hornets, and numerous other peculiar feats.

Much is known about insects, but there's still much more to learn. The great advantage of insect study is that you can go about it in your own way—learning by staying quietly at home, if that's your inclination, like a French Jean Henri Fabre or an American Edwin Way Teale, or by travelling to the ends of the world if you have ambitions in that direction.

BOOKS ON INSECT LIFE—Arend T. Bandsma and R. T. Brandt, *Amazing World of Insects*. New York, The Macmillan Company.

Edwin Way Teale, *Strange Lives of Familiar Insects*. New York, Dodd, Mead & Company.

J. Henri Fabre, *The Insect World of J. Henri Fabre*. Edwin Way Teale, ed. Greenwich, Connecticut, Fawcett Publications.

Insects. U.S. Department of Agriculture Yearbook 1952. Catalog No. A 1.10:952. $6.50. From Superintendent of Documents, U.S. Government Printing Office, Washington, D.C. 20402.

Peter Farb, *The Insects*. Chicago, Time-Life Books.

Working with Others

It would be possible for you to go on for years, occupying yourself with whatever phase of insect life has caught your fancy, inventing your own approach and methods for arriving at conclusions. But you can, almost certainly, save yourself a great deal of effort by finding out from others what methods they have used in similar work. Also, sooner or later, you will want to share your findings with others. You can kill both of these birds with one stone by joining a local or national entomological society and taking part in its deliberations.

SOCIETIES—Entomological Society of America. Headquarters: 4603 Calbert Road, College Park, Maryland 20740. Periodical: *Annals of the ESA*.

American Entomological Society. Headquarters: 1900 Race Street, Philadelphia, Pennsylvania 19104. Periodical: *Entomological News*.

Lepidopterists' Society. Headquarters: Department of Zoology, Southern Illinois University, Carbondale, Illinois 62901. Periodical: *Journal of the LS*.

Very probably, there are insect students right in your own vicinity with whom you can exchange views. A local biology teacher or museum director may put you in touch with them.

In addition to needing study and collecting helps, you may need aid in identifying some of your species. When local experts give up, send your specimen to the entomology department of a nearby museum or university, your state entomologist, or to the Bureau of Entomology and Plant Quarantine of the U.S. Department of Agriculture, Washington, D.C.

Note—Be sure that your specimen is *dead* before sending it for identification. It is against federal law to send live specimens of insects through the mails. However, certain specified live insects may be sent, but only by permit obtained from the Bureau of Entomology and Plant Quarantine.

INSECTS IN THE FIELD

Equipment for Insect Study

Lutz, in his *Field Book of Insects*, gives the requisites of a successful insect enthusiast: "eyes, fingers and an inquiring mind. . . ." With those three things a firm foundation can be laid for getting close to the life of the six-leggers.

STUDY EQUIPMENT—Magnifiers—When it comes to studying

minute insects and to distinguishing among tiny species, the naked eye is not sufficient. A magnifying glass is needed. The simplest kind for field work is one of the folding-type pocket magnifiers.

The most popular pocket magnifiers are made with one, two, or three lenses in individual mountings. The two-lens magnifier makes it possible for you to choose between three magnifications—such as $5\times$, $7\times$, or $10\times$—depending on whether you use one lens, the other, or both together. The three-lens magnifier, similarly, gives you seven choices—usually from $5\times$ to $20\times$.

Another pocket magnifier is the Coddington type. This consists of a single lens of special construction. Four models are available with magnifications of $7\times$, $10\times$, $14\times$ and $20\times$.

The most efficient—and most expensive—is the Hastings triplet. It is made up of a combination of highly corrected lenses, and has a wide angle of view. Here, also, you can take your choice between models of four magnifications.

Knife—You will need a knife to dig out the insects that live in bark and dead wood or in the ground. A Scout sheath knife or hunting knife will be your best bet.

¶ *Tip*—Or why not try this stunt: File down one side and the tip of a small, narrow garden trowel into a cutting edge. In this way you have a combination cutting and digging tool.

Insect books—You will need a good field book to find your way in the insect world. When you know that more than 650,000 species have been described, and that new ones are still being found and added to the list, you will realize that it takes an outstanding expert

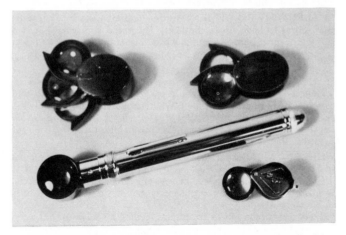

Three types of magnifiers: pocket magnifiers (top), Coddington, illuminated (center), Hastings triplet (bottom).

to make a positive identification of anything but fairly common species.

But don't let that scare you away from identification. The field of insect study is wide open for people who have the patience and necessary power of observation to become experts in any of its multitudinous branches.

BOOKS FOR FIELD IDENTIFICATION—Frank E. Lutz, *Field Book of Insects*. New York, G. P. Putnam's Sons.

Ralph B. Swain, *The Insect Guide* (Orders and main families). New York, Doubleday & Company.

Donald J. Borror and Richard E. White, *Field Guide to the Insects of America North of Mexico*. Boston, Houghton Mifflin Company.

OTHER BOOKS—Alexander B. Klots, *Field Guide to the Butterflies*. Boston, Houghton Mifflin Company.

Paul R. Ehrlich, *How to Know the Butterflies*. Dubuque, Iowa, William C. Brown Company.

Robert Mitchell and Herbert S. Zim, *Butterflies and Moths*. New York, Golden Press.

W. J. Holland, *The Moth Book*. New York, Dover Publications.

Notebook—Carry a convenient-sized loose-leaf notebook, and make immediate notes of your field observations.

In insect observation, even seemingly unimportant happenings or actions may have significance. A change in temperature as a cloud passes before the sun, the appearance of another insect on the scene, a suddenly encountered obstacle across the insect's path—these may each give an insight into the insect's reactions. Most of such observations will be lost unless they are recorded on the spot.

COLLECTING EQUIPMENT—For a close-up study of insects, you generally have to catch them. The same equipment—and a number of other items—are used when you set out to make an insect collection. See section starting on page 180.

Finding Insects

Generally speaking, the answer to Where? and When? to find insects is "Anywhere—anytime." Wherever you are, you will always be able to find *some* insects. But when it comes to locating *certain* insects, you need to know their feeding habits, their way of propagating, their life cycles.

WHERE? With eyes trained to see, you will notice insects in almost any outdoor locality you visit—and many indoor places as well.

Grasses and weeds harbor numerous crawling and jumping insects. Even in midwinter, colonies of insects may be found in grass tufts and in weed rosettes.

Trees and shrubs—Look for insects feeding on leaves or hiding in bark furrows.

Flowers attract the large airborne insects—butterflies, moths, bees, flies—as well as numerous minute species.

Shallow mud puddles also draw butterflies, bees, and a number of other insects.

Streams and lakes contain hundreds of species—some of them scurrying over the surface, some swimming, others crawling on the bottom or burrowing in the mud, hiding under stones. The debris that has floated up on the windward shore of a lake may prove a regular treasure trove.

Numerous species—especially beetles—may be found by turning over **rocks, debris, leaf piles, loose bark, cow dung and other manure, dead animals, and birds.**

Still other must be dug out of the ground, or cut out of **rotting wood, fungi, galls, plant stems, fruits.**

And then there are the HOUSEHOLD PESTS—the insects you find in woodwork and in food, in wool and in books, in warm attic and moist cellar.

Anywhere is right!

WHEN?—Time of year—A great number of insects go through the complete metamorphosis of egg-larva-pupa-adult. Others have incomplete metamorphosis of egg-nymph-adult. The time when the insect changes from one form to the next varies with the species, but you can be sure to find one, two, or all of these forms the year round.

Eggs are most readily located from fall to spring, larvae and nymphs from spring to late summer, pupae from fall to spring, and adults in spring and summer. Some insects winter over in the larval stage. A number hibernate as adults, but the majority of adult insects die as soon as eggs have been laid to ensure a new brood.

Time of day—Weather—Insects that move about by day prefer warm sunny weather. They are sluggish in the cool of morning, get more active in the middle of the day, become inactive as night approaches. They hide in rainy weather.

Warm, sultry, overcast nights are the best for discovering the insects that travel by night. You will see very few when the night is cool. Similarly, you will have little success on clear nights—especially nights with a brilliant moon—no matter whether they are warm or not.

Attracting Insects

Instead of going hunting far and wide for insects, you may prefer to take it easy and persuade the insects to come to you—and by so doing, you may possibly even pick up species that you wouldn't come upon in your hunts.

You have your choice among several methods of attracting. Each of them is effective in its own way, bringing in insects that may not be attracted by any of the other means.

SUGARING—Sugaring is especially good for drawing moths and other nocturnal insects. It attracts them with a bait consisting mainly of various kinds of sugars and slightly fermented fruit pulp.

Sugaring is a popular method for attracting moths. It is done by smearing a sweet sugar bait onto trees and posts.

Making the sugaring bait—The three requirements for a successful mixture are these: It must *smell* sweetish; it must *taste* sweet; it must *paint well* without running too much. Here are several suggestions that may help you develop your own patent formula:

Stir a teaspoonful of rum or rum flavoring into heavy molasses or honey. Or dissolve brown sugar in stale beer. Or mash overripe bananas, mix with sugar, stand in warm place to ferment. Or rub pitted peaches, plums, or apricots (fresh, canned, stewed or dried) through a sieve; let the pulp stand a day or so to ferment, then add white or brown sugar. The consistency of the final product should be like that of a fairly thick paint.

Method of sugaring—Set out just around dusk, before the moths are on the wing, on a sultry evening or even on a night with a warm drizzle. Bring along a can of bait, a 1-inch paintbrush, and a flashlight. You will have an exciting night ahead of you, particularly if you bring a friend to keep you company.

Choose a territory with trees or posts, preferably on the outskirts of woods or orchards. Select a circular route of about half a mile—one you can cover in fifteen minutes or so.

Paint a palm-sized dab of your sugaring bait on the lee side of some of the tree trunks, at shoulder height. Use trees that stand about 50 feet apart—more or less.

Collecting the specimens—When you have finished the painting, start from the beginning. Play your flashlight over the tree and take your pick from the moths and other insects that have arrived and cling to the tree around the edge of the sticky patch. Make your rounds several times during the night, each time adding to your collection.

Some of the insects will let themselves fall into your collecting jar if you hold the jar directly under them. Others may need a slight poke with the edge of the jar before they let go and drop in.

¶ *Tip*—Go back over your "trap line" during daylight the following day. Your bait may prove equally irresistible to a number of butterflies, wasps, bees, and other day-roaming insects.

LIGHTS—Most of the night fliers are subject to *phototaxis* or, in simpler language, are attracted by light. You remember having seen moths by the hundreds—and gnats by the thousands—fluttering around a street lamp or a porch light, mostly on warm humid nights.

You can make use of this phenomenon in several ways.

Dishpan method—Place a large dishpan on the ground. Pour in 1 inch of water. Put three small stones on the bottom of the pan in a triangle, and place a lighted kerosene or gasoline lantern on the stones, thus keeping it raised above water surface. If you are near a house, run a wire from an outlet and hang an electric bulb over the pan. Wait for the insects to fly around until they drop exhausted into the water.

Sheet method—Hang up a sheet or other white cloth over a clothesline between two trees or posts, with 1 foot of the lower edge flat on the ground. Or if you are in camp, simply use a white tent. Suspend a kerosene or gasoline lantern 3 to 4 feet in front of it. Or even better, run a wire from the house, if possible, and use an electric bulb.

Place a reflector (a piece of tin can) behind the light source, so that the light falls on the sheet.

¶ *Tip*—Experiment with different-colored light bulbs. Blue light may prove most effective.

¶ *Tip*—Your car gives you a quick light source. Drive it up in front of the sheet, and train the headlights full on it.

Some insects will finally come to rest on the sheet, others will drop to the ground in front of it—hence the turned lower edge.

Light traps—The best method for drawing a number of insects is to use a light trap that will attract them and keep them imprisoned so that you can watch their reaction, or until you are ready to take them out.

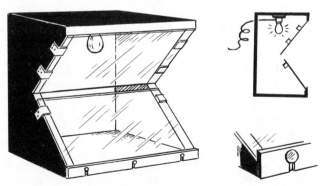

A light trap may be made from wood or from a square can, fronted by two pieces of glass with an opening between.

Such a trap may consist of a box made from plywood or from a five-gallon can, with a front of two pieces of glass arranged with an opening between them, and at such an angle that the insects can get in but cannot find their way out (see drawings on page 155).

The light source may be an ordinary electric bulb wired to the house circuit or a flashlight bulb powered by two or three flashlight batteries.

GROUND TRAPS—Many insects—particularly roaches, crickets, and beetles—may be caught in baited ground traps.

Molasses traps—Sink pint jars or tin cans into the ground with their tops level with the surface. Pour in about 1 inch of a mixture of two parts molasses and one part water, or one of the concoctions suggested for sugaring. Cover the top with a piece of bark or wood scrap, raised high enough on three or four small stones to permit the insects to crawl under.

The insects are attracted by the sweetness, drop in, and drown. Lift them out with a tea strainer and wash them free of molasses.

¶ *Tip*—You can establish a trap line by placing a number of these traps, 20 to 30 feet apart, in a circular course. Mark the locations clearly with sticks. Make your rounds once a day.

Carrion traps—Certain burying and scavenging beetles are attracted to decaying meat and fish.

Place a dead mouse, or other dead animal, a slice of meat, a pat of hamburger, or a piece of fried fish on the ground. Cover it loosely with a board to prevent carrion-eating birds from stealing it. Inspect it a day later and take your pick from the insect assortment that has congregated.

Carrion traps can also be sunk into the ground as suggested for molasses traps.

Catching Insects

The method for catching insects depends on the life habits of the species you are after. The necessary equipment may be bought through a biological supply house (page 27). In most instances you can make it yourself.

SWEEPING—Sweeping usually produces quicker results than any other method for catching insects. It consists in swinging a net back and forth, like a sweeping broom, over and through grasses and other vegetation to scoop up the insects.

Sweeping net—The net used for sweeping is literally meant to "take a beating." It must therefore be made of sturdy material: lightweight canvas, unbleached muslin, or, better still, nylon bolting cloth. The diameter of the net is about 12 inches, its depth approximately 28 inches, with a 2-inch pocket-hem along the top. Thirty inches of material in the commercial width of 38 inches will suffice. Cut it to pattern and sew as shown on page 157. Reinforce the pocket-hem with a 4-inch-wide strip of muslin.

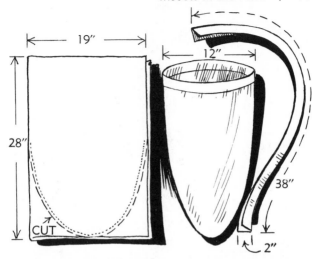

Fold material for a sweeping net in half before cutting. Reinforce the edge with strip of material four inches wide.

¶ *Tip*—If you want to be able to see your catch, make the bottom quarter of the bag of marquisette or bobbinet.

The frame consists of a piece of spring steel wire, 8 or 10 gauge, 45 inches long. Bend approximately 38 inches of it into a circle, 12 inches in diameter, leaving the ends of the wire straight—one for 3 inches, the other for 4 inches. Bend ½ inch of each tip at a 90-degree angle.

¶ *Tip*—Many entomologists swear by the angler's "landing net,"

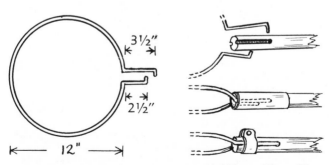

Frame for sweeping net is a wire ring. Hold in position with ferrule (right, center) or hose clamp (right, bottom).

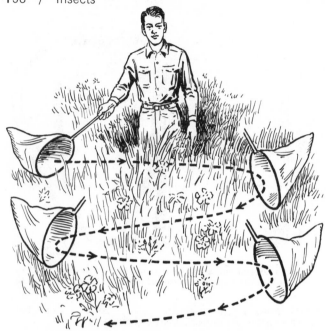

Sweeping consists in moving the net vigorously from side to side with its opening always in direction of stroke.

using its collapsible frame with inset netting instead of the regular cotton mesh.

Make the handle from a ¾-inch hardwood dowel stick or an old broom handle. The usually preferred length is 18 to 24 inches, although you may find some other length more suitable for your sweeping style. Gouge out two grooves at one end of handle, on opposite sides, to fit the straight ends of the frame wire. Bore two holes in the handle into which the bent tips of the wire will lock. Wrap thin wire around the frame ends and handle, or hold in position with electrician's tape or adhesive tape. Even better, keep it in place with a hose clamp, or place a brass ferrule around the handle. Clamp or ferrule makes it possible to remove the frame from the handle.

Sweeping technique—Make a few practice sweeps. Grasp the end of the handle. Sweep the net from right to left, with the frame opening toward the left, using a forehand stroke. At the end of the sweep, twist the wrist so that the frame opening now is toward the right, and make a left-to-right sweep, using a backward stroke. Continue sweeping back and forth in this manner, in an uninterrupted, smooth movement.

Stop with the handle in a horizontal position, twisting it quickly so that the frame opening is toward the ground. This causes the lower part of the net bag to fall over the rim of the frame, with the result that everything swept into the bag is now "locked" in. Get into the habit of doing this final twist automatically whenever you stop sweeping. It is one of the marks of the expert collector.

After a small amount of practice, you are ready for the "real thing": In your first strokes, sweep through tops of weeds and grasses. In subsequent strokes, sweep closer to the ground. After a few sweeps, stop and investigate.

BEATING—Some insects stick so closely to tree branches and brushes that sweeping doesn't loosen them. Beating the branches may dislodge them.

Beating equipment—The necessary equipment consists of a club and a beating cloth—or an old umbrella.

The club is a stout stick, about $1\frac{1}{2}$ inches thick, $2\frac{1}{2}$ to 3 feet long. Cut it in the field or bring it from home.

The *beating cloth* is made from a piece of unbleached muslin or sheeting, a yard square. Hem the edges. Sew a 6-inch piece of tape in each corner. Make the frame from two sticks $4\frac{1}{2}$ feet long. Tie them together in the middle to form a cross. Stretch the cloth under the frame by tying the four tapes to the four stick ends.

¶ *Tip*—Instead of rustic sticks, you may prefer to use two pieces of lath, $\frac{1}{2}$ inch thick, $1\frac{1}{2}$ inches wide, $4\frac{1}{2}$ feet long. Drill a small hole in the middle of each. Fasten them together crosswise with a small bolt and wing nut. When the frame is not in use, loosen the bolt, fold the frame together, and roll it in the beating cloth.

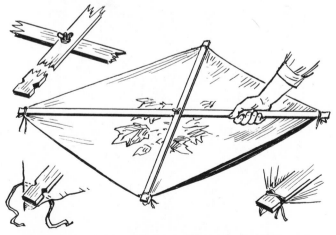

Beating cloth is a yard square. Tie to rustic sticks or to pieces of lath, held together with bolt and wing nut.

Beating method—Beat the branches with the club in one hand. With the other hand, hold the beating cloth horizontally below the branches to catch the insects as they fall.

¶ *Tip*—To keep the more vigorous insects from jumping out of the beating cloth, place some dead leaves and other debris in the cloth for them to hide under.

AIR NETTING—The main use of this method is for catching butterflies and moths in flight. Whereas sweeping is an indiscriminate process, air netting is a highly selective one, with more of the thrill of real hunting.

Aerial net—The aerial net can be made to the same simple pattern and in the same manner as the sweeping net (see page 157). A better net results when you sew together four pieces, following the pattern suggested below. To cut down air resistance, use a medium-mesh netting—bobbinet, marquisette, brussels of cotton, nylon, or Dacron —available from biological supply houses.

Reinforce the pocket-hem with muslin. Sew a 4-inch-wide strip of this material along the top.

Make the handle of a length to suit yourself—2½ or 3 feet or longer.

¶ *Tip*—An emergency aerial net may be improvised by pinning a

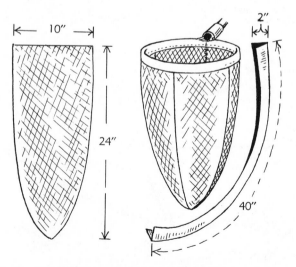

A strong aerial net results when you sew it together from four pieces of material, of the dimensions shown above.

piece of mosquito netting or cheesecloth into a bag, and attaching it with more pins to a ring made from a wire clothes hanger.

Method of netting—In hunting for butterflies and moths, you will find it of great help to know botany. By locating the right plants at the right season, you are certain to have a successful hunt of flower-visiting insects.

Wait for the insect to settle on the food plant. Then swing the net in an easy, forehand stroke sideways toward the flower, with the net frame vertical, the opening toward the insect. Scoop the insect into the net, reverse the stroke, stop, twist the handle so that the bag locks over the rim.

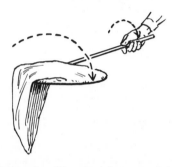

After sweeping or air netting, lock in your catch by twisting net handle so bottom of net falls over frame.

If you miss, don't go on a wild chase after your intended victim. Stay where you are. The butterfly will probably return—only to be picked up the next time.

Some butterflies have the habit of dropping when disturbed; others fly straight up. You will soon learn their habits so that you will know where to aim.

With a little practice, it is possible to "draw a bead" on an insect. Hold on to the bottom of the net with one hand, slingshot fashion, while straining the handle and frame with the other. If the net hand is suddenly let go, the net—if correctly aimed—will pick up the insect in a lightning swoop.

¶ *Tip*—On an automobile trip through new territory, suspend a net from a window, frame opening to the front. Cruise at about 30 miles per hour, or less, and empty the net every five minutes or so.

WATER NETTING—Most water insects are caught by netting, although a number of them may be picked up with the fingers.

Aquatic net—The aquatic net is constructed in the same way as the aerial and sweeping nets, but it need not be as deep since the insects that are caught do not have to be "locked in." A depth of 18 inches is sufficient for a bag 12 inches in diameter.

The material used should be extra sturdy. Nylon netting is particularly good for this kind of net.

The wire for the D-shaped frame should be of ¼-inch thickness, preferably of coppered steel so that it will not rust (see page 201).

Using the net—Use the aquatic net in a manner similar to that used with the sweeping net, moving it from side to side in the water, with a hand twist at the end of each stroke.

Begin at the surface—or even above it if plants grow out of the water—then sweep deeper and deeper, finally into the mud of the bottom.

In a fast-moving stream, wind up by placing the net firmly on the bottom, with the frame opening upstream. Have a companion move rocks and stones, or dig into the bottom above the net. The insects will be swept into the net by the flowing water.

¶ *Tip*—A couple of pie plates, painted white, make it easy for you to examine your catch.

Hand screen—A simple screen or sieve may be improvised from a piece of ⅛-inch plastic window screening, 2 feet long, 1 foot wide. Tack each narrow side to a 2-foot stick, leaving the upper part free for a handle. Point the lower end of the sticks.

To use it, hold it against the bottom of the stream bed and have a helper turn over stones upstream. Or push the handles into the bottom and turn over the stones yourself with a pole.

DIGGING AND TURNING—Great numbers of species of small insects live in the ground, in decaying wood, in moss and dead leaves, under stones and logs. You can locate them only by digging or turning.

Equipment—Carry a strong trowel or sheath knife, or the combination digging-cutting tool described on page 151.

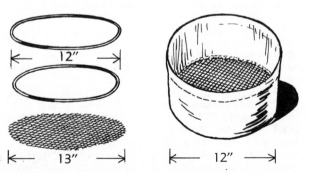

A collapsible sieve is made from two wire rings, a piece of quarter-inch wire mesh, and a cylinder sewn from cloth.

To separate insects from dirt and debris, use an *insect sieve* made from ¼-inch galvanized wire mesh. Cut the mesh into a circle, 13 inches in diameter. Make two rings, 12 inches in diameter, of ¼-inch steel wire. Bend the edges of the mesh circle around one ring, solder into position. Sew a piece of heavy muslin, 38 inches long, 10 inches wide, into a cylinder. Sew one edge of this cloth cylinder around the mesh-covered wire ring, the other to the free ring.

¶ *Tip*—A wire basket used for popping corn may be used for sifting small quantities. Or use a shoe box with its bottom cut out and replaced with wire mesh.

Sifting—Throw a thin layer of dug-up dirt or dead leaves into the sieve. Sift a small amount of it onto a piece of white cloth. Study the siftings carefully, pick out the insects, throw the debris away, then sift more.

SUCTION—Some of the insects you want to collect may be so tiny that they cannot be picked up with the fingers. Use a suction bottle or aspirator. This consists of a glass or plastic vial, closed with a two-hole rubber stopper through which two metal tubes lead. One

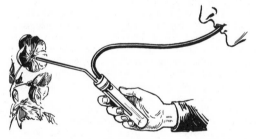

Tiny insects may have to be picked up with suction bottle or "aspirator." Air current sweeps them into vial.

short tube ends just below the stopper; the other, longer tube goes almost to the bottom of the vial.

By placing the opening of the longer tube near the insect and drawing in the air sharply through a rubber tube attached to the short metal tube, by mouth or rubber bulb, you create an air current that sweeps the insect into the vial.

¶ *Tip*—To keep yourself from inhaling the insects, tape a tiny piece of gauze onto the end of the smaller metal tube.

Insect Lists

The moment you start making notes of the insects you see and catch, you have taken your first step toward making a personal inventory of the insect world.

REGIONAL LISTS—Make a determined effort, through your own investigation and with the help of other insect enthusiasts, to discover and catch confirmatory specimens of the insects that inhabit a certain region—not in terms of square miles, but of a specific locality, such as a garden, an orchard, a campsite. Don't bite off more than you can chew. Dr. Frank E. Lutz found 1,402 different species in his 75-foot-by-200-foot suburban-home lot.

A thoroughgoing listing of the insects of your locality and recording of unusual species found may be of great interest to the department of agriculture or of conservation of your state. You may have found species not previously recorded. Such a discovery has occasionally meant the stamping out of a newly introduced insect pest before it had a chance to become established.

LIFE LISTS—For your own satisfaction, list all the insects you encounter in your entomological pursuits. Use your *Field Book of Insects* for this record. Write the date and place where an insect is seen, in the margin of the page that carries the description of it.

Field Observation

The books by famous Jean Henri Fabre, Maurice Maeterlinck, Edwin Way Teale, and many others suggest the discoveries that the insect world may reveal to you if you have the necessary patience and keenness of observation. Those books will also suggest methods to employ in the field study of insects. You will find ideas for further study on almost every page of Lutz's *Field Book of Insects*.

The number of opportunities for special field observations is so immense that any list of suggestions can only scratch the surface. Nevertheless, here goes:

Life cycles—The life cycles and lifespan are known for comparatively few insects. This field is wide open for investigation.

"Social life"—While the lives of ants and bees have been thoroughly investigated, little has been done with other gregarious insects.

Feeding habits—Larvae of a certain species generally feed on a specific food plant. Can feeding habits be changed artificially—from cultured plants to weeds, for instance?

Locomotion—Influence of light and shade, temperature, moisture, etc., on speed of crawling and running insects. Flight patterns of winged forms, influence of wind.

¶ *Tip*—Tiny dabs of different-colored enamel or nailpolish may be placed on the back or "thigh" of the hind legs to identify certain insects for the purpose of determining whether they return repeatedly to the same locality.

Insect homes—Kinds of insect homes found locally—nests, tubes, etc. Galls as insect homes; types of abnormal plant growth associated with various insects (see Lutz's *Field Book of Insects*).

"Music"—Influence of temperature, moisture, and so on, on rate of chirps of "music-making" insects, such as grasshoppers, crickets, katydids, and other Orthopterae. Does formula worked out for snowy tree cricket:

$$T = 50 + \frac{N-40}{4}$$

where: T—temperature in degrees Fahrenheit,
N—number of chirps per minute
work with others?

RECORDINGS—*The Songs of Insects.* Cornell University Records, Ithaca, New York.

Light of fireflies and other light-bearers. Purpose. Effect of temperature on number of flashes. And the tremendous accomplishment awaiting achievement: producing the same kind of "cold" light synthetically—but that's chemistry, not entomology.

Migration of the monarch and other migrating butterflies. Finding local gathering spots—"butterfly trees." Develop marking method for following their flight in cooperation with entomologists throughout the country.

REFERENCE—For information about the study of monarch butterfly migration, drop a line to Zoology Department, Scarborough College, University of Toronto, West Hill, Ontario, Canada.

Insecticides—Effectiveness on different species.

Other studies—Protective coloration. Mimicry. Intelligence and senses.

REARING INSECTS

One of the most intriguing features of insect study is that you are able to follow and watch the life cycle of many of them from egg to adult insect. It is difficult to do this out-of-doors—in many cases impossible. The solution is to rear the insects in which you are interested, in captivity.

Some species are suitable for study in this way; others are not. It is exceedingly interesting to watch the social life of ants and bees, for instance. But you would hardly have the patience to follow the cicada eating its way through a seventeen-year diet of roots, nor might you care to introduce a colony of termites into your house.

With hundreds of thousands of species to choose from, it is obviously impossible to suggest methods for raising them all. We have to concentrate on a few of the more important orders.

REFERENCE—Hung-fu Chu, *How to Know the Immature Insects.* Dubuque, Iowa, William C. Brown Company.

ROACHES, GRASSHOPPERS, ETC.—The most accomplished insect musicians belong in this group. You may want to raise these hardy creatures for the sake of listening to their sweet (?) music, in addition to watching them go through their incomplete metamorphosis from eggs through nymphs to the adult stage.

Roaches and crickets—These insects may be reared in almost any kind of glass or plastic container, from a 1-quart mason jar to a 1-gallon mayonnaise jar. You can even use a plastic refrigerator dish.

Spread about 2 inches of soil or sawdust on the bottom, and place a watch glass on top of this for a water trough. Cover with a lid of screen wire.

Feed them bread soaked in water, corn mush, mashed potatoes, bits of lettuce, and occasionally a delicacy such as peanut butter or library paste. Keep the watch glass filled with water.

Grasshoppers and walking sticks—Use the same kind of containers as for crickets, but instead of putting in plain soil, cut a sod of grass, about 2 inches thick, and line the bottom with this. Water the grass from time to time. The grass provides food, the soil a place for the female to deposit her eggs.

Praying mantis—In fall or winter, you may find the many-chambered egg case—oötheca—of the mantis. It contains hundreds of eggs. Bring it indoors and place it in a container similar to that used for crickets.

The young mantises (mantes or mantids—whichever plural you prefer) emerge after a few weeks. They are carnivorous, feeding on live insects. Give them aphids for their "baby" diet, later on, house-flies, bees, roaches. If you don't feed them enough, they turn cannibal and eat one another.

Adult mantises may be caught—often by hand—in late summer. They may live into the early winter if the temperature and humidity are right. If you can't manage to provide them with live insects, try feeding them tiny pieces of liver or chopped meat. Serve it on the tip of a toothpick or hold loosely between two fingers. They may take water from the end of a medicine dropper.

BUTTERFLIES AND MOTHS—Butterflies and moths may be reared from larvae or pupae. You can also rear them from eggs, laid by captive females or found in the fields.

CATERPILLARS—The important secret for raising butterflies and moths from caterpillars is to keep them supplied with their food plant. The adult female lays her eggs on a specific plant, peculiar to her species, and the emerging larvae seldom touch any other plant, but rather die from starvation. Therefore, if you are collecting larvae for rearing, it is very important to identify the food plant, bring home some leaves, and know where to find more to satisfy the larvae's voracious appetites.

¶ *Tip*—Lutz's *Field Book of Insects* lists the food plants of most common caterpillars.

The food plant must be kept fresh—either by keeping it growing where it is, by potting it, or by placing cut stalks in water. The more airtight the container in which the plant and larvae are kept, the longer the leaves remain fresh and palatable. Have no fear of suffocating the larvae. They need very little air to exist.

Outdoor cages—The larvae may be left on their food plant and prevented from straying by enclosing the plant in a piece of cheese-cloth or tobacco cloth, tying it up top and bottom.

If you want to observe your captives, make a transparent cage

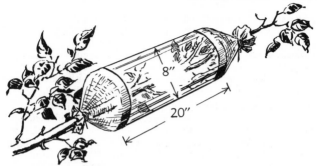

A transparent rearing cage, around caterpillars on their feed plant, makes an unusual display on the nature trail.

from a piece of cellulose acetate, 20 by 25 inches (one-half sheet, commercial size). Roll it into a 20-inch-long cylinder. Overlap the two edges about ¾ inch, and glue them together with fast-drying acetate cement. Glue (or sew) a 12-inch-wide sleeve of muslin or netting to each end of the cylinder. Slip the cage over the food plant, and tie the two sleeve ends around the plant.

Flowerpot cage—The flowerpot cage is of appropriate size for rearing a couple of larvae of a single species.

Fill a flowerpot or coffee can with soil. Plant one or more of the food plants in the soil, if they are small. Otherwise, sink a small mayonnaise jar into the soil as a container for water and for stalks of the plant. Punch holes in the cover in which to place the stalks. Place the larvae on the food plant.

Obtain an old-fashioned lantern globe or make up a cylinder of

A lantern globe or a plastic sleeve makes a rearing cage when placed around feed plant and larvae, in can of sand.

acetate sheet or window screening. Push the lower edge of the globe or cylinder into the soil. Cover the top with a lid of fine wire mesh or screening, or with a plastic lid from a can.

Aquarium cage—An old aquarium tank is excellent for raising a large number of larvae. Cover the bottom with a couple of inches of moist soil. Plant food plants in this, or place jars with stalks in water in the cage. Put in the larvae. Cover with a glass plate.

PUPATION—The larvae will pass through several moltings, and will finally reach the pupation stage. They will be "off their feed" figuratively, and may possibly literally be off their food plant, if they are the kind that go underground to pupate (hence the dirt on the bottom of the rearing chamber). Leave them alone, but study their activities carefully. Make notes or take photographs. Keep the pupae for the adult insect to emerge.

Note—You will sometimes discover that instead of raising larva to pupa, you are raising a brood of ichneumon wasps or tachinid flies. Most of these parasitic wasps and flies lay their eggs in caterpillars. The parasitic larvae feed on the flesh of their live host, and finally they pupate as the host dies. The wasp pupae often look like eggs attached to the outside of the caterpillar.

PUPAE—It should not be hard for you to locate a few pupae in the open, in addition to those that you may have "grown" yourself. Although chrysalids are generally rather hard to find, the cocoons of the larger species of moths make easy hunting—if you know what to look for and where.

REFERENCE—Lois J. Hussey and Catherine Pessino, *Collecting Cocoons.* New York, Thomas Y. Crowell Company.

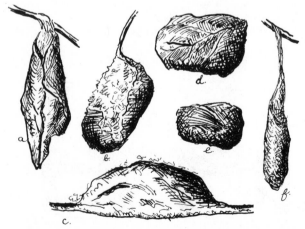

Cocoons of our spectacular moths: (a) Cynthia, (b) polyphemus, (c)cecropia, (d) luna, (e) io, (f) promethea—half size.

Finding cocoons—The cocoons of the *polyphemus* moth usually fall to the ground under the fruit or willow tree on which the larvae fed. Similarly, *luna*-moth cocoons may be found beneath the hickory and walnut trees. Leaf-wrapped *cynthia* and *promethea* cocoons dangle by one end from branches of their favorite host trees: ailanthus and spicebush respectively, and also wild cherry and some other trees. *Cecropia* cocoons are firmly attached at their full length to the branches of one of a great variety of host trees. *Io*-moth cocoons, on the other hand, are found mostly in cornfields on the ground among dead leaves.

¶ *Tip*—You can tell if a cocoon has a live pupa inside by the feel of it and by listening as you gently shake it. The cocoon with a live pupa will feel comparatively heavy, and you can hear a soft bumping when you shake it. A cocoon with a dead, dried-up pupa will feel light and will give off a dry rattle.

Rearing pupae—Almost any container will do for a rearing and emerging case, as long as it has room for a couple of branches onto which the emerged adult can crawl to dry and spread its wings.

A half-gallon-or-larger glass or plastic jar is good—even a large tin can. Or you can roll up a piece of wire mesh and provide it with a bottom and top by using a couple of plastic lids, or simply place it inside an empty ice cream or cottage cheese container with a window cut in its side. Even simpler: Cut a window in the container, drop the container into an old nylon stocking, and hang it up someplace where you can watch what goes on inside.

Place a 1-inch layer of dirt or sphagnum moss on the bottom of the container. Lay the pupae on it. Plant a few short sticks. Put on the cover.

Sprinkle pupae and dirt with water regularly—once a week or so—to keep them from drying out. The air in the container should be humid, but it should not be so moist that the contents get moldy.

¶ *Tip*—Instead of placing the pupae on the ground, many entomologists prefer to glue the pupae to the sticks with a couple of drops of glue to keep them from actually touching the dirt.

Controlling the emergence—Regulate the temperature so that the adults will emerge at a time to suit your purposes.

Pupae found in late fall and brought into a warm room will provide butterflies or moths, as the case may be, in two months' time—in midwinter.

¶ *Tip*—You can make a moth announce its emergence by wiring up the cocoon to a dry-cell electric buzzer. Remove the button and arrange the wire ends so that the emerging moth pushes one wire against the other.

If you intend to obtain eggs and to raise larvae, you should delay the emergence until the normal time when the natural food plants are available. You can do this by keeping your container between a regular window and the storm window on the north side of the house, in a glass container placed on the ground in the garden, or even by storing your pupae in the humidifier compartment of your refrigerator. In the latter case, bring them out as late winter turns into spring. To get fertile eggs, of course, you need to have both sexes emerge from your collection of pupae.

¶ *Tip*—A newly emerged female moth has a magnetic attraction for the males. Put it in a cheesecloth-covered glass jar. Place this outdoors in the evening and wait for the males to come around.

BEETLES—It is comparatively easy to study the life cycle of almost any beetle. Simply keep the specimens confined in a container with a fairly high humidity, and provide them with their favorite food.

As an example, you may want to follow the cycle of the tenebrio beetle—the mealworm beetle—and, while studying insect metamorphosis, at the same time produce the favorite food of aquarium fish, pet birds, and small reptiles.

Mealworm culture—Fill a half-gallon glass or plastic jar half full of ordinary breakfast bran or a mixture of bran and bread crumbs. Lay a piece of crumpled newspaper or paper toweling on top of it, and on this, place a thick slice of apple, a scraped carrot, or half a potato—partly for food, mostly for moisture. Wrap the jar in black paper.

The tenebrio is an insect pest often found in granaries or even in home-stored cereals, where you may be able to find specimens to start a culture. Otherwise, purchase a culture from a biological supply house (for addresses, see page 27). This will consist of bran containing adults, eggs, pupae, and larvae of all sizes.

Dump the culture in your container; cover the container with wire screening or close it with the lid punctured with a few nail holes. Place it in a warm location—best temperature is around 85 degrees—and let nature take its course. Replenish the apple slice, or whatever you are using, when it dries up.

Dermestid beetle culture—The raising of a culture of dermestid beetles is another double feature. You can follow the life-cycle of a beetle, and in feeding it its favorite food, you can use it for cleaning up skulls and small skeletons for a mammal collection.

It is a simple matter to start a dermestid colony. Just expose a piece of old hide, a dry carcass, or cheese, outdoors in warm weather. The beetles will soon make their appearance. Catch a number of them and keep them in a wide-mouth gallon jar prepared for them by placing a couple of layers of corrugated cardboard on the bottom to provide hiding places for them. Close the jar with a lid perforated with a number of small nail holes. Place the jar in a dry, warm room, and keep the jar dark by placing a paper bag over it.

¶ *Tip*—If you have no luck establishing a dermestid colony on your own, you can obtain a starter colony from one of the major biological supply houses (for addresses, see page 27).

ANTS—The social life of ants provides the greatest amount of entertainment and the best possible opportunities for learning to make careful and detailed observations in the field of *myrmecology*—the scientific study of ants.

Two types of ant house—or *formicarium*, if you want to be technical—are popular: the dirt-filled anthill house that gives you a chance to follow the ants' tunnel-digging prowess, and the dirt-free house that gives you an unobstructed view of the ants' comings and goings.

Anthill house—In its simplest form, the anthill house consists of two pieces of window glass of commercial size—10 by 14 inches or 12 by 18 inches—attached to the two sides of a wooden frame made up of strips of wood, ¾ inch square. The top side of the frame is removable and provided with three holes—each closed with a small piece of tin or strip of wood, turning on a nail. The whole house may be glued together with epoxy cement or taped together with masking tape. It rests, on one edge, on a couple of wooden blocks, in slits cut to fit. Cover both panes of glass with pieces of cardboard to keep the interior dark. Remove the cardboard during observation.

Filling the anthill house—You should have no special difficulty obtaining ants in the field any time during spring, summer, or fall. The best time is between late July and early September when not only workers but also winged males and females are present in the nests.

Locate an anthill. Dig into the side with a trowel or with rubber-

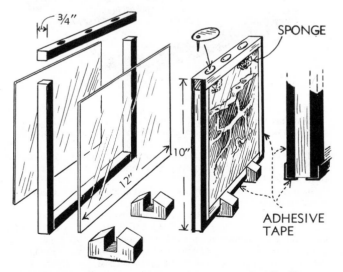

Two sheets of glass, a few strips of wood, and a bit of tape are the ingredients for creating an anthill house.

gloved hands. Scoop out a couple of handfuls of ant-dirt mixture and place them in a screw-top glass jar. Include eggs, larvae, pupae ("ants' eggs"), and if possible, a queen—you will know her by her larger size.

At home, pour the ant mixture into the house through the open top. Before replacing the top, hang a small sponge under two of the openings.

Ants need moisture and food. Provide the moisture by dropping water from an eyedropper onto one sponge; provide food by placing drops of honey and water (half and half) on the other sponge. From time to time, throw in a few flies or other insects. For a special treat, drop in a twig covered with aphids.

Dirt-free ant house—The best known dirt-free ant house is the Fielde design. This consists of a flat, glass-covered tray, approximately 12 inches long, 8 inches wide, 1 inch deep. Half of it is the

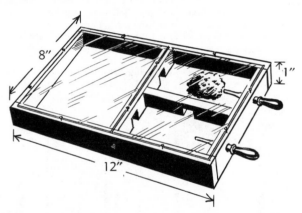

Dirt-free ant house is a wooden frame covered with sheet of glass. The ants are watered and fed from eye droppers.

living compartment. The remaining space is divided into two smaller rooms—one a moisture room that contains a damp sponge, the other the feeding room.

Such ant houses are commercially available. But you can readily make your own.

Use six strips of ½-by-1-inch wood—two 12-inch pieces, three 7-inch pieces, one 5-inch piece. Tack four strips into a frame, then partition it off as shown on working drawing on this page. Gouge ½-inch doorways to connect main room and two small rooms. Bore two holes through the outside wall into each small room—of such size that ordinary eyedroppers will fit snugly in them. Tack the frame to a piece of plywood, 12 by 18 inches, with the "doorways" down. Varnish or shellac inside and outside. Put the eyedroppers into position, one with water, the other with the feeding mixture (page 172). Place a small piece of sponge at the tip of the water dropper. Cover the whole thing with a piece of glass, and lay a sheet of cardboard over this to darken the interior.

¶ *Tip*—Instead of cardboard, use pieces of red glass, acetate, or cellophane, cut to fit over each room. You can easily follow the activities of the ants under this transparent cover. They behave in red light as if they were in the darkness they desire. Removing the red cover from any one of the rooms will cause the ants to move into the other two.

Introducing the ants—Purchase an ant colony of fifty ants with a queen, or collect the ants as suggested on page 171—dirt and all. The trick now is to get the ants into the house, leaving the dirt outside. To do this, spread a newspaper on a table. Place the house on the middle of it. Place a piece of cardboard over the house to darken the interior. Remove both eyedroppers after having moistened the sponge in the "moisture room." Along the edge of the newspaper, make a smooth, 1-inch-high ridge of dry plaster-of-paris powder, creating a so-called Forel arena. Then dump your ant-dirt mixture in the arena and watch the proceedings. As the dirt dries out, the ants try to get away. They soon give up their attempts to climb the plaster wall, and seek shelter in the house where moisture and darkness await them. When they are in, put the eyedropper "door" back in, place the ant house in its permanent location, carefully, without jarring, and remove the newspaper and plaster.

BEES—The observation beehive—or *apiary*—like the ant house, will provide endless opportunities for observations. It may be purchased from a biological supply house, bees and all, or you can make your own.

SUPPLIES—Biological supply houses. (Addresses on page 27.)

A. I. Root Company, Medina, Ohio 44256.

Herman Kolb, P.O. Box 183, Edmond, Oklahoma 73034.

Observation hive—If you desire to construct your own hive, make the acquaintance of a local bee fancier. Get his help and his suggestions. And persuade him to let you buy a few of his beekeeper's supplies. He gets his brood frames and supers by the dozen or by the hundred and buys beeswax brood foundations and super foundations by the pound—whereas you need only a couple.

The construction of the hive depends on the supplies you succeed in getting. In the main, the hive consists of a lower compartment with one or two brood frames with brood foundations attached where the young are raised, and an upper story with two supers provided with foundations for storing surplus honey. Build an outside frame to enclose the parts, with runway and entrance hole at the bottom and with glass front and back. Cover the glass with cardboard when the bees are not under observation.

¶ *Tip*—Construct the hive with the entrance runway at one side,

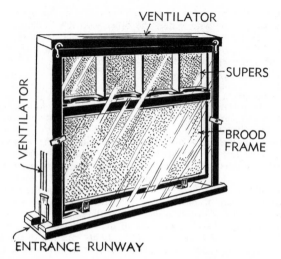

VENTILATOR

SUPERS

VENTILATOR

BROOD FRAME

ENTRANCE RUNWAY

Secure supers and brood frame for bee observation hive from a local bee keeper or from a biological supply house.

rather than front or back. This makes it possible to place the hive on a windowsill, at a 90-degree angle to the windowpane, with the runway extending into the open under the almost closed lower sash.

Stocking the hive—In stocking the hive, again depend on your beekeeper friend. He may be able to supply you with a few hundred bees and a queen. Otherwise, purchase bees by the pound from a mail-order house or from a biological supply house.

FLIES—You have probably already had a chance to watch the life cycle of the ordinary housefly—from eggs laid in garbage, through wriggling maggots and pupae, to adult flies. The whole business may take a month—or only a couple of weeks, under favorable conditions.

Blowflies—Blowfly larvae, pupae, and adults provide excellent food for aquarium fishes and for terrarium frogs and lizards. You can quickly and easily raise them in quantity by placing a strip of meat on which eggs have been laid in a jar, on top of a few inches of moist sand. Cover the jar with a piece of cheesecloth. As the larvae emerge, they feed on the meat and finally bury themselves in the sand to pupate. The adults appear about a week later.

Drosophila flies—The raising of the tiny vinegar flies, *Drosophila melanogaster*, has become an important means of studying heredity and demonstrating the Mendelian ratio.

SIMPLE REARING—Starting a culture is easy enough. All you have to do is to mash a piece of ripe banana and leave it in the open. In a short while vinegar flies appear and deposit their eggs. The larvae emerge in a couple of days and feed on the banana for about a week. They then pupate, to emerge as adults after another five days.

CONTROLLED REARING—For the study of genetics, such a crude method of raising your laboratory "animals" is not adequate. Instead, you need to develop your culture in sterile bottles, on a medium not readily subject to molds. Such a medium may be obtained from biological supply houses. Or you can make your own according to the Bridges' formula: Boil together for 10 minutes 10 g of agar, 50 g of cornmeal, 35 ml of molasses, 500 ml of water.

Pour approximately 1 inch of this medium into pint jars or half-pint milk bottles, or $\frac{1}{2}$ inch into 4-ounce, wide-mouth bottles. Insert a strip of paper toweling in each bottle in such a way that a couple of inches of it is above the medium—for the larvae to pupate on. The jars are closed with wads of cotton and sterilized in a pressure cooker.

After the bottles cool, drop one drop of a yeast and water mixture on the medium, and place a number of drosophila flies in the bottle. The mated females lay their eggs in the medium, and your culture is under way.

The new adults, emerging ten days to two weeks later, are anesthetized with ether. For your first controlled mating, a male and a female with decisive characteristics—red eyes and white eyes, for instance—are then picked out and placed in a bottle with the medium, as soon as they revive.

REFERENCE—Free leaflets on Drosophila culture are available from Ward's, General Biological Supply House, Carolina Biological Supply Company. (For addresses, see page 27.)

AQUATIC INSECTS—A number of insects spend their lives as larvae or nymphs in water. Some of them become airborne when they reach adulthood; others remain in the water. To do a successful rearing job, you should keep these insects in captivity under conditions that imitate their natural surroundings as closely as possible.

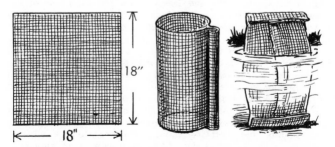

Insects from quickly moving streams do not survive in an aquarium. Rear them instead in a Needham pillow cage.

BOOK—Elsi B. Klots, *New Field Book of Freshwater Life*. New York, G. P. Putnam's Sons.

Insect aquarium—Insects from quiet waters, such as ponds and lakes, may be raised in a miniquarium (see page 211).

Insect water cages—Insects from swiftly moving streams cannot be reared too successfully in an aquarium. They are more easily raised directly in their home stream.

The simplest way of keeping them captive is to put them in a *pillow cage*, as suggested by James G. Needham. This cage is made from a piece of wire window screening, 18 inches square. Bring two opposite edges together and fold them into a tight hem. Flatten one end of the cylinder thus formed, and close it by folding over the edges. Put the insects into the cage with some of their natural foods, and close the top by folding (see illustration page 175).

Anchor the cage in the stream with a string, leaving a couple of inches of it above water. Visit it every couple of days to check the progress of your captives.

INSECT PHOTOGRAPHY

Insect photography is one of the most rewarding of all the many kinds of nature photography. Your results will amaze other people, and may even astonish you.

With a camera, you can catch and keep the grace of a dragonfly and the beauty of a moth. You will discover details in the structure of the tiniest insect which would evade you otherwise, even under the magnifying glass. And you can create the exciting effect of gigantic, prehistoric monsters by blowing up heads of insects into 8-by-10-inch enlargements or by filling a motion-picture screen with them.

REFERENCE—Edwin Way Teale, *Grassroot Jungles*. Chapter on insect photography. New York, Dodd, Mead & Company.

Stills

EQUIPMENT—Camera and lenses—With the exception of the larger insects, the photography of insects involves macrophotography in which the film image is up to fifteen times larger than the subject photographed.

For this kind of photography, you need a camera that permits you to shoot at a distance of a couple of inches from the subject, with a device for critical focusing, a diaphragm that can be closed down to almost pinhole size to ensure the greatest possible depth of field, and with shutter speeds from fractions of a second to time.

If you have a double-extension-bellows camera or a camera with so-called macro lens especially designed for close-up photography, you should be able to get close enough to an insect to get a full-sized image on your negative or slide. But that, usually, is not enough in insect photography. You may have to resort to extension tubes and rings and adjustable bellows.

Courtesy: Zeiss-Ikon-Voigtlander, Inc.

Macro-photograph of left eye of ordinary housefly.

William Hillcourt

Close-up of praying mantis in the process of laying her eggs.

William Hillcourt

Color slide reproduced in black-and-white gives only weak idea of brilliant colors of the original butterfly.

In close-up work, the ordinary camera viewfinder becomes useless. The only way in which you will know the field the lens is covering, is by focusing on ground glass or, in the case of some miniature cameras, by using a special focusing attachment. You will have no focusing problem with the single-reflex camera.

Because of the extreme close-up, the depth of focus will be exceedingly shallow. It is imperative, therefore, to make your focusing as exact as possible. Then, to add to the depth, close down the diaphragm as far as it will go.

Other equipment—For practically all kinds of insect photography you will need a tripod—preferably with a tilting or a ball-jointed head—and a cable release to prevent your shaking the camera when you make the exposure.

Exposures—The smaller the diaphragm opening, the longer the exposure. This doesn't make much difference if you are photographing dead specimens, but live insects may not cooperate by holding their pose as long as you would like them to.

The two ways of shortening the exposure is to use a fast film and to light up the subject as brilliantly as possible, using sunlight or photofloods or flash, and metallic reflectors of postcard size or smaller.

¶ *Tip*—In taking a reflected light reading, remember that the insect is so small that it will be the background that will register. Take your reading, therefore, by substitution, against a piece of gray cardboard. For outdoor shots, you may prefer to use incident light readings.

OUTDOOR PHOTOGRAPHY—You will have no trouble photographing the more or less stationary insects outdoors—caterpillars, aphids, and other leaf-eating or sap-sucking insects. Simply set up your camera on its tripod, focus, and shoot.

To photograph the insects that move about—butterflies, bees, and so on—don't run your legs off chasing them. Instead, study the landscape and notice the flowers that are especially effective in attracting the insects in which you are interested. Pick the most photogenic of these flowers, set up your camera at the proper distance and focus it on the flower. You will probably have scared away any insect that was visiting it, but the same insect or another will be along in a few moments. Wait for it to assume a desirable pose, then shoot. If you move slowly and carefully you will probably be able to make several exposures before the insect takes off.

Our most spectacular insects, the moths, must be photographed at night, using flash for illumination. Start your preparations in the daytime by locating the night-scented flowers of neighborhood or garden: honeysuckle, flowering tobacco, garden heliotrope. Return in the evening with your camera and with a helper carrying a flashlight. Set up your camera and focus it tentatively. When a moth settles on the flower, have your helper illuminate it briefly with the flashlight for a final, critical focusing. Then shoot.

¶ *Tip*—To encourage butterflies, moths, and bees to sit still long enough to pose for several shots, dab a little diluted honey in the center of the flower.

To be positive that you will get what you want, it often pays to catch the insect first. Anesthetize it by keeping it for a few minutes in a jar containing a wad of cotton with a few drops of ethyl acetate (nailpolish remover). In the meantime focus on a suitable plant part. When the insect has become stupefied enough, arrange it on the plant, and let it cling. Recheck the focus. Snap the shutter.

INDOOR PHOTOGRAPHY—Generally speaking, you will have much better success photographing your insects indoors rather than outdoors. You have a far better control over the situation—including background and the most attractive angle for composition.

Set up your props as you would for tabletop photography: plants in a vase or pot, a sod of grass, a piece of bark on the table. Put up a sheet of gray or colored construction paper for a background, or a piece of black velvet, if you prefer a dead black background in black-and-white photography.

Arrange a single floodlight or flash to imitate sunlight. Light up shadows with metal reflectors.

¶ *Tip*—A shaving mirror makes a good reflector for small subjects.

When everything is in order, bring out your anesthetized insect model, pose it, and shoot.

¶ *Tip*—Move fast after the insect is out of the jar. The heat from the floodlights will quickly revive it.

Why not take your shots of dead collection specimens that will stay quiet? OK—for detail shots, such as of head, mouth parts, antennae. Otherwise, NO—partly because it is almost impossible to arrange them in a lifelike pose, partly—well, to real nature photographers, it just isn't cricket.

WHAT TO PHOTOGRAPH—Insect subjects suitable for photographs are legion. Most photographers have concentrated on the more spectacular or better known subjects. So the field is wide open.

The most valuable photographs are *series* showing the life cycle of the insect from egg to adult, and *sequences*—such as of a caterpillar turning into a chrysalis, a moth emerging from its cocoon (see pages 168 and 169).

¶ *Tip*—For a life cycle or a sequence, don't depend on a single caterpillar or pupa. It may die before your series is complete. Be certain to have several stand-ins on hand.

Movies

Insect movies are considerably tougher to make than insect stills. They require infinite patience and a great amount of inventiveness.

EQUIPMENT—**Camera and attachments**—A camera that can be focused through the lens is an absolute necessity. You also need supplementary lenses, close-up attachments, extension rings and tubes, and bellows extensions—depending on how ambitious you are!

MOVIE TECHNIQUES—Generally speaking, the suggestions for taking stills apply equally well for movie making—with the one exception that shots are more easily taken outdoors by sunlight than indoors under artificial light.

The usual method in movie making of taking "long shot, medium shot, close-up" needs to be modified when insects are the actors to "close-up, close-close-up, ultra-close-up." The effect will be striking.

To get the most lifelike action—or any action at all—out of your actors, you will have to vary the camera speed to fit the insect. Some insects, such as butterflies, grasshoppers, bees, are fast moving. Slow down their action to keep them on the screen by shooting them at 32 frames per second. Other insects are slow moving: praying mantises, locusts, katydids. Speed up their action by taking them at 8 frames per second.

The pupation of a caterpillar or the emergence of a butterfly needs to be taken by time-lapse, single-frame exposures, to cover the action within the limits of the usual movie footage. (See page 339.)

INSECT COLLECTIONS

One of the most absorbing hobbies in the nature field is the creation of a permanent insect collection. Many youngsters begin collecting for the fun of it. As they grow older, their insect hobby becomes an engrossing activity that brings them out into the open, and often puts them in touch with other people who have the same interest.

You can, of course, start a collection by pinning insects in cardboard boxes with ordinary pins. But don't! It takes no more effort and costs little more to do the job right—using correct methods and good equipment, most of which you can make yourself.

The important steps in making an insect collection consist in catching the insects by one of the methods described previously (pages 153–63), killing them without damaging them, preparing them correctly, mounting them properly, displaying them attractively.

REFERENCES—*How to Make an Insect Collection.* Ward's, Rochester, New York 14603; Monterey, California 93940.
U.S. Department of Agriculture. *Collection and Preservation of Insects.* Catalog No. A 1.38:601. Twenty-five cents. From Superintendent of Documents, U.S. Government Printing Office, Washington, D.C. 20402.

SUPPLIES—see addresses on page 27.

Killing Insects

KILLING JARS—Insects for collections are killed by exposing them to fumes of various chemicals in tightly closed "killing jars." Some of these chemicals are nonpoisonous for human beings; others are dangerous poisons. Obviously, the nonpoisonous killing jar is recommended for young insect hunters. Since the poison jar is more effective, it is preferred by advanced entomologists.

Nonpoisonous killing jars—For a perfectly safe killing jar, start by making a small batch of plaster-of-paris mixture (see page 120) and pouring it into a screw-top pint jar to a height of $\frac{3}{4}$ to 1 inch. Let it harden, then dry it out completely by placing the jar in the sun (without the lid on it) for a couple of days, or by baking it in a very slow oven until all moisture has been removed, followed by cooling. Now pour $\frac{1}{2}$ inch of ethyl acetate (nailpolish remover) onto the plaster, cover the jar, and allow it to stand for about a day for the plaster to soak up the liquid. Pour off the excess liquid and wipe the inside of the jar dry with tissue or paper towel. Cover plaster with two circles of heavy blotting paper cut to fit snugly inside the jar.

¶ *Tip*—While you are at it, make two killing jars—one for butterflies, the other for beetles and other insects. Never put delicate and robust insects together in the same jar if you want good specimens.

¶ *Tip*—For a simplified killing jar, use a circle of cotton batting instead of plaster of paris layer.

Poison jar—The killing agent in the poison jar is sodium or potassium cyanide—an extremely potent poison in two ways: by itself and by its fumes.

It doesn't pay to make your own poison jars. Instead, purchase them, ready-made, from a biological supply house (see page 27)—two or more pint-size killing jars for larger insects, and an unbreakable killing tube for small species.

Put strips of blotting paper or paper toweling in the jar to absorb moisture and to keep the specimens from shaking around—except in a jar meant for butterflies or moths.

¶ *Tip*—For added safety, wrap strips of 1-inch adhesive tape around the jar to reduce the chance of breakage.

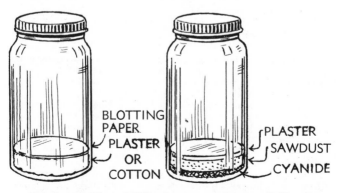

Two types of insect killing jars: nonpoisonous (left) using ethyl acetate; poisonous cyanide jar (right).

Stinging insects may be subdued by placing net corner in killing jar. Paralyze butterflies by squeezing the thorax.

WARNING!—Keep the poison jar away from children and mark it conspicuously: POISON!!! If the jar cracks or breaks, dig a hole for it a couple of feet deep, smash it completely at the bottom of the hole, then bury it. Wash hands thoroughly afterward.

Using the killing jar—When you pick up insects with your hands, simply drop the insects into the jar and cover it tightly.

Many insects will let themselves drop into the open killing jar if it is pushed in under them. This method usually works well when "sugaring" (see page 154).

To get an insect from a net into a jar, hold the insect in a small fold of the netting with a couple of fingers of the left hand. Slip the opened killing jar into the net with the right hand. Drop the insect into the jar. Grasp the jar through the netting with the left hand. Bring the cork or cover into the net and place it on the jar.

¶ *Tip*—If the insect is a wasp or other stinging insect, push the corner of the net in which it is imprisoned into the jar and put on the cover. In a few moments the insect will be overcome by the fumes, and you can take it out without fear of being stung.

¶ *Tip*—To stop a butterfly or moth from beating its wings to bits before it succumbs in the killing jar, demobilize it while it is still in the net. Hold it by the body with the wings together over its back. Pinch the sides of the body under the wings (the thorax) between two fingers without crushing. This paralyzes the insect and quickly stops its movements. Then drop it into the killing jar.

Alcohol vials—Insects that shrivel up when dried—stone flies, mayflies, and the like—and insects in immature stages are dropped directly into vials containing 80 percent ethyl alcohol or 70 to 80 percent rubbing alcohol (isopropyl alcohol).

Temporary Storage

Insects killed in the field should be removed from the killing jar as soon as they are dead—half an hour to one hour—and transferred to a container for temporary storage.

¶ *Tip*—Never take insects out of the jar with your fingers. Instead, use a pair of forceps, 4 to 5 inches long. Some insect collectors prefer forceps with thin curved tips; others like the broad-tipped variety. Take your choice.

Storage boxes—Beetles, grasshoppers, and similar "hard-shelled" insects may be stored temporarily in small plastic boxes between layers of glazed cotton batting (jeweler's cotton) or cellulose cotton.

Papering—Butterflies, moths, and dragonflies are "papered" in individual paper containers. The traditional container is a triangular envelope formed by folding a rectangular piece of smooth paper in the manner shown in the drawing below. The proportion between the width and length of the paper used is two to three. Medium-sized butterflies take papers 4 by 6 inches. Make a supply of triangles for varying sizes of specimens.

¶ *Tip*—Glazed paper envelopes and envelopes of cellophane are on the market. They will save you the trouble of making triangles, but they cost quite a bit more.

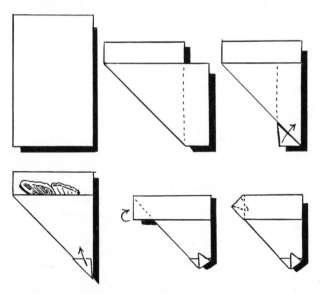

Butterflies, moths, and dragonflies are "papered" in individual envelopes, folded, as shown, from pieces of paper.

When the insects are papered, write data on the outside of the envelopes. Bring them home in a box, such as a plastic sandwich box, for pinning later.

Preparing Insect Specimens

It pays to go about the job of preparing the insect specimens with great care. The result will be an attractive and workmanlike exhibit.

RELAXING—If at all possible, you should prepare the insects the same day you collect them, before they dry up and become brittle. You won't often accomplish this. Your harvest will be too large, or the hour too late.

The alternative is to store the insects, then relax them before working with them by placing them in a damp container until they become soft again.

Relaxing boxes—Relaxing boxes are available through biological supply houses, but almost any covered glass or metal container can be used. A plastic refrigerator dish with a close-fitting lid or an empty coffee can will do the trick.

Place a 1-inch layer of cotton or paper toweling on the bottom of the container. Moisten it with water. Cover it with a couple of layers of paper toweling. Place the insects in the box on top of the dry toweling, then close the box. Leave the specimens in the relaxing box until the legs and wings can be moved freely.

Small butterflies usually relax overnight, larger insects in a couple of days.

¶ *Tip*—To prevent mold from forming, use a 1 percent phenol (carbolic acid) solution instead of plain water for moistening. Or place a layer of paradichlorobenzene or naphthalene flakes at the bottom of the relaxing box.

PINNING—The most common method for displaying insect specimens is to use pins.

Pins—Never use regular pins for your insects, even if you happen to be the rankest beginner. They are too coarse and bend and rust too easily. From the very start, use *insect pins*. These are slender pins, made of stiff steel wire, japanned to be practically rustless. They come in a standard length of 37 mm (almost $1\frac{1}{2}$ inches), numbered according to thickness from 000 to 7.

¶ *Tip*—Keep several sizes of insect pins on hand: No. 2 for small to medium-sized butterflies, wasps, and insects of similar size, No. 3 for grasshoppers and large butterflies, No. 4 or 5 for large beetles.

Pin locations—Insect pins are not pushed indiscriminately through any part of the insect body. They are systematically placed—partly to ensure a uniform appearance, partly to leave identifying marks undisturbed.

The place at which pins are inserted varies with the insect orders:
Butterflies, moths, dragonflies—through the center of the thorax, the body part to which wings and legs are attached.

Insect killing jar used by amateurs should preferably be the nonpoisonous kind using ethyl acetate. The killing agent is squirted onto cotton in container attached to lid of jar.

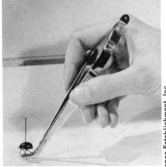

Pin holder, with holes for holding pins of different diameters, simplifies the work of pinning insects for adding to collection.

Pinning forceps are used for pressing the mounting pin into the pinning bottom of an insect box and for removing a specimen.

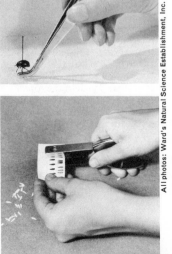

Point punch punches out mounting points of uniform size. Several models are available: for points with straight base, blunt point; straight base, sharp point; rounded base, sharp point.

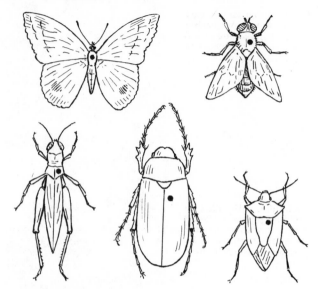

Insect pins are placed systematically, their locations depending on the insect orders, to insure a uniform look.

Bees, *flies*—through the thorax, slightly to the right of center.

Grasshoppers, *crickets*—through the back section of the thorax, slightly to the right of center line.

True bugs—through the triangular shield, the scutellum, slightly to the right of center.

Beetles—through the right wing cover, near the front edge and close to the inside edge.

Placing the pin—Hold the specimen firmly, between two fingers, on top of a piece of balsa wood. Place the tip of the pin on the back of the insect, at the correct spot for the order to which it belongs. Then thrust the pin through the body in such a way that the insect is at right angles to the pin—crosswise as well as lengthwise.

Finally, adjust the insect on the pin so that ½ inch of the top of the pin protrudes from the insect's back. You do this by bringing the insect up near the pin head, then pushing it down to the correct height. You will soon learn to judge the distance by eye.

¶ *Tip*—Or use a "setter" for adjusting the height. This is simply a thin piece of wood or plastic with a fine hole bored in one end, ½-inch deep, wide enough to fit over the head of the pin.

¶ *Tip*—To prevent a heavy specimen from sliding down on the pin, turn the pinned insect over and place a small drop of clear nail-polish or white shellac from the tip of a toothpick at the point on the underside where the pin emerges.

After the insects are pinned, handle them with special care when transferring them from one location to another. Don't use your fingers, grabbing the head of the pin. Instead, use forceps, grabbing the pin near its point. Use regular insect pinning forceps or long-nose pliers that have jaws at a 90-degree angle.

SPREADING—Butterflies, moths, and dragonflies are mounted with their wings spread out flat. To accomplish this, you have to dry them on spreading boards.

Spreading boards—A spreading board consists of two strips of soft wood, fine-textured wallboard or fiberboard, or even corrugated cardboard, nailed or glued parallel on a couple of crosspieces, with a groove between them as wide as the body of the insects to be spread. A pinning strip of cork, balsa wood, or corrugated cardboard is tacked under the groove.

The wood strips can be flat. But most collectors prefer them slanted toward the middle to counteract the tendency of butterflies to droop their wings when taken off the board.

Standard spreading boards are 19 inches long, of widths varying from $3\frac{1}{16}$ inches with a $\frac{1}{16}$-inch groove, to $7\frac{3}{4}$ inches with a $\frac{5}{8}$-inch groove. The most useful size is $4\frac{3}{8}$ inches wide, with a $\frac{3}{8}$-inch groove (see design below).

¶ *Tip*—Make a number of spreading boards of different groove widths.

Method of spreading—Pick up the recently killed or relaxed butterfly with forceps. Squeeze the thorax slightly to open up the

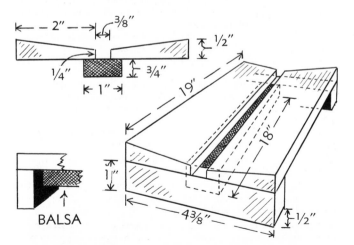

Spreading boards for butterflies and moths are made of two strips of wood, nailed parallel, and a pinning strip.

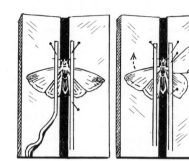

In spreading, hold down wings with paper strings. Open up wings. Keep in place with (a) glass plates or (b) strips.

wings, then push an insect pin through the center of the back of the thorax. Place the insect body in the groove of the spreading board, and press the pin into the pinning strip. The back of the butterfly should be slightly higher than the surface of the spreading board. Anchor the body by pushing a pin in next to the thorax on the side to be spread first, to prevent the insect from swinging on its pin when you start moving its wings.

Cut a number of strips, ⅛-inch wide, from a good grade of writing paper. Pin one end of a strip to the spreading board, ahead of the butterfly's forewing. Move the wing forward by pushing against one of its heavy veins with a fine insect pin until the rear edge of the wing is at a right angle to the insect's body. Move up the hind wing in a similar manner until its forward edge meets the forewing. Be careful not to puncture either wing. Hold the paper strip firmly down over both wings while adjusting them, then fasten it down by putting a pin through the loose end. Treat the opposite wing pair in the same manner.

The wings are next covered with two more strips of paper, placed farther out toward the wing tips. Some collectors prefer strips of glass for this purpose and use standard microscope slides, 1 by 3 or 2 by 3 inches.

If necessary, brace antennae, legs, and rear of butterfly with a few pins, so that they will dry in a natural position.

¶ *Tip*—Use ordinary pins for fastening down the paper strips or, better, stiff glass-headed mounting pins.

Put the spread butterflies away to dry, from a couple of days to a full week, in a place where they are protected against attacks from ants and other insects and from mice.

SETTING—Beetles, true bugs, grasshoppers, and other "hard" insects are prepared on a setting board which may be a piece of balsa wood or styrofoam or several layers of corrugated cardboard.

After pinning the insect, push the pin into the setting board until

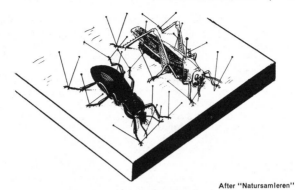

After "Natursamleren"

Beetles, grasshoppers, and other "hard" insects are dried in natural position by pinning them onto a setting board.

the body of the insect is slightly above the board. Position the legs and antennae with the help of a pin. Anchor them in place by bracing them with pins. Leave the insect alone until its legs are completely dry and stiff, then transfer the insect to your collection.

POINTING—Tiny insects are not pinned on regulation length insect pins. They are occasionally pinned on short (about ½ inch long), especially fine pins—*minuten nadeln*—and attached by them to small pieces of cork or pith or balsa wood which in turn are impaled on No. 3 insect pins. More often, tiny insects are "pointed"—glued to the tip of small triangular paper points.

Paper points—Insect points are cut from stiff white paper or thin cardboard. They may be purchased by the thousand.

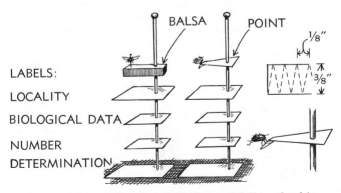

BALSA   POINT

LABELS:

LOCALITY

BIOLOGICAL DATA

NUMBER

DETERMINATION

⅛"

⅜"

Tiny insects are pinned on "minuten nadeln" or glued to paper points. Place labels properly, as shown to the left.

You can make them yourself by punching them out with a special "insect point punch," or simply by cutting them from a $\frac{3}{8}$ inch (8 mm)-wide strip of stiff paper or Bristol board with scissors or an old razor blade. Do a neat cutting job, making each point $\frac{1}{8}$ inch (3 mm) wide at the base.

Attaching the point—Push a No. 3 insect pin into the point near its base. Adjust the point to the usual height of an insect on a pin, $\frac{1}{2}$ inch below the pin head. Bend the tip of the point downward about 45 degrees. Touch the tip to a drop of clear nailpolish, then to the right side of the insect. Adjust the insect so that its head points straight forward with its body at a right angle to the axis of the point. Put it aside until the polish has dried.

INFLATING CATERPILLARS—It is sometimes desirable to display the caterpillars of butterflies and moths next to the adults of the same species. The most attractive way of doing this is by eviscerating the caterpillars, inflating the skins during the drying, and mounting them on pins.

The first step is to remove the innards. Place the caterpillar on a piece of paper. Make a slit at the vent with a pin or with the tip of a knife, then roll a round pencil gently over the body from just behind the head to the tail, thus pressing out the contents.

Insert the tip of a glass tube in the hole at the vent, and fasten the skin to the tube with a tiny wire clip. Inflate the skin by blowing air into the glass tube through a piece of rubber hose, using a double rubber bulb or your mouth. While you are inflating the skin, dry the caterpillar slowly over a safe heat source—a piece of metal or a tin can with a couple of inches of sand on top of an alcohol lamp or a Bunsen burner, an electrical hot plate, an upturned electrical iron, or in a special oven. Turn it from time to time, and watch against scorching. Completely dry, the skin will hold its shape when the blowing stops.

Remove the dried skin from the glass tube. Insert a balsa wood plug in the hole at the tail and glue it in place with a drop of shellac. Push a No. 3 insect pin through the balsa, and adjust the caterpillar to the proper pin height.

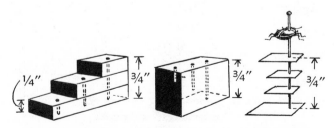

Two pinning blocks: step block with quarter-inch steps and solid block. Right: correctly placed insects and labels.

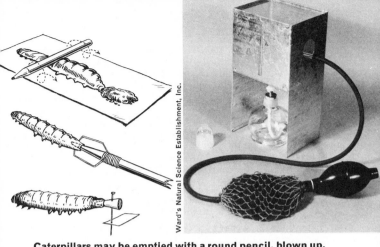

Caterpillars may be emptied with a round pencil, blown up, dried in "oven," fastened to small plugs of balsa wood.

LABELING—The notes that have followed the specimens through their temporary storage and their preparation are finally attached permanently to the pins on which the insects are impaled. Here custom has established a procedure that provides for exactness and uniformity.

Labels—The labels considered necessary for satisfactory description consist of:

LOCALITY LABEL, $\frac{1}{4}$ by $\frac{1}{2}$ inch, with space for the name of the locality where found, the date, and the finder's name. This may be handwritten, but it is more satisfactory if printed. (A few of the major biological supply houses make these available with three lines of 4-point type, according to your specifications. You can also make them yourself by filling a sheet of paper with typewritten lines of the legend, then having the sheet reduced photographically to make the individual labels the correct size.)

BIOLOGICAL DATA LABEL, a tiny label containing information on the host plant or habitat. Though not always used, it adds to the value of your collection.

NUMBER LABEL, a small label with the file number of the insect. Used only in large collections.

DETERMINATION LABEL, $\frac{5}{16}$ by $\frac{11}{16}$ inch or $\frac{1}{2}$ by $1\frac{1}{16}$ inches, generally with a black border line, containing the scientific name of the specimen, the original authority, and the name of identifier. Also, if ascertained, the sex of the insect.

Placing the labels—The labels are placed in their proper positions on the pin by the use of a *pinning block*, a small block of wood, $1\frac{1}{8}$ inches thick, 1 inch wide, 3 inches long, with three holes bored in it to depths of $\frac{1}{4}$ inch, $\frac{1}{2}$ inch, and $\frac{3}{4}$ inch respectively.

Another type of pinning block is steplike, with the steps $\frac{1}{4}$ inch,

½ inch, and ¾ inch high, and the holes bored through to the bottom.

The locality label is placed over the ¾-inch-deep hole, and the pin pushed through the center of the label to the bottom of the hole. This sets the label at the proper height.

The biological data label, when used, is set in a similar way, using the ½-inch hole.

The number label is pinned over the ¼-inch hole.

The determining label is placed on the bottom of the storage box, and the pin is thrust through it.

Permanent Storage

Good specimens deserve good storage, in well-constructed boxes with tight-fitting covers to protect them against dust and insect attacks.

STORING THE SMALL COLLECTION—The most popular storage box for the small collection is the Schmitt box. This is a wooden box with hinged top that fits tightly over an inside collar. It has a pinning bottom of cork or balsa wood, and it is lined with white glazed paper. It is made to a standard size of 13 by 9 by 2½ inches.

Making your own storage box—A fair facsimile of the Schmitt box may be made from ½-inch pine boards, cut to size and nailed to top and bottom sheets of Presdwood, Masonite, or ½-inch plywood (see the design below). Glue a pinning bottom of Celotex (wallboard), pressed cork (entomological cork), balsa wood or corrugated cardboard to the bottom of the box. Paint the inside white or cover it with white paper. Give the outside a double coating of shellac or plastic spray.

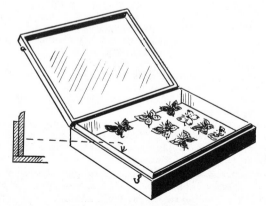

The Schmitt box is the most popular box for small insect collection. Inside collar helps keep box dust-free.

STORING THE LARGE COLLECTION—As your collection grows, it will pay you to transfer your specimens to drawers in a storage cabinet. The larger biological supply houses carry several models of such cabinets in stock. Two important models are the U.S. National Museum model with drawers of 18 by 18 by 3 inches outside measurements, and Cornell University model with drawers 19 by 16½ by 3 inches.

When drawers are used, the insects are rarely pinned to the drawer bottom. Instead, they are placed in unit pinning trays of certain standard sizes which, in turn, are placed in drawers. The trays for the drawers of the U.S. National Museum cabinets are all 1⅝ inches high and 4 inches wide, but of varying lengths: 1¼, 1⅞, 3$\frac{13}{16}$, and 7⅝ inches. This unit system permits you to keep your whole collection perfectly arranged at all times.

PROTECTING THE COLLECTION—Certain small insects take special pleasure in feeding on dried insect specimens. You need to protect your collection against them.

Repelling pests—Naphthalene, the ordinary moth repellent, is commonly used in insect collections. It may be used in the form of mothballs or as flakes placed in a small cheesecloth bag or a perforated cardboard box in one corner of your collection box.

¶ *Tip*—To prevent mothballs from rolling around in the box, pin them in place. Heat the head of a pin in a flame. When it is red hot, push it into the mothball. As the pin cools, the ball sticks to it. The pin with its mothball head is then pushed into the bottom of the storage box.

Killing pests—Fine sawdustlike powder in your storage box tells you that the enemy pests have already made their inroads. Kill them off immediately.

Paradichlorobenzene is an effective killing agent. It comes in flakes like naphthalene. Spread a teaspoonful of flakes on the bottom of the storage box, and close it tight.

¶ *Tip*—A number of entomologists use a mixture of equal parts of naphthalene and paradichlorobenzene flakes to do the double job of repelling and killing. Paradichlorobenzene cannot be depended on to do the job alone because it volatilizes rather rapidly.

Displaying Your Insects

Instead of storing away your insects, you may be more interested in putting them on display for yourself and others to enjoy. Several display methods are old-time favorites with thousands of insect collectors. New methods make their appearance occasionally.

Riker mounts—Riker mounts are shallow, cotton-filled cardboard boxes with glass covers. They are usually ¾ to 1 inch deep, ranging in size from 2½ by 3 inches to 12 by 16 inches. The insects are arranged on the cotton, then the box is covered with the glass and sealed.

Homemade Riker mounts—To make your own Riker mount, buy a piece of windowpane in one of the standard sizes—6 by 8 inches,

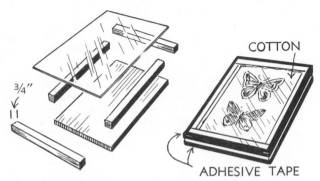

3/4″

COTTON

ADHESIVE TAPE

A homemade Riker mount is constructed from a frame of wood strips, a plywood backing, and a sheet of glass.

6 by 12 inches, or 12 by 16 inches. Make a frame from strips of wood, $\frac{1}{2}$ inch thick, $\frac{1}{2}$ inch wide, of the same outside measurements as your glass. Tack this frame to a bottom of heavy cardboard or $\frac{1}{4}$-inch plywood.

When you are assembling the mount, start by placing a pinch of paradichlorobenzene crystals on the bottom. Next, put in layers of cotton batting. On top of the cotton, arrange your insects and the labels that go with them. Cover it with the glass plate, and seal it with strips of 1-inch adhesive tape. Finally, paint the bottom, the sides, and the adhesive tape with enamel—black or any other color you prefer.

Improvised Riker mounts—For an even simpler homemade Riker mount, cut the top off a ladies' nylon stocking box, leaving a $\frac{1}{2}$-inch-wide frame. Fill the bottom of the box with cotton batting, arrange the insects, cover them with an acetate sheet, replace the top, and seal the box with 1-inch masking tape.

Plastic butterfly mount—A simple rigid mount for display and easy handling of individual butterflies can be made from a sheet of styrofoam, $\frac{1}{2}$ to $\frac{3}{4}$ inch thick. Cut it in squares of appropriate sizes. Carve an indentation in each square to fit the butterfly's body. Place the butterfly on the square and cover it with a glass plate of the same size as the styrofoam. Tape around the edges.

Flexible butterfly mount—For the use of students in identifying various butterflies, the quickest trick is to put them in a flexible mount.

For protection, first place the butterfly between two pieces of the clinging kind of plastic wrap: Saran or Handi-Wrap. Trim the wrap to within $\frac{1}{4}$ inch of the outline of the butterfly. Place the wrapped insect on the sticky surface of a piece of clear transparent self-adhesive plastic such as Con-Tact. Cover with a similar piece and rub smooth.

CHAPTER 7

Water Life

A BODY of water under the open sky brings out the kid in each of us—the desire to while away some sunny hours lying on the belly in front of a lazy pond, watching striders skating across the "dry" surface, diving beetles squirming up and down, tiny fishes moving among the water plants; or wading in a tide pool looking for shells and starfish and sea anemones; or following a stream with rod and reel in hand hoping for a prize strike; or rocking gently in a boat on the ocean waves with a school of mackerel flashing by below.

The world under the water's surface is a world by itself, a world of extremes . . . of microscopic creatures in every water drop, and giants in the expanses of the open sea . . . of brilliant beauty and repulsive ugliness . . . of creatures that spend a lifetime burrowed in the bottom mud, and others that travel across an ocean to mate and die.

Once your interest has been aroused, you will find water life an unending source of new and intriguing activities. Each body of water is different from any other body, and each deserves your study—whether lake or pond, brook or river, meadow or swamp, beach or open sea.

You will quickly have to decide whether your main interest lies in *limnology*—the study of life in fresh water—or whether you favor *oceanography*—life in salt water. Within each of these fields, the opportunity for specialization is tremendous. Just check the possibilities:

In *freshwater*, you will find numerous microscopic and near-microscopic animals, and then, in ascending scale: sponges—hydras—flatworms—threadworms—bristle worms—leeches—fairy shrimps, scuds, crayfish—aquatic insects—snails, mussels—lampreys, fishes—salamanders, frogs, toads—turtles, water snakes.

In *salt water*, the variety is just as great. Here, in addition to discovering a multitude of minute organisms, you will come upon: sponges—jellyfish, sea anemones—flatworms—starfishes, sea urchins, sea cucumbers—snails, limpets, mussels, clams, oysters, squids—sandworms, bloodworms—barnacles, shrimps, crabs—fishes.

But do not let the immensity of the subject scare you away from it. Get started, then follow the line that catches your fancy.

BOOKS ON WATER LIFE—James G. and Paul R. Needham, *A Guide to the Study of Freshwater Biology*. San Francisco, Holden-Day.

Rachel L. Carson, *The Sea Around Us*. New York, Oxford University Press.

Augusta F. Arnold, *The Sea Beach at Ebb Tide*. New York, Dover Publications.

Edward F. Ricketts and Jack Calvin, *Between Pacific Tides*. Stanford, California, Stanford University Press.

Leonard P. Schultz and Edith M. Stern, *Ways of Fishes*. New York, D. Van Nostrand Company.

Leonard J. Grant, ed., *Wondrous World of Fishes*. Washington, D.C., National Geographic Society.

F. D. Ommanney, *The Fishes*. Chicago, Time-Life Books.

Working with Others

There are many phases of water life that you can undertake on your own—special studies, photography, collections of many kinds. There are others that need to be developed into group projects, still others for which you may require assistance.

Because of the tremendously varied aspects of water life, there may not be any person in your vicinity specializing in the subject you have picked. Nevertheless, it should be worth your while to check with the local biology teacher or biology professor to get whatever suggestions they may have to offer.

If your main pursuit involves fishes, contact your local game warden and find out whether any federal, state, or private hatcheries are located nearby.

For a more scientific approach to water life, join a national society specializing in the subject, and take part in its work.

SOCIETIES—American Society of Limnology and Oceanography. Headquarters: Oregon State University, Corvallis, Oregon 97331. Periodical: *Limnology and Oceanography*.

American Society of Ichthyologists and Herpetologists. Headquarters: United States National Museum, Washington, D.C. 20560. Periodical: *Copeia*.

FIELD STUDY OF WATER LIFE

Equipment for Water-life Study

CLOTHING—Any type of outdoor clothing will do for water-life study, where it is a matter of walking along a lake shore, wading along the beach, rowing or boating. But since you will have to risk getting wet, pick a material that will dry easily.

To protect your feet against cuts from shells and barnacles, use a pair of sneakers or, better, for walking on wet rocks, a pair of old leather shoes. For certain jobs, you may decide to bring along rubber waders.

For more intensive work, where you may have to submerge in

order to get hold of specimens, you will, of course, get into a bathing suit.

SKIN-DIVING EQUIPMENT—Skin diving provides the greatest possible thrill in studying water life.

For ordinary skin diving, you need only a few pieces of simple equipment: a diving mask fitting close around your eyes and nose, with an oval window of safety glass; a snorkel consisting of a plastic or aluminum tube with a hard-rubber mouthpiece; swimming fins for easy propulsion.

While ordinary skin diving requires only a fair amount of swimming ability, scuba diving (with self-contained underwater breathing apparatus) is ABSOLUTELY and POSITIVELY for only expert swimmers in excellent health who have a clear judgment of the dangers involved. Scuba divers use specialized breathing equipment made up of a diving mask connected to an air tank containing compressed air. Other equipment may consist of swimming fins, a rubber suit for prolonged stays in the water, a waterproof watch to determine the length of your stay, a waterproof compass to show directions taken underwater, a weighted diving belt with quick-release buckle for easier descents.

BOOKS ON SKIN DIVING—Jacques-Yves Cousteau and others, *Complete Manual of Free Diving*. New York, G. P. Putnam's Sons.

A. P. Balder, *Complete Manual of Skin Diving*. New York, The Macmillan Company.

George Sullivan, *The Complete Book of Skin and Scuba Diving*. New York, Coward-McCann.

Wheeler J. North, *The Golden Guide to Scuba Diving*. New York, Golden Press.

STUDY EQUIPMENT—Waterscope—Light reflected from the water surface makes it almost impossible to observe the life below unless you provide yourself with a waterscope. This is simply a waterproof box or tube with a transparent bottom. To use it you push the bottom under the water's surface and bring your eyes close to the upper, open end.

A WOODEN WATERSCOPE can be made from a bucket or a box. Cut a square hole in the bottom. Cut a piece of plate glass slightly larger than the hole. Fasten it in position with strips of wood, making it watertight with putty or aquarium cement. Then paint the inside of the waterscope black. To use it, simply float it on the water.

A METAL WATERSCOPE can be made from a 2-foot length of 4-inch stovepipe by providing it with a window of $\frac{1}{16}$-inch plexiglass, cut to a diameter of 4 inches. Seal the seam of the pipe and attach the window in one end with waterproof adhesive tape. Shape the upper edge of the stovepipe to fit your face and cover it with adhesive tape for protection. Blacken the inside.

¶ *Tip*—For a quickly made *plastic waterscope*, use a half-gallon plastic bleach bottle. Cut off the top and shape the edge to fit your face. Spray the inside with black enamel. Cut out the bottom to within ½-inch of the side, and cement a piece of plexiglass into position as a transparent bottom. Even simpler: Instead of using a plexiglass bottom, place the bottle in a bag of clear, heavyweight plastic and hold the top of the bag in place around the top of the bottle with a strong rubber band.

Flashlight—For night hunting of frogs, salamanders, crayfish, and night insects, you will need a good flashlight.

¶ *Tip*—You can use your flashlight for observing underwater life at night. Place the lighted flashlight, with the light switch locked, lens down, in a glass jar. Add a couple of stones for ballast. Screw the jar top on tightly. Tie a line around the neck of the jar. When the jar is lowered into the water, the flashlight will light up the surroundings.

Magnifiers—For the identification of many of the minute specimens you come upon, you will need a good magnifying glass. A folding-type pocket magnifier, magnifying up to twenty times, will serve you in most cases (see page 151). A great number of water creatures are so small that they can be seen only in a microscope under laboratory conditions; this takes them out of the realm of field study.

Water-life books—To satisfy your curiosity, you will want to take along on your field trips a guide book designed to give you an idea of the multitude of things you see at lake, stream, or seashore.

BOOKS FOR GENERAL IDENTIFICATION—FRESHWATER—Elsie B. Klots, *New Field Book of Freshwater Life*. New York, G. P. Putnam's Sons.

Leon A. Hausman, *Beginner's Guide to Fresh Water Life*. New York, G. P. Putnam's Sons.

SALT WATER—Roy Waldo Miner, *Field Book of Seashore Life*. New York, G. P. Putnam's Sons.

Leon A. Hausman, *Beginner's Guide to Seashore Life*. New York, G. P. Putnam's Sons.

In case you specialize in certain features of water life, choose a book that treats your specialty comprehensively.

BOOKS FOR FIELD IDENTIFICATION—FISHES—Ray Schrenkeisen, *Field Book of Fresh-Water Fishes of North America*. New York, G. P. Putnam's Sons.

Charles M. Breder, Jr., *Field Book of Marine Fishes of the Atlantic Coast*. New York, G. P. Putnam's Sons.

Lionel A. Walford, *Marine Game Fishes of the Pacific Coast*. Berkeley, California, University of California Press.

AMPHIBIANS—Albert H. and Anna A. Wright, *Handbook of Frogs and Toads of the United States and Canada*. Ithaca, New York, Cornell University Press.

Roger Conant, *Field Guide to Reptiles and Amphibians*. Boston, Houghton Mifflin Company.

MOLLUSKS—See page 226.

AQUATIC REPTILES—See Snake chapter.

AQUATIC INSECTS—See Insect chapter.

Notebook—Your notebook will get wet from time to time—you won't be able to help it. So pick a book with a sturdy waterproof cover and with pages of good quality paper that won't soak up water and thus obliterate your notes.

CATCHING EQUIPMENT—See section starting on page 200.

Finding Water Life

"Where'll I find water life?" The answer seems obvious: "Wherever there is water!" Such an answer might be satisfactory in your early hunts.

But the moment you want to find specific water creatures, it no longer suffices. You have to look for them in the kinds of water they favor, and the part of such water that suits their living conditions.

WHERE?—Freshwater—The depth of the water and the speed with which it moves have a profound influence on freshwater life.

You will want to search all types of waters, but you will probably find the greatest variety of freshwater life in the quiet waters of a pond. A POND, as defined by Ann Morgan, is "a body of water that is so shallow that rooted water plants can grow all the way across it." This definition fits bodies of water in meadows and woods, swamps and marshes. In such ponds, you may locate the whole gamut of freshwater life from microscopic protozoans to large fishes.

Even within a pond, there are several comparatively well-defined zones, depending to a great extent on the plant life. Plants that emerge from the water—cattails, rushes, pickerel weed, and others—harbor certain kinds of animal life attached to their stalks. Plants with leaves that float on the surface shelter a number of fishes, and provide rafts topside for small turtles and young bullfrogs, bottomside for snails and water mites, sponges and eggs. The tangled growth of completely submerged plants is the lurking place for still other types of water creatures. In addition, there are the animals that dig themselves into the pond bottom or hide under rocks, those that travel on or just below the surface, those that spend part of their lives in the water, part of it on the surrounding land.

For other kinds of freshwater life you will turn to our various types of LAKES. Our more prominent freshwater fishes—salmon, trout, whitefishes—are found in deep, cold lakes, scientifically known as *oligotrophic*. Lakes that are shallower and warmer—*eutrophic* lakes—have a greater variety of water life. Brown and acid lakes—*dystrophic* lakes—have their own kind of plant and animal life.

As you study moving waters, you will find that certain animals are thoroughly at home in the slow waters of a wide RIVER, others prefer a fast-moving STREAM, still others the rushing waters of a mountain BROOK.

WHERE?—Salt water—Starting from the SPLASH AREA, where marine fauna meets land fauna in the sea wrack of high tide, you can travel seaward, finding different types of creatures as you move farther and still farther out.

The LITTORAL ZONE takes in the shore area from high-tide to low-tide level, continuing along sea bottom to a depth of about 300 feet. Its animal life, to a great extent, can be classed as *benthos*—"of the bottom"—moving slowly along the sea bottom or attached to it.

The PELAGIC ZONE is the open sea, as deep as light will penetrate, with its numerous forms of swimming animals—*nekton*—and still more numerous passively floating forms—*plankton*—ranging from microscopic creatures to jelly fishes up to 7 feet in diameter.

The ABYSSAL ZONE refers to the ocean depths, where sea animals live in the darkness under enormous water pressure.

You will have little chance to study the life of the abyssal zone unless you happen to be an "aquanaut." As far as the pelagic zone is concerned, your studies will have to be by boat or through the cooperation of the fishermen along our shores. The littoral zone is your most satisfactory hunting ground. Within this zone, the character of the shore and the tide determine the animals you will find.

Generally speaking, shores may be classified as muddy, sandy, or rocky, although there often is some overlapping among them. In mud flats, you will find mostly clams, snails, certain worms, and crabs. The same animals are found along sandy shores. Some of them are on top of mud or sand; most of them you will have to dig for. Rocky shores—especially shores with small tide pools—will give you a far better harvest. Here you may find barnacles and periwinkles, limpets and chitons, sea urchins and starfish, sea anemones and crabs, and often specimens of small fishes. Some of the animals are in plain sight; others you discover by turning over rocks and looking among seaweeds. In addition to looking on the shore itself, look for animal life on wharf piles, and on jetsam and flotsam found along the shore.

WHEN?—Time of year—The best seasons are spring and summer, when water life is at its busiest. Fall is fair, and observations can be made even in winter. There is plenty of life to study in open brooks and under the icy surface of ponds and lakes, although many of the animals have gone into winter quarters deep in the bottom's mud.

Time of day—The majority of water animals are active in the daytime—especially if the weather is sunny. Some make their appearance mostly at night—frogs, some of the salamanders, crayfishes, certain insects.

Catching Water Life

With such great variation in water life, a great variety of catching methods is necessary. Pick the method that best suits your purpose or combine a number of them to accomplish your aim.

Note—Remember that federal and state laws prohibit certain catching methods and govern the taking of some fishes, lobsters

Ward's Natural Science Establishment, Inc.

Apron net keeps debris away from your catch. Aquatic dip net resembles insect net but has D-shaped frame.

and crayfish, edible frogs and turtles, oysters and clams, and a few other water animals. Find out what the laws are and get the necessary permits.

WATER DIP NETTING—Netting with a dip net is a common method of catching water life.

Dip net—The aquatic net used for catching water insects (see page 161) is suitable for catching other water creatures as well. Many collectors prefer a somewhat smaller net—about 9 inches in diameter, 10 inches deep; or even smaller, 5 inches in diameter and 5 inches deep. The handle should be 3 to 4 feet long. The same frame may be provided with several replaceable nets of coarse, medium, and fine silk bolting cloth or brussels netting.

¶ *Tip*—A kitchen wire strainer makes an excellent dip net. It may be attached to a handle of suitable length. If the wire screen is too open, line it with cheesecloth.

Using the net—The dip net can be used to scoop up small swimming animals. Or it can be used for general water sweeping—moving it back and forth among water plants, from the surface of the water to the bottom, eventually picking up some of the bottom mud.

From time to time, empty the net into a container in which you can study your catch.

PLANKTON SWEEPING—The tiny animals which, with various algae, float in the water are collected with a special type of net.

Plankton net—The plankton net consists of a conical bag made of a rather tightly woven material that permits the water to run through but retains the minute solid matter. You can make it from silk bolting cloth or woven nylon.

Use 15 inches of yard-wide material. Cut it diagonally, then sew the two pieces together into a triangle. Sew the two sides of the triangle together, in this way forming a cone. Cut the tip off the cone, making an opening about ¾ inch in diameter. Hem the material around this opening, and sew on here a 6-inch piece of tape to be used to tie up the opening. Sew the open end of the cone to a brass wire ring, 9 inches in diameter. Fasten three pieces of mason line or thin brass chain, 2 feet long, to the wire ring, equal distances apart. Tie the free ends of the lines together.

Using the plankton net—For sweeping a pond, tie the lines of the plankton net to a pole, and move the net, with the tip tied up, slowly back and forth in the water. For sweeping in lake or ocean, attach a rope to the net lines and tow the net behind a boat.

After a couple of minutes of sweeping, pull the net out of the water. Let the water drain out until only a small amount is left. Open up the tip of the net and drop the remaining water with its concentrated plankton contents into a jar.

DIGGING AND TURNING—A great number of freshwater and marine animals spend their lives hiding on the bottom. To find them, you must dig up sand or mud and turn over rocks.

For investigating small quantities of mud, the dip net or a sieve may be used. In digging for worms and clams, you will need a more substantial tool—a short-handled shovel or a narrow-bladed spade.

¶ *Tip*—A strong garden rake comes in handy for digging up clams—unless you prefer to use a regular clam rake specifically designed for the purpose.

PRYING—Animals attached to rocks or wharf piles—sea anemones, barnacles, chitons, limpets, mussels, and others—usually can be pried or cut loose with the point of a strong knife. In collecting abalones, a light wrecking bar or a tire iron is in order.

ANGLING—For medium- and large-sized fishes, you may have to resort to one of the many forms of angling: *still fishing* with pole and bait, *trolling* from a slowly moving boat, *bait casting* with rod, reel, and plug, *surf casting* along the ocean shore, *fly casting* with wet or dry flies.

OTHER METHODS—In addition to the more conventional methods, others may be devised for special purposes.

Jacklighting—You can catch frogs and other amphibians most easily at night—especially during the breeding season of early spring—by hunting for them along the water's edge. Wade slowly, a few feet from the shore, equipped with a flashlight and a bag for carrying your catch. When you locate a frog by its singing, blind it temporarily by playing the flashlight beam in its eyes, then pick it up by hand.

¶ *Tip*—If you are interested in seeing one of the most beautiful sights in nature, place the battery end of the flashlight at your nose tip while you bend over until the light shines in the bullfrog's eyes. As the frog moves its eyes slightly, you will see brilliant flashes of topaz, emerald, ruby, and sapphire.

¶ *Tip*—Try a "frog raft": Fasten a lighted candle to the middle of a 1-foot piece of 1-inch board with candle drippings. Float it in the water. Watch for passengers.

Trapping—Lobsters, crabs, and octopi are usually caught in box-like traps—"lobster pots"—made of wire netting or slats, with one or two entrances. The traps are baited with fish heads or entrails and lowered to the sea bottom. "Minnow traps" are used for small fishes.

Baiting—Strips of meat, anchored at the edge of a pond, are almost certain to attract various freshwater worms and nymphs of aquatic insects.

"Weeding"—Numerous species of water life attach themselves to stalks and leaves of plants growing in the water. The simplest way of obtaining them consists in "weeding" the plants by pulling with the hands or with a rake, then picking off the specimens or scraping them off with a fingernail or a dull knife into a dish of water.

Commercial methods—A number of special methods for catching water animals—specifically in the ocean—are employed by professional fishermen. Obtain their help if your studies involve the water life of the open sea.

INVESTIGATING YOUR CATCH—Catching water life is to a great extent a matter of "catch-as-catch-can." You grab—and what you get, you get. Your next job is to separate your catch into its component parts and pick out the animals you intend to study.

The simplest method is to drop your catch into a shallow pan—a white-painted pie plate or something larger—with a small amount of water.

¶ *Tip*—Photographic developing trays, 6 by 8 inches, 9 by 11, or 12 by 15, make excellent study trays.

For larger specimens and jumping amphibians, use a deep white-enameled dishpan or an enamel pail.

TRANSPORTING YOUR CATCH—Carry home your catch in mason or mayonnaise jars. It is not advisable to put the top on. Instead, fit a screen-wire lid over the opening. Tie a line around the neck so that you can carry the jar in a hanging position. In this way, there is less chance of the water swishing out.

¶ *Tip*—A long narrow bag of a sturdy plastic may serve your purpose. It is easy to carry: You just attach it to your belt.

Fishes may be transported in a pail covered with a perforated lid or in a live-bait container such as is used by fishermen.

Mollusks and crustaceans should not be carried in water. You have a better chance of keeping them alive if you pack them in wet moss or seaweed. The same goes for many of the salt-water creatures, with the exception of fishes.

Frogs and salamanders, similarly, should be carried home packed in moist moss to keep their skin from drying out. Their eggs and tadpoles, on the other hand, must be transported in water.

Water-life Lists

In trying to find out about the water life in your territory, you will soon discover that you will have to specialize. The amount of material is just too immense and unwieldy. You can approach the subject from a couple of angles.

You may decide to concentrate on one specific phylum (mollusks, for instance), or a class within that phylum (as represented, in this case, by chitons, snails, tusk shells, bivalves, and squids), or an order within one of these classes (among bivalves, you have the choice of mussels, clams, scallops, oysters, and shipworms), or even a single family within an order—and you will still have plenty to do.

Or you may take an ecological approach and attempt to find out all you can about the water life of a tide pool, a forest lake, a brook, a drainage ditch, or whatever strikes your fancy.

LISTING—The only way you can achieve results is by keeping a careful check of your discoveries. Make thorough notebook records of each field trip, with complete listing of species, their location, and the conditions under which you found them. By making such a listing on a yearly basis, you will be able to ascertain the fluctuation in water life through the seasons.

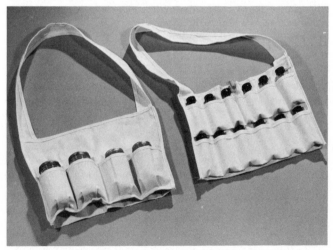

Ward's Natural Science Establishment, Inc.

For water life study, buy or make up your own collecting "apron" with pockets for unbreakable plastic containers.

Field Observations

Because of the difficulty of studying water life in the field, there are great gaps in our knowledge regarding aquatic animals. Your chances of filling some of these gaps are excellent. The following listing may suggest some avenues you may want to pursue.

Influence of surroundings on water life—What are the differences between life in a forest pond, marsh bog, lake, meadow stream, mountain brook, and so on? What causes these differences?

Influence of weather—How are water animals influenced by temperature, sunlight, wind, and other weather conditions?

Locomotion—What fins are used by various fishes, and how, at different speeds, for backing, breaking, stopping? Certain burrowing water animals are said to disappear with "lightning speed" when exposed. What is their actual speed?

Senses—What is the reaction to visual stimuli, to sounds produced in and out of the water, to food of various smells and flavors, to touch?

Sites of various fishes used for feeding, resting, nesting.

Mating habits—Courtship, if any; fertilization.

Egg deposits—Fish eggs, unprotected, hidden, or in nests. Eggs of insects, snails, amphibians. What methods of attachment, arrangement, numbers?

Length of time for incubation of eggs. Length of immature stage—nymph, larva, tadpole, etc.

Depth studies—What water levels are preferred by game fishes, by forage ("rough") fishes? What conditions influence these levels?

Length-weight-age relationship in fishes. What effect has water mass, amount of food, number of specimens, and so on, on fish growth?

Note—Just as a tree's age is revealed by growth rings, the age of certain fish can be read in their scales, through a magnifier. At various times during the year, minute rings, circuli, form on the surface of the scales. These rings develop close together in winter, farther apart in summer, thus forming yearly growth patterns, annuli. The number of annuli tells the age of the fish.

"Music" of frogs and toads—Uses of calls—warning, courtship, no apparent use, and so on. When does singing start; when does it stop—dates, time of day?

RECORDINGS—*Voices of the Night.* Calls of twenty-six frogs and toads of Eastern North America. Cornell University Records, Ithaca, New York.

Special problems—Feeding cycles and habits. Parasites and diseases. Hibernation, aestivation—reaction to freezing and drought.

KEEPING WATER LIFE

By keeping fishes and other water animals, you can establish a small world and observe the life that goes on in it. The opportunities are as great as your fancy dictates—from a small tumbler for a culture of mosquito wrigglers, through an aquarium and a garden pool, to a specially constructed pond.

BOOK—James G. Needham, *Culture Methods for Invertebrate Animals*. New York, Dover Publications.

Conventional Freshwater Aquarium

The conventional freshwater aquarium is easy to establish and easy to keep up if you follow the simple requirements that are necessary for success in regard to size of tank, temperature, light and feeding.

BOOK—William T. Innes, *The Modern Aquarium*. Norristown, Pennsylvania, Aquarium Publishing Company.

PERIODICAL—*Aquarium Magazine* (monthly). Norristown, Pennsylvania, Aquarium Publishing Company.

SOCIETY—Aquarium Society. Headquarters: American Museum of Natural History, Seventy-ninth Street and Central Park West, New York, New York 10024.

AQUARIUM TANKS—The size of the aquarium is governed by the type and amount of water life you expect to study.

All animals require oxygen to sustain life. Water animals meet their needs from the oxygen absorbed by the water through its surface contacts with the air. The larger the water surface, the more oxygen can be absorbed and subsequently the more life sustained. Stating it differently: More animal life can be supported in a certain amount of water in a shallow tank where the surface is large, than can be supported in the same amount of water in a deep tank with a much smaller water surface.

The important thing, then, is to obtain a tank that is large enough in water surface area, and at the same time deep enough to make observation possible. Some expert aquarists recommend 10 square inches of surface for each inch (not counting the tail) of our native fishes and a depth of not much beyond 12 inches, unless artificial aeration is provided by an "aerator"—an electrically powered pump that forces air up through the water to ensure oxygen saturation. Other experts suggest 1 inch of fish (exclusive of tail) per gallon of water without aeration, and double the amount of fish with aeration.

All kinds of aquarium tanks, stands, and other aquarium equipment may be bought from most of the biological supply houses, as well as from local firms and business houses specializing in aquarium supplies.

SUPPLIES—Look in your telephone book under "Aquarium" and under "Pets." Also check local variety stores.

Biological supply houses. (Addresses on page 27.)

Jewel Aquarium Company, 5005 West Armitage Avenue, Chicago, Illinois 60639.

Aquarium Stock Company, 27 Murray Street, New York, New York 10007.

Ward's Natural Science Establishment, Inc.

Frameless aquarium is constructed of clear glass joined with a cement that is invisible, leakproof, and permanent.

Jewel Aquarium Company

Conventional aquarium tank has welded angle-iron frame and glass in correct thickness to provide maximum safety.

Aquarium Systems, Inc., 1450 East 289th Street, Wickliffe, Ohio 44092. (Specializes in marine aquaria.)

Common aquarium tanks are of the following dimensions:

Approx. capacity	Length	Width	Depth	Square-inch surface area
5 gal.	14″	8″	10″	112
8 gal.	18″	9″	12″	162
10 gal.	20″	10″	12″	200
15 gal.	24″	12″	12″	288
20 gal.	30″	12″	14″	360
25 gal.	36″	12″	14″	432
30 gal.	36″	14″	14″	504
40 gal.	36″	16″	16″	576

¶ *Tip*—To find out the capacity of a tank, multiply the length in inches by the width and depth, then divide that figure by 231 to get the number of U.S. gallons.

For most purposes, you will be better off with several smaller tanks, of 10 gallons, say, rather than with one or two large tanks.

Frameless tanks—In the all-glass frameless tank, all sides are clear plate glass with their edges firmly joined with invisible, leak-proof, permanent cement. The result is distortion-free vision.

Fiberglass tanks—These tanks have three sides and bottom made of chemically inert fiberglass. The front is a heavy plate-glass window firmly cemented in place.

Metal-frame tanks—The metal-frame tank is the most popular. Modern commercial tanks are usually made with frames of stainless steel or welded angle iron, plate-glass sides, and blackboard-slate bottoms.

ESTABLISHING THE CONVENTIONAL AQUARIUM—Before starting the aquarium, make sure that the tank is waterproof. Fill it and let it stand overnight. If the tank leaks, make the necessary repairs. Then place the aquarium tank in its permanent location and set out to equip it with a sandy bottom, water, water plants, and animal life.

Location and light—Place the aquarium where the temperature will be fairly constant; 60 to 70 degrees Fahrenheit is ideal. The proper temperature is important for the health of the water life—not just for keeping it normally active, but also for providing the proper amount of oxygen. At higher temperatures, water loses some of its oxygen and does not absorb it as readily.

A certain amount of light is necessary—enough to "read fine print by." Sufficient light is particularly important if you intend to have plants in your aquarium. Sunlight is unnecessary; indirect light throughout the day is better. A window to the north or east is an excellent aquarium location.

¶ *Tip*—If exposure to daylight is not sufficient or feasible, use an electric light instead—whether an incandescent bulb, a fluorescent tube suspended over the tank, or a commercial aquarium reflector.

Putting in sandy bottom—For anchoring water plants and for providing spawning beds for fishes and hiding places for certain water animals, place a thin layer of coarse sand or fine gravel on the bottom of the aquarium. Clean the sand first by washing it a number of times until ʰthe washing water comes out clean. Put it in position in such a way that the layer is 2 inches at one end of the tank, decreasing to about 1 inch at the other. Debris in the finished aquarium will tend to move toward the lower level from which it can be removed.

Water—When the sand bottom has been firmed down, pour in the water, half filling the tank. The water used can be clear pond water, rainwater, or tap water.

¶ *Tip*—To prevent the water pouring from stirring up the sand, place a piece of paper on top of the sand, and pour the water on it. Or place a saucer in one corner and pour slowly into this.

Plants—Plants are not essential, but they add greatly to the appearance of the aquarium by making it look more like the fishes' natural habitat.

The most popular aquarium plants are two ready-rooters with tapelike leaves: tapegrass or eelgrass, *Vallisneria*, and narrow-leaved arrowhead, *Sagittaria*. Also popular are three nonrooting, plumelike plants: water milfoil or foxtail, *Myriophyllum*; fanwort, *Cabomba*; and waterweed, *Anacharis* (formerly known as *Elodea*).

You may be able to find some or all of these in a local pond or lake. Otherwise, buy bundles of one or more plants from each of the two groups from a supply house.

In planting, place the rooting plants in such a way that the sand just covers the roots up to the crown. In the case of the nonrooting plants, push the bottom part of the stalks well down into the sand. If the nonrooters don't seem to stay put, keep them down by tying them to small stones. Do not overplant. A dozen sprays or so is enough for a 5-gallon aquarium.

When the planting is completed, pour in more water until it comes to a point just above the lower edge of the frame. Be careful in this final pouring or you may uproot the plants. Hold one hand just under the water surface and pour the water into this hand from a pitcher held in the other hand.

Stocking the aquarium—Leave the aquarium for a couple of days to permit the water to clear and the plants to get themselves established. Then introduce the fishes or other water animals.

MAINTAINING THE AQUARIUM—If the aquarium has been properly established, you should have little trouble maintaining it and keeping your water animals healthy.

Feeding—In the case of fishes, find out what food they eat in their natural surroundings by your own investigation or from a field book. If no information is available, experiment. You can be fairly certain that some or all of the following live foods are acceptable: daphnias, cyclops, tubifex worms, aquatic insect larvae and nymphs, mealworms. Most of these you can scoop out of a local pond. Of some of them, you can keep a culture going for all-year feeding—daphnias (water fleas), see page 213; tubifex worms, see page 213; mealworms, see page 170.

Earthworms also rank high as fish food—whole, cut in pieces, or chopped.

¶ *Tip*—You may be accustomed to digging for earthworms. It is easier to locate them at night, especially after a rain or a garden-hose soaking when they come up to the surface. Search for them with a flashlight, with the beam covered with red cellophane.

¶ *Tip*—You can establish an *earthworm culture* in a wooden box or tub, protected against rotting with a coating of melted paraffin, or in a deep plastic basin. Fill it with about 10 inches of good garden soil, moistened but not wet. Place 50 to 100 earthworms on the soil; cover them with a thin layer of decaying leaves. Every week or so, replenish the diet, varying it with wet coffee grounds, cornmeal, powdered milk, bread crumbs, leftover boiled vegetables. Keep the soil moist, but never let it get soggy. Check evaporation by covering the container with a damp burlap bag or several sheets of wet newspapers. In the wintertime, keep the container in a cool cellar. In the summer, embed it outdoors in the ground to within a few inches from the top in a cool shady place.

¶ *Tip*—Enchytra worms, "white worms," may be raised in the same manner. Collect the specimens for starting from around a compost heap, or buy them from a supply house.

Although you will probably prefer to use native food for your aquarium animals, you may occasionally have to resort to chopped raw meat, or hard-boiled egg yolk, or commercial aquarium fish food purchasable from a local pet shop.

The main point in feeding is: DON'T OVERFEED. Feed only once a day. Sprinkle a little of the food on the water and see how it is accepted; then add a little more.

Any food not eaten after about ten minutes should be removed from the bottom of the tank with a glass tube. Cover one end of a regular glass tube or an aquarium dip tube with your finger. Bring the other end down to the refuse on the bottom of the tank. Raise your finger. The water will rush into the glass tube, carrying the refuse with it. Again close the top end of the tube. Lift the tube out of the tank and get rid of its contents.

"Green water"—Occasionally, aquarium water turns green, and a green film settles on the glass sides and plants. This does not affect the health of the water animals, but it makes observation difficult.

The color is caused by green algae. The reason for their development is usually that the aquarium has been exposed to too much light. Therefore, the best remedy is to remove the tank to a less lighted location where the condition generally clears itself up.

To help clear the water, scrape the algae off the glass sides with a razor blade pushed T-wise into a short stick of wood. When the algae have settled on the bottom, take them out with a dip tube.

¶ *Tip*—The introduction of half a dozen pond snails into the

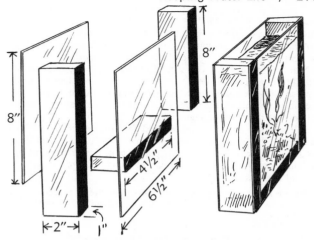

A miniature aquarium for small water animals and aquatic insects made from glass and wood, or pieces of plastic.

aquarium will help to check the green water conditions. The snails eat the algae. In addition, they eat the remains of fish food and act as general scavengers.

Water changing—It should be your aim to have an aquarium that will maintain itself without any water changing. If you follow the recommendations given above, no changing should be necessary. All you have to do is add a little water from time to time to keep the water level constant.

¶ *Tip*—To keep the evaporation low and to prevent dust from falling into the water, cover the tank with a piece of window glass. Cement small pieces of cork to the corners so that the glass plate will be raised slightly to permit free access of air, or use commercial clips designed for this purpose.

Special Aquariums

Practically all freshwater animals will thrive well in the conventional aquarium. But for a number of them, a much simpler arrangement can be used. Also, in some instances, a much smaller water container is preferable. These can range in size from a miniature aquarium—"miniquarium"—of ½- to 1-quart capacity, to a small aquarium of up to 2-gallon capacity, glass or clear plastic.

Whatever you place in these smaller aquariums, do not keep any animals in the same container with the enemies that prey on them— unless you are planning to study their reaction to each other.

MINIQUARIUM—Tiny animals thrive in an ordinary water glass or in a jar, and you can readily observe them there. The chief disadvantage of this kind of "miniquarium" is that the cylindrical glass wall makes observation uncertain by distorting the view.

A far superior miniquarium can be made from two pieces of glass or clear plastic, 6 by 8 inches, and three pieces of $\frac{3}{4}$-inch plexiglass or wood, 2 inches wide, two side pieces 8 inches long, and a $4\frac{1}{2}$-inch-long bottom piece. Cement the three pieces together with epoxy to form a U. (If you use wood, apply cement, nail them together, then shellac them and let them dry.) Cement the two glass pieces to the frame. (See illustration, page 211).

Still another miniquarium method for studying water life is the "Living Lab" principle developed by Ward's Biological Supply House. This makes use of strong plastic bags that can be put up on individual cardboard frames or can be hung on wire brackets on a vertical pegboard panel.

¶ *Tip*—For the kind of small animals you intend to raise, a deep plastic refrigerator storage container or vegetable crisper may be just right.

Raising Water Animals

SMALL WATER ANIMALS—For some small water animals, you will make use of a miniquarium or other small aquarium. For others, different arrangements are more suitable.

Some of the animals feed on minute plant and animal life in the water from the pond in which they were found; others like a supply of daphnias.

Hydras—Hydras, which look like half-inch pieces of string with one end frayed, can be picked off the undersides of waterlily leaves or from submerged plant stems in freshwater ponds. You will probably also find them in a scoopful of bottom material, with many other freshwater creatures, among decaying leaves.

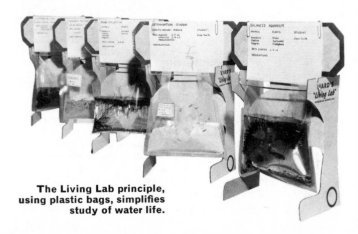

The Living Lab principle, using plastic bags, simplifies study of water life.

Bring them home in some of the water in which you find them. Keep them in a miniquarium and feed them daphnias.

Planarians—These quarter-inch to half-inch worms, used extensively in biological regeneration studies, hide in shallow water under stones and trash, or hang onto grasses that trail into the water from the streamside.

You can bait them by placing several thin strips of raw meat or liver along the edge of a slow-flowing stream, with part of the meat out of the water. Check from time to time, and shake the planarians that may have gathered into a jar of water.

¶ *Tip*—Try using a planarian trap: Cut the top and bottom off a frozen-juice can. Flatten the can to within $\frac{1}{2}$-inch by stepping on it. Make two nail holes through the flattened part, opposite to each other. Push a sliver of meat into the can and keep it in place by pushing a nail through the holes in the can and through the meat. In the evening, anchor the trap near the water's edge in a pond or a slow-moving stream. Tend the trap in the morning.

Raise the planarians in clear pond water in an enamel or plastic pan about 3 inches deep. Cover the pan with a piece of cardboard to shut out the light. Every few days, feed the planarians with a small piece of meat. When they have gorged themselves, remove the remaining food and change the water.

Tubifex worms—Tubifex worms—also called sludge, red, and mud worms—live in tubes they form in soft mud in stagnant pools. You can catch them by the hundreds by screening mud through a fine-meshed net or sieve.

You can establish a tubifex culture in a shallow dishpan. Pour in a 2-inch-deep layer of mud in which the worms are found. Add an extra inch of pond water.

Leeches—Leeches hang on to rocks or submerged logs with the help of strong suckers. If you wade in a leech-infested pond, some of them will probably attach themselves to your bare legs or even to your wading boots. You can remove them easily by pushing a knife point under the suckers.

Leeches can be kept in clear pond water—or in tap water, for that matter—in an ordinary gallon jar. Place the container in a dark spot. Feed them every couple of weeks by netting them out of their container and putting them in a finger bowl or cup in which you have placed a piece of raw beef or liver. When they have had their fill, wash them off with clean water and return them to their container.

Leeches have a way of crawling out of the container in which they are kept. So keep it covered with a piece of gauze held in place with string or rubber band.

Daphnias—These tiny creatures, commonly known as water fleas, are important as food for other forms of water life. For a small culture, sweep them out of the pond in which they live with a dip net of rather fine nylon, then place them in pond water in a small glass container.

¶ *Tip*—You can raise a large culture of daphnias to be used as fish food in a wood tub or a plastic garbage pail placed in a cool location. Add 1 ounce of dried sheep, cow, or horse manure per gallon of water; throw in a few lettuce leaves from time to time.

Crayfish—Crayfish can be raised in a gallon jar or in a couple of inches of water in a dishpan. Place a few handfuls of pebbles on the bottom to provide hiding places. Feed them water insects, chopped earthworms, or tiny pieces of raw meat.

¶ *Tip*—If some of the crayfish you catch in the fall or early spring happen to be females with eggs attached to their swimmerets, you may have the chance to see the eggs hatching into tiny crayfish.

Aquatic insects—Insect larvae, nymphs, water bugs, and water beetles can be raised in quart jars or miniquariums. Place a small amount of sand on the bottom and insert a spray of some water plant. Part of the plant should be above water so that an emerging adult of dragonfly or damsel fly, for instance, may be able to crawl out of the water. Cover the container with a lid of wire screening to prevent a flying insect from escaping.

¶ *Tip*—By using a plastic shoe box for an aquarium for water boatmen, water striders, back swimmers, and whirligig beetles, you will have an excellent chance of following their antics.

Some of the insects will feed on plant particles and on the algae in the pond water. Others are carnivorous and require small insects, mosquito wrigglers, daphnia, and the like. Dip-net sweepings should satisfy most of them.

The peculiar "houses" of caddis larvae can be observed best in a shallow pan, such as a photographic developing tray.

Freshwater snails—Snails will get along well in a container, quart-sized or larger, filled with the "green water" of a stagnant pool, or with an inch or so of bottom mud and a couple of water plants.

AMPHIBIANS—Raise salamanders, frogs, and toads from eggs. Locate the eggs yourself during the spring and early summer. Eggs of most salamanders are attached singly on water plants, with a leaf bent down over each of them. Pickerel and leopard frogs lay their eggs in large tapiocalike masses attached to some water plant, bullfrogs and green frogs in floating surface films. The eggs of toads are laid in long double "pearl" strings. Bring home the eggs in water in a jar.

Place the eggs in water in an ordinary gallon jar. Or use a white-glass battery jar. These jars come in three sizes—1-gallon (6 inches diameter, 8 inches deep), 2-gallon (8 inches diameter, 9 inches deep), 3-gallon (9 inches diameter, 12 inches deep).

When the tadpoles begin to come out, plan to keep only a couple of dozen; return the remaining eggs to the pond where you got them.

Salamander larvae feed on insects and insect larvae; tadpoles live on algae and other water plants. All of them will get along beautifully on dip-net sweepings.

¶ *Tip*—The job of feeding tadpoles becomes even simpler if you raise them on cornmeal. Sprinkle a little meal in the water daily. Remove excess food with a dip tube.

When the tadpoles approach the adult stage, you need to make it possible for the fully grown amphibians to leave the water. Place a stone in the water with part of it above the surface, or float a piece of wood in it. The metamorphosis of most amphibians takes place in the same year. The green frog and the red-legged frog require two years, the bullfrog two to four years.

As the salamanders, frogs, or toads come out of the water, transfer them to a shallow aquarium in which one side of the sand bottom has been built up into an above-water bank, or better, to a woodland terrarium (see page 242) containing a shallow dish of water. The adult amphibians are carnivores. Feed them live, moving insects, caterpillars, mealworms, earthworms, slugs, or dangle tiny pieces of lean meat or liver in front of their eyes.

TURTLES—Small turtles may be raised in the same type of aquarium or terrarium as adult amphibians. They get along on a diet of snails, tadpoles, and small fishes.

Marine Aquarium

While keeping the freshwater aquarium is a fairly simple matter, the marine saltwater aquarium presents two problems that are often hard to overcome.

The first of these is the problem of temperature. Sea animals are accustomed to much lower temperatures than freshwater animals. Unless you can manage to keep the water temperature around 50 to 60 degrees Fahrenheit, you cannot expect the animals to thrive. You may be able to keep the proper temperature in the wintertime but it will prove a major concern during the summer months.

¶ *Tip*—You can lower the temperature of aquarium water by placing in it a leak-proof ice bag or hot-water bottle filled with ice water or crushed ice.

The second problem is that of sufficient oxygen. Wind and waves whip air into ocean water. The oxygen content is therefore much higher than in freshwater. You may succeed in keeping marine life alive in fresh ocean water for a couple of weeks. But unless the higher oxygen content can be maintained, your animals will eventually die. You can solve this problem by artificial aeration—by installing an electrically driven air-pump aerator. Such a pump may be purchased from any company handling aquarium supplies.

If you think you can lick these two problems, by all means go ahead with plans for developing a marine aquarium.

REFERENCES—Robert P. L. Straughan, *The Salt Water Aquarium in the Home*. New York, A. S. Barnes and Company.

Try a Salt-Water Aquarium. Free. Carolina Biological Supply House.

ESTABLISHING THE MARINE AQUARIUM—Tanks—Obtain a tank of fairly good size—absolute minimum, 15 gallons.

Seawater has a corroding effect on metal. For this reason, a frameless tank or a fiberglass tank is superior to a metal-frame tank. If you do use a metal-frame tank, be certain to check the inside for places where the metal may be exposed. Cover exposed spots with asphalt paint or with aquarium cement.

Water—Bring home salt water from the ocean in glass or plastic containers. If you live inland, make your own by dissolving in distilled water a mixture of the various salts found in seawater. Such a salt mixture is available from biological supply houses.

Pour the water into the tank. Cover the tank with a glass plate and mark the water level on the outside of the tank with a piece of tape. These are important precautions. Some of the water will eventually evaporate, with the result that the mineral concentration will increase, to the detriment of the tank inhabitants. By filling up with distilled water to the marked water level, you can make sure that the mineral concentration remains constant.

Sand and plants—There is no advantage in putting sand into a marine aquarium—unless it is needed for burrowing animals. Similarly, plants are unnecessary—unless you want them for looks. In that case, float a few pieces of sea lettuce, *Ulva*, or other green algae in the water, or anchor them on the bottom by tying them to small stones.

Include a couple of stones for some animals to attach themselves to, for others to hide under.

Stocking the marine aquarium—Stick mainly to smaller marine animals such as you may be able to catch yourself in a tidal pool: sponges and sea anemones, crabs and shrimps, whelks and periwinkles, sea stars and sea urchins, perhaps a few small fish.

Bring them home in sea water in a jar or in a strong plastic bag.

Marine animals require a larger amount of oxygen than freshwater animals; therefore, they need a larger water surface. The exact number you can keep can be found only by experimenting. But in any event, watch out for overstocking.

MAINTAINING THE MARINE AQUARIUM—With proper temperature and aeration taken care of, feeding becomes your only other concern.

Feeding—Most marine animals will get along on a diet of small pieces of clams, mussels, oysters, and fish.

For sea urchins, sea cucumbers, barnacles, and crabs, place the food next to the animals, with aquarium forceps—two 18-inch strips of wood held together at one end over a thin, wooden wedge, tong fashion. For sea anemones, place the food in the center of the expanded animal. For fishes, drop the food on top of the water so that the fishes may pick it up as it sinks toward the bottom. Food particles not consumed within about fifteen minutes should be removed with a dip tube before the food has a chance to decompose.

In feeding starfishes, place a whole live clam or mussel next to each specimen. Starfishes have their own way of opening shells and getting at the contents.

Marine snails feed on the algae that settle on the sides of the tank.

PHOTOGRAPHING WATER LIFE

In water-life photography you run up against a snag that you do not often encounter in photography: the problem of overcoming the reflections from a water surface when you are shooting outdoors, from the side of a glass tank when shooting indoors. If you keep on watch against picking up these reflections with your camera lens, you should be able to produce some striking underwater shots.

Stills

EQUIPMENT—Camera and lenses—To get close enough to your objects and to be positive that you get what you are aiming for, you need a camera with ground-glass focusing and tripod support.

Your regular camera lens will be adequate for some shots, but for most, you will have to use supplementary lenses, extension tubes, or bellows. If you hanker to photograph the minute creatures of plankton and of pond mud, you may have to take the step into microphotography, posing your models under a microscope. But that is a science in itself, outside the realm of regular photography.

Polarizing screen—There is one accessory that you will bless a hundred times over in your water-life photography: the polarizing screen. By placing this screen in front of your lens and adjusting it, you are able to cut down a large percentage of reflections and glare, in this way penetrating below the surface film of water and behind the glass of a tank. Some polarizing screens are visually adjusted: you turn the two sections of the screen while looking at your scene until reflections disappear. Others are provided with a pointer to be turned toward the light source.

In using a polarizing screen, you do not have to increase the exposure as is the case for other filters. Simply take the meter reading and set the diaphragm and speed accordingly.

Exposures—In exposure meter readings, again watch out for reflections. In attempting to take the reading of a fish hovering close to the water's surface, you may actually be getting the reading of the sky reflected in the water. For safety's sake, use the substitution method, taking your reading on a piece of gray cardboard.

OUTDOOR PHOTOGRAPHY—In outdoor pond photography, concentrate on the life of the water film—striders or whirligig beetles skimming over the surface—and of the first few inches of water just below it. A saltwater tide pool gives you a better chance, provided the weather is still. Ripples on the water will blur your subjects, but they may, in some cases, provide an interesting effect.

If you insist on going deeper, use a waterscope as described on page 197. Add an arrangement for attaching the camera on the inside of it so that you can move the scope about.

Underwater shots—If you are a skin diver, underwater photography will add greatly to the enjoyment of your sport. For this kind of photography, you need various pieces of extra equipment.

The most important of these, of course, is a waterproof camera housing of sufficient strength to withstand the water pressure at the maximum depth at which you may be operating. Such housings, in metal or plastic, are available commercially.

Because it is almost impossible to focus and set the diaphragm under water and because of the need for a deep depth of focus, you should use a wide-angle lens on your camera. Even then, you may require a special correction lens.

To provide sufficient illumination and to correct, to a certain extent, the excessive blue in an underwater photograph, you may want to resort to the use of a flash. This will, necessarily, call for a special underwater flashgun.

REFERENCES—Hank Frey and Paul Tzimoulis, *Camera Below—The Complete Guide to Underwater Photography*. New York, Association Press.

D. Rebicoff and P. Cherney, *Guide to Underwater Photography*. Philadelphia, Chilton Book Company.

Here's How AE 87. Eastman Kodak, Rochester, New York 14650.

SUPPLIES—Underwater Photographic Service, Inc., P.O. Box 884, Marathon, Florida 33050.

Mako Products, 2931 Northeast Second Avenue, Miami, Florida 33137.

Ikelite Manufacturing Company, 3301 North Illinois Street, Indianapolis, Indiana 46208.

INDOOR PHOTOGRAPHY—Many of your stills of water life will have to be taken indoors, where you can control your subjects and your light.

Aquarium photographs—Use a tank with a front of flawless plate glass. Set up the camera on a tripod and arrange your floodlights. The important thing is to place the lights in such a way that they do not reflect against the glass front of the tank into the camera, and do not light up the camera itself so that it is mirrored in the tank. You may have to keep the lights above or at each end of the tank, perhaps even place a large cardboard frame around the front window. A polarizing filter will prove of great help.

¶ *Tip*—To keep fishes and other water life in focus, place a sheet of glass in the tank 1 or 2 inches from the front glass. Confine your models between the two glass surfaces.

¶ *Tip*—Turn off the floodlights when you are not shooting, to prevent them from heating up the aquarium water unnecessarily.

The shallowness of the depth of field will generally throw the back of the tank out of focus. If it doesn't, place a neutral gray background (blue for color photography) or even a few potted plants on the other side of the tank.

Tray photography—Some subjects photograph well from above—directly above or at an angle. Place them in a shallow glass tray with a couple of inches of water. Set the tray on a thin layer of pebbles, sand, or dirt to provide a suitable "natural" background.

Movies

With a focusing motion-picture camera, supplied with suitable lenses, you will find water-life moviemaking one of your most satisfying experiences. You can shoot according to a script and make use of a variety of shooting methods.

MOVIE TECHNIQUES—Whether you want to take a movie dealing with a whole water-life community of brook or lake or sea, or with the life cycle of a single animal—"From Egg to Frog," for instance—you will almost certainly want to use a combination of outdoor and indoor shots—outdoor shots to establish the locale, indoor for close-ups.

In a movie of, say, "The Quiet Pond," you may establish a mood of tranquillity by starting with "atmosphere shots" of the pond shimmering in the sunlight, of plants along its shores waving softly in the summer breeze. The camera eye then moves down into the water, roaming here and there, finally showing scene upon scene of dramatic close-ups of the far-from-quiet life-and-death struggles of the pond's inhabitants.

For the mood shots, you will, of course, make use of the usual technique of the long-medium-close-up shots. When entering the water, use the methods suggested in the previous pages for stills—employing the waterscope for outdoor shots, the aquarium tank for the dramatic sequences taken indoors.

WATER-LIFE COLLECTIONS

DRYING—A few water animals make good collection specimens by the simple process of drying—sea horses, starfish, and crabs.

Ward's Natural Science Establishment, Inc.

By using standard-size jars, you can build up a collection that is not only attractive but makes study easy.

By embedding your specimen in clear plastic—Bioplastic or a similar product—you can produce real museum pieces.

Place the animals for a couple of days in a half-and-half mixture of rubbing alcohol and water, or give them a quick boil in freshwater. Lay them out on a board, arrange them in a natural manner, and let them dry in the sun.

LIQUID PRESERVATION—All sea animals can be preserved in formalin or alcohol.

Sea anemones and jellyfish close themselves up; starfish pull in their tube feet when touched or placed in a conserving fluid. By anesthetizing them first, you can keep them extended. To do this, place them in a small amount of seawater, say, 1 quart. Slowly add one quarter of this amount ($\frac{1}{2}$ pint) of a saturated solution of magnesium sulphate, Epsom salt—made by dissolving 1 pound of the salt in 1 pint of water. Leave the animal in the liquid for six to ten hours until it no longer contracts when touched.

Worms, leeches, and small fishes are usually drowned in alcohol.

Frogs and toads die quickly in freshwater shaken up with ether— 1 teaspoon ether to 1 quart of water. When a specimen is dead, arrange it in a natural position in a shallow pan containing 10 percent formalin (one part commercial formaldehyde, three parts water) and leave it overnight. If the specimen is large, make slits in the stomach wall and the underside of the leg to give the preservative a chance to penetrate.

Finally, place the specimens in tightly closed jars in 10 percent formalin or 70 percent alcohol (rubbing alcohol, isopropyl alcohol). In the case of jellyfishes and other species that have a large water content, the preserving fluid will have to be replaced a couple of times before the jars are permanently closed.

¶ *Tip*—For an especially good-looking display, tie or glue your specimens to pieces of regular or opal glass and place in standard biological display jars, as described for snakes (pages 146 and 219).

PLASTIC EMBEDDING—Small specimens of water life make spectacular displays when embedded in blocks of clear plastic.

Pick a watertight mold somewhat larger than the specimen to be embedded. A small glass mold with tapering sides is good. Or assemble and use a special commercial take-apart mold made of aluminium strips. Coat the mold with mold release paste.

Embedding in Bioplastic: Place dry specimen in uncatalyzed plastic overnight (right). Put together mold and apply mold release compound (below). Mix right amount of plastic with catalyst (below, right).

All photos: Ward's Natural Science Establishment, Inc.

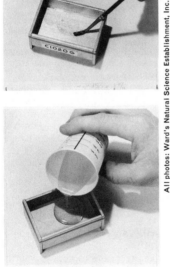

Pour a base layer into mold; set aside two hours (above). Place specimen in position; cover with catalyzed plastic; set overnight (above, right). Cure in "light bulb oven" four hours, then cool (right).

Mix enough uncatalyzed plastic and catalyst (hardener) to make a supporting layer, $\frac{1}{3}$ the thickness of the final job. Set aside to gel for a few hours, covered to keep the dust out.

When the plastic has gelled to the point where it no longer flows, place on it the dry specimen, previously soaked in uncatalyzed plastic. (A specimen preserved in alcohol or formalin must be air-dried before soaking.) Again cover the mold and wait for the specimen to be firmly anchored—about two hours.

Mix another batch of uncatalyzed plastic with catalyst and pour over the specimen to a thickness of double that of the supporting layer. Again cover and set aside overnight.

The final process is the hardening of the plastic. This is done by baking it for three to four hours at about 140 degrees Fahrenheit, in the electric oven provided in the material kits or in a homemade oven.

¶ *Tip*—A simple light-bulb oven may be improvised from an oatmeal carton. Cut a hole in the bottom to fit over the socket of a light bulb. Screw a 40–60-watt light bulb into the socket from inside the carton. Make two vent holes the size of a quarter next to the light socket. Invert the carton and bring the open end down over the mold. Turn on the light and bake at 140 degrees for three to four hours. If you are in doubt about the correct temperature, keep checking with a candy thermometer.

After the hardening process, turn off the heat and let the plastic cool inside the oven. In cooling, the plastic shrinks away from the mold, thus making it easy for you to remove the cast.

The cast may be further shaped with a fine-toothed saw. If necessary, it may be ground and polished, using various grades of emery paper, liquid abrasive, and polish.

SUPPLIES—*Bio-Plastics*. Ward's.

Castolite. General Biological Supply House.

Caroplastic. Carolina Biological Supply Company.

(For addresses, see page 27.)

Fish Displays

If you are a fisherman, you may like the idea of turning your prize catch into a display. It can be done by casting, mounting, or printing.

Fish prints—For an artistic portrayal of a good-sized fish make a print of it in the Japanese style—called a *gyotaku*, from *gyo*, fish, and *taku*, rubbing.

Rub down the fish thoroughly with salt to remove all slime. Dry and place on newspapers. Prop up the fish on crinkled paper so that it lies horizontal, with fins spread. Even better, use a sand bag as described on page 302. Then quickly brush a coat of thick Japanese carbon black ink—*sumi*, available in art stores—onto all top surfaces of the fish, except the eye. Make all brush strokes in the same direction: head to tail or tail to head.

Yoshido Hiyama

You can make an artistic Japanese-style fish print—"gyotaku"—of your prize fish by using India ink and rice paper.

¶ *Tip*—If you have difficulty getting *sumi* ink, use poster paint in a color according to your taste.

Cover the ink-smeared fish with a sheet of Japanese rice paper. Place a cloth on top of this and rub down firmly with your fingers and palm over all parts of the fish. Remove the cloth and peel off the rice paper carefully, starting at the head. Pat the paper with a moist sponge, if necessary, to facilitate removing. Paint in the eye and touch up any weak spots. When dry, mount on cardboard and frame.

REFERENCE—Yoshido Hiyama, *Gyotaku—The Art and Technique of the Japanese Fish Print*. Seattle, Washington, University of Washington Press.

Fish casts—Get or make up a cardboard box that will hold your fish with room to spare. Fill the box to within 2 inches from the top with moist sand. Smear a thin layer of petroleum jelly over one side of the fish—the side to be cast. Lay the fish on the sand, ungreased side down, and press this side completely down into the sand. Make a batch of plaster-of-paris mixture (see page 120). Pour it over the fish to the top of the box and leave it to set. When it is completely hardened, lift this negative cast off, brush the inside of it with vaseline and make a positive cast in the same way that a positive track cast is produced (see page 122). Paint the finished product in natural colors with oil paint.

Fish mounting—Instead of a plaster facsimile, you may want to keep the fish itself. You can do it if your catch happens to be one of the tough-skinned varieties.

First, skin your fish carefully. Make a cross cut near the tail fin, a lengthwise cut up one side. Using a dull knife and taking your time, skin out the body. Scrape the skin to remove the remaining flesh, and rub it thoroughly with salt or powdered borax.

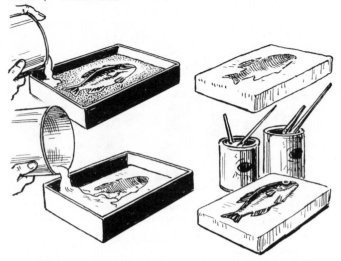

Making a fish cast: pouring plaster on the fish, half-embedded in sand; negative; pouring positive; painting.

Sew up the incisions carefully. Then, while someone holds the skin, pour in dry sand. Place the sand-filled fish on its side in a natural position; prevent the sand from running out by placing a wad of cotton in the fish's mouth. Use long pins to keep the fins in place. Leave the skin to dry thoroughly.

When the skin is dry, pour out the sand. Replace it with cellulose cotton or excelsior, or pour in a plaster "batter," made by mixing plaster of paris and sawdust, half and half, with sufficient water. Shellac when this is dry. Finally, mount the fish on a plywood panel and retouch the colors.

Fish-head mounts—A rather interesting display can be made of "pickled" fish heads—as was suggested by Dave Dunbar.

Cut off the head around the gills and scrape out any remaining flesh. Rub table salt into the head, inside and out, getting it into all crevices. Put a match stick in the mouth to keep the jaws open. Hang up the head by the match stick to dry in the sun for about a week. Brush off the salt and give the head two coats of clear varnish. Mount the head by tacking it to a piece of wood cut to fit inside the gills.

Shell Collecting

The study of mollusks is called *malacology*. The study and collection of their shells is called *conchology*. The latter has been a popular activity for hundreds of years—with children picking up native species on home shores, sailors bringing back rare forms from trips around the globe. As in insect collecting, it is common for shell collectors to get together to increase their collections by swapping and bartering.

SOCIETY—American Malacological Union. Headquarters: Route 2, Box 318, Marinette, Wisconsin 54143. Periodical: *Annual News Bulletin*.

WHERE?—Shells found empty are seldom satisfactory. They are usually wave- or weather-beaten and chipped. To obtain perfect shells, you must seek out and collect the live animals in their natural habitat, and clean out the shells.

Certain of the mollusks—the land snails—are found on dry land. But most mollusks are denizens of fresh and salt waters. The more prominent ones are found along rocky and sandy ocean shores.

WHEN?—Time of year—In northern waters, look for mollusks throughout the summer, after the waters have warmed up following the winter's cold. In southern waters, you can, of course, collect them year round.

Time of day—The best time for collecting sea mollusks is between one hour before low tide until one hour after. Since tides run about fifty minutes later each day, check local paper or radio for the time.

COLLECTING EQUIPMENT—Some of the mollusks you find, you can pick up with your fingers. A small rake will uncover shallow-burying mollusks, a small shovel those that hide deeper in the sand. A knife is handy for prying certain mollusks off the rocks or pilings to which they are attached. A kitchen strainer or sieve can be used for sifting tiny mollusks out of the sand. And then, of course, you need a bag for carrying your loot home.

¶ *Tip*—A waterscope (page 197) will help you see the mollusks you must locate below the water's surface.

In preparing a fish for mounting, cut along one side, remove carcass, sew up skin, fill with sand, dry and stuff.

CLEANING TECHNIQUES—Chitons and limpets—You can clean these one-shelled mollusks by scraping off their flesh with a knife.

Snails—Place snails in cold water and heat the water to the boiling point. The soft body can then be pulled out with a bent pin or a small knitting needle. Be sure to keep the "door," operculum, that the live snail may have used for closing itself in. Glue it in position with household cement after the shell has dried.

Tiny snail shells need not be cleaned out. Place them in alcohol overnight, then dry them in the sun.

Bivalves—Clams, mussels, and oysters open when you pour hot water over them. Scrape out the meat thoroughly.

Some collectors separate the two shells. It is better to keep intact the elastic band that holds the shells together and dry one set of shells spread out flat, another set of the same species closed up. To do the latter, tie a string around the shells during the drying.

¶ *Tip*—Many of the bivalves open up readily when placed in carbonated water—plain soda water.

ARRANGING THE COLLECTION—In developing your collection and displaying your shells, you can use your own ingenuity.

Tiny shells are best kept in small vials with screw caps or corks. Medium shells may fit into matchboxes. Larger shells may be kept in cardboard trays of suitable size. The whole collection can then be arranged in shallow drawers. For a large collection, you may want to make use of a system similar to that used in rock collections (see page 304).

¶ *Tip*—A light rubbing with mineral oil restores the natural luster of shells.

Instead of having shells loose, you may prefer to mount your collection. You can attach the shells to a piece of cardboard with household cement. Even better is the use of strips of glass.

Each shell should, of course, be identified and labeled. Write a small catalog number on the shell with India ink. Protect the writing with a dab of white shellac or clear nailpolish.

BOOKS—Percy A. Morris, *Field Guide to the Shells of Our Atlantic and Gulf Coasts. Field Guide to Shells of the Pacific Coast and Hawaii.* Boston, Houghton Mifflin Company.

R. Tucker Abbott, *Seashells of North America—A Golden Field Guide.* New York, Golden Press.

A. Hyatt Verrill, *Shell Collector's Handbook.* New York, G. P. Putnam's Sons.

SHELL PHOTOGRAPHY—Shells are excellently suited for table-top photography. Pose them individually on a small mound of sand. Sidelight or backlight them in such a way that their texture is brought out to the greatest advantage. Shoot from above, or from a low angle, against a neutral background.

Shells may also be shot by shadowless photography (see page 310).

CHAPTER 8

Flowers and Flowerless Plants

THE moment you leave city streets behind and set out in the open, you enter into the land of plants. There's the green of the fields, the colors of a multitude of flowers, the arching canopy of trees. Even where nature is not too lavish with her gifts of fertility—on mountain tops and in deserts—you will find plants that make a brave stand under adverse conditions.

Life would be pretty dreary if we couldn't turn to fields and forests, parks and gardens, for recreation and enjoyment—if the green of the out-of-doors should turn to withered brown forevermore.

But even more important, human life would end if plant life should die. The food we eat, the clothing we wear, the air we breathe, the houses in which we live, depend on the plants that grow around us. Even the heat in our homes, the electric light that turns our nights into day, the power of our motors are possible only because of plants of prehistoric days transformed into coal and oil and gases.

There is wonder in the structure of plants, from microscopic bacteria to the tallest tree in the world. There is beauty in colors, excitement in odors, piquancy in flavors. There is healing for body and mind in planting a seed in the good earth and seeing it grow.

And there is everlasting mystery in the ability of plants to pick up the energy of the sun and to store it—not just for their own use, but for ours. We are still far from solving the great riddle of plant life: How can a plant take carbon dioxide from the air and water from the ground, and under the power of sunlight and by means of the green matter in its leaves—chlorophyl—combine them into sugar, releasing free oxygen for animals and humans to breathe? Not limited to even that magic, the plant goes on building other substances: starches and cellulose, oil, protein, complex vitamins. How? Eventually we may know.

BOOKS ON PLANT LIFE—Harry J. Fuller and A. B. Carothers, *The Plant World*. New York, Holt, Rinehart & Winston.

Frits W. Went, *The Plants*. Chicago, Time-Life Books.

Herbert S. Zim, *Plants: A Guide to Plant Hobbies*. New York, Harcourt, Brace & World.

Donald Culross Peattie, *Flowering Earth*. New York, Viking Press.

Working with Others

Probably no other field of nature has as many followers as the field of botany—plants from the most primitive to the most highly developed, plants of a thousand purposes.

Your local biology teachers will be able to suggest people in your community who are interested in wild plants. Or you may drop a line to the department of botany of your state university, to your state agricultural experiment station, or to your county agent.

You are almost certain to find, right in your own locality, a member club of one of the national garden clubs meeting regularly. Although the garden clubs are concerned mainly with cultivated plants, they are also interested in the preservation of native plants. There are people within most of these clubs who specialize in wild flowers and their conservation. Join a congenial group of such people for field trips and other activities.

SOCIETIES—Garden Club of America. Headquarters: 598 Madison Avenue, New York, New York 10022. Periodical: *The Bulletin.*

National Council of State Garden Clubs. Headquarters: 4401 Magnolia Avenue, St. Louis, Missouri 63110.

Men's Garden Clubs of America. Headquarters: 50 Eaton Street, Morrisville, New York.

And then there are scientific organizations working in certain fields of plant life. Many of them publish bulletins and magazines on their special subjects. These organizations and societies are open to interested people.

SOCIETIES—GENERAL—Botanical Society of America. Headquarters: Botany Department, Indiana University, Bloomington, Indiana 47401. Periodical: *American Journal of Botany.*

Torrey Botanical Club. Headquarters: New York Botanical Garden, Bronx, New York 10458. Periodical: *Bulletin of the TBC.*

FLOWERS—Wild Flower Preservation Society. Headquarters: 3740 Oliver Street, NW, Washington, D.C. 20015.

FERNS—American Fern Society. Headquarters: 415 South Pleasant Street, Amherst, Massachusetts. Periodical: *American Fern Journal.*

MOSSES—American Bryological Society. Headquarters: University of Colorado Museum, Boulder, Colorado 80302. Periodical: *The Bryologist.*

FUNGI—Mycological Society of America. Headquarters: Department of Plant Pathology, Cornell University, Ithaca, New York 14850. Periodical: *Mycologia.*

PLANTS IN THE FIELD

Equipment for Plant Study

Little equipment is needed to penetrate into the world of plants. As in every other phase of nature, your most important tools are observing eyes—not just eyes that see, but eyes that notice the many details that, together, tell the whole story.

STUDY EQUIPMENT—Magnifiers—Many plant parts are so tiny that they cannot be seen clearly with the naked eye. Some of them may be the final points that determine the plant you are studying—whether tiny hairs, seeds, or number of stamens.

For most work, you can get along with one of the folding-type pocket magnifiers that magnify from five to ten times (see page 151).

If you specialize in plants that have minute parts, you may have to resort to the more expensive Coddington-type pocket magnifier, or the Hastings triplet. These will give you magnifications up to twenty times.

Knife—A penknife with a small blade is satisfactory for opening most flowers to lay open their inside structure, and for making cross sections of stems or branches.

Dissecting needle—For very small plants, the knife may be too coarse, and you may have to use a dissecting needle instead. This is just a fine metal point in a small handle of wood or metal, available in scientific supply houses at a dime or a quarter.

¶ *Tip*—You can make your own dissecting needle by pushing a sewing needle, eye first, into a 3-inch length of ¼-inch dowel stick, with a pair of pliers.

Trowel—A sturdy hand trowel with a blade about 6 inches long, for studying the root system of the plant.

Rule—For measuring, use a 6-inch pocket rule, graduated along one edge in eighths of inches, along the other in millimeters. The most popular type is of a flexible transparent plastic.

Plant book—The number of books for identifying plants is immense. Some of them are simple, others are intended only for experts. Very few cover the whole subject of all plants. Most of them specialize—some in flowers, others in certain flowerless plants.

If you are a beginner, your best bet is a well-illustrated book in the subject in which you are interested. With such a book, you can arrive at your identification by comparing your plant with the illustrations, checking it against the text that accompanies the most likely picture.

BOOKS FOR FIELD IDENTIFICATION—Harold W. Rickett, *New Field Book of American Wild Flowers.* New York, G. P. Putnam's Sons.

Roger Tory Peterson and Margaret McKenny, *Field Guide to Wildflowers of Northeastern and North-Central North America.* Boston, Houghton Mifflin Company.

Margaret Armstrong, *Field Book of Western Wild Flowers.* New York, G. P. Putnam's Sons.

Edgar T. Wherry, *Wild Flower Guide.* New York, Doubleday & Company.

M. Walter Pesman, *Meet the Natives.* (Rocky Mountain Flowers.) Published by author, 372 South Humboldt Street, Denver, Colorado.

Edmund C. Jaeger, *Desert Wild Flowers.* Stanford, California, Stanford University Press.

FERNS—Herbert Durand, *Field Book of Common Ferns*. New York, G. P. Putnam's Sons.

Boughton Cobb, *Field Guide to the Ferns*. Boston, Houghton Mifflin Company.

Edgar T. Wherry, *The Fern Guide. The Southern Fern Guide: Southeastern and South-midland United States*. New York, Doubleday & Company.

MOSSES—A. J. Grout, *Mosses with a Hand-Lens*. Distribution: Chicago Natural History Museum, Chicago, Illinois.

Henry S. Conard, *How to Know the Mosses*. Dubuque, Iowa, William C. Brown Company.

FUNGI—William S. Thomas, *Field Book of Common Mushrooms*. New York, G. P. Putnam's Sons.

Alexander H. Smith, *Mushroom Hunter's Field Guide*. Ann Arbor, Michigan, University of Michigan Press.

LICHENS—G. G. Nearing, *The Lichen Book*. Ashton, Maryland, Eric Lundberg.

Mason E. Hale, *Lichen Handbook: A Guide to the Lichens of Eastern North America*. New York, Random House.

ALGAE—Lewis H. Tiffany, *Algae, the Grass of Many Waters*. Springfield, Illinois, Charles C. Thomas.

Valentine J. Chapman, *Algae*. New York, St Martin's Press.

ADVANCED BOOK FOR IDENTIFICATION—Asa Gray, *New Manual of Botany*, rev. by M. L. Fernald. Flowering plants and ferns of Central and Northeast United States. New York, American Book Company.

Note—For books on the flowers or flowerless plants of your region or your home state, consult your state university or state museum.

Notebook—And then, of course, the ever-present notebook and pencil. In the notebook, you can keep track of each plant you find—its name, the date you found it, its location, its habitat, and so on.

COLLECTING EQUIPMENT—For the equipment you will need for establishing a herbarium, see page 249.

Finding Plants

The study of plants has two advantages over the study of most other living things. First, plants stay put; you don't have to sneak up on them as you do on animals, or watch them from afar through field glasses as you do birds, or hunt them with net or line. And second, you can find plants any time during the year.

WHERE?—The best place to start looking for plants is **here**—right in your own backyard, your garden, or if you live in the city, the nearest park. These places may be well tended, nevertheless, they will all contain a fair abundance of wild plants. You may think of them as weeds—"a weed is a plant out of place"—but any of them, whether dandelion or mustard, plantain or ragweed, can start you off on your study of plant families.

When you have become acquainted with the plants of your own immediate surroundings, set out on field trips into the different types of plant communities that are found within a couple of miles of your home—whether FOREST, GRASSLAND, MARSH, LAKE SHORE, SEASHORE, DESERT, or whatever they happen to be.

Study each type in turn. Discover its dominant plants and become thoroughly familiar with each plant community.

WHEN?—There is no closed season on plants; any time of the year is plant time. There is always something to find. But to find the things that specifically interest you, you may need to pick a certain time of the year.

The season for FLOWERS starts in early spring—mostly with plants of the Lily and Crowfoot families—to wind up in late summer with domineering members of the Composite family.

You can follow the growth of FERNS from spring to fall.

LICHENS and MOSSES may be found in the heat of midsummer and under the snow of midwinter, ALGAE wherever there is open water—fresh or salt.

Some FUNGI may be located throughout the year. Late summer and early fall are the times for the more spectacular species.

Plant Lists and Calendars

LIFE LISTS—By listing in your notebook, or in the margin of your field book, every plant you discover and identify on your field trips, with a notation of date and place, you are building yourself a life list of plants.

Such a listing may be mostly for your own satisfaction, but it may occasionally prove of interest to a much larger audience.

Regional lists—Your state, through the extension service of its department of agriculture, its department of conservation, or its state university, may already have made a listing of the plants of your region. But conditions change over the years. An old plant community may have given way to a new; plants not previously common to the region may have made their appearance. Many new discoveries are possible; you may be the one to make them!

¶ *Tip*—Obtain from the departments listed above any pamphlets that may have been published on the flora of your state.

CALENDARS—"The flowers that bloom in the spring, tra-la" are possibly the most welcome of all plants. In addition to their beauty, they provide you with a chance to compare their current dates of appearing with dates of previous years, in this way giving you an idea of climatic conditions from spring to spring.

Flower calendars—The simplest way of keeping track of flower openings is to jot down the notes about them in your regular notebook, during daily spring walks:

April 7.   Weather: Sunny.   Temp.: Appr. 50
Hepatica.   Rue anemone

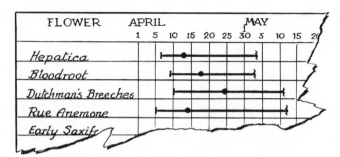

In a flower calendar, aim for three dates: petals open (left mark), pollen shed (dot), petals shed (right mark).

April 10. Weather: Showery. Temp.: Appr. 55
    Bloodroot. Adder's tongue. Dutchman's breeches
Later on, at your convenience, transfer the notes to file cards or loose-leaf sheets, one for each flower:

HEPATICA
    April 7.
      Weather: Sunny. Temp.: Appr. 50
BLOODROOT
    April 10.
      Weather: Showery. Temp.: Appr. 55

For a more complete study of spring flowers, aim to get three dates for each flower: (1) opening of petals; (2) shedding of pollen (scientifically, a flower is not considered in full bloom until the anthers release their pollen); (3) all petals dropped. In all cases, keep track of weather conditions.

Calendar charts—For ready reference, the calendar notes may be transferred to a chart, with flower names opposite the respective dates.

A better system is the use of ruled paper (millimeter paper) on which a line may be drawn opposite each flower name to indicate the full period of flowering.

¶ *Tip*—A simple calendar chart can be used to advantage in club, school, and Scout work. Rule off a large sheet of cardboard with spaces for:

DATE   NAME OF FLOWER   WHERE SEEN   DISCOVERER

Such a chart may be the basis for a competition.

Field Observations

Field trips for the purpose of learning new flowers, or for checking the progress of the seasons, will always have a certain fascination. But the field trips will be even more productive of results if the opportunity is taken to peer into ever different phases of plant life.

Plant diaries—Keep track of the development of a single genus of flowering plant through daily observations from budding to fading.

Young shoots—How do shoots of plants push out of the ground—straight up, spearlike, or arched, with bent "backs"? Power of young shoots—moving stones, breaking through concrete, etc.

Desert plants—Year round, but specifically a couple of weeks after heavy spring rains: "Belly-flowers"—flowers so tiny that you hardly see them unless you lie on your stomach.

Mountain plants—Effect of altitude on flower growth.

Effect of increasing shade—Transformation of forest carpet as year advances. Plant succession as shade increases.

¶ *Tip*—To determine relative light, use a photographic light meter. Take a reading against a piece of gray cardboard on sunny days of observation at the same hour each time.

WILD FLOWERS AROUND YOUR HOME

Lucky you, if you are close enough to nature to have a piece of dirt of your own for flowers, fruits, and vegetables. Whether yours is a suburban garden or a country estate, a section of it should be set aside for a display of native wild flowers and ferns.

On the other hand, if you happen to be an apartment dweller you can still get a lot of satisfaction from wild flowers by raising them indoors and following their growth.

Your Wild Flower Garden

You can turn the wild-flower corner into the most fascinating part of your whole garden. In doing so, you get more than the usual enjoyment out of gardening. You have the added thrill of the hunt—of hiking through neighboring or faraway fields and forests in search of specimens and of matching your skill against nature in your efforts to effect a successful transplanting.

BOOKS—Kathryn S. Taylor and Stephen F. Hamblin, *Handbook of Wild Flower Cultivation*. New York, The Macmillan Company.

George D. Aiken, *Pioneering with Wildflowers*. Englewood Cliffs, New Jersey, Prentice-Hall.

Edwin F. Steffek, *Wild Flowers and How to Grow Them*. New York, Crown Publishers.

DEVELOPING THE WILD FLOWER CORNER—To be a successful wild-flower gardener, you need to start out by developing a section of your garden to fit the living conditions of the plants you intend to introduce.

Many wild plants transplant with gusto to the perennial border of the ordinary garden, but they look out of place there and often take on a different character. Wild columbine, for instance, dainty in the wild where it lives on a lean diet, becomes husky in company with its cultivated relatives.

If you want to have your wild plants look the way they do in their natural habitat, you must imitate that habitat as closely as possible in your garden. This means special attention to exposure, moisture, and soil reaction.

Exposure—Some wild flowers are open-field plants exposed to the sun all day long; others grow in the deep shade of dense forests. You should have no trouble in providing for the former. The latter need to be shaded—preferably under the spreading branches of native shrubs and trees that are their natural neighbors.

Moisture—From desert plants to floating bog specimens, your choice is great. You will have to decide whether you want to use your garden as you have it, or whether your ambition calls for the development of a desert section, a rock garden, a marshy area. If your space is limited, you may solve the problem by a series of terraces, separating them by rocks or old logs.

Soil reaction—Some wild flowers are at home in alkaline soil, some like their soil neutral, others prefer acid soil. In spite of their apparent native preferences, a number of plants will get along seemingly well in whatever soil you provide. Others are more fussy: They will go on a hunger strike and die unless the reaction of the soil to which they are transferred matches their original surroundings.

¶ *Tip*—Alkalinity and acidity are described in chemical language by pH numbers: pH 1 to 6 indicate acid reactions, pH 7 neutral, pH 8 to 14 alkaline conditions. The reaction is determined by the change in color of certain dyes. Purchase a soil-testing set. Or, cheaper, a soil-test paper. Use long-range 4- to 9-pH test paper. Mix a small amount of soil with an equal amount of rainwater or distilled water. Immerse a strip of paper in the mixture. Match the color the paper has turned against a scale that comes with the paper, to find pH number.

The safest way to satisfy your wild flowers is to bring them into the garden with plenty of the soil in which you found them growing.

If that is not possible, you may have to change the reaction of your garden soil.

You can make it *more alkaline* by adding crushed limestone.

You can make it *more acid* by mixing in leaf mold from oak or coniferous forest. Or by raking sulphur into the top—3 to 5 pounds to 100 square feet. Or by sprinkling aluminum sulphate on the surface—3 to 5 pounds to 100 square feet. Or by watering with a solution of 1 pound tannic acid to 5 gallons of water.

OBTAINING PLANTS—With the garden spot prepared, you are ready to move in the plants.

Plants from the wild—It used to be a fairly simple matter to obtain plants for a wild flower garden from woods and fields. It isn't anymore—unless you happen to be or to know an owner of country property.

Respect other people's property. Trespass by arrangement only, and get permission in advance to remove those plants that you would like to transfer to your own garden.

¶ *Tip*—You can often do a service for the protection of wild flowers by removing them (with permission) from places where real-estate development or highway construction threatens their complete destruction.

Know and follow the laws of your state in regard to wild flowers. In order to protect rare and disappearing species of wild flowers, several states have enacted laws for their protection. Some states protect all wild flowers along the highway right-of-way and forbid the moving of plants from public lands.

But whether your state has such laws or not, you will certainly want to do your part to perpetuate its wild plants. Find out which flowers in your territory are so plentiful that they can be picked freely, those that should be picked only in moderation, and those that should be left undisturbed in their natural habitat. Choose your flowers from the first category, and with care from the second, but leave those in the third alone.

REFERENCES—*Helpful Hints on Conserving Wild Flowers.* Free. Conservation Committee, The Garden Club of America, 598 Madison Avenue, New York, New York 10022.

Wild Flower Protection Lists—Northeastern, Southeastern, and Western editions. Wild Flower Preservation Society, 3740 Oliver Street, NW, Washington, D.C. 20015.

Transplanting equipment—You will need a few pieces of equipment for transferring plants from the wilds to your garden: a small garden trowel, newspaper or aluminum foil to wrap around the roots, a notebook for writing down the living conditions of each plant, a flat basket or a large plastic bag for carrying home your loot.

Transplanting—Your success in transplanting depends on your care in digging up the plants, the way you transport them and replant them.

Remove dead leaves, debris, and stones from around the plant. Make a circular cut with your trowel around it, then lift it very carefully, with the roots as nearly intact as possible and with a fair-sized ball of soil attached to them. Wrap the roots immediately in newspaper or, far better, in heavy-duty aluminum foil.

In bringing your plants home, protect the top against damage, and the plant as a whole against wilting. You may want to transport them in the flat basket favored by many gardeners. Or you may use a large bag of a tough plastic, or even a vasculum (see page 250). If you have a long trip before you, wet down the paper- or foil-wrapped roots to prevent them from drying out.

With each plant, place a scrap of paper with information of where picked, whether in an open field or shade, in what kind of soil.

Plant the flowers as soon as possible after you get home. Set them to the same depth as you found them in the wild and in the same general living surroundings. Water them, then mulch around them with leaves or grass clippings to prevent too quick evaporation.

Buying plants—Occasionally, you may be able to obtain plants that appeal especially to you through bartering with another wild flower enthusiast. More often, you may have to buy them from a nursery specializing in wild flowers. Usually it is much easier to work with nursery-grown plants than with wild specimens. They will have been transplanted several times, and therefore they will have a root system that can be disturbed without ill effects.

NURSERY PLANTS—Putney Nursery, Putney, Vermont 05346.

Sky Cleft Gardens, Camp Street East, Barre, Vermont 05641.

Mincemoyers, Route 4, Box 482, Jackson, New Jersey 08527.

Vick's Wildgardens, Box 115, Gladwyne, Pennsylvania 19035.

Three Laurels, Marshall, North Carolina 28753.

Garden of the Blue Ridge, Ashford, North Carolina 28603.

Lounsberry Gardens, Oakford, Illinois 62672.

Ferndale Nursery and Greenhouses, Askov, Minnesota 55704.

Siskiyou Rare Plant Nursery, 522 Franquette Street, Medford, Oregon 97501.

PROPAGATION OF WILD PLANTS—Once you have your wild flower garden established, you can increase the number of plants by various types of propagation—among them division, slips, layering, and seeds.

DIVISION—The simplest way of propagating many wild flowers is by division. This consists in digging up the roots, after one or two growing seasons, dividing them into several parts, and planting these separately. The job should be done in late summer, after the foliage has turned brown, or in early spring.

Crowns—If the root system appears like a tangled clump of rootlets (day lily, phlox, certain daisies), all you have to do to get several sections, is to break or cut the crown vertically. If it is

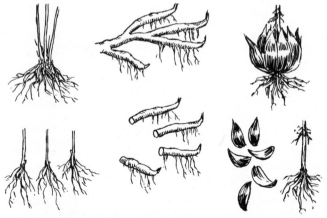

Propagation by divisions: breaking crown apart, cutting rootstock into sections, separating scales of lily bulbs.

particularly large and tough, thrust two forking spades into the middle of the clump, back to back, and lever them apart.

Rootstocks—Branching, horizontal rootstocks or rhizomes (iris, wild ginger, trillium) are cut in portions with a strong knife, each portion with a bud. Plant the sections horizontally.

Offsets—Bulbous plants (spring beauty, wild onion) often form small offsets, bulblets, below ground—some even bulbils (tiger lily) above ground at the leaf bases. Each of them is a potential new plant. If the bulb is scaly (certain lilies), break off the scales and replant them separately along with the core.

Runners—Some ground-hugging plants (wild strawberry, moneywort) send out special slender horizontal side branches whose tips develop roots and anchor themselves. Separate the runners from the mother plant and plant them.

Stolons—In some plants (mints, thyme), regular branches bend down to the ground and form roots where they touch. Here again, the rooted parts may be separated from the mother plant.

CUTTINGS—Root cuttings—Some plants with deep taproots (milkweed, butterfly weed, chicory) may be propagated by root cuttings. In the fall, cut the root into 2- to 3-inch-long sections. Bury these outdoors, to form calluses, in a mixture of garden soil and coarse sand. Transplant them vertically the following spring.

Green cuttings—Green cuttings, or slips, can be taken in early summer from numerous juicy-stemmed plants and rooted. Snip off tips of branching plants to a length of 3 to 4 inches. Pull off most of the leaves. Prepare a soil mixture of equal parts loam (garden soil), peat moss, and sand or vermiculite. Pour the mixture into a clay or plastic pot, or into a tin can with drainage holes cut into the bottom. Moisten the soil mixture, make holes in it with a pencil, insert the cuttings, firm the soil around them with your fingers. Place the pot in a plastic bag and close the bag with tape or wire.

¶ *Tip*—To speed up rooting, dip the bases of the slips in plant hormone for rooting, such as Rootone, before planting them.

SEEDS—Wild-flower seeds may be collected in the fall and sown like ordinary seeds.

The simplest way of getting seeds in quantity is by putting a small plastic bag over the ripening flower head and tying the mouth of the bag around the stem. When the seeds are completely ripe, cut off the flower head, retaining the plastic bag around it, and hang it up to dry.

You will simplify matters for yourself by purchasing seeds from one of the seed houses that specialize in wild-flower seeds.

SEEDS—Harry E. Saier, Dimondale, Michigan 48821.

Claude A. Barr, Prairie Gem Ranch, Smithwick, South Dakota 57782.

Clyde Robbin, P.O. Box 2091, Castro Valley, California 94546.

Growing wild flowers from seeds—Sow tiny seeds in "flats"—

shallow boxes about 3 inches deep, 8 inches wide, 12 inches long. Fill to within an inch from the top with a mixture of moist sand and leaf mold. Scatter the seeds over the soil, and firm them down with a flat board. Place a sheet of glass over the flat to retain the moisture. Keep it in a shady location until shoots appear, then expose it to the sun part of the day without letting the soil dry out. When it is of sufficient size to be moved, "prick out" the plants with a small flat stick and transfer them to another flat. From this they are finally transplanted to the outdoors, when they have reached a suitable height.

¶ *Tip*—An egg container is excellent for raising pricked-out plants, each in its own compartment. They are easily transplanted when they have reached sufficient size.

Large seeds are more easily sown in a seedbed in the open. Sow them in the fall so that they will be exposed to all kinds of winter weather. Sift a layer of sand over them to double the thickness of the seeds themselves. Firm it down with a flat board. Moisten the seedbed and cover it with burlap or plastic.

¶ *Tip*—Seeds of most wild flowers in the northern states drop to the ground in the fall and spend the winter exposed to freezing and thawing, snow and rain. Seeds collected from such flowers may not germinate unless they have gone through this natural process of "stratification." To stratify them, prepare the seed flats in the fall and place them in the ground outdoors. Cover them with burlap to protect them against driving rain and with window screening to save them from rodents.

¶ *Tip*—You can accomplish artificial stratification by keeping the seeds in a refrigerator for a month or so, and shifting them between the freezing compartment and humidifier from time to time.

RAISING FERNS—Ferns are raised from spores collected from the spore cases found on the fronds. Because of the way in which ferns develop, their cultivation is quite different from that of seed plants.

Fill a flat bulb pot half full of pebbles. Cover this with a layer of mixed sand and leaf mold. On top of this, sprinkle fine sand. Sterilize everything by baking the pot in an oven for ten minutes or more. Cool it completely. Place it in a pan of water. When the soil is moist throughout, sprinkle the spores thinly over the surface. Then cover the pot with a piece of glass and place it in a warm shaded spot.

¶ *Tip*—Or use the Costello method: Fill a flowerpot with sphagnum moss (peat moss). Sterilize it with hot water. Also sterilize a saucer and a bell jar or a plastic dome. Cool. Invert the flowerpot in the saucer. Sprinkle spores on the wet surface of the pot. Fill the saucer with water. Cover the pot with bell jar or dome.

In a few weeks, a green film forms on the surface. Look at it closely with a strong magnifier, and you will see that it consists of numerous flat, generally heart-shaped *prothallia*—minute plants a single cell layer thick. In another week or more, tiny fronds begin to appear.

Ferns may be raised from spores in a covered bulb pot, or on the outside of a flower pot, covered with a jar.

When the small new fern plants are large enough to be moved, transplant them to a seed flat, and treat them as regular seed plants. Eventually, set them out in your fernery.

WILD PLANTS IN YOUR ROOM

Wild flowers brought indoors are always welcome. In the spring, they herald sunny days ahead. In the fall, they tell of Indian summer.

LIVE PLANTS—Cut flowers—A myriad of decorative schemes are possible using cut flowers—from floating a single waterlily in a glass bowl, to arranging a spectacular display of autumn asters.

Gather the flowers in the early morning before the sun gets too hot. Cut the stems at a slant with a sharp knife or with scissors. Place them in water in a suitable vase or other container, after first pulling off any leaves that may be under water.

Potted flowers—You may want to raise a few wild flowers indoors to follow their blooming closely, from budding to fading.

One way to do this is to pot the plants in the spring, as soon as they show the earliest sign of life. Dig them up carefully, with a good ball of earth adhering to the roots. Plant them in ordinary, unglazed clay pots, 6 to 8 inches in diameter, with about 1½ inches of pebbles on the bottom for good drainage. Keep the soil moist by placing the pots in saucers with a small amount of water.

For an earlier bloom, plant your pots in the fall, but leave them outdoors all winter, dug down with the top flush with the ground. Bring them into an unheated room or porch early in February, then into a warmer room when the buds show.

DRIED PLANTS—Dry weed stalks—There is a very special beauty in the winter stalks of many of our wild plants—cattails, milkweed, yarrow, evening primrose, jimson weed, goldenrod, and pampas grass.

Most of them can be brought indoors and arranged with no preparation. To prevent shedding, treat the grasses by spraying them with a fixative of thinned lacquer or shellac. You can keep cattail heads intact by giving them a quick dip in the fixative.

¶ *Tip*—Look into the windows of commercial florists in the winter, and you will see large bouquets of prepared dry flower stalks, many of them in bright colors. You will recognize many weed stalks among them, painted or sprayed with quick-drying enamels. If you prefer the pastel tones, try some of the new water paints, either painting or dipping the stalks.

DRIED FLOWERS—You can preserve some wild plants with especially large flowers in their natural shape and with their natural color by drying them in sand or a chemical called silica gel.

Sand method—Place a pan of clean fine sand over the burner of a kitchen stove. Heat it until it is warm but not hot—you should be able to place your hand in it without discomfort.

Pour a layer of the warm sand into a cardboard box. Place the flowers you want to dry on top of the sand, then sift the dry sand all around them until they are completely covered. Leave the box in a warm place for a couple of weeks. Or speed up the drying process to six to eight hours by placing the box in a very slow oven with the door open.

When the drying is complete, remove the sand by cutting a hole in one corner of the box and letting the sand run out.

Silica-gel method—Depending on whether you want to dry full-length flower stalks or just the flower head with part of the stem, use a tall, narrow tin can or a flat plastic box or a cake tin.

Start the process by pouring a thin layer of the sandlike silica gel into the container. Position the flowers; then carefully pour silica gel around and into each flower until it is completely covered. Put the cover on the container and seal it airtight with a strip of tape. Allow a week for the drying. Then open up the container and slowly pour out the silica gel. Lift out the dried specimens with great care.

¶ *Tip*—Silica gel may seem expensive initially, but it can be used again and again. After each use pour it into a metal pan in a thin layer and heat it in a 240-degree oven for thirty minutes. Pour it back into its container, close the container and tape it airtight.

¶ *Tip*—Biological supply houses advertise "indicating silica gel." This contains crystals of cobalt chloride, a chemical that is blue when dry, red when moist. When the indicator shows red, dry the silica in the oven before using it.

Terrariums

An even more spectacular display is possible with a terrarium—a covered glass container with a miniature garden of soil and plants.

Nathaniel Bagshaw Ward, an English doctor, started the terrarium idea more than a hundred years ago. Ward noticed that ferns and grasses kept right on growing in a tightly closed glass container in his home. He realized that the plants stayed alive because the water that transpired from the leaves and evaporated from the soil condensed, and kept the moisture content constant. The principle made possible the successful transportation of plants on long ocean journeys—rare specimens from everywhere to botanical gardens in

England, coffee plants from Arabia to Brazil, rubber plants from South America to the East Indies.

TYPES OF TERRARIUMS—Almost any glass container that can be made fairly airtight can be turned into a terrarium, or "Wardian case."

Bell jars—A bell-jar terrarium is probably the easiest one to make. Simply develop a miniature garden in a glass or metal tray that fits the circumference of the bell, then place the bell over it. Be sure that the plants do not touch the sides. Somewhat Victorian, and rather expensive.

¶ *Tip*—For a modern counterpart, make the garden in a circular cake tin or plastic tray. Cover it with a transparent plastic plant cap or with a "bell" made by cutting the top off a large plastic mayonnaise jar.

Bottle gardens—All kinds of bottles and glass containers can be used for decorative indoor gardens—from 10-gallon carboys, 5-gallon distilled water bottles, to carafes, globular glass bowls, brandy inhalers, even burned-out and cleaned-out TV tubes.

It takes a bit of imagination, patience, and ingenuity to develop this type of terrarium. Begin by lining the bottom of the container with a thin layer of moss, green side down, for looks. Then pour in, through a paper funnel, a layer of pebbles for drainage and a layer of dry leaf mold. Smooth this in position with a teaspoon on a long handle. Then insert the plants with the help of slender wooden forceps, homemade to fit your container. Tamp down the soil with a dowel stick. Fit in small pieces of moss to hold plants in place and give a more finished look to your planting. Then water, using a rubber bulb spray or a plastic squeeze bottle. Finally, cork the bottle or cover the containers. Place it in good light but not in direct sunlight.

Numerous types of bottle gardens are possible. Good is a gallon mayonnaise jar cradled on two wooden supports.

¶ *Tip*—You can make an interesting bottle garden from a 1-gallon mayonnaise jar. Lay it on one side, cradled on two wooden supports. Then arrange the soil and plants in it.

Commercial terrarium case—The most common terrarium is a rectangular glass case, either of solid glass or of glass panes fitted into a framework of metal molding. Ready-made terrariums of this type, of different sizes, are available commercially through scientific supply houses, as well as through stores selling aquarium supplies.

¶ *Tip*—An old, discarded, even leaky, aquarium tank will make an excellent terrarium case.

PLANTING THE TERRARIUM—With the container secured, the satisfying job of planting it is before you. In planting, remember that your goal is to create a bit of nature that will greet you daily during the lean months between October and May. You have the choice of many different habitats, from humid bog to arid desert.

Woodland terrarium—A 2-inch layer of gravel or pebbles first—mixed with a bit of charcoal, if you like, to keep the terrarium "sweet." On top of this, put a couple of inches of leaf mold, moistened so that it forms a ball when squeezed in the hand. Then put in woods plants, the number depending on the size of the case; arrange them in a pleasing, natural manner, placing the taller specimens toward the back. Finally, put down a thin layer of green moss as a plush carpet around the base of the other plants, and maybe a couple of small rocks and lichen-spotted sticks to clinch the effect.

Keep it covered with a sheet of glass or clear plastic. Place it in the cool semishade most of the time. If "sweating" occurs, push a match stick under the cover to raise it slightly and let the excess water evaporate.

Bog terrarium—Place 2 inches of gravel in a waterproof terrarium case. Cover with 2 to 3 inches of wet sphagnum moss. On top of this, fill in several inches of the soil you collected with your bog plants. Set the plants as deep as you found them in the wild. Keep the terrarium covered with a piece of glass or plastic.

¶ *Tip*—A bog terrarium permits the growing of the interesting insect-eating plants—venus's-flytrap, pitcher plant, and sundew. Place small insects with the plants and watch developments.

Desert terrarium—Cover the bottom of the terrarium with 2 inches of gravel, then with 2 to 3 inches of a mixture of sand and soil. Plant cacti and other desert plants to the original soil lines that show on them. Place a few stones, pieces of dead cactus and yucca stems, and the like on the ground, to give an "artistic" effect. Place the terrarium, uncovered, in a sunny location. Sprinkle the ground around the plants with water every ten days or so.

Survey terrarium—A terrarium provides an opportunity for a thorough survey of the small plants of a given area.

Make a terrarium case that will enclose 1 square foot (144 square

Jewel Aquarium Company

A terrarium case with aquarium base makes all kinds of plantings possible. Slanting front gives easy viewing.

inches) of ground (12 by 12 inches, or 10 by 14.4 inches), or $\frac{1}{2}$ square foot (6 by 12 inches, or 8 by 9 inches). Cover the bottom with 1 inch of gravel. Place on top of this a 3-inch-thick sod of grass, or piece of forest carpet, cut to the size of the terrarium. Make every effort to keep the sod intact while putting it in.

Sprinkle it thoroughly with water. Cover and keep it in semishade in a fairly cool spot. See what develops. You will discover much animal life, in addition to plant life, in your survey terrarium. Keep a record of the insects—centipedes, spiders, mites, and others—that may emerge.

If moisture condenses on the inside, remove the glass entirely.

FLOWER PHOTOGRAPHY

"WORK WANTED—Photographic model of exceptional beauty, with natural, inborn grace, colorful, able to pose untiringly without temperamental upsets, no compensation asked. . . ." The photographer's dream come true!

Few human beings would fit such a description. But most flowers do. That is what makes flower photography such a pleasant occupation.

Stills

EQUIPMENT—Camera and lenses—For flower photography, use a camera that makes it possible for you to fill the whole negative with a single flower head. You will not always want to do this, but it should be possible for you to do so.

That means a camera with close-up lenses, macro lenses or telephoto lenses, and probably also extension tubes and bellows. It also means a device whereby knife-sharp focusing can be done—either on the camera's own ground glass or by means of a focusing attachment.

Tripod—For focusing purposes, you also need a tripod. The ordinary tripod is of no help unless its legs can be folded all the way out, completely flat. Best is a special low tripod, the kind used for tabletop photography. Flower photography is belly photography. You need to get down where you can be at "plant-eye level" with your models.

Flash—On overcast days or when photographing in deep shade, you may have to resort to a flash—electronic or bulb.

TAKING STILLS—Lighting—Your best lighting is forenoon and afternoon sunlight; the best time is a couple of hours before and after high noon. At those hours, the light strikes the flowers from the side, modeling them with a rather soft shadow effect. Noon itself is not very satisfactory because the light is harsh; it hits your flowers from above and casts dense, unpleasant shadows.

Move around the flower you intend to photograph. Look at it from all angles until you have found the most striking effect. Sidelighting accentuates the shape of most flowers. Many photograph especially well when backlighted, with the sun shining through their petals.

¶ *Tip*—To soften the shadows, use a metal reflector, 10 by 14 inches, or so. Crinkle up a piece of aluminum foil; smooth it out somewhat; paste it on cardboard. Prop up the reflector with the help of a short stick.

¶ *Tip*—Use a polarizing screen for white flowers in bright sun, for better modeling of their structure.

Background—The proper background is of great importance in flower photography. The subject should stand out clearly against its surroundings.

A single brilliantly colored flower may stand out against almost any background, but a less conspicuous plant will disappear in a jumbled net of crisscross lines unless you give it special attention:

The sky as background—Tall plants appear even taller and more spectacular when photographed from a low angle against a blue sky or a sky with a few scattered clouds. Shoot through a light or medium-yellow filter in black-and-white photography.

Out-of-focus background—A sharply delineated flower will stand out effectively against a background of soft, blurred masses. To achieve this effect, focus critically on the center of the flower,

Sky background will make every flower show up sharply. If photographed in color, blue sky will provide spectacular effect.

Eastman Kodak Company

Diffused background makes specimen stand out clearly. It results from focusing sharply, opening up diaphragm, using increased speed.

Close-up of single specimen reveals intricate design. 35-mm slide, shown on a 32-by 48-inch screen, will give a magnification of 1000× area size.

William Hillcourt

then open up the diaphragm wide enough to throw everything else out of focus.

SHADOW BACKGROUND—Compose your shot, with the camera lens slightly higher than the flower. Look through the focusing device and determine what surroundings constitute the background. Throw a shadow over those surroundings with a piece of cardboard. In this manner, your flower stands out brightly against a much darker background—as long as you watch out that the shadow does not hit the flower itself.

Whatever you do about backgrounds, p-l-e-a-s-e use nature's own. Don't detract from a good flower portrait with a cardboard or cloth background—except in those rare instances where an artificial background may mean the difference between a picture and none at all.

Exposures—In taking an exposure reading with a meter, remember that you get the reading not just from the flower itself, but also from its surroundings. So use the substitution method, taking your reading on gray cardboard. If the flower is light, close down the diaphragm accordingly.

The correct exposure is, of course, especially important in color photography. Although frontlighting is usually preferred, you can get striking effects with side- and backlighting. If you have arrived at the proper stop for frontlighting, open up one full stop for a side-lighted, two full stops for a backlighted subject.

¶ Tip—Flowers with finely veined white petals, or of a pale hue, often appear "washed out" in color, even though the exposure is correct. By underexposing slightly—one-half stop, for instance—you are able to deepen the color. But don't overdo it!

Watch your time setting. If you decide on a small aperture, you may have to shoot at $1/20$ or $1/10$ of a second. This is OK on a perfectly still day, but not on a windy day. A slight breeze will require $1/50$ of a second or less. If the wind is stronger, protect the plant with a screen of clear plastic sheeting, wait for a lull, or come again some other day.

WHAT TO PHOTOGRAPH—Instead of setting out on an indiscriminate hunt, specialize from the beginning.

Flowers around the year—Starting in early spring, photograph the flowers as they appear.

Flowers of a certain region, of a certain plant family, of plants of certain specific uses.

Symmetry of nature—The almost architectural effect of opening buds, unrolling fern fronds, venation in flower petals, structure of seedpods, and so on.

Series—Whole plant, leaf detail, flower, fruit of a number of different plants—probably the most revealing and profitable kind of plant photography.

Sequences—From tight bud, through blossoming, to seed, of the same plant.

The unusual—The tiny dark purple flower in the middle of a Queen Anne's lace's flat-top flower cluster, the real flower of skunk cabbage or jack-in-the-pulpit, the violet flower that never opens, tiny ferns, and many more.

¶ *Tip*—When you are photographing small plants, it is often well to include a familiar subject in the picture—a leaf, a twig, or the like—to indicate the relative size.

Movies

EQUIPMENT—**Camera and lenses**—In photographing movies, as well as stills, you will find wild flowers easy to work with, provided you have the right camera. You need to get close to your subject for best effect. The lens for the usual family movie camera won't get you there.

In the beginning, you can make use of a portable titler. Compose your picture within the frame. What you have in your frame is what you get in your shot.

Sooner or later you will want to get closer to your flowers for more spectacular effects. You will then require supplementary lenses, extension tubes, or bellows, possibly telephoto lenses. Unless the camera has through-lens focusing, you will need a focusing device to ensure getting what you aim for, and getting it in sharp focus.

Tripod—For most of your flower shots, you will want a low tripod.

MOVIE TECHNIQUES—With much nature moviemaking, you have to grab what you can get, when you can get it. For flower movies, you can develop and follow a script for a complete film. It can be simple—"A Day in Spring"—or complex—"The Glory of Creation." It can be close to home—"Our Wild Flower Garden"—or of social significance—"Saving Our Heritage."

Sequences—As you take your shots, you will probably work in sequences of medium shot, close-up, extra close-up. But don't stop with a single angle. Move around your subject and shoot it from several sides. Add a few distance shots to establish locale and provide atmosphere.

Mood—There are moods to flowers. Try to catch them. The proud sunflower—make it look taller by shooting it from a low angle. The shy arbutus—show it hiding among dead leaves. The pink lady's-slipper—make those colors sing! The Cinderella idea: a casual shot of a dandelion—then a single head filling the whole screen in its golden glory!

¶ *Tip*—"Dew-kissed" flowers photograph well. If nature doesn't supply the dew, a window-spray bottle or an atomizer will.

Motion—Movies should be motion pictures. The breeze that might spoil a still is your best ally in taking movies. A soft stir is pleasing, but watch out for gusts that may throw your subject out of the view of your lens.

Stooges—Where there are flowers, there are insects. Let them come around, then shoot while they visit your flower subject. They will add further motion and interest to your film. But don't get insects into every one of your shots. It is a flower film you are aiming for, not an insect picture.

PLANT COLLECTING

Plant collecting is probably the easiest and least expensive of all types of nature collecting. You can start anywhere, and the equipment for preparing a satisfactory collection is found in the ordinary household.

Note—Know your state laws in regard to protected flowers, and respect other people's property when you are collecting. A true botanist and plant lover is eager to "Save the wild flowers." Therefore, never pick a flower unless six are seen, never collect a plant with root unless ten are found. *Refrain from collecting rare plants threatened with extinction* (see page 235).

The Herbarium

The most popular type of plant collection is the herbarium—pressed, dried plants, mounted on sheets of thin cardboard. When carefully put together, a herbarium may be valuable for years to come to show the plant life of a certain region; some European herbariums established almost five hundred years ago are still in excellent condition.

You can start a simple herbarium around your home or around camp with whatever materials you have on hand, or you can go in for expert methods from the start, developing or purchasing the necessary equipment.

Whatever you do, there are four simple rules you need to follow to make a good herbarium: 1. Collect whole plants. 2. Dry them thoroughly under pressure. 3. Mount them carefully. 4. Label them correctly.

Simplified Herbarium Methods

If you are interested mostly in making a collection of plants from your immediate vicinity, you can generally dispense with the kind of collecting equipment that an expert botanist would take along. As a matter of fact, if you are working with a group of youngsters, you will find it a deterrence to collecting if you insist on carting equipment along every time you go hiking. Although expert botanists will frown on the idea of bringing home a wilting bouquet of field flowers, it is the simplest way of getting started—provided your bouquet consists of carefully collected whole plants. The specimens may have wilted a bit on the way home, but they will usually regain their freshness if placed in water for a short while, whereupon they are ready for pressing.

Pressing the finds—Make up two pressing boards, 12 by 17 inches, by nailing together a few pieces of scrap wood or slats from an orange crate. Open up some newspapers and make 16-by-23-inch sheets—the standard newspaper size—by cutting along the left folds. Tabloid newspapers are already cut to size and need only be taken apart.

Put one of the pressing boards on the table. Fold three newspaper sheets in half and lay them on the pressing board.

Spread a newspaper sheet before you, and place your first plant on the right half of it, arranging it in a natural manner. Fold the left half of the paper over, and write the name of the enclosed plant in the right-hand corner of this folder. Place this specimen folder on the press, and cover it with a layer of three newspaper sheets folded in half. Continue in this manner, alternating specimen folders with layers of newspaper.

When your stack is $\frac{1}{2}$ foot high (or less), place the other pressing board on top of it. Finally, put a weight on top—stones for instance—or strap the whole pile tightly together with two straps—web or leather—or Scout belts.

Give the plants a first pressing for about fourteen to eighteen hours. Then replace all papers in the pile with fresh dry sheets. This goes for your specimen folders as well as for the drying sheets. Rearrange the specimens, if necessary, in the new specimen folders. Remember to transfer the plant names to the outside of the new folders.

After another twenty-four hours, open up the pile again. This time, leave the specimen folders intact; simply renew the drying sheets.

Follow the same procedure every twenty-four to forty-eight hours until the plants are thoroughly dry. The job should be completed in a week or ten days unless the weather is exceptionally humid.

Standard Herbarium Methods

Herbarium methods vary somewhat among the experts, but generally they follow these lines:

COLLECTING EQUIPMENT—Field press—For collecting, the most common piece of equipment used today is the field press. Several models are available commercially.

You can easily make your own from two pieces of heavy cardboard or $\frac{1}{4}$-inch plywood, cut to a standard size of 12 by 18 inches. Or rivet or nail $1\frac{1}{2}$-inch-wide, $\frac{1}{4}$-inch-thick strips of wood together into two 12-by-18-inch lattice frames, keeping the strips approximately $1\frac{1}{2}$ inches apart.

Between the two sections of the field press, place a dozen or more specimen folders made from unprinted newsprint or old newspapers, and just as many pieces, plus one, of "driers"—heavy blotting paper, gray "building felt," or "carpet paper," cut to 12 by 18 inches, or standard herbarium driers. Hold everything together with two web straps equipped with adjustable buckles. For comfort in carrying, you may want to add a shoulder strap.

Vasculum—The collection box, or vasculum, once the trademark of the botanist, is now used mainly for bringing home fresh specimens that are to be studied and analyzed. If you prefer to do the arrangement of plants and preparation for pressing at home rather than in the field, you will need a vasculum of metal or a modern-day equivalent made of plastic.

¶ *Tip*—A bag of heavy-duty plastic will protect your plants against drying out as well as will a vasculum. It is lightweight and can be folded up when not in use.

Other equipment—In addition to needing a field press or vasculum, you will need a trowel for digging up roots and a sharp pocketknife for snipping large plants into sections and for trimming down bulky specimens.

Bring a number of thin cards for identifying the spot where each plant was found. Place the card in the field press next to the plant, or make a slit in the card and push it up over the plant stem.

And then there's your perpetual companion: your notebook for keeping notes of plant names, locality, growing conditions, and so forth.

COLLECTING TECHNIQUES—To be perfect, a specimen should show all the features of the plant: root, stem, leaves, bud, flower, fruit. If the plant is dioecious, that is, has male and female flowers on separate plants, get both plants.

Dig up each plant carefully, then place it in a specimen folder of newsprint. Spread out the plant to reveal as much as possible of the structure. Make it look natural. Keep away from the outdated and unlovely "walking stick" style. Arrange some flowers faceup, others face down, and some of the leaves with the underside showing. The latter is especially important when pressing ferns.

Small species will fit readily into your specimen folders. So will any plants up to 3 feet—provided you bend their stems into a sharp-angled V or N.

¶ *Tip*—If the springiness of a bent stem tends to throw part of the plant outside the folder, cut a slit in a small piece of stiff paper and bring the slit paper down over the bend.

Write a serial number on the front of each specimen folder, and jot down all necessary data about the plant in your notebook under the corresponding number.

Place the specimen folders in the press, alternating them with herbarium driers. Close the press and tighten the straps around it.

The plants may be kept in the field press until the morning after your field trip, but preferably not any longer. They should be transferred to the drying press as soon as possible.

PRESSING—The usual drying press is similar to the lattice-work field press, only made of heavier material—$\frac{1}{2}$-inch wood strips, spaced about 1 inch apart.

Plant presses come in a wide variety of designs. Simplest field press consists of two pieces of plywood held together with two webbing straps with buckles.

Metal field press is made up of two reinforced metal sheets perforated with a number of large holes for ventilation. Held together with two webbing straps.

Lattice-work field press is assembled from $\frac{1}{4}$-inch-wide strips of wood, bolted together about $1\frac{1}{2}$ inches apart. It is provided with two adjustable webbing straps.

All photos courtesy: Carolina Biological Supply Company

Plant press for laboratory work requires heavy-duty construction. Frames are made from 5-ply wood. Pressure is applied by turn-handles on metal screw rods.

Place a herbarium drier on one of the press sections. Put on top of it a specimen folder with the first plant in place in it. Then another drier, another specimen in its folder, and so on, finishing with a drier and the other press section. Strap tightly together or place heavy weights on top of the pile. The pressure will prevent the leaves from wrinkling as the plant dries.

After about twenty-four hours, replace the herbarium driers with fresh sheets, and strap up the pile again. Dry the moist driers for future use. Repeat with twenty-four-hour intervals until the specimens are thoroughly dried. They are dry when they no longer feel cool to the touch, when the leaves are stiff and a stem snaps when bent.

¶ *Tip*—The drying process may be speeded up by the use of "ventilators" of double-surfaced corrugated cardboard—bought or cut out of cardboard boxes—with the corrugations running crosswise. The sheets are then placed in the press in the following order: ventilator, drier, specimen folder, drier, ventilator, drier, specimen folder, drier, ventilator, and so on.
For extra-quick drying, the "ventilated" press may be placed in direct sun, on top of an idling automobile motor, or at a safe distance over a stove.

When the plants are dry, go carefully through the specimen folders and write out a 2-by-3-inch label for each plant, with the name of plant, where collected, the date, the collector's name.

MOUNTING—For mounting, use regular herbarium mounting paper. This is thin cardboard, cut to standard size of 11½ by 16½ inches. It pays to buy a good quality if you intend your collection to last.

Drying press of latticework. Notice order of driers and corrugated ventilators, above and below specimen folders.

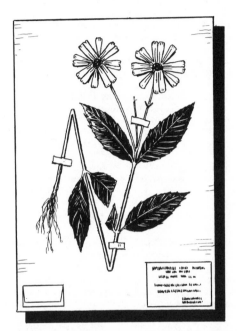

A well-arranged, well-pressed, well-mounted plant specimen. Note N-shape of stem, seed envelope at left, label.

The specimens are mounted on the mounting sheets by gluing, taping, or tying—whichever method you think best.

Gluing—The method of gluing the whole plant to the sheet is easy after a little practice, and undoubtedly produces the neatest display. The disadvantages of this method are that you can never transfer the plant to another sheet without damaging it, and that you can study only one side of the plant. Nevertheless, it is a method commonly used by expert collectors.

To do a good mounting job, use a sheet of glass, 12 by 17 inches, or a smooth cookie sheet. With a broad brush, spread a thin layer of herbarium glue or slightly diluted LePage's glue evenly over the glass.

Pick up the plant specimen with forceps. Place it, bottom side down, on the glue. Use the forceps to press all parts down into the glue. Lift up the specimen and lower it carefully to the mounting sheet in a pleasing arrangement. Moisten the specimen label and paste it in the right-hand corner. Cover the sheet with a piece of unprinted newsprint or other white paper. Place a heavy book or a marble or cement slab on top of it to hold it down while drying.

Continue mounting your specimens in this manner, placing one finished sheet over the other with protecting sheets of newsprint between them. Run the brush over the glass from time to time to keep the glue layer smooth and even.

Taping—Taping is a more tedious process than gluing. In this method, the specimen is fastened to a herbarium sheet with thin strips of gummed cloth in strategic locations, across stems and, occasionally, leaves.

Gummed cloth comes in sheets and in tapes $\frac{3}{4}$ inch and $1\frac{1}{2}$ inches wide. Cut a supply of $\frac{1}{8}$-inch-wide strips, and keep a wet sponge handy for moistening them.

Tying—Especially coarse plant parts may refuse to be stuck to the mounting sheet with glue or tapes. In that case, you will have to tie them on.

Thread a needle with a piece of strong green thread. Push the needle through the mounting sheet, from the top, at one side of the plant part. Bring the thread in from the back on the other side of the plant part. Tie the two ends of the thread together over the plant part, then trim off the excess thread. Use as many loops of this kind as may be necessary.

SPECIAL METHODS—Most flowering plants and such flowerless plants as ferns give no trouble in pressing and mounting. But some plants and plant parts require special treatment.

Fleshy plants—Plants with thick succulent stems and leaves will dry slowly, at best. They often keep on living even in the drying press—sending out new shoots, refusing to give up. Before placing them in the press, dip them in boiling water for a few moments. That kills the cells and makes drying easier. As far as possible, keep the flowers of such plants above the surface of the boiling water, or pick extra flowers to press separately.

Plants with thick parts—Some plants have heavy stems, thick roots,

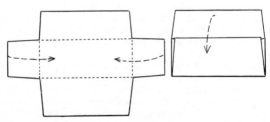

Seed envelope may be made from a piece of white paper, cut and folded as shown. Glue to the left on mounting sheet.

Delicate algae are floated onto their mounting papers so that they will have a chance to spread out naturally.

large flower heads, bulky fruits that do not press flat. Trim down the thickness by slicing off the back half—the part that will not show when the plant is mounted. Then press in the usual manner.

Seeds—Seeds are often important in the identification of a plant, but they have the bad habit of falling off the specimens. They are therefore placed in small envelopes of white paper, cut and folded as shown in the diagram on page 254 or in small cellophane envelopes. Paste seed envelopes in the left-hand corner of the mounting sheets.

Mosses and lichens—Mosses and lichens should be picked in "fruiting" condition, as far as possible. They can be kept in clear plastic boxes without pressing. If they are to be mounted, they need a certain amount of flattening.

Smaller specimens must be dried under light pressure, otherwise important characteristics of growth may be obliterated. Small specimens are usually kept in envelopes of a standard size of 4 by 5½ inches.

Larger specimens will take more pressure. They may be mounted on regular mounting sheets.

Algae—In collecting algae, get, as far as possible, all parts: foliage, stem (called stipe), and holdfast. If the algae are from salt water, soak in fresh water for about half an hour before mounting. Otherwise the salt will prevent them from drying completely.

Coarse seaweeds are dried in the usual manner. But delicate algae, with thousands of threadlike parts, would look miserable if pulled out of the water and slapped onto a piece of mounting paper.

Instead, float the alga in fresh water in a shallow dish. Slip a piece of mounting paper under the alga. Hold the end of the stalk against the paper, at an appropriate point. Move the paper gently, setting the alga in motion. When it has feathered out neatly, bring the paper with the alga slowly out of the water. Let the water drain off by placing the paper on a slanting surface. Cover the alga with a piece of unbleached muslin the size of the mounting paper, then with a piece of blotting paper. Place it in the drying press, and press it in the usual way. No gluing is necessary. The gelatinous substance of the alga takes care of the mounting. When it is completely dry, peel off the muslin.

LABELING—Attach a label to the lower right-hand corner of the herbarium sheet and write on it the necessary information. This should include the name of the plant (scientific and common), the name of the plant family, where collected, the date collected, the name of collector, ecological data, and reference number.

STORING—When your mounting sheets are ready, sort out your plants, following the order in your botany manual.

Place all the plants of one genus together in a *genus folder*—all the goldenrods, all the asters, and so on. This is a manila folder slightly larger than the mounting sheets, 12 by 17 inches.

The genus folders, in turn, are placed in *family folders* or portfolios made of cardboard sides with cloth backs.

The complete herbarium is finally stored in a suitable container—a cardboard or wooden box for a small collection, a cabinet with $12\frac{1}{2}$-by-$17\frac{1}{2}$-inch shelves or drawers for the large collection.

¶ *Tip*—To protect the collection against insects, place a small amount of a mixture of paradichlorobenzene and naphthalene crystals, half and half, in a cloth bag on the bottom of your storage container.

Displaying Pressed Plants

You may consider it a pity to store away some of your most beautiful specimens on a shelf or in a drawer, where few will have a chance to see them. Also, you may need your specimens for demonstration or instruction—yet want to protect your plants against injury. There are several ways of solving these problems.

Cellophane sheet covers—For handling mounted plants safely, cover the mounts with a thin sheet of cellophane. Such sheets may be cut out of rolls, or bought, cut to a size of $12\frac{1}{2}$ by $17\frac{1}{2}$ inches, from a scientific supply house.

Lay a cellophane sheet over the mounting sheet. Fold about 1 inch of cellophane over at the top, and glue this to the back of the mounting sheet. Fasten the lower front edge of the cellophane to the herbarium sheet with a couple of short strips of scotch tape.

Botanical Riker mounts—A Riker mount for a botanical specimen is easily prepared. All you need is a piece of glass or sheet plastic, a piece of cardboard of the same size, a thin layer of cotton batting, also cut to size, and a few feet of black masking tape.

Place the cardboard on the table, and cover it with the cotton batting. Arrange the plant specimen on the cotton, and press the glass down over it. Seal it along the edges with masking tape.

Plastic mount—You may make an airproof mount by placing your plant specimen between two layers of clear transparent self-adhesive plastic, such as Con-Tact.

Cut two pieces of plastic to whatever size you prefer. Remove the covering from one piece and place the plastic on a smooth surface, sticky side up. Arrange the pressed plant specimen carefully on the plastic and press it firmly in position with a finger. Cover it with a second piece of plastic, starting from the top edge and carefully smoothing it down as you go.

¶ *Tip*—Instead of using two sheets of plastic, you can use one sheet with a backing of acetate sheet or glazed cardboard.

¶ *Tip*—For instant display, use fresh plants. The mounted plants may retain their color and natural look for a year or more.

Other Collections

SEEDS—Small seeds and flat seeds may be kept in cellophane envelopes. Seeds with fluff, spines, wings, or the like might suffer from this treatment; they are better off in short, round, straight-walled vials with corks or screw caps.

¶ *Tip*—Many collectors keep all types of small seeds in vials, labeling around the top with narrow labels—Dennison No. 261, for instance.

For display purposes, seed vials may be wired to sheets of plywood or heavy cardboard.

FLESHY FRUITS—Fleshy fruits that would shrink up and become unrecognizable in drying may be preserved in glass jars in 10 percent formalin.

¶ *Tip*—The trouble with formalin is that it almost always bleaches out the natural colors of specimens kept in it. To keep some of this color, try adding 10 per cent ordinary cane sugar to the solution.

FUNGI—Mushrooms and other fungi present one of the toughest problems for the collector. Here are a couple of methods.

DRIED MUSHROOMS—**Air and heat drying fungi**—The most common way of preserving mushrooms is to dry them. One way of doing this is by stringing them on heavy thread and suspending them in the sun or over a hot stove until they are dry.

For a more efficient method, spread the specimens on a piece of cloth over an open rack. Place them in the oven. The proper temperature for drying is between 130 and 160 degrees. To get the desired temperature, you must set the oven at its lowest heat and keep the oven door open. It is a matter of slow drying, not baking.

When thoroughly dry, the specimens may be kept in cellophane envelopes. Or you may decide to flatten them down a bit and mount them on regular herbarium sheets or special cards.

Silica-gel drying fungi—To retain the shape of the mushroom—although in reduced size—use silica gel.

Pour a $\frac{1}{2}$-inch layer of silica gel into a container of plastic or glass. Place the mushrooms on the silica gel, top of cap down. Pour additional silica gel around and over the mushrooms. Close the container and make it airtight with a strip of adhesive tape. Leave it undisturbed for a couple of days, then pour out the silica gel and remove the mushrooms for storage in plastic boxes.

Dry the silica gel for repeated use (see page 240).

Protected against draft, the spores from a gilled mushroom will fall into a spore print of intricate pattern.

SPORE PRINTS—During the mushroom's short lifespan, spores by the millions drop from its gills. Catch the spores as they fall, for they create an intricate and beautiful pattern. But great care is needed in doing this since the slightest draft sends the microscopic spores flying.

Mucilage method—Spread a very thin coat of a mixture of mucilage and water, half and half (or egg white, stirred to liquid with a fork), over a piece of thin cardboard. Cut the stem of a mature, fully opened mushroom directly under the cap. Place the cap, bottom down, in the middle of the cardboard.

¶ *Tip*—If the gills protrude below the edge of the cap so that they will fold under when placed on the paper, the whole cap needs to be kept slightly raised over the paper. Push three toothpicks into the side of the cap and keep it suspended on these by resting them on small wood or cork supports.

Cover the layout with a turned-over glass dish, and leave it undisturbed for twenty-four hours.

During this time the spores will fall down and will stick in the mucilage, made moist from the natural moisture of the mushroom. Lift the cap off, and let the sheet dry in the air.

You can further fix the spore print by spraying it with ordinary fixative.

Colors of spores vary from white, through pink and rusty brown, to black. To have your spore prints show up, use a dark-colored or black paper for mushrooms with light spores, and vice versa.

¶ *Tip*—No mushroom has blue spores. So why not use a medium-blue paper for all your spore prints?

Wax-paper method—Instead of mucilage-coated cardboard, use a piece of wax paper, and proceed as above.

When the spore print is completed, fix the spores in the wax by transferring the paper carefully to an electric hot plate. Leave it until the wax has melted, then remove it and let it cool.

CHAPTER 9

Trees

F̲OR recreation and pleasure, we take to the woods. There's a certain primitive enjoyment in walking along a half-hidden trail under the green canopy of tall trees, listening to the forest murmurs . . . the wind in the treetops, the calls of birds . . . the footfalls of animals scampering away before your approach.

In almost all nature activities, sooner or later you will be drawn to the woods—into the closely knit community of trees and shrubs, with the myriads of other plants that make up the forest carpet, the soil from which they all spring, the creatures that live in it, the lakes and streams that traverse it. The forests of our country hold an unending fascination for all who enter them.

And then, some day, you may stop under a mighty tree in wonder, thinking of the forces that send the sap surging from the deepest root tip to the highest twig, the power of the green leaves to pull nourishment out of the air, the riddle of bud opening and leaf falling, and a hundred other things.

Or you may listen to the voice of the trees, as expressed by an unknown author:

Ye who pass by, harm me not. I am the heat of your hearth on cold winter nights, the friendly shade screening you from the summer sun. My fruits are refreshing draughts quenching your thirst as you journey on. I am the beam that holds your house, the board of your table, the bed on which you lie, the timber that builds your boat. I am the handle of your hoe, the door of your homestead, the wood of your cradle, the shell of your coffin. I am the gift of God and the friend of man. Ye who pass by, listen to my prayer.

In spite of the fact that we depend so much on trees, we have not played fair with our natural treasures. We have cut and burned and wasted a large part of our original heritage.

Fortunately, we are waking up! Today the importance of conserving and perpetuating our forest resources is recognized by every thinking citizen.

BOOKS ON TREES—H. Kleijn and B. K. Boom, *Glory of the Tree*. New York, Doubleday & Company.

John Kieran, *Introduction to Trees*. New York, Doubleday & Company.

Trees. U.S. Department of Agriculture Yearbook, 1949. Catalog No. A 1.10:949. $4.00. From Superintendent of Documents, U.S. Government Printing Office, Washington, D.C. 20402.

Working with Others

Getting to know the trees may be a personal pursuit—whether you do so by taking walks in the woods or by growing trees in your home garden or wood lot. On the other hand, you may be one among the many who have their interest in forestry awakened to the point of determined community action. The need for such action is becoming more and more evident—not just for the sake of beautification, but also for the sake of environmental quality—to provide recreational facilities and forestry products for the future.

You will find youth groups, schools, and service clubs willing to listen to suggestions for projects for planting trees, and eager to get to work. Plans of this type, carried out successfully in numerous communities, have involved such varied aspects as establishing a memorial grove, improving school grounds, ball park, and Scout camp grounds, creating a springtime display of flowering dogwood along the main approach to the town, planting willows along riverbanks to stop erosion, developing a community forest.

In all such projects, whether for your home grounds or on a community scale, your county agent and the agricultural experiment station of your state are ready to help you with expert advice. In many instances, they are also able to provide you with seedlings free or at low cost. You can learn further ideas from the U.S. Forest Service of the Department of Agriculture, the National Park Service of the Department of the Interior, both with headquarters in Washington, D.C., and from national associations interested in trees.

SOCIETIES—American Forestry Association. Headquarters: 919 Seventeenth Street, NW, Washington, D.C. 20006. Periodical: *American Forests.*

Wilderness Society. Headquarters: 729 Fifteenth Street, NW, Washington, D.C. 20005. Periodical: *Living Wilderness.*

TREES IN FIELD AND FOREST

Equipment for Tree Study

The main pieces of equipment for tree study are the same as you would use for studying herbaceous plants.

STUDY EQUIPMENT—Magnifiers—Any of the magnifiers described on page 151 is suitable. You may never need one for the identification of a tree, since most trees have a number of readily seen identifying marks. But you may want it to catch the beauty of often tiny and inconspicuous tree flowers, and to study wood and tree rings.

Knife—A penknife with a strong, sharp blade is necessary for making cross sections of branches to find out their structure and to determine the color and consistency of their sap.

Measuring devices—Foresters use special gadgets for measuring diameter, height, and board-foot volume of trees—caliper, tree scale, or cruiser's stick. You can get along with a tape measure for measuring diameter, and a foot rule for finding the height.

Measure a tree's diameter at breast height (dbh for short)—$4\frac{1}{2}$ feet above the ground. Take the girth of the tree with your tape measure, then divide by 3 to get a rough diameter, by π (3.1416) for a more exact measurement.

To measure the height of a tree, make a chalk mark on the trunk at your own height. Step back. Hold the ruler upright with your hand outstretched at full arm's length before you. Close one eye. Continue to step back until $\frac{1}{2}$ inch of the ruler covers the distance from the ground to the chalk mark on the trunk. Now measure the whole tree, on the ruler, from the same position. Multiply the number of half-inches by your height to get the height of the tree.

Tree books—For the specific trees of your region, drop a line to the forestry service of your state. It probably has available, free or at low cost, a booklet on the forest trees of your section.

For a more comprehensive view, get a good field book of common trees, and carry it with you on your field trips.

BOOKS FOR FIELD IDENTIFICATION—F. Schuyler Mathews, *Field Book of American Trees and Shrubs*. New York, G. P. Putnam's Sons.

C. Frank Brockman, *Trees of North America—A Golden Field Guide*. New York, Golden Press.

George A. Petrides, *Field Guide to Trees and Shrubs*. Boston, Houghton Mifflin Company.

William M. Harlow, *Trees of the Eastern and Central United States and Canada*. New York, Dover Publications.

Edward E. McMinn and Evelyn Maino. *Illustrated Manual of Pacific Coast Trees*. Berkeley, University of California Press.

J. B. Perry, *Western Forest Trees*. New York, Dover Publications.

Charlotte H. Green, *Trees of the South*. Chapel Hill, North Carolina, University of North Carolina Press.

When it becomes a matter of identifying trees of the rather uncommon species, you may have to resort to Gray's *New Botany* (see page 230) or to Sargent.

BOOK FOR ADVANCED IDENTIFICATION—Charles S. Sargent, *Manual of the Trees of North America*. New York, Dover Publications.

Notebook—Your notebook may be a small bound volume or a loose-leaf book in which you can keep a record of the names and important details of the trees you discover. Include a number of map sketches among your notes, with the location of prominent trees clearly indicated so that you can find them again.

¶ *Tip*—In addition to learning about trees on your field trips you may locate the thickest tree, the tallest tree, the tree with the widest spread, within your community. Record them carefully.

Finding Trees

WHERE?—The answer to the Where? is easy: "Wherever they are!" If they are found at all in your locality, you will certainly know about them.

In the beginning, get to know the trees of your immediate vicinity. Find out what species associate to make up your local woods, and learn some of the reasons why these specific trees grow and thrive in your region—soil conditions, temperature, light, rainfall, and so on.

Having once started on the subject of trees, you will want to expand your circle of knowledge ever farther and farther afield—to your county, your state, eventually to famous trees and forests of our country.

Your vacation trips will take on new meaning as you add to your list of tree acquaintances. You have a lifelong hobby before you, with breathtaking sights and quiet excitement—Eastern dogwood and Southern magnolia in bloom, scarlet fall flames of sugar maples over New England, splashes of golden-yellow aspen among the dark-green ponderosas on a Rocky Mountain slope, cypresses of Monterey with their gnarled limbs, royal palms of the Everglades in their slender beauty, mangroves and sequoias and mesquites and joshua trees. Historical trees, unusual trees, the world's tallest or oldest trees—you will find them scattered throughout the length and breadth of our country, in state and national forests and parks.

WHEN?—If you are concentrating on a single phase in the lives of trees, you will have to watch your season. Otherwise, trees are there to be studied year round: the unfolding of the leaves in the spring, formation of flowers and fruit in summer, fall coloration of foliage, twigs, and wintering buds—and, starting all over again with the sap running in the old trees, the first tiny sprouts of the new seedling.

Tree Lists and Surveys

LIFE LISTS—Your list of trees discovered and observed will grow from field trip to field trip—in the beginning in spurts, then slowly, until you have located and become familiar with all local species.

You will, of course, keep a record of your finds in your field notebook. In addition, develop a separate list to be left at home, to which you can add new species as you come upon them in your wanderings. Such a listing may take the form of marginal notes in your field book of trees, or it may occupy a special notebook.

SURVEYS—It often becomes of interest to make a thorough tree survey of a given area—school grounds, city park, camp. The effectiveness of such a survey depends on the size of the area covered, and the number and skill of the people participating in the survey.

¶ *Tip*—Get the cooperation of local groups interested in nature—nature clubs, biology classes, Boy Scouts and Girl Scouts, garden clubs, and others.

General tree survey—For a thorough, general tree survey of an area, divide the area into squares with sides approximately 100 feet long (40 average walking steps), marking the corners of each square in a conspicuous way, such as, for example, with sticks with paper streamers if the survey is in an open area, with strips of gauze bandage tied around trees in a forest. Place two or more investigators in each square, with instructions to pick a leafy twig of each different tree and shrub they find, and to bring their haul to a central spot at a certain time. Arrange all specimens according to species and have the experts catalog them.

Tree census—A census of local trees is another job that a nature club or youth group might undertake.

Get a street map of your community or a topographic map of the area. Divide it into sections—in town by the middle of streets, in the field by paths, streams, or other landmarks. Send a couple of investigators into each section, with instructions to count all trees present that are at least 4 inches thick, indicating the number of each species. Tabulate the result.

TREE CALENDARS—A tree calendar may be developed along the lines suggested for flower calendars and calendar charts (page 231).

The notes here may include: (1) unfolding of first leaf; (2) flowers in bloom (shedding of pollen); (3) fruits ripe; (4) first indication of fall coloration; (5) all leaves shed.

Field Observations

Your early field trips will be mostly for the sake of locating and identifying the trees of your neighborhood. When that has been accomplished, you may want to delve deeper into the life of a single tree or of a tree association—trees that live together because they require the same living conditions of soil, moisture, and light.

Tree associations—What are the main tree associations in your area—beech-maple-hemlock, oak-hickory, pine, or what? How do they differ? Why do they differ?

Tree diary—The life of a tree for a full year, based on once-a-week observations.

Tree community—Not just the tree itself, but other plants and creatures that live on and in it.

Budding and leafing—How are leaves arranged in the bud? How does the bud open?

Flowers—How pollinated? By insects? Wind? Self-pollination?

Seed dispersal—How dispersed? By wind, water, animals, birds?

Other reproduction—By suckers, sprouts from stump, and so on.

Barks—How do they differ? Thickness of bark—thickest in what compass direction?

Fall colorations—Listing of trees by colors—from light yellow of poplars and birches, through orange and red of sugar maple, to flaming scarlet of scarlet oak and tupelo. Influence of weather—light, moisture, temperature.

Trees in winter—Recognition by silhouettes, bark, buds, leaf scars.

Stump detecting—Study stumps and, by observation and deduction, decide the facts of the tree's life and death. The following questions, adapted from William Gould Vinal's *Nature Recreation*, show the possibilities:

1. What kind of tree was this?
2. How old was it when cut?
3. How much was its average annual increase in diameter?
4. In what year did it grow most rapidly?
5. Approximately when was it cut?
6. (a) What tools were used? (b) In what order?
7. (a) Number of workmen? (b) Amateur(s) or woodsman (or men)?
8. Where did he (or they) stand?
9. In what direction did the tree fall?
10. Was it cut during a strong wind or a calm?

GROWING NATIVE TREES

In deciding on trees for your home grounds, keep in mind that the trees you plant will thrive only if your locality provides the climate that matches their natural living conditions. You will have no luck attempting to grow a species native to the North in the all-year warmth of southern Florida. Neither can you expect a Southern tree to survive the harshness of a New England winter.

Before you plant, therefore, note what trees are already doing well in your locality, or check with local nurserymen or other authorities and get their recommendations. Write to your state forester or contact your local agricultural agent. Their advice is yours for the asking.

TRANSPLANTING TREES—You will know that the climate is suitable if you transplant native trees or shrubs into your garden from your immediate vicinity—with permission, of course, if they are from someone else's property.

Time for transplanting—The best time for transplanting trees is when the running of the sap is at the lowest ebb—from September or October to early in the year. Late fall is the generally recommended time, but much transplanting is done in early spring.

Don't accept this as an arbitrary rule. Trees can be moved successfully at almost any time of the year, if the proper care is taken.

Transplanting hints—As a general hint for transplanting—don't bite off more than you can chew. In other words, don't attempt to move a tree that's too large to stand successful transplanting. As a rule of thumb, it is not wise to try to move any tree larger than 1 inch in diameter—unless the job is handled by expert tree movers.

Select a sound tree with strong buds. Make a circular cut in the ground around it, 1 foot or more in diameter, depending on the size of the tree. Then cut in under the roots. During transplanting, it is very important that the roots be prevented from drying out. Keep as large a ball of earth as feasible attached to them, and tie up the ball in burlap for transporting.

In spite of all care taken in digging out a tree, it often happens that the dirt falls away from the roots, especially in dry weather. Don't despair at this. Wrap the roots tightly in wet burlap, bring the tree home, and plant it immediately.

For planting, dig a hole large enough to permit the roots to spread out in their natural position. Hold the tree upright, and fill in around it with dirt taken from the spot where the tree grew. Add *no* fertilizer. Give a plentiful soaking with water. Keep watering thoroughly for several weeks to encourage root growth.

If a number of roots have been cut off in digging up the tree, compensate for them by pruning back the top to a similar extent.

NURSERY STOCK—Rather than attempting to transplant wild trees, you may have more success with planting nursery-grown stock. From a nursery, you may purchase local trees of almost any size you desire—from a few large ones for your garden corner, to thousands of seedlings for the establishment of a wood lot, for reforestation, or for creating a community forest.

For an extensive planting, the recommended stock is one-year-old hardwood seedlings and two- to four-year-old conifer seedlings or transplants (transplants are plants that have been grown for one or two years as seedlings. then been moved to another bed for further growth).

¶ *Tip*—Many states make available seedlings and transplants free or at cost. Write to your state forestry service for information. It is advisable to file your request in the fall for spring delivery.

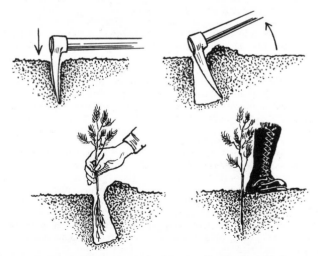

In planting with a mattock, drive mattock straight down, raise handle to widen hole, place seedling, firm the dirt.

Planting seedlings—Determine the location of the wood lot. Figure out the size of it; then order the right number of seedlings, figuring on planting them 4 to 6 feet apart.

When the seedlings arrive, get them into the ground as quickly as possible. Keep their roots moist in the meantime by "puddling"—placing them in a pail in a liquid mixture of dirt and water.

A mattock or grub hoe makes a good planting tool. Drive the blade straight into the ground, with the handle horizontal. Raise the end of the handle, thus widening the hole at the bottom. Remove the mattock. Flick the roots of the seedling into the hole, with the root "collar" at ground level. Use the mattock to push the dirt in around the seedling. Finally, firm the dirt with the foot. Be sure that no air space is left around the roots at the bottom of the hole.

TREE CUTTINGS—A number of wild deciduous trees and shrubs can be propagated from cuttings.

Spring cuttings—Thin branches of a number of trees and shrubs are suitable for spring forcing and rooting, expecially those that have catkins: willow, poplar, alder, hazel.

Collect them when the buds have started to swell—late January or February. Place them in water in a not-too-warm room.

Within a week, you will have a touch of early spring to enjoy in your room—and, in a couple of weeks, possibly rooted cuttings. Let them get a good start, then plant them out in your wild garden.

Summer cuttings—In the middle of the summer, *softwood or greenwood cuttings* may be taken from a great variety of shrubs and trees and rooted in a simple version of a "Wardian case" (see page 237—green cuttings): an ordinary plastic bag.

These cuttings must be of the current season's growth. You can recognize them by their light-green, rather than brown, coloring and by the fact that they snap like fresh stringbeans when broken between the fingers.

Make a rooting mixture of equal parts peat moss and clean sand. Add water—just so much that a handful of the mixture when squeezed will give off only a few drops. Put some of this moistened mixture, to a height of 4 inches, into a large plastic bag, such as a 2-quart polyethylene freezer bag.

Use a sharp knife to take cuttings—preferably terminal shoots—4 to 6 inches long, with about five or six leaves on each. Pull off the lower leaves. Make a straight cut across the base of the cutting and take a thin sliver off the side. Dip the base of the cutting first in water, then in a rooting hormone.

Make 3-inch-deep holes in the rooting mixture, using a pencil. Insert the cuttings and firm the soil around them with your fingers. Space them so that their leaves don't touch.

Close the plastic bag with a rubber band and set it in a spot where it will have plenty of daylight but no direct sunlight—such as a northern window.

Check them after eight weeks. By then the roots should be ½ to 1 inch long.

When they are rooted, condition the cuttings to the outside, less humid atmosphere by opening up the bag more and more over a period of a week. Water, to keep the moisture content of the rooting mixture constant. Then transplant the rooted cutting into individual pots, later into their places in your garden.

Winter cuttings—The time to take winter cuttings—*hardwood cuttings*—is late fall, after the leaves have fallen, or any time during the winter.

Choose sound, pencil-thick twigs for your cuttings. Cut the twigs into pieces, 6 to 8 inches long. Tie the cuttings into bundles of a dozen or so, and bury them in sand. Store them for the winter in a cool cellar, keeping the sand moist but not wet.

In the spring, set out the cuttings in a rather sandy soil bed. Transplant them after a year into a nursery or permanent location.

TREE PHOTOGRAPHY

Tree photography has an appeal not only to the person whose main interest is a set of documentary shots of tree details, but also to the landscape photographer who may look at a tree mainly as a valuable prop to improve the composition of his pictures.

Whatever your approach, you will find that one of the great advantages of tree photography is that it can be an all-year hobby. There is always some phase of tree life in season to be photographed.

Stills

EQUIPMENT—**Camera and lenses**—Tree photography is one of the few types of nature photography in which the average snapshot camera feels at home. If you know what to photograph and how to go about it, you should be able to take an excellent series of shots of tree silhouettes and of tree trunks even with the cheapest camera. But be certain to use a yellow filter to darken the sky if you are shooting black and white, and a fine-grain film so that good enlargements can be made.

For complete coverage of a tree, from its shape to the tiniest flowers, you need a better camera, equipped with the same features for close-up photography as are required for flower photography (see page 244).

WHAT TO PHOTOGRAPH—If you are familiar with trees and have an eye for their pictorial possibilities, you will never run out of subjects.

BOOK OF TREE PHOTOGRAPHS—G. H. Collingwood and Warren D. Brush, *Knowing Your Trees*. American Forestry Association, Washington, D.C.

Walter E. Rogers, *Tree Flowers*. New York, Dover Publications.

Sequences and series—Single casual tree pictures are of little value. Think from the start in terms of *sequences*—several shots of the same tree, its shape, trunk, bark, buds, leaves, flowers, fruits; and of *series*—silhouettes of a number of different trees, close-ups of as many types of bark, tree flowers, fruits. Sequences and series develop together; by the time you have taken a number of sequences, you automatically have your series as well.

Tree silhouettes—A set of twin shots of the same tree—one taken in summer, the other in winter—has a greater appeal than a single shot. Such sets are most effective when taken from the identical spot, so that there is no question of the shots being of the same tree. If they are taken at the same time of day, so much the better.

¶ *Tip*—Don't stake your spot. The stake won't be there when you return half a year later. Instead, add to your exposure notes the compass bearing from which the shot was taken, determined with a pocket compass, and the distance in number of steps.

You generally take silhouette shots of trees growing in the open to get their characteristic forms—the vase shape of the American elm, the wind-blown effect of the sycamore, the dense, globular crown of the sugar maple, the cone shape of firs and spruces, and so on.

As far as possible aim to have the sun strike the tree at an angle somewhere between 30 and 60 degrees to the line between camera and tree. Sidelighted to this extent, highlights and shadows of trunk and crown will give the tree a molded and alive aspect.

Watch your background. Place your camera in such a position that you avoid distracting background features of buildings, wires, poles. You may eliminate many of them by taking the photograph from a low angle. Your best background is a blue sky, clear or with scattered clouds. Use a medium-yellow filter for black and white.

¶ *Tip*—An unusual set of tree photographs results from using infra-red film and red filter. The green foliage will appear almost white against a black sky background.

Trunk and bark—The rough bark of many trees will test your photographic skill. In strong light, the deep fissures will turn into black masses. To get details in the shadows, you should photograph tree trunks and barks in diffused light—by waiting until a cloud covers the sun, shooting on a hazy day, or throwing a shadow on the bark with a scrim or gauze screen.

Buds, leaves, flowers, and fruits—Follow the same procedure as for photographing flowers (page 244). You may find it necessary to tie down the branch you are photographing, to keep it in focus, and to tie up overhead branches to prevent them from casting distracting shadows.

Fall foliage—All the above subjects are suited to color photography as well as to black-and-white. When it comes to photographing fall foliage, it is a different matter. The brilliant colors add little to a black-and-white photograph, but they make all the difference in a color transparency. A series of such transparencies, thrown on the screen, is a marvelous sight. But stick to close-ups for your greatest effects.

Tree flowers show up well on a diffused or sky background.

Photo by U.S. Forest Service

Tree silhouette, to tell shape, should be of a solitary tree.

Leaf and fruit sizes are given in inches on marked background.

Tree bark details become sharp when trunk is sidelighted.

Tree Movies

EQUIPMENT—Camera and lenses—The motion-picture camera with the standard lens for amateur movies can be used to excellent effect for taking tree movies.

Shoot the whole tree the way you would a medium landscape, the trunk the way you would photograph a person full size. A wide-angle lens will come in handy for silhouette and crown shots.

By placing a portrait lens over the camera's regular lens, you should be able to get within about 2 feet for photographing leaves, flowers, and fruits. These features will not fill the picture area as in a real close-up, but will give you satisfactory medium shots. A portable titler can be used in a similar manner, and it has the advantage that the framing device tells you exactly what you get.

For close-ups of tree flowers and fruits, you may have to use extension tubes, or bellows, or telephoto lenses, and a focusing device.

YOUR TREE MOVIES—For making movies of trees, it pays to develop a script in advance. Individual shots may be technically perfect, but it is the way they are tied together that makes entertainment or education out of them.

The variety of possibilities is inexhaustible. It ranges the whole way from "Trees in Spring" or "Flames of Autumn," through "Our American Forests" or "Mighty Sequoias," to "At Home in the Woods."

Use your imagination in making the script. If you do, you come to realize fully that a tree is not just a tree—it is a wildlife community in itself, exposed to the elements and probably inhabited by mammals birds, insects, and flowerless plants such as mosses and lichens. You can build a whole film around a tree. Take a cue from Joyce Kilmer and show the tree through the seasons—in winter with snow on its "bosom," in summer as it "intimately lives with rain." Mix medium shots of the tree lifting its "leafy arms to pray," with close-ups of the "nest of robins in her hair," and of flowers and fruits.

¶ *Tip*—One of the few times when slow panoraming may be justified is when you are showing the height of a tree, sweeping the lens from the base up into the crown.

TREE COLLECTIONS

Collecting tree specimens offers a greater variety of possibilities than other types of nature collecting. You can make a herbarium with exhibits showing all the parts of individual trees, or you can specialize in different aspects of trees—in their leaves, twigs, roots, or fruits.

The Tree Herbarium

The making of a herbarium of tree specimens follows closely the development of a plant herbarium, as described on pages 249 to 255.

The equipment is the same, and the procedure follows the same general pattern, with only a few variations.

Special methods—Cut sprays of branches and twigs to a length of 10 to 12 inches so that they will fit properly on the regular herbarium sheet. If at all possible, get branches with flowers and with fruits in their early development, as well as leaves. This is not always possible. In some trees, the flowers appear and fade before the leafing; in others, the pollen-bearing and seed-bearing flowers are found on separate trees. In such cases, it will be necessary to get several sprays to include all features of the tree. Prune off excess twigs and leaves so that those remaining will show up clearly.

In drying the specimens, you may have some trouble with the woody stems because of their thickness. They just won't press flat, with the result that the leaves shrivel up instead of drying flat. You can solve this problem to a certain extent by whittling down the back of the stem to half thickness. If that is not enough, have on hand pads of newspaper strips of various sizes that you can build into the same thickness as the stems and place these over the leaves to flatten them down.

In mounting your specimens, you may find that you will have to use a combination of the mounting methods described on pages 252 to 254. If you prefer to stick to a single method, you will probably have to resort to tying.

Small flat seeds and fruits can be mounted on the herbarium sheet with the specimen itself. Large dry fruits will have to be stored in boxes, fleshy fruits in glass containers in a formalin preservative (page 257).

Leaves

Leaves may be pressed or reproduced in a number of different ways. Leaf reproductions may have little scientific value, but they combine enjoyable activities with gratifying results.

PRESSED LEAVES—It is easy to make a good collection of pressed leaves. All you need in the line of collecting and pressing equipment is a couple of pulp magazines among whose pages you can place the leaves, and some heavy books for keeping them flattened. Change the leaves into another magazine after a first pressing of about twenty-four hours, and finish the drying there.

For perfect specimens, pick your leaves in early summer, before they have been chewed by insects. Or maybe you will like to make a collection of leaves in their most spectacular fall coloration.

Cardboard mounts—Individual leaves may be glued to full-sized or half-sized herbarium sheets, or to thin cardboard of any size you like—5 by 7 filing cards, for instance.

Plastic mounts—In plastic mounting, you can use dry, pressed leaves or fresh leaves right off the tree. Cut two pieces of clear transparent self-adhesive plastic to size, then proceed as described on page 256.

¶ *Tip*—Pressed leaves have many decorative uses, from lampshades to glass-covered tabletops and even "stained-glass windows."

LEAF RUBBINGS—As a child you probably learned to take a "rubbing" of a coin. You did this by the simple process of placing a piece of paper over the coin and rubbing a pencil over the paper to pick up the design of the coin. The same method can be used for taking rubbings of leaves.

Crayon rubbings—Place the leaf, veiny side up, on a smooth surface and cover it with a piece of thin writing paper. While holding the paper firmly in position so that it won't shift, rub a wax crayon over it, bringing out on the top surface of the paper the veins and margins of the leaf that lie under the paper. Make the strokes of the crayon parallel and exert just enough pressure to bring out the details of the leaf.

¶ *Tip*—Burnishing wax (used by shoemakers for finishing heels, shanks and edges of shoes) is superior to crayon for taking rubbings. You should be able to get a block of this from a local shoe repair shop.

Carbon-paper rubbings—If you happen to have sheets of used carbon paper around, use them to make leaf rubbings.

Place the leaf, veiny side up, on a smooth surface. Cover it with a piece of carbon paper, carbon side up. Cover this, in turn, with a piece of white paper. Rub over the top surface of the white paper with a teaspoon, pressing the white paper firmly against that part of the carbon paper that is directly over the leaf. The result is a complete image of the leaf on the underside of the white paper.

LEAF PRINTS—You can make a leaf print in a rather casual manner by pressing a leaf against any smeared surface, then transferring the ink or paint that has been picked up by the leaf veins to a piece of clean paper. If you want better prints, use a more exacting inking method, or go in for photographic reproductions.

For smoke printing, smoke up cardboard. Press leaf in soot. Move leaf to white paper, press firmly to make print.

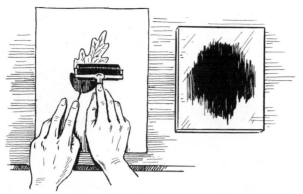

In ink printing, spread ink on glass plate. Roll ink on leaf. Place leaf on white paper. Transfer ink by rubbing.

Settle on a definite size for all your prints—5 by 7 inches is especially good. Photographic papers come in that size.

Stamp-pad prints—Stamp pads are available in stationery stores in many sizes and in various colors. Get a pad of sufficient size to accommodate the size of the leaves you expect to print.

Place the leaf, veiny side down, on the pad. Cover with a piece of newspaper. Press the leaf firmly and completely against the pad by rubbing your fingers over the newspaper. Remove the newspaper.

Pick up the leaf and place it, inked side down, on a piece of white paper. Again place a piece of newspaper over it, and again, press the inked leaf firmly against the white paper by rubbing your fingers over the newspaper, being careful not to shift it. Remove the newspaper and leaf, and let the print dry.

Smoke prints—Smoke printing is a backwoods method for which you need only a few pieces of white paper and a candle stub. Rub candle wax in a thin layer over a sheet of paper. Smooth it down with a finger, rubbing it in thoroughly. Light the candle stub. Move the paper horizontally through the flame, with the waxed surface down. If this is done carefully, the paper will pick up a thin layer of soot. Place the paper on a smooth surface, sooty side up. Lay the leaf on the paper, veiny side down. Cover it with a sheet of newspaper. Rub the leaf through the paper to make it pick up a thin coating of soot. Place the leaf, sooty side down, on a piece of white paper, cover it with another sheet, and rub firmly but carefully with the fingers of one hand while keeping the leaf in place with the fingers of the other.

Ink prints—For ink printing, purchase from an art supply store a tube of linoleum-block printing ink—black, green, or brown, water soluble or oil base—or get a dab of regular printer's ink from a local printer. You also need a small rubber roller (brayer), a piece of glass,

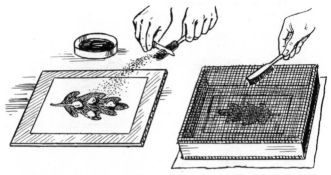

Two ways to make spatter print: with toothbrush and leaf held in position with pebbles and with spatter screen box.

several sheets of soft-textured white paper (mimeograph or construction paper is good), and pieces of newspaper.

Squeeze half an inch of printing ink onto the glass plate. Spread it into a thin, even layer by rolling the roller over it, back and forth and crosswise. Place a leaf, veiny side up, on a piece of newspaper. Ink the veins with the rubber roller. Place the leaf, inked side down, on a sheet of clean paper. Cover it with a piece of newspaper. Roll the rubber roller over the newspaper, pressing the leaf under it firmly against the printing paper. Remove the newspaper. Pick up the leaf carefully so that you do not smudge the print.

BOOKS—David S. Marx, *Learn the Trees from Leaf Prints*. Cincinnati, Ohio, Botanic Publishing Company.

David and Jean Villasenor, *How to Do Nature Printing*. Foster Art Service, Laguna Beach, California.

Carbon prints—Carbon prints made with carbon paper require the use of an iron, preferably an electric one, for satisfactory results.

Place the leaf, veiny side up, on a padding of several sheets of newspaper. Cover with a sheet of carbon paper, carbon side down. Place a sheet of newspaper over the carbon paper and press with a medium-hot iron. Remove the newspaper and the carbon paper.

Place a sheet of white paper on top of the blackened leaf. Cover with a sheet of newspaper and press with the medium-hot iron.

Spatter prints—Toothbrush method—Spatter printing is an outlining process. The finished print shows the leaf in white silhouette against a background of minute ink drops. Ordinary ink is not suitable. You need a thicker-flowing ink, such as India ink, or slightly diluted poster paints.

Place a leaf on a piece of construction paper or mimeograph paper, holding it down with pebbles or pins. Dip the tip of an old toothbrush—preferably one with stiff nylon bristles—in a small amount of ink in a saucer. Shake off the surplus ink. Point the toothbrush at an angle toward the leaf, bristles up. Rub a nail or stick or a knife blade over the bristles, from the tip of the brush toward the handle. As the bristles snap back, they spatter drops of ink on the paper. Continue until a satisfactory print has been made.

¶ *Tip*—The spatter process can be greatly simplified and speeded up with the use of a *spatter screen box*. For this, remove the top and bottom of a cigar box or any similar wooden box. Replace the top and bottom with two pieces of wire screening, stretching the screening over the frame and tacking it in position. Arrange a leaf on a sheet of paper. Place the screen box over it, with the bottom screen holding the leaf in position. Rub the inked toothbrush over the top screen until the print is completed. The screen adds an interesting pattern to the print.

Spatter prints—Spray-can method—Aerosol spray cans containing enamel provide the simplest and quickest method for making spatter prints. Because of the air current by which the enamel is spewed out, the leaf to be printed must be held firmly to the paper. This can be done, horizontally, by placing small pebbles on it, vertically, by pinning it to the paper against a cardboard backing.

Experiment with the spray can to determine the best distance for producing a spray of fine droplets. When you have arrived at the proper distance, aim the can and shoot.

¶ *Tip*—Rubber cement is superior to pebbles and pins for holding the leaf down firmly and providing a closer fit. Smear a light coating of rubber cement onto the bottom side of the leaf. Stick the leaf to the paper and spray it. Let it dry completely. Peel off the leaf and rub off any rubber cement that may have stuck to the paper.

Dryprints—Dryprinting is a photographic process—but without the use of a camera. The seemingly miraculous way in which the print appears intrigues young and old alike: The printed paper is dry-developed by simply exposing it to ammonia fumes. Depending

ADHESIVE TAPE HINGES

A simple printing frame for printing out light-exposed leaf prints and ammonia developing jar for making dryprints.

on the type of paper used, the result is a brownish-red, blue, or black silhouette against a white background.

The paper for dryprinting is a light-sensitized paper commonly used by architects. It may be purchased from architects' supply stores under various trade names—Diazo, Driprint, Ozalid. Most of it comes in large rolls, but it is also available in cut sheets. *All handling of dryprint paper must be done in subdued light.*

¶ *Tip*—If the store has outdated paper in stock, it may let you have it at a greatly reduced price. It is useless for architectural purposes but all right for leaf printing.

In addition to the paper, you must have a printing frame.

You can, of course, buy a photographic printing frame. But you can get along just as well with a homemade frame. For this, get a 6-by-8-inch piece of corrugated cardboard or $\frac{1}{2}$-inch plywood and hinge onto it, with a strip of masking or adhesive tape, a pane of glass of equal size. Use a couple of spring clothespins or large rubber bands to clamp the parts together.

In subdued light, pull out a piece of dryprint paper from the lightproof envelope in which you keep it. Place the leaf to be printed on the coated (yellow) side of the dryprint paper, and put both of them in the printing frame with the leaf against the glass. Close the frame and clamp it.

Expose it to direct sunlight or to a photoflood bulb until the yellow color of the paper has bleached to white.

Then, back in subdued light, take the paper out of the frame, roll it up with the exposed side to the inside, and slip it into a quart-sized mayonnaise jar or tin can of a circumference slightly larger than the length of the paper. Place the jar or tin over a small dish—eggcup, plastic cup, bottletop—containing a wad of cotton soaked with strong household ammonia or, better, concentrated ammonia from a drugstore. Fume the print for a few minutes until a clear image has formed. That's it! No washing or anything else is needed afterward.

¶ *Tip*—Always keep the developing container bottom up. Ammonia is a gas lighter than air. If you turn the developing container right side up, the ammonia escapes. This slows down the process for the next printing.

Blueprints—Blueprinting is another photographic process without the camera. The finished product—after exposure, developing in water, and drying—shows the leaf in white silhouette against a blue background. Blueprint paper, like dryprint paper, is used by architects and may be purchased from architects' supply stores. It comes mostly in large rolls, but you will probably be able to persuade the dealer to sell you a few feet. Cut it to whatever size you want for your collection. *All handling of blueprint paper must be done in subdued light.*

For the printing, proceed as in dryprinting. Expose the paper to direct sunlight or a photoflood bulb until the paper has turned from cream through blue to an ashen gray. Remove the paper.

Leaf prints are of many different kinds. Top left: ink or stamp-pad print. Top right: spatter print using printing box. Center, left: blueprint or photographic print (short exposure). Center, right: dryprint. Bottom, right: photographic print (long exposure).

Place the exposed paper face down in a pan of water for ten minutes or more. During the washing, the exposed part of the paper turns blue again. Blot it between pieces of newspaper, and dry it between more sheets under light pressure.

¶ *Tip*—When you are making the print, place a small rectangle of paper in the right-hand corner. When it is completed, you will have a white space here for your identification notes.

Photographic prints—Instead of using dryprint or blueprint paper, use proof paper, such as portrait photographers use for making preliminary prints of their negatives. This is a printing-out paper, turning dark when exposed to the sun. It is not developed afterward, only fixed. *Handle printing-out paper in subdued light.*

The printing method is similar to dryprinting. A short exposure to the sun or a strong artificial light will result in a white leaf outlined against an almost black background. By a longer exposure, you will get a complete negative photograph of the leaf, with all veins showing.

When the exposure is completed, fix the paper for five to ten minutes in regular photographic acid fixer (hypo), then wash it for fifteen minutes or more before drying.

¶ *Tip*—If you have a photographic darkroom at your disposal, you can do the printing there, using contact paper and contact printer or enlarging paper and enlarging easel. You may place small leaves in the enlarger head itself and project as a regular negative to make an enlarged print.

¶ *Tip*—You may use a photographic leaf print as a paper negative to produce a positive print. Place it face to face with a piece of unexposed paper in the printing frame, with the back of the original print toward the glass. Expose it, then fix it and let it dry.

Photo-developer prints—In this trick method, you use regular photographic paper in whatever size you prefer, plus developing and fixing solutions.

Pull out a sheet of paper and expose it completely to the light.

Dip the leaf in developer, then take it out and shake off the excess liquid. Place the leaf, veiny side down, on the exposed side of the paper. Cover it with a couple of sheets of newspaper. Press the leaf firmly against the photographic paper by rubbing your fingers over the newspaper. Remove the newspaper and the leaf. Watch the image develop. When the paper is completely developed, drop it in the fixer. When it is fixed, wash and dry it.

Electrostatic prints—If you have access to an electrostatic copying machine—Xerox, IBM, A. B. Dick, or the like—you can make a set of leaf prints in short order. Simply lay the leaf on the glass surface and expose, following the directions for the machine.

LEAF CASTS—You can use leaves to make interesting, decorative plaster plaques.

Drop a wad of modeling clay (plasticine) on a smooth surface. Place two strips of wood, $\frac{1}{2}$ inch thick, on either side of the modeling clay, about 5 inches apart. Using the wood strips as supports and thickness guides, roll the modeling clay flat with a straight-sided bottle.

Place the leaf, veiny side down, on the flattened modeling clay. Press it into the clay by rolling the bottle over it. Then remove the leaf.

Place a collar of cardboard around the leaf impression and proceed to make the plaster cast as described on page 120.

SKELETON LEAVES—Skeleton leaves are occasionally found in the woods, where insects, fungi, and moisture have done the skeletonizing. You can do a quicker job yourself.

Pick a leaf with rather tough veins. Place it on a piece of cloth or soft felt. Hold one end of a hand brush or hairbrush loosely between the fingers of one hand. Tap the bristles of the opposite end of the brush firmly and repeatedly against the leaf. The bristles will slowly pick out the fleshy part of the leaf, leaving even the finest veins intact. When the leaf is completely skeletonized, dry it under pressure the way you would an ordinary leaf. Mount the pressed leaf between glass or cellophane.

¶ *Tip*—For a quicker job, boil the leaf for a couple of minutes in a solution of 4 ounces household lye in 1 pint of water—in an enamel or glass pot, NOT in aluminum. Wash thoroughly in water before using the brush.

Twigs and Winter Buds

Twig collections—Select a twig that is truly representative of the tree, then cut it off. Trim it with a sharp knife to fit the size of the

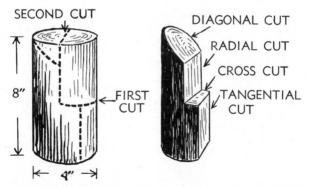

Make wood specimens to size shown or to your own standard size. Cut as indicated. One half of cuts may be varnished.

sheets on which you plan to mount your twigs. Make the trimming cut on the slant, and in such a way that it will face out, when the twig is mounted, to show the inside structure.

Mount the twig on the sheet with strips of gummed cloth or adhesive tape or by tying it (see page 254).

¶ *Tip*—Instead of mounting the twig in a separate collection, you may want to place each twig next to the leaf of the same species in your leaf collection.

Bark

Bark rubbings—Do not cut or pull the bark off a living tree; it will disfigure it and possibly kill it. Instead, take a rubbing of the bark.

Tape a piece of writing paper onto the bark at the spot that most truly shows its particular texture. Then rub the paper with the side of a piece of black crayon until you have a good impression of the details of the bark. Even better, use shoemaker's burnishing wax (see *Tip* on page 272) for taking the rubbing.

Wood Specimens

Wood collections—If there is lumbering, clearing, or thinning going on in your neck of the woods, you have a good chance of obtaining a collection of wood samples of local trees. No nature lover would cut down a live tree just for the sake of adding a wood specimen to his collection.

Cut foot-long sections out of thick branches or young trees, 2 to 4 inches in diameter, leaving the bark intact. When you get the blocks home, trim them down to the standard length you have set for all your wood samples—6 to 10 inches. Season them for a month or more in a spot where they will dry slowly.

Finally, turn each of your samples into a display piece that will show the different grains: Make a crosscut to the center, half the length of the block down, then a radial cut from the top until the saw meets the crosscut. Saw off half of the bottom "step" in a tangential cut. Cut the top diagonally, at a 45-degree angle. Sandpaper all cut surfaces.

¶ *Tip*—If you like, you can leave the left half of the exposed surfaces unfinished, and coat the other half with varnish or lacquer to show how the grain of that particular wood takes a finish.

Mount the specimens by wiring them to plywood panels or by standing them upright, secured with screws, on pieces of 1-inch board. Or hang them by screw eyes under a shelf.

CHAPTER 10

Rocks, Minerals, and Fossils

L OOK wide over the countryside—and whether you stand on the highest peak of the Rockies or the lowest point of Death Valley, in the most undulating part of New England or the flattest of Kansas, all around you are rocks, rocks, and more rocks. Some of those rocks are the solid masses of the hardest granite, others the loose powder of the softest sand. Some of them are the original bedrock or "country rock" of the landscape, others make up the mantle rock of loose material, formed from the bedrock on which it lies by weathering or carried in from afar by ice or wind or waves.

Rocks are of a thousand uses. They give us directly the stones for building blocks and the coal for our furnaces. Through various processes they supply us with our metals—iron for our skyscrapers and our cars, copper for our electrical fixtures, aluminum for our cooking pots and our planes, silver for our coins, uranium for our atomic reactors. They give us the chemicals for our industries, the fertilizers for our farms, the plastics for our homes. They provide us with the implements of peace and the arms of war. But more important than anything else: They indirectly sustain our life—the soil in which our plants grow is made up of particles of rocks and fragments of minerals, mixed with decomposed plant matter and animal remains.

The moment you become interested in rocks, and in the minerals or prehistoric plant and animal life that form them, the whole field of *geology* opens up before you in a vista of a score of roads all leading out from a main center.

In the beginning, your interest may consist in hunting for the most beautiful or most unusual rocks or minerals in your locality and preparing them for the most effective display. But collecting alone will soon prove of little satisfaction to you unless you can identify your specimens—and so you delve into *mineralogy*, *petrology*, or *lithology*. With your interest once aroused, you may start wondering about the origin of your rocks and minerals and fossils. How were they formed? By what forces did they come into being? This curiosity of yours may lead you into a study of the formation of the landscape and its underlying structure, *geomorphology*, or of the past ages of the world, of *historical geology* and *paleontology*. Or you may wonder about the uses to which rocks and minerals are put and look into *economic geology* as it deals with metal ores or coal mines, quarries or mineral fields, oil or gas deposits, or some other of its multitudinous phases.

The field of geology is as big as the earth—it *is* the earth!

BOOKS ON GENERAL GEOLOGY—Kirtley F. Mather, *Earth Beneath Us*. New York, Random House.

Gary G. Croneis and William C. Krumbein, *Down to Earth*. Chicago, Illinois, University of Chicago Press.

ROCKS—Carroll L. Fenton and Mildred Fenton, *The Rock Book. Rocks and Their Stories*. New York, Doubleday & Company.

MINERALS—George L. English and D. E. Jensen, *Getting Acquainted with Minerals*. New York, McGraw-Hill Book Company.

Paul E. Desautels, *The Mineral Kingdom*. New York, Grosset and Dunlap.

FOSSILS—Carroll L. Fenton and Mildred A. Fenton, *The Fossil Book*. New York, Doubleday & Company.

Ruben A. Stirton, *Time, Life and Man: The Fossil Record*. New York, John Wiley Sons.

METEORITES—Harvey H. Nininger, *Out of the Sky*. New York, Dover Publications.

Working with Others

It is, of course, possible for you to pursue your interest in geology alone. But you might as well realize from the beginning that the instant you show the least bit of interest in rocks, minerals, or fossils, you have automatically entered the vast fraternity of "rockhounds," or at the junior level, "pebble pups."

As a rock-and-minerals enthusiast, join with others in a local branch of one of the national societies. If no nearby branch exists, find out through your state university or natural history museum the addresses of local organizations. Practically every state has one or more of them. Then sign up and take part in the deliberations of the group, and in its field trips.

SOCIETIES—American Federation of Mineralogical Societies. Headquarters: 3418 Flannery Drive, Baltimore, Maryland 21207. Periodical: *Gems and Minerals*.

Mineralogical Society of America. Headquarters: U.S. Museum, Washington, D.C. 20025. Periodical: *The American Mineralogist*.

Geological Society of America. Headquarters: 231 East Forty-sixth Street, New York, New York 10017.

In addition to meeting and exploring with like-minded individuals, the true rockhound spends much of his time in correspondence and in exchanging his own specimens for specimens from rock-and-mineral collectors in other states or other countries. If you are interested in this kind of pursuit, you will find a great number of addresses in a current issue of one of the periodicals that cater to hobbyists interested in geology.

PERIODICALS—*Rocks and Minerals.* Box 29, Peekskill, New York 10566.

The Mineralogist. 329 S.E. Thirty-second Avenue, Portland, Oregon 97215.

The Earth Science Digest. Box 1357, Chicago, Illinois 60690.

Lapidary Journal. Del Mar, California 92014.

The Desert Magazine. Desert Press, Palm Desert, California 92260. Of special interest to Westerners.

If your interest in geology runs toward exploring the more exciting aspects of the subject rather than to the usual type of field trips and collecting, you may want to get in touch with mountain-climbing geologists who scale the highest peaks of our country, or with speleologists—"spelunkers" for short—who penetrate into the wonderland of the deepest underground caves.

SOCIETIES—American Alpine Club. Headquarters: 113 East Ninetieth Street, New York, New York 10028. Periodical: *American Alpine Journal.*

National Speleological Society. Headquarters: 2318 North Kenmore Street, Arlington, Virginia 22210. Periodical: *NSS Monthly News.*

GEOLOGICAL FIELD WORK

Equipment for Field Work

CLOTHING—The usual kind of outdoor clothing is suitable for average geological field work. But if you intend to go in for more intensive work, it will pay you to buy clothing that is tough enough to take it. Excellent is an outfit of sturdy, extra-heavy denim, as long as it does not fit too snugly—you have a lot of bending to do. For climbing, it is important that your clothing be without any kind of trim that may snag on projecting rocks.

¶ *Tip*—Reinforce the knees of trousers with patches of soft leather to strengthen them for all the kneeling you will be doing.

For footwear, pick a pair of sturdy hiking shoes or climbing boots.

Much of your field work will be under the open sun, so protect your face with a broad-brimmed hat or a visored cap. If you expect to be working under a protruding overhang, bring a hard fiber hat.

TRAVELING EQUIPMENT—Rock hunting will take you far afield, way off the beaten track. It is important for you to get there and back safely.

Maps—Take along a map of the territory you expect to cover. Before setting out, study the map and familiarize yourself with the main features of the landscape so that you will have a general idea of the lay of the land—the direction of its ridges, the streams and main roads that traverse it. In addition to using the map for finding your way, use it for marking your route and the locations of your finds.

Excellent for your purpose are the topographic maps produced by the U.S. Geological Survey to the scale of 1:24,000 (1 inch on the map is equal to 2,000 feet in the field). Drop a postcard to Map Information Office, United States Geological Survey, General Services Building, Eighteenth and F Streets, NW, Washington, D.C. 20405, and request a free *Topographic Map Index Circular* of the state in which you are traveling. From this index, decide on the maps you need, then order them, following the instructions for ordering given in the index circular.

Compass—When traveling cross-country you will need a compass for "orienting" your map—that is, turning the map so that north on the map points in the same direction as north in the field—and for guiding you along your route. You will also need a compass for determining the directions in which certain geological features run and for preparing a simple sketch map that will make it easy for you to return some other time to your "strike"—if any. A compass can also be used to determine whether a mineral is magnetic or not.

The most suitable compass for these various purposes is one based on the "Silva" system, such as the Pathfinder, Explorer, or Huntsman. The built-on base plates of these compasses function as a protractor and simplify the job of determining your bearings.

REFERENCE—Bjorn Kjellstrom, *Be Expert with Map and Compass— The Orienteering Handbook*. La Porte, Indiana, American Orienteering Service (soft cover); and Harrisburg, Pennsylvania, Stackpole Books (hard cover).

First-aid items—Bring along a few adhesive bandages. Since a sprained ankle is always a possibility while climbing, include the

Good maps and compass follow the geologist wherever he goes. Silva 15-TD-C1 compass has built-in clinometer.

materials for making a sprained-ankle bandage—a bandana or a Scout neckerchief.

Special equipment—For mountain climbing, you may need climbing boots with crampons, mountain ax, pitons, spring hooks, and climbing rope.

REFERENCE—Kenneth A. Henderson, *Handbook of American Mountaineering*. Boston, Houghton Mifflin Company.

For cave exploring, you will need the same kind of special equipment as for mountain climbing and, in addition, flashlights (head type) and spare lights (candles and matches). As an added safety feature, most spelunking parties equip themselves with field telephones by which they keep in continuous contact with a post at the cave entrance.

REFERENCES—Franklin Folsom, *Exploring American Caves*. New York, Collier Books.

Roy Pinney, *Complete Book of Cave Exploration*. New York, Coward-McCann.

Charles E. Mohr and Howard N. Sloane, eds., *Celebrated American Caves*. New Brunswick, New Jersey, Rutgers University Press.

STUDY AND COLLECTING EQUIPMENT—In the beginning of your geological pursuits, you can get along very well with an ordinary hammer, a cold chisel, a couple of newspapers, and a knapsack. When you have decided that rock hunting is the hobby for you, you will probably want to get better equipment.

EQUIPMENT—See addresses on page 27.

"Mineral hammers" are of two kinds: one has chisel-shaped head; the other is pick-pointed. Many geologists use both.

Hammers—The favorite geology hammer or "mineral hammer" weighs about $1\frac{1}{2}$ pounds. It comes in two different shapes. In both, one end of the head is square and flat. But in one, the opposite end is chisel-shaped; in the other, the opposite end terminates in a sharp pick point. The chisel-shaped hammer is particularly suited for splitting stratified rocks (limestones, shales, etc.). The pick-pointed hammer is excellent for digging out minerals and for loosening fossils. Many rock hunters carry both.

¶ *Tip*—For more extensive work, a regular pick, a chisel-pointed steel bar ("moil"), a sledgehammer, and a spade may be called for. They are heavy, so watch your transportation problem.

Chisels—A $\frac{7}{16}$-by-$\frac{1}{2}$-inch and a $\frac{5}{8}$-by-$\frac{3}{4}$-inch cold chisel are valuable in cases where more exact chipping is necessary than can be done with the edge of the mineral hammer, or in places, such as cavities, where the hammer will not reach.

Pocketknife—An ordinary pocketknife will be found helpful for digging crystals or small fossils out of soft rocks.

Gloves—If your hands are tender-skinned, protect them with a pair of cheap cotton gloves when handling rock specimens.

Goggles—If your work involves much pounding or chipping with the hammer, it is advisable to protect your eyes with a pair of goggles.

Labeling material—Use adhesive tape or masking tape for marking the specimens you collect.

¶ *Tip*—Cut $\frac{1}{2}$-inch tape in as many $\frac{3}{4}$-inch pieces as you expect to need. Stick them to a piece of wax paper or plastic for easy carrying. Number them with India ink.

Notebook—Carry a pocket-sized notebook for taking general notes of the trip as well as detailed notes on the specimens collected. Number the notes to coincide with the numbered labels you stick on the specimens.

Magnifier—One of the magnifiers described on page 151 with magnifications from about $5\times$ to $10\times$ will make it possible for you to see the individual mineral crystals of which many rocks consist.

Field book—For tentative identification in the field of rocks and minerals which you come upon, you will probably want to bring along a suitable field book.

BOOKS FOR FIELD IDENTIFICATION—Frederic B. Loomis, *Field Book of Common Rocks and Minerals*. New York, G. P. Putnam's Sons.

F. H. Pough, *Field Guide to Rocks and Minerals*. Boston, Houghton Mifflin Company.

D. K. Fritzen, *The Rock-Hunter's Field Manual*. New York, Harper & Row.

Richard M. Pearl, *How to Know the Minerals and Rocks*. New York, McGraw-Hill Book Company.

Herbert S. Zim and Paul R. Shaffer, *Rocks and Minerals*. New York, Golden Press.

F. H. T. Rhodes, H. S. Zim, and P. R. Shaffer, *Fossils*. New York, Golden Press.

Wrapping materials—Bring old newspapers for wrapping rock specimens, paper toweling or cleansing tissue for minerals, cotton for protecting crystals.

¶ *Tip*—Some rock collectors place their rock specimens in individual paper bags (No. 1) after wrapping and put all rocks found in a single locality in a larger bag (No. 5).

Field bag—For carrying home your loot, take a sturdy canvas musette bag, preferably divided into several compartments, with a strong shoulder strap; or a stout knapsack. You should be able to pick up one at a nearby army surplus store or in the Boy Scout or Girl Scout section of a local department store.

¶ *Tip*—Many collectors pack a cigar box in their field bag for the safe carrying of rocks that have a tendency to crumble or rocks with loosely embedded crystals. A molded wood pulp egg box, with separate compartments, is particularly good for safeguarding delicate minerals. Small plastic boxes or glass vials may be needed for sediments, soils, and crystals.

SPECIALIZED EQUIPMENT—The days of the old-time prospector with his burro are long past. Modern prospecting—exploring for commercially valuable deposits of rocks and minerals—has become a highly specialized part of economic geology.

Only a couple of items used by professional prospectors are of interest to amateurs.

Ultraviolet lamp—A portable ultraviolet lamp (see page 308) will permit you to locate fluorescent minerals in a rock pile, but only in the blackness of a dark night.

Geiger and scintillation counters—These instruments—ranging in price from $100 to $1,000 and more—are indispensable to the geologist or prospector specializing in locating radioactive minerals—minerals containing uranium and thorium.

REFERENCES—Max W. Von Bernewitz, *Handbook for Prospectors*. New York, McGraw-Hill Book Company.

Barry Storm, *Practical Prospecting*. Storm-Jade Books, Chiriaco Summit, California 92201.

Prospecting with a Counter. U.S. Geological Survey. Catalog No. Y 3.At7:2C83. Thirty cents. From Superintendent of Documents, U.S. Government Printing Office, Washington, D.C. 20402.

Finding Rocks and Minerals

WHERE?—Where to start? Right outside your door if you live in the country; down the street at the nearest building excavation or in the nearest park if you live in town. Everywhere you go, geological formations lie before you.

Whether you are interested in the field of geology as a whole or in collecting geological specimens, start off by getting a thorough understanding of your own immediate vicinity—how its hills and valleys, its mountains or plains, its bedrock and its soils came into being. Such an understanding will help you immeasurably to know what outcrops may occur and where you have your best chance of finding specimens of certain rocks and minerals or fossils.

When you know your own locality and your own state, your eyes will have a keener perception of the geological wonders of our country's variegated surface and its hidden underground treasures. You will thrill to the sight of Mount Washington rising in the mist and to the Half Dome of Yosemite silhouetted against a blue sky. You will marvel at the incredible immensity of the Carlsbad Caverns in New Mexico and at the puzzling pinnacle of the Devil's Tower in South Dakota, at the seemingly bottomless gully called the Grand Canyon and at the hot springs of Yellowstone. You will ponder the forces that shaped the granite coast of Maine and the sandstone caves of southern California, the delta of the ever-flowing Mississippi and the dried-up ocean bed that is now the salt flats of Utah. And you will marvel at the rich mineral wealth of our country—from its soft, humus-laden soil to its massive building blocks, from its lusterless metal ores to its brilliant gem stones, from its coal deposits to its reservoirs of petroleum (literally "rock oil").

REFERENCES—*Geologic Map of the United States.* Four sheets, each 27 by 47 inches, showing more than 160 rock units, distinguished by patterns printed in 23 colors. U.S. Geological Survey, Washington, D.C. 20025.

Geological Maps of your state. Write to your state geological survey department at your state capital for lists of geological folios and reports.

Rock sources—Wherever you travel through the countryside there will be rocks aplenty. Some of them may form the very surface on which you walk; others may be outcrops laid bare by erosion or by the work of man. "Layered" *sedimentary* rocks are distributed throughout America. The heat-formed *igneous* rocks and the "changed" *metamorphic* rocks crop out mostly in mountain territory; you will have no luck searching for them in the Mississippi Valley or in the Great Plains regions. In the northern section of our country, you will come upon boulders and rock fragments and sediment which were not part of the native ground but which were carried in by glaciers and deposited during the glacial age.

You can start your study and collecting practically anywhere. But for the greatest yield, look particularly in places such as these:

RAW CUTS of completed roads or roads under construction.

EXCAVATIONS for new buildings, highways, railroads, bridges; tunnel construction; harbor deepening.

Waste heaps of broken rocks around QUARRIES; slag dumps around MINES.

WARNING—Never enter quarries or mines without explicit permission of those in charge. There may be danger of rock slides, blastings, or unexploded charges. Quarry and mine foremen are often exceedingly helpful to rockhounds; they may even have on hand especially interesting samples which they themselves have collected.

WELL CUTTINGS and DRILLINGS from water wells and oil wells.

Eroded HILLSIDES, RIVERBANKS and GORGES, CANYONS and "BADLANDS."

BEDS of stony streams, whether water-filled or dry.

Exposed CLIFFS and the debris slopes below them—TALUS SLIDES.

OUTCROP LEDGES on cliffs, in hillside pastures.

In parts of the country once covered by glacier, investigate GRAVEL PITS, GLACIAL TILL, LOOSE BOULDERS, edge-of-glacier MORAINES.

Mineral sources—Where you find rocks, you find minerals—that's what the rocks are made of. The listing above of places for finding rocks holds true, then, for minerals as well. But when it comes to discovering good specimens rather than tiny crystals and poor fragments, you need to keep your eyes peeled for special conditions or special formations:

CRACKS and CAVITIES—"vugs"—in granite and trap rock, in lavas and limestone.

CONTACT LINES between two kinds of igneous or metamorphic rocks, or between an intrusion of igneous rock into sedimentary rock.

PEGMATITE DIKES—the coarsely crystalline veins that cut the mountain face in light bands with almost parallel sides.

GRAVEL and SAND in stream beds, draws and gullies, and on ocean beaches.

Deposits in CAVES and around HOT SPRINGS in limestone districts.

Odd-looking pebbles or rocks, loose or in residual clay, may prove to be mineral-lined GEODES, or mineral-filled AMYGDULES, or agate NODULES; break them open.

On going dry, the temporary lakes—called PLAYA—of some of our Southwestern states may yield water-soluble minerals, such as halite (common salt) and borax.

In desert territory, look for "FLOATS," minerals found lying loose, eroded out of the ground by wind action. Where you find floats, you may hit upon still better specimens by digging. Or you may come upon the abandoned dumps of oldtime prospectors.

REFERENCE—Price List, PL 15. Free. From Superintendent of Documents, U.S. Government Printing Office, Washington, D.C. 20402. Contains lists of pamphlets and circulars describing rock and mineral locations throughout the United States.

Fossil sources—Probably the smartest procedure for finding fossils is to eliminate first the places where you will NOT find them: in igneous rocks. Fossils are the petrified remains of plant and animal life of ages past, and it is obvious that they could never have survived the heat of the molten magmas and lavas that formed the igneous rocks. You need to search for them in sedimentary rocks.

LIMESTONE and SHALE DEPOSITS, in natural outcrops or exposed in road cuts, quarries, excavations, mines, tunnels, would be your prime choices for investigation. The finer the grain of limestone or shale, the more successful you will probably be; but don't expect to find fossils in all limestone or shale.

Fine-grained SANDSTONE DEPOSITS may contain fossils; coarse sandstone seldom does. But yours may be the exception, so you had better examine it anyway.

VOLCANIC TUFA—rock formed from the ashes of volcanic eruption—sometimes contains fossils.

Around COAL MINES, check the slate and shale debris around the breakers. Also look for "coal balls"—hard masses occurring in coal seams.

Occasionally, fragments of fossilized bones are found in debris at the foot of CLIFFS of sedimentary rock, in gorges, badlands, canyons. They may lead to the discovery of the layer in the cliff above where the remaining parts are deposited.

Working in shale, you may come upon CONCRETIONS—rounded masses, harder than the surrounding shale—in which fossils may be embedded.

Fields of PETRIFIED FORESTS in the West, not under federal, state or local protection, will yield silicified or opalized wood.

Fossil sharks' teeth are found in great numbers in PHOSPHATE BEDS in our Southern states and along the SEASHORE in certain sections of the country.

Preserved footprints of prehistoric animals come to light from time to time, such as in the RED SANDSTONE DEPOSITS of New England.

REFERENCE—Richard Cassanova, *Illustrated Guide to Fossil Collecting*. Naturegraph Company, Healdsburg, California 95448.

SOCIETIES—Paleontological Society. Headquarters: Department of Geology, University of Illinois, Urbana, Illinois 61801. Periodical: *Journal of Paleontology*.

Society of Vertebrate Paleontology. Headquarters: U.S. National Museum, Washington, D.C. 20560.

Meteorites—On one of your field trips you may accidentally stumble upon a meteorite—the unburned or unevaporated remains of a meteor or "shooting star" from outer space. Meteorites are more commonly found in desert or plains territory than anywhere else. This is so not because more of them fall there, but simply because they are more conspicuous there, and therefore are more easily spotted than in mountainous or wooded areas.

SOCIETY—Meteoritical Society. Headquarters: Smithsonian Institution, Washington, D.C. 20560. Periodical: *Meteoritics*.

WHEN?—Time of year—Any season is geology season. The landforms are always there to study—the hills and mountains and plains. As far as collecting is concerned, rockhounds are busy the year round, with the possible exception of collectors in the northern parts of the country in the dead of winter, when snow covers their hunting grounds.

Time of day—The proper light conditions play an important part in finding rocks and minerals. A cliff wall with a western exposure would be in deep shade in the forenoon but lighted by the sun in the afternoon. Therefore, obviously, the afternoon is your choice for studying it. Horizontal ledges on a bluff facing south cast readily seen shadows when the sun is at its zenith, but vertical fissures will show up much more clearly in the slanting rays of the sun in early morning or late evening. Frontlighted permatite dikes may look of little promise, while the same dikes sidelighted may reveal a wealth of worthwhile specimens. The same holds true for floats on desert plains; they are most easily found by the shadows they cast in morning and evening.

A period of clear weather immediately following a heavy rain is particularly propitious for rock hunters. The rain will have washed exposed surfaces free of dust; this makes it much easier to locate good specimens. Also, a heavy rain may have exposed a new batch of minerals from the sand or clay in which they were embedded on hillsides or in stream banks.

If your hobby is collecting fluorescent minerals, you may want to go hunting for them at night, with a portable ultraviolet ray lamp.

Field Observations

Although the United States Geological Survey and your state geologist have probably made a general study of the geology if the territory in which you do your field work, there is still much detail work to be done. The findings of amateur geologists may help toward a clearer understanding of the landscape, and toward a more exact listing of local rocks, minerals and fossils. Many valuable museum finds have been made by amateurs.

Land forms—Find out by personal investigation the formations of the bedrock of your territory, and the mantle-rock that covers it. With this knowledge, you have the basis for making conclusions on the underlying formations, and for determining what rocks and minerals you are likely to find, and whether fossils are present.

Rock formations—Make a listing of the deposits you investigate, with notes of their location, types of rocks, detail sketches of bedding, layers, folds, faults, joints, dikes, and so on.

Outcrops—Map the main rock outcrops of your area by "walking the outcrop" to determine the direction of each "strike"—the direction in which the outcrop extends from one edge to the other. Measure its width. Determine the amount of the "dip"—the angle expressed in degrees at which the outcrop rises from the ground. You can find the directions of the strike with a compass and the angle of the dip with a clinometer—from the Greek *klino*, to incline, and *metron*, measure.

¶ *Tip*—You can make a simple clinometer from a piece of thin wood, 4 by 4 inches, a five-and-ten-cent-store protractor, a small nail, a thin string, and a small lead sinker with an eye. From the protractor cut a quarter circle marked from zero to 90 degrees, and tack it to the board in such a way that the zero is at the bottom

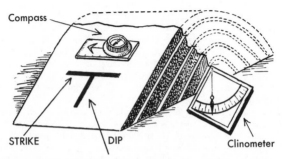

The "strike" (direction of an outcrop) is determined by a compass; the "dip" (angle of outcrop) with a clinometer.

edge. Hammer the small nail into the board at the center of the protractor circle, and suspend the sinker (whittled into a small plumb bob) in the string from this nail as a pointer. When measuring, place bottom edge of clinometer on the dip, and read the degrees where the pointer indicates it to be.

Mineral deposits—Visit the location of the more important minerals of your state to ascertain the conditions under which they are found, what varieties occur together, and their relative abundance.

Weathering—Study the effects of weathering on the surface of rocks found in your region.

Age of sediments—Locate deposits of shale and slate, and attempt to determine their age from the fossils found in them.

Soil profiles—Measure the depth of each type of soil as it appears in a raw road cut, or in a hole dug in the ground—from the top layer of darker-colored loam, through the layers below it of lighter-colored subsoil, for a distance of a couple of feet or until you strike bedrock.

Well logs—In oil regions, you may have a chance to join the "mud smellers"—the geologists who investigate the core and sludge from rotary drills, or the cuttings from churn drills, and interpret the information gained. In this investigation, it is particularly important to know from what depth the material is brought to the surface, the type of material, the character of it, the depth at which the material changes from one type to another.

GEOLOGICAL COLLECTIONS

The collecting of rocks and minerals and fossils is about the least expensive hobby you can think of. To start with, your equipment may be only an old hammer and an old chisel, and your storage cabinets a few cigar boxes. It is only when you go deeper and still deeper into the subject that you may decide to get more adequate

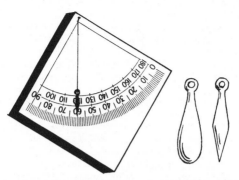

A clinometer may be made from an inexpensive protractor, a piece of wood, and a sinker whittled into a plumb bob.

collecting equipment and better facilities for storing and displaying your specimens.

By then, you will also have to make up your mind in what direction your collection should go—before the ever-growing piles of rocks and minerals drive your family from house and home.

A beginning collector is apt to pick whatever comes his way or whatever catches his fancy. But he soon becomes critical and starts to choose only perfect specimens. At the same time, since he realizes that he cannot hope to cover the whole field of geological collecting, he concentrates on those rocks and minerals that fit into the type of collection he visualizes for himself.

BOOK ON COLLECTING—William B. Sanborn, *Crystal and Mineral Collecting*. Menlo Park, California, Lane Book Company.

Types of Collections

A great number of possibilities open themselves up for specialization within the fields of rocks, minerals, and fossils. The following cover only a few of the many possibilities.

ROCKS—Specimens of all rocks from a certain locality—township, mine district, county, state.

Specimens of all igneous or sedimentary or metamorphic rocks from a given area.

Rocks of a certain geological formation or era.

Samples of ores from one state; or different ores from around the country containing a certain metal—iron, silver, copper, etc.

Soil samples from a given area.

Representative rocks, personally collected, from states and foreign countries visited.

MINERALS—Specimens of all minerals from a certain locality—township, mine district, county, state.

Minerals of one certain distinguishing characteristic, such as color, luster, hardness, fluorescence, etc.

REFERENCE—Fritzen's *The Rock-Hunter's Field Manual* (see page 286) has the minerals arranged according to color: black, blue, brown, gray, green, purple, red, white, yellow, colorless.

Specimens to show all the main crystal systems; or minerals representing one single crystal system—cubes, tetragons, hexagons, etc.

Minerals representing all the groups, according to chemical composition, of Dana's system of classification; or minerals of one single chemical group—sulphides, oxides, carbonates, silicates, etc.

REFERENCE—Pough's *Field Guide to Rocks and Minerals* has the minerals arranged according to Dana's system.

Note—A complete "Dana" collection is hardly within the reach of the amateur collector. It would involve a specimen of each of the more than 4,000 minerals described in the three-volume standard work on minerals: James D. Dana's *System of Mineralogy*, rev. by Charles Palache, Harry Berman, and Clifford Frondel. New York, John Wiley & Sons.

Specimens of the several forms in which a single mineral may be found—various forms of calcite, for instance, or quartz, garnet, barite, etc.

Minerals containing a certain metal—calcium, zinc, iron, etc.

Gem stone minerals.

FOSSILS—Specimens of all fossils from a certain locality—township, county, state.

Collection of specimens of fossilized plants or invertebrates or vertebrates from a given area.

Fossils representing the main geological eras, or fossils from one single era—Pre-Cambrian, Paleozoic, Mesozoic, Cenozoic; or from one single period within an era—Cambrian, Silurian, Devonian, etc.

Collecting Techniques

The methods of collecting various types of geological specimens vary somewhat, calling for an ever-increasing amount of care in the field preparation.

ROCK SPECIMENS—Find a place on the rock surface (outcrop) where the texture of the fresh, unweathered rock appears characteristically and to best advantage. Then break loose, with hammer and chisel, a specimen that shows, in the case of igneous rock (granite, basalt), the alignment of the grain; in the case of sedimentary rock (sandstone, limestone), the layering; in the case of metamorphic rock (slate, marble), the banding or folding. Trim the specimen down roughly to the standard size which you have set for your collection (see page 300).

¶ *Tip*—Expert collectors do little field trimming, preferring to do the job at home. For amateurs, it may be advisable to do the

Use newspaper for wrapping a rock. Fold sheet up from bottom, then over from sides, finally roll rock up in paper.

trimming on the spot. If you spoil one specimen, there are others available.

Next, stick a number marker on the specimen—a numbered strip of adhesive tape or masking tape (see page 286). Immediately open your notebook and write down details pertaining to the specimen: (1) its number; (2) name—if you know it; (3) exact location where found so that you might be able to return to the same spot again; (4) structural feature of the rock mass of which the rock is a sample and of other types of rock associated with it; (5) date of collection.

Finally, wrap the rock specimen in a half section or quarter section of a newspaper sheet to prevent it from getting damaged rubbing against other specimens. Put the package in your knapsack for transportation home.

If you are collecting sediments, sands or soils, newspaper wrapping is unsuitable. Instead, use small screw-cap jars. Stick the number marker on the outside of the jar.

MINERALS—Exert great care in collecting and transporting minerals to prevent them from being scratched or broken.

In the case of a float, stick a number marker on it as for a rock specimen (see above). Then wrap it in tissue and place it in a box (cigar box or egg box) in your knapsack.

When it comes to a mineral attached to a rock formation, do not attempt to knock the mineral itself off with a hammer. Instead, use the chisel and hammer at a safe distance around the base of the mineral and remove a piece of the rock to which it is fastened—the "matrix." Refrain from any further trimming in the field. Stick a number marker on the specimen and wrap it carefully.

Especially fragile minerals should be placed in cotton—or in moss or grass if you didn't bring cotton—before they are wrapped in tissue. Tiny crystals are better transported in small vials, stoppered with cotton to prevent them from shaking around and breaking.

FOSSILS—Where fossils appear in fairly soft rock, they may be exposed by splitting open the layers between which they lie with chisel or wedges and hammer. Be certain to keep both of the counterparts; one may contain the fossil itself; the other may bear an impression of it. Don't skimp on size, even in the case of small fossils. A slab showing how such fossils as trilobites and ammonites lay on the ocean floor is more valuable than a single perfect specimen.

If your fossil occurs in a hard-rock substance, don't attempt to chisel out the fossil. Instead, cut well beyond the outline of the fossil so that there will be no danger of damaging it, and leave the main job of trimming to be done at home.

As in the case of rocks and minerals, stick a number marker on each fossil specimen and make notes of all pertinent information, including details about the strata between which it was found.

Fossil skeletons—Of all geological specimens, fossil bones require the greatest care in their collection. As a matter of fact, if you should ever have the luck of hitting upon the skeleton of a prehistoric animal, you may do a great service to science if, instead of attempting to dig it out yourself, you report your find to the nearest museum and let its trained paleontologists do the job of recovering it.

Adding to Your Collection

Few rockhounds are content with just the geological specimens they find themselves. Sooner or later they want to complement their collection with rocks and minerals from other states or countries around the world. The most interesting way of doing this is by personal bartering with local collectors or by swapping through correspondence with rockhounds at home or abroad (see page 282).

Where personal contacts or correspondence are not feasible, the solution to the problem is to purchase through a reputable dealer in rocks and minerals.

REFERENCE—*Rockhound Buyers Guide*, published annually by *Lapidary Journal*, 3564 Kettner Boulevard, San Diego, California 92112, contains an extensive listing of dealers. Addresses may also be found in the magazines listed on page 283.

MINERAL DEALERS—Ward's Natural Science Establishment, P.O. Box 1712, Rochester, New York 14603; P.O. Box 1749, Monterey, California 93940.

Schortmann's Minerals, 6 McKinley Avenue, Easthampton, Massachusetts 01027.

Odoms, Star Route A, Box 32C, Austin, Texas 78710.

The Prospector's Shop, 201 West San Francisco Street, Santa Fe, New Mexico 87501.

Scott Scientific, Inc., P.O. Box 2121, Fort Collins, Colorado 80521.

Identifying Your Specimens

Before preparing your specimens for storage or display, you want to have them correctly identified. In the beginning, seek the help and advice of some local geologist or a fellow rockhound. Then, as you become more proficient, you will be able to do your own identifying.

EQUIPMENT FOR IDENTIFICATION—For complete identification of your specimens, you will turn to books, sample collections, and various types of testing equipment.

Books—Books are available on all phases of geology. For general identification, almost any of the field books on rocks and minerals listed on page 286 will suffice. For exact identification, you may require a more technical book that describes the various physical and chemical tests that will definitely establish the identity of a rock or mineral specimen.

BOOKS FOR LABORATORY IDENTIFICATION—Pough's *Field Guide to Rocks and Minerals* (see page 286) explains the tests for identifying most American rocks and minerals.

E. S. Dana and C. S. Hurlbut, *Manual of Mineralogy. Minerals and How to Study Them.* New York, John Wiley & Sons.

Sample collections—Book descriptions and illustrations are not always sufficient for identifying a rock or mineral. A better method consists in comparing your specimen with the specimens in a fairly large and correctly labeled study collection. You will probably be welcome to use such a collection at your nearest university or natural history museum, but you may prefer to have your own. Inexpensive student reference collections with small specimens of common rocks and minerals are available through some of the larger rock and mineral dealers.

REFERENCE COLLECTIONS—Send for catalog to the nearest of the mineral dealers referred to on page 296.

TESTING EQUIPMENT—For testing the physical and chemical properties of geological specimens, you may need some of the equipment described in the following, depending on how far you intend to pursue the subject.

Hardness—The hardness of a mineral is one of the most important points of identification. The hardness is determined by comparing the mineral with the minerals of Mohs scale (named for the German mineralogist Friedrich Mohs):

10 Diamond	6 Feldspar	3 Calcite
9 Corundum	5 Apatite	2 Gypsum
8 Topaz	4 Fluorite	1 Talc
7 Quartz		

According to this scale, a mineral of a certain number will scratch a mineral that has a lower number, and will, in turn, be scratched by a mineral with a higher number. A mineral that scratches fluorite (hardness 4) but is itself scratched by apatite (hardness 5) has a hardness somewhere around 4.5.

Mineral supply houses carry inexpensive collections of sample hardness minerals (generally exclusive of diamond—for obvious reasons). They also have available so-called hardness points, consisting of small mineral points of hardnesses 5 to 10, mounted in the ends of short brass rods.

¶ *Tip*—An easy and costless test for hardness can be done with fingernail, hardness 2.3; copper penny, 3; knife blade, 5.5; piece of glass, 6.5. A mineral that scratches your knife blade, for instance, but is itself scratched by glass will have a hardness of approximately 6.

Streak—The color of a mineral's "streak"—the powder mark it leaves when a corner of it is rubbed against an abrasive surface—is another important means of identification. The color of the streak of a mineral will often be found to differ from that of the mineral's surface. Black limonite, for instance, makes a brown to yellow streak, whereas metallic-yellow pyrite makes a black streak.

"Streak plates" for such testing are made of unglazed porcelain. They are hexagonal or square, about 2 inches wide and $\frac{1}{4}$ inch thick. They are available by the half dozen and dozen from mineral supply houses.

¶ *Tip*—The unglazed back of a bathroom tile or the edge of a broken china plate may be used to check the streak of a mineral.

Magnetism—A small horseshoe or bar magnet will help to identify such minerals as magnetite and pyrrhotite. They are magnetic and are therefore attracted to the magnet. A number of other minerals are attracted to a magnet after being heated.

Density—Some rocks are heavy to the feel, others comparatively light. It is a matter of their density or specific gravity—the weight of the rock in relation to the weight of the same volume of water. For determining the density of a rock, a balance is used on which the rock can be weighed first in the air, then submerged in water. For most amateur purposes, an estimate is enough: very heavy, medium heavy, light, very light.

Fluorescence—The ability of a rock or mineral to glow in the dark when exposed to "black" light can be determined by the use of a lamp giving off ultraviolet rays. See page 308.

Radioactivity—The radiation of radioactive minerals can be tested with a Geiger or scintillation counter. See page 287.

Reaction to heat—Some minerals can be made to fuse (melt) in the heat from a match flame, others when heated in a hot gas flame. The metal in the chemical composition of certain minerals colors an almost colorless flame with a characteristic color and also colors distinctively a small bead of melted borax or of salt of phosphorus. For such tests, you will need a Bunsen burner or a pocket blowtorch, a blowpipe, charcoal blocks, a nichrome or platinum wire mounted in a glass rod, borax and salt of phosphorus (sodium ammonium phosphate).

Chemical reactions—Dilute hydrochloric acid is commonly used for testing rocks and minerals; it causes fizzing of carbon dioxide bubbles when dropped on limestone, chalk, marble, and other mineral carbonates. Numerous other chemicals are used in the testing of

Hardness points for determining relative hardness of minerals come, commercially, in sets of eight cut minerals, mounted at each end of four 3-inch brass rods.

Streak plates are two-inch-square, unglazed porcelain. The color of the streak resulting when a specimen is rubbed over the plate is important for identification.

All photos: Ward's Natural Science Establishment, Inc.

Magnet, mounted at one end of aluminum tube the size and shape of a pencil, is handy gadget for testing and distinguishing between magnetic and nonmagnetic minerals.

Goniometer is an instrument for measuring the angles of crystals. It consists of a protractor scale with 1° intervals and swivel arm with window for reading angle.

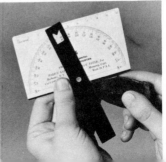

rocks and minerals. The methods are described in advanced books on mineralogy; few of them are within the scope of the amateur geologist.

Preparing Your Specimens

When a specimen has been identified, prepare it for inclusion in your collection by trimming it to final size, marking it and cataloging it.

ROCK TRIMMING—The more uniform the size of your rock specimens, the easier it is to compare their physical features, and the more attractive your collection. Decide on a standard size and stick to it. The size you pick will be determined by the amount of storage space you have available. Traditionally, rock specimens are cut to a thickness of about 1 inch and trimmed to a rectangular pillow shape, about 3 inches wide, 4 inches long—so-called hand specimens. You may decide to follow the same dimensions or to make your specimens smaller—2 by 3 inches, for example.

Cut your specimen to thickness first, then shape it to an even-edged rectangular form. The square end of the head of your geological hammer is particularly suited for trimming the harder rocks, the chisel-edged end for the softer kinds. Hold the piece in one hand and strike sudden, well-planned blows along the edge nearest to you. A number of light taps will usually do the job. When the specimen has become rectangular, break off chips from the top and bottom edges to make it pillow-shaped. Trim the back side—the least attractive side—in such a way that the specimen will lie flat without wobbling.

¶ *Tip*—Protect the palm of the hand in which you hold the rock with a glove or a piece of soft leather.

¶ *Tip*—A pair of pliers may be found helpful in the final shaping of a specimen.

After trimming it, wash the rock with detergent and water, using a hand scrubbing brush if necessary. Then rinse and dry it.

Most collectors trim their rock specimens into uniform size and cut them into the shape of a small pillow.

¶ *Tip*—Persistent rust stains on a rock can usually be removed by leaving the rock for a few hours in a solution of oxalic acid in water—3 ounces to 1 quart. Rinse thoroughly in several sets of water. Dry.

MINERALS—Wash your minerals free of adhering dust, soil, or clay with detergent and water. Rinse. Dry. Then select for your collection the specimens that have the best shape, the most perfect crystal form, brilliancy, transparency, luster.

CAUTION—Do not use water for cleaning water-soluble materials (such as halite, sylvite, thenardite, epsomite, borax, and a few others) and on minerals that are damaged by water (such as pyrite, marcasite, and other iron-containing minerals). Instead, use alcohol or cleaning fluid.

Loose crystals need no further preparation. In cases where crystals are attached to a piece of rock ("matrix"), you may want to trim this down to a suitable size. Do it with extreme care so that you do not detach the crystals—mineral crystals attached to a matrix are far more valuable than loose crystals.

¶ *Tip*—An old dental scraping tool is excellent for cleaning minerals from adhering rock.

GEM MINERALS—Gem preparation is an art in itself. Numerous collectors attracted to this specialized branch of mineral collecting —*lapidary*—have become expert "lapidarists," turning their gem minerals into true gems.

Traditionally, such minerals as agate, bloodstone, jade, jasper, and turquoise are classified as ornamental rocks; amethyst, aquamarine, kunzite, topaz, and tourmaline are semiprecious stones; emerald, ruby, sapphire, and diamond are precious stones.

Note—The U.S. Bureau of Internal Revenue classifies minerals of a hardness of 6 or more on Mohs scale as semiprecious and precious stones, subject to excise tax, on purchase, unless unsuitable for cutting and polishing into gems.

If you decide to take up lapidary as a hobby, you will need special lapidary equipment to saw, grind, or lap, sand, polish, and buff your stones.

LAPIDARY EQUIPMENT—Ward's Natural Science Establishment (addresses on page 27).

Grieger's Inc., 1633 East Walnut Street, Pasadena, California 91109.

Hillquist Lapidary Equipment, 1545 Northwest Forty-ninth, Seattle, Washington 98107.

Get the help of other lapidarists in your locality and learn by doing, by following the instructions in a lapidary manual.

REFERENCES—G. F. Herbert Smith, *Gemstones*. New York, Pitman Publishing Corporation.

Richard T. Liddecoat, Jr., *Handbook of Gemstone Identification*. Gemological Institute of America, Los Angeles, California.

Russell P. MacFall, *Gem Hunter's Guide*. New York, Thomas Y. Crowell Company.

J. Sinkankas, *Gem Cutting*. New York, D. Van Nostrand Company.

PERIODICALS—*Lapidary Journal*, 3564 Kettner Boulevard, San Diego, California 92112.

Gems and Minerals. 3418 Flannery Drive, Baltimore, Maryland 21207.

SOCIETY—Gemological Institute of America, 11940 San Vicente Boulevard, Los Angeles, California 90049. Periodical: *Gems and Gemology*.

FOSSILS—Obviously, no standard size can be set for trimming fossil specimens. Each of them should be trimmed to such a size that the fossil will show to best advantage.

When you are trimming fossils, it is important to prop up the rock matrix in which the fossil is embedded, to prevent the matrix from shifting during the delicate trimming process. For this, a sandbag comes in handy. Fill a small bag of some strong material about three quarters with soft sand, then tie up or sew up the top. Lay your sandbag flat on the table. Set the rock matrix with the fossil firmly on it with the side to be trimmed to the top. Perform coarse trimming with chisel and hammer, more intricate trimming and cleaning with an awl.

¶ *Tip*—If there is little contrast between the fossil and the matrix,

When freeing a fossil from the matrix in which it is embedded, prop up the matrix on sandbag to hold it firmly.

you may want to tint the surrounding rock with a water- or alcohol-soluble color to make the fossil more discernible.

Plaster casts—In many cases, plants and animals have left impressions in rocks and have themselves disappeared. To find out how they looked, make a plaster cast of the impressions. Brush the rock with a thin layer of mineral oil, then make a cast in the same manner in which a positive cast of an animal track is made (page 122).

"Turning"—Shells in soft limestone are often embedded in such a way that only the smooth inside shows, and break to pieces if you try to pry them loose. The Danish Dr. Carl Malling has suggested a method for "turning" this kind of fossil. Make certain that it is absolutely dry. Then drip into it ordinary sealing wax until it is completely covered. When the wax has hardened, place the specimen in cold water for a few minutes. Pry off the sealing wax—the fossil shell comes out with it and now shows its "right" side.

MARKING—When the rock or mineral specimen has been made ready for inclusion in your collection, the temporary number which you placed on it on finding it should be replaced with its permanent number. In the case of a rock specimen, the number is sometimes placed in the lower left-hand corner, but more often on the back. On a mineral, it is placed where it will detract the least from the looks.

The number may be written on paper or adhesive tape and stuck to the specimen. But this method is risky since the number may come off. A better and safer method is to write the number on the specimen itself.

Using white, quick-drying enamel, paint a small rectangular or oval spot about $\frac{1}{4}$ by $\frac{3}{8}$ inch, at the proper location. When it is completely dry, write on this marking spot, with India ink, the number you have given the specimen in your collection. Let it dry. Then cover the India-ink number with clear nailpolish to protect it.

¶ *Tip*—For the sake of simplicity and uniformity, you may want to make a stencil of your standard-sized marking spot and use this, with a stencil brush, when marking your specimens.

CATALOGING—For each numbered specimen, prepare a file card, 3 by 5 inches, or a page of a loose-leaf notebook, with all the pertinent information.

Minimum information should contain the following items (compare with the list on page 295: (1) number of the specimen in your collection; (2) name of the specimen; (3) topographic location where found; (4) geological environment and associations; (5) date collected; (6) source, if obtained by barter or purchase; (7) date received—purchase price, if any.

To add to the interest of yourself and others, you may further wish to include some of the following information, extracted from a book on rocks and minerals: (8) number in Dana system of mineralogy; (9) distinguishing characteristics; (10) physical properties; (11) chemical composition; (12) interesting facts: industrial uses, etc.

Storing Your Specimens

Store your specimens so that they are protected from damage and dust and so that they can be readily studied. This means keeping them in separate compartments in suitable containers.

TEMPORARY STORAGE—Cigar boxes may be used for temporary storage of the small collection. Divide the box into compartments by notched strips of heavy cardboard, pieces of a dismantled cigar box, or $\frac{1}{8}$-inch plywood.

PERMANENT STORAGE—ROCKS—The best way of storing your rock specimens permanently is to use individual cardboard trays of suitable size, arranged in shallow drawers of the proper depth, fitted in some kind of cabinet. The complete facilities for this type of storage are available from mineral supply houses. They are expensive, so you may prefer to make your own.

Individual trays—Start by figuring out the size of the individual trays you need. Consider the idea of settling on a standard size for large specimens, half that size for medium specimens, quarter size for small specimens. With this system, it is possible to fill up a drawer in such a way that no space is wasted.

Pasteboard trays that fit this system may be purchased from mineral dealers at a reasonable price. The most popular sizes are: $2\frac{15}{16}$ by $3\frac{15}{16}$

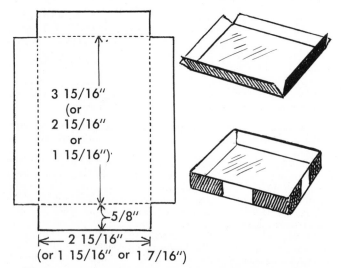

3 15/16"
(or
2 15/16"
or
1 15/16")

5/8"

2 15/16"
(or 1 15/16" or 1 7/16")

You can make your own trays for individual rocks from cardboard. Diagram indicates the three most popular sizes.

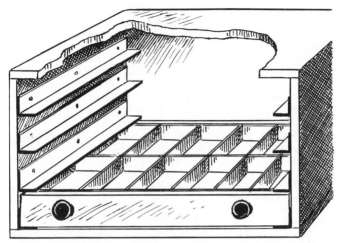

For a simple, homemade rock cabinet, use angle irons to support the drawers. Cabinet itself must be solidly built.

inches, $1\frac{15}{16}$ by $2\frac{15}{16}$ inches, and $1\frac{7}{16}$ by $1\frac{15}{16}$ inches. They have the standard height of $\frac{5}{8}$ inch.

You can easily make similar trays yourself from stiff cardboard and masking tape. Draw a rectangle of the proper size on the cardboard. Draw another rectangle with its sides $\frac{5}{8}$ inch from the first. Cut out this rectangle. Remove a small square from each corner. Use this first cutout as a template for cutting out the others. To form the tray, score the sides, then bend them up and secure the corners with strips of masking tape. For extra strength, you may decide to run the masking tape the full length around all four sides of the tray.

Drawers—Rocks and minerals are heavy; therefore, don't attempt to make the drawers of your projected cabinet too large. Also consider the most effective way of fitting the largest number of individual trays into the drawers.

Drawers commercially available are made to the following inside dimensions which many collectors consider ideal: $20\frac{1}{4}$ by $13\frac{1}{4}$ by $1\frac{1}{4}$ inches. A drawer of this size will take 36 standard-sized trays, 72 medium-sized, 144 small-sized.

You can make up such drawers yourself from $\frac{1}{4}$-inch plywood and strips of $\frac{1}{2}$-by-$1\frac{3}{4}$-inch lumber. Assemble the pieces with nails and flathead screws.

Cabinet—The cabinet, fundamentally, is a strong wooden box placed on its side. It should, of course, be of sufficient width to fit your trays. Its height depends on the number of trays you expect to use; you should figure on a height of 3 inches for each tray.

To support the drawers, use pieces of $\frac{1}{2}$-inch angle iron or $\frac{1}{2}$-inch aluminum corner molding, as long as the cabinet is deep. Screw these supports horizontally onto the inside of the cabinet sides, 3 inches apart.

The illustration (page 305) will give you a general idea of the simplest kind of cabinet possible. If you are any kind of a cabinet-maker, you will be able to work out your own embellishments.

¶ *Tip*—To keep out dust, make doors for the cabinet or provide each drawer with a front, 3 inches wide, that will completely cover the open space between the drawer and the one above it. Drawers made up in this way will need pulls.

PERMANENT STORAGE—MINERALS—In a storage cabinet containing a mixed collection of rocks and minerals, the minerals will find their way into the pasteboard trays intended for small specimens. If you are mainly a mineral and gemstone collector, you may prefer a less elaborate storage arrangement.

Mineral collection boxes—Rather than have a cabinet with drawers, many mineral collectors use separate shallow boxes with hinged or lift-off lids. Such boxes are easily moved around and can be readily stacked on a bookshelf or in a sideboard or kept in a file drawer.

Mineral collection boxes of this type are obtainable from most mineral dealers. Two common sizes are $16\frac{1}{2}$ by 13 by $1\frac{3}{4}$ inches (with space for 45 $2\frac{1}{2}$-by-$1\frac{3}{4}$-inch trays) and $13\frac{1}{4}$ by $10\frac{1}{4}$ by $1\frac{1}{4}$ inches (with space for 36 2-by-$1\frac{1}{2}$-inch trays).

It is quite a simple matter for you to make up similar boxes at home from $\frac{1}{4}$-inch plywood and $\frac{1}{2}$-by-$1\frac{3}{4}$-inch lumber, assembling them along the same lines as the drawers for a rock cabinet. An overlapping lift-off lid may be made in the same fashion by cutting the plywood 1 inch longer and wider and using $\frac{1}{2}$-by-1-inch lumber instead of $\frac{1}{2}$-by-$1\frac{3}{4}$-inch.

The box may be partitioned by strips of heavy cardboard or $\frac{1}{4}$-inch plywood. But the use of separate specimen trays (see page 304) is preferable to permanent partitions.

Metal drawer cabinets—Metal drawer cabinets for minerals are available from mineral dealers. But you may be able to find just what you need locally in a hardware store (metal chests for small tools), in an office supply house (legal blanks cabinets, "junior" blueprint cabinets), in a jewelry store (drawer cabinets for silverware), in a photographic shop (35-mm negative files, microfilm files), in a dry-goods store (spool cabinets).

Plastic boxes—Plastic boxes of all sizes and shapes are on the market. You may be able to find small plastic boxes of just the right size to hold your individual mineral specimens and cabinets of crystal-clear lucite or plexiglass for storing your entire collection.

Displaying Your Specimens

Some day you may want to put your collection—or parts of it—on display in your home or at a hobby show or special exhibition.

Display trays—The simplest way to show off your rock and mineral specimens is to use the regular trays and drawers in which you store them. Place in each specimen tray a label with just enough information on the specimen to be of interest to the general public. If you desire, provide each drawer with a glass top.

Display shelves—An old bookshelf may be used for displaying large specimens—so-called cabinet specimens, 4 by 5 inches or larger; or "museum specimens," 5 by 10 inches or more. Even better is a case with adjustable glass shelving. If desired, appropriate lighting may be installed.

¶ *Tip*—A local showcase company may have suitable secondhand showcases on sale at reasonable prices.

Display charts—A small number of specimens may be displayed on a piece of $\frac{1}{8}$-inch plywood. Cut the plywood to the desired size and arrange the specimens on it. Drill small holes through the plywood to each side of the specimens and fasten them in place with thin wire.

Individual mountings—Especially beautiful mineral specimens may be mounted on bases of $\frac{1}{8}$- or $\frac{3}{16}$-inch clear plastic or squares of styrofoam. Attach the specimens with plastic cement.

Micromounts—"Micromount boxes," $\frac{7}{8}$ by $\frac{7}{8}$ inch, made of plastic, are available through many mineral supply houses, for displaying tiny mineral crystals.

Ward's Natural Science Establishment, Inc.

Cabinets for rock collections using standard-size trays are available through dealers of rocks and minerals.

Plastic embedding—Minerals make excellent objects for plastic embedding, as described on page 221. Before embedding, clean them thoroughly in carbontetrachloride to remove finger marks, then let them dry completely.

Fluorescent minerals—Fluorescent minerals should be displayed in such a way as to show off their remarkable qualities. To do this, you need two kinds of lighting—the ordinary light of a common electric bulb and the ultraviolet light from a special light source.

LIGHT SOURCES—The *argon bulb* is the cheapest source for the special light required. It screws into the ordinary lamp socket and emanates light in the range between 3,300 and 3,700 Angstrom units. Other light sources are the long-wave-light ultraviolet tube (with a range of 3,400 to 3,800 Angstrom units) and the short-wave-light quartz tube (of 2,540 Angstrom units).

SUPPLIES—Argon bulbs may be in stock at your local electrical dealer. If not, he can order one for you.

Ward's Natural Science Establishment (addresses on page 27).

Ultra-Violet Products, Inc., 5114 Walnut Grove Avenue, San Gabriel, California 91778.

East Coast Mineral Corporation, 440 Columbus Avenue, New York, New York 10024.

¶ *Tip*—Ward's catalog FM-12 contains a chart of the more important fluorescent minerals and the way in which they react to the three different light sources.

SETTING UP THE DISPLAY—For greatest effectiveness, the display of fluorescent minerals should be arranged in a room that can be darkened completely. Set it up on a table around which your audience

Ward's Natural Science Establishment, Inc.

Make cardboard viewing box for studying fluorescent minerals. Provide it with viewing slit and two socket holes.

can move; arrange the two light sources directly overhead in such a way that you can turn them on and off alternately. Or display your specimens in a "shadow box," arranging your lights accordingly.

¶ *Tip*—If conditions do not permit any elaborate arrangement, fluorescent minerals may be studied in a simple viewing box made of cardboard or wood. Paint the inside of the box with a dull black paint and cut in the lid a viewing slit and two socket holes— one for an ordinary electric light bulb, the other for an argon bulb. See illustration page 308.

ROCK AND MINERAL PHOTOGRAPHY

Of all the photographic models with which you have to deal in nature photography, rocks and minerals are the easiest to handle. They stay put. Nothing disturbs them. They patiently wait for you to adjust your lights, if necessary, and take their picture. And the results are often breathtaking—from the gigantic sweep of a mountain range extending through the intricate texture of a rock specimen to the colorful brilliance of an almost microscopic crystal.

Geological photography challenges you to roam the country for shots of the granite rocks of Acadia National Park, Maine; the stalactites and stalagmites of Carlsbad Caverns, New Mexico; the opalized wood of the Petrified Forest, Arizona; the geyserite formations at the mouth of Old Faithful in Yellowstone National Park, Wyoming; the red sandstone cliffs in the Garden of the Gods, Colorado; the crumbling slate of the Delaware Water Gap, Pennsylvania and New Jersey—and hundreds of other photogenic, geological wonders.

And when you are tired of roaming, geological photography gives you the chance to spend many quiet evenings at home shooting the specimens of your collection.

Stills

EQUIPMENT—Camera and lenses—Any camera you would use for taking the ordinary pictures of landscapes and members of the family will do for taking long shots of distant geological formations and medium shots of outcrops. When it comes to taking close-ups of rock details and of minerals, you will require the same features in your camera as you need for insect photography (see page 176).

Other equipment—Your hands are probably steady enough to permit you to take long and medium shots with a hand-held camera. But for close-ups, you need a tripod. And further, for indoor shots, you need suitable lighting and various props for placing and posing your specimens.

WHAT TO PHOTOGRAPH—In your travels, you will soon build up a *series* of photographs of geological formations. At home, you will be developing further series of shots of the rocks and minerals you have gathered.

As a record of each of your excursions, you may decide that a *sequence* is in order—several shots of the geological formation in question: the formation as a whole, details of its structure (bands, folds, faults, dikes, etc.), close-ups of its component parts (minerals and mineral-like matter).

¶ *Tip*—To make it possible to determine comparative size, you may want to include an object of known size in your photographs: in your medium shots, your mineral hammer or a pick; in close-ups, a ruler, a coin or other familiar subject.

OUTDOOR PHOTOGRAPHY—In taking photographs of geological formations, consider composition, light, and sky. A routine head-on photograph of a mountain, taken on a dull day against an overcast sky, may be all right for a record shot—but how much more effective the shot would be if taken from the most attractive angle, with sunlight and shade emphasizing rock texture, and with a dark sky sharply outlining the silhouette.

Backlighted geological formations photograph poorly. For best effect they should be front- or sidelighted. The time of day suggested for finding rocks and minerals (see page 290) is also the time of day for getting the best lighting for your photographs.

¶ *Tip*—In black-and-white photography, a yellow filter will increase the contrast and add crispness to a medium shot. A yellow or orange filter will darken the sky in a distant shot. Always use a haze filter when taking color shots of distant objects.

INDOOR PHOTOGRAPHY—Your indoor photographs all will be close-ups of rock and mineral specimens. Posing, background, and lighting become your main considerations.

Posing—Study the specimen you want to photograph from all angles and decide on its most photogenic side. Then place the specimen on the background you intend to use with the chosen side to the lens. Use blobs of modeling clay to prop it up if necessary.

Background—For background, use a piece of material or a sheet of cardboard—of a neutral gray if you are shooting in black-and-white; of a contrasting color if you are using color film. Arrange the material or curve the cardboard against an upright support in such a way that the background completely fills the negative.

¶ *Tip*—For the background and to indicate comparative size, Pough, in his *Field Guide to Rocks and Minerals*, very cleverly posed his specimens on pieces of wide-waled corduroy of about $5\frac{1}{2}$ stripes to the inch (each stripe approximately 5 mm).

Lighting—Use two floodlights and one spotlight for bringing out the shape, texture, and color of the specimen to greatest advantage and for illuminating the background. Modify the light arrangement for each specimen. Take your light-meter reading by substitution, against a piece of gray cardboard.

¶ *Tip*—For shadowless photography, arrange your setup as follows: Lay the background material on the floor and place two boxes (1 foot high) on it, 1 to 2 feet apart. Lay a sheet of glass as a "bridge" between the two boxes. Pose your specimen on the glass.

Minerals photograph well when lighted by two floodlights and a spot. Translucent specimens (such as rock crystal) should be backlighted for spectacular effect.

Fossils need a careful lighting arrangement for bringing out details. Shadowless photography shows distinction between fossil and matrix of this "Isoletus gigas."

Rocks can be compared to size if photographed on cloth with a pattern of known dimensions—such as this obsidian with christobalite on corduroy with 3-mm stripes.

Light it so that the shadows fall outside the section of the background that fills the negative.

Be especially careful with minerals that are translucent or have a lustrous surface. You may have to use a polarizing filter to eliminate light reflections. Crystals may show up especially well if illuminated from below. The cat's-eye effect (chatoyancy) of certain minerals and the "star" (asterism) of certain gemstones may be brought out with a spotlight focused to a pinpoint.

Fluorescent minerals—In the case of fluorescent minerals, you will want to take two photographs: (1) under ordinary light; (2) under ultraviolet light to show their fluorescence. Your light meter will give you the correct exposure for the shot under ordinary light. Only experimentation will give you the correct exposure for the shot under ultraviolet light; your light meter will probably not even register.

Movies

OUTDOORS—All landscape shots may be considered parts of a geological movie since they cannot help but show some of the geological features of the area photographed. But they will make up a geological movie only if tied together with medium shots, showing forms and structures, and close-ups, showing textures and colors.

A wide-angle lens makes it possible for you to photograph a geological feature from a location much closer to the object than the usual 1-inch lens permits. A telephoto lens at the proper distance will give you your medium shots. You can also use it for taking the close-ups.

In shooting a landscape, beware of the tendency, so prevalent among movie amateurs, of "spraying the hose" on it—of moving the running camera across it from side to side. Instead, focus on the left part of the landscape, and while holding the camera still—on a tripod, preferably—run it for approximately 5 seconds. Stop the camera. Shift its position until the viewfinder is framed on the section to the right of the first shot. Shoot again for 5 seconds. And so on until you have covered the whole subject.

It is only in very special cases—such as making a horizontal sweep of the Grand Canyon or a vertical sweep of the Devil's Tower—that you are justified in very slow panning.

INDOORS—In taking movies of rock and mineral specimens indoors, use the same technique as for photographing stills indoors (see above).

Add movement to some of the shots by having a helper turn a specimen in his hand, or by placing the specimen on the slowly turning turntable of a record player, or by moving the light source that illuminates it.

CHAPTER 11

Weather

WEATHER affects all of us at all times. We enjoy it when it is fair, grumble about it when it turns foul. We cover ourselves up against it when it becomes cold, strip down to a minimum of clothing when it turns hot. We talk about it incessantly, listen to the radio and watch TV for weather forecasts, govern our outdoor activities according to its whims.

Knowledge of the weather is an important factor in our economy. It helps contractors to plan the day's job, farmers to decide on the right time for planting and harvesting, shippers to protect perishable goods. It tells the electric, gas, and oil industries what energy and heat will be needed. It informs merchants what sales to anticipate, travel agencies and resorts what attendance to expect. It tells airplane pilots the routes to follow for safe and fast flying.

Man has always had an exalted notion about his own importance. But when it comes to weather, we are quite helpless. We live, like fish, on the bottom of a vast ocean—the ocean of air that surrounds our globe. The air of the atmosphere sustains our life; without it there would be no life on earth at all. But the atmosphere does far more than that. It is a shield that protects us against the deadly effects of cosmic rays and the bombardment of millions of meteors, against being burned up on the sunlit side of the earth or frozen to death on the dark side. Without the atmosphere, there would be no wind or rain, no sound or smell, no fires or water power to produce energy.

The study of weather—meteorology, from the Greek *meteoron*, phenomenon in the sky—is the study of the atmosphere and what happens in it. Meteorology involves the effects of the heat of the sun and the rotation of the earth. It is a science that depends for its complete understanding on earthbound observers, radar and upper-air sounding stations, high-flying planes, space-conquering satellites.

But in spite of its global ramifications, it is a science you can enjoy wherever you happen to be and to which you can contribute by staying right at home, using your powers of observation and recording your findings.

BOOKS ON WEATHER—H. Neuberger and F. B. Stephens, *Weather and Man.* Englewood Cliffs, New Jersey, Prentice-Hall.

C. E. Koeppe and G. C. DeLong, *Weather and Climate.* New York, McGraw-Hill Book Company.

R. M. Fisher, *How About the Weather?* New York, Harper & Row.

Working with Others

You will get a certain amount of satisfaction out of a solitary pursuit of the many phases of meteorology. But you will get far more enjoyment if you share your interest with others. It may be fun for you to come up with weather-eye forecastings for your own benefit, but it's far more fun if you can compare your conclusions with the predictions of friends and associates. It may give you a certain gratification to establish a weather station of your own with purchased equipment, but you may get far more pleasure out of helping a group of youngsters put up a whole set of homemade weather gadgets at school or in camp.

You will have little difficulty getting in touch with people interested in meteorology. Many industries have their own weather experts. So have airports across the country. A local science teacher or professor may know of weather-interested people in your community.

By joining the American Meteorological Society, you will have a chance to meet a great number of people who share your interest, and you will be able to keep up with the latest developments in the field of meteorology.

SOCIETY—American Meteorological Society. Headquarters: 45 Beacon Street, Boston, Massachusetts 02108. Periodicals: *Publications Bulletin* and *Weatherwise.*

And if the day should come when you are able and willing to give regular hours and sustained effort to the cause of meteorological and climatological observation, the U.S. Weather Bureau may welcome you among its corps of more than 12,000 volunteer "cooperative weather observers" who devote more than 1,000,000 hours each year to observing and recording the weather for the benefit of all of us.

WEATHER-EYE WEATHER FORECASTING

Your early interest in meteorology will probably be spurred by a desire on your part to look into the future, to be able to cock an eye at the sky and tell what the local weather will be tomorrow—or even this afternoon. Oldtime mariners and farmers were able to do it with a fair degree of accuracy without instruments. Why not you? Shakespeare gave the clue to the procedure:

> Men judge by the complexion of the sky
> The state and inclination of the day.

Becoming a fairly good weather prophet is mostly a matter of having an observant mind, of being able to read a few weather signs, and of concentrating mainly on the western half of the sky, whence comes the weather in our latitudes. If, in addition, you possess a certain degree of the gambling spirit and a willingness to stick your neck out, so much the better.

Weather Signs

For weather-eye weather forecasting, you need to take into consideration such things as the clouds and their sequence of formation, the color of the sky, the direction of the wind, the atmospheric pressure, and perhaps a few other weather signs.

BOOK—Eric Sloane, *Eric Sloane's Weather Library*. New York, The Meredith Press.

CLOUDS—Think of the ten major cloud types under three heads: HIGH CLOUDS—cirrus, cirrocumulus, cirrostratus; MIDDLE CLOUDS—altocumulus, altostratus; LOW CLOUDS—stratocumulus, stratus, nimbostratus, cumulus, cumulonimbus. The first eight form an orderly, although not always consistent, sequence generally leading to rainy weather.

¶ *Tip*—For a sharper view of clouds, study them through dark sunglasses. This darkens the blue background of the sky and makes white clouds stand out. Such glasses are, of course, useless for layered clouds that completely cover the sky.

REFERENCES—*Cloud Code Chart*. U.S. Weather Bureau. Catalog No. C30.22:C62/2/958. Ten cents. From Superintendent of Documents, U.S. Government Printing Office, Washington, D.C. 20402.

Be Your Own Weather Prophet. Cloud chart by Louis D. Rubin. Free from Metropolitan Life, Madison Square, New York, New York.

Clouds in forecasting—Each of the major cloud types has its own way of indicating the weather. The simplest way of keeping track is to memorize some of the age-old weather sayings and rhymes that have proved generally reliable:

CIRRUS: In sailor lore, cirrus has many names—mares' tails, fillies' tails, hen scratches, painter's brush. Hence the rhyme:

> Hen's scarts and filly tails
> Make tall ships carry low sails.

If cirrus forms in a clear sky and does not increase, it signifies a likely continuance of fair weather. On the other hand, if cirrus grows and thickens into cirrocumulus and cirrostratus, it foretells a decided change in the weather, with rain within twenty-four to thirty-six hours, particularly if the wind is from the northeast.

CIRROCUMULUS: Its scalelike cloudlets have given cirrocumulus its common name of "mackerel clouds":

> Mackerel sky, mackerel sky—
> Not long wet, not long dry.

Cirrocumulus is not too dependable as a weather sign, except as a warning of change. It may dissipate in hot weather according to an old weather rule: "All signs of rain fail in dry weather." It usually indicates a windy day, except when it continues into the sequence of cirrostratus, altostratus, nimbostratus resulting in rain within eighteen to twenty-four hours.

CIRROSTRATUS: The thin veil of cirrostratus lets the outline of the sun and the moon shine through and often gives rise to halos. And when halos form, the rhyme tells what comes next:

> When sun or moon is in its house
> Likely there will be rain without.

This weather rhyme has an .800 batting average of being correct. Expect rain within fifteen to twenty hours.

ALTOCUMULUS: Generally considered fair-weather clouds. But watch out: When woolly altocumulus clouds thicken, or their edges join, and a steady northeast wind blows, expect rain or snow—depending on the temperature—within fifteen to eighteen hours:

> Woolly sheep in a dappled sky
> Will bring you raindrops by and by.

ALTOSTRATUS: A thin veil, similar to cirrostratus, but denser so that the sun behind it looks as if it were seen through frosted glass. It is a harbinger of rain, if the wind is northeast to south, probably within ten to fifteen hours. If the wind blows from another direction, the sky may simply remain overcast.

STRATOCUMULUS: This heavier form of altocumulus spreads wide in long cotton rolls across the sky and may show blue sky in spots. If it appears in the evening, the sun may break through in the familiar "sun drawing water" phenomenon. Rain may follow in the night.

STRATUS: When stratus descends over the landscape, its watery companion, nimbostratus with rain, is not usually much more than a few hours away:

> When hill or mountain has a cap
> Within six hours we'll have a drap.

NIMBOSTRATUS: No forecasting is necessary for this type of cloud: a low, nearly uniform layer of a dark gray color. You'll know what it means when it is upon you: a continuous rain or snow.

CUMULUS: The heaps of white cotton with flat bases are the clouds of fair summer weather:

> When woolly fleeces spread the heavenly way,
> No rain, be sure, will mar the summer day.

When cumulus clouds decrease in numbers and size during the afternoon, there is continued fair weather ahead. But watch out if cumulus starts building up vertically.

CUMULONIMBUS: On a hot summer's day cumulus may grow into towering cumulonimbus—"thunderhead." A violent drenching may be upon you within an hour or less, perhaps with hail, thunder, and lightning:

> When the clouds appear like rocks and towers
> The earth's refreshed by frequent showers.

Cirrus "Feather"

Cirro-cumulus "Mackerel"

Cirro-stratus "Tangled web"

Alto-cumulus "Sheep"

Alto-stratus "Curtain"

Strato-cumulus "Twist"

Stratus "Spread sheet"

Nimbus "Umbrella"

Cumulus "Wool pack"

Cumulo-nimbus "Thunder"

Rain from cumulonimbus will generally be over as quickly as it began:

A sunshiny shower won't last half an hour.

This fits in with a meteorological saying of major importance:

Short notice, soon past.
Long foretold, long last.

SKY COLORS—The relationship between sky colors and weather has been recognized for more than two thousand years: "When it is evening," it says in the Bible (Matt. 16:2–3), "ye say, It will be fair weather for the sky is red. And in the morning, It will be foul weather today for the sky is red and lowering . . ." The old sailor rhyme tells the identical story:

Red sky at night,
Sailors' delight,
Red sky in morning,
Sailors take warning.

The same prediction, in a more complete form, goes like this:

Evening red and morning gray
Send the traveler on his way.
Evening gray and morning red
Send the traveler wet to bed.

The latter fits in with another old weather saying:

When the sun goes down in a sack
[setting behind a bank of clouds]
It comes up in a wellspring
[rain next day].

ATMOSPHERIC PRESSURE—For predicting weather with instruments, the barometer is of prime importance. It shows the changes occurring in air pressure, with rising pressure indicating fair or improving weather, falling pressure indicating weather changing to storm or rain. In nature, air pressure is often indicated by the flight pattern of certain birds and by the way smoke and sounds and certain odors behave.

Bird flight—Swallows and swifts—bats, too, for that matter—are in-flight feeders on insects. At high atmospheric pressure insects are carried high by air currents. At low pressure they are carried downward by cool air and their wings are heavy with moisture:

Swallows flying way up high
Mean there's no rain in the sky.
Swallows flying near the ground
Mean a storm will come around.

Smoke—The same principle holds true for smoke particles rising from a chimney or a campfire:

If smoke goes high
No rain comes by.
If smoke hangs low
Watch out for a blow.

Sounds—Sounds carry farther at low pressure, when there is a moist atmosphere:

> Sounds traveling far and wide
> A stormy day will betide.

The sound of a train whistle from a nearby railroad, not usually heard, may carry to your ears at certain times when pressure and resulting wind direction are just right and may tell you about weather ahead.

Smells—The same goes for smells. Odors from a marsh or barnyard may become more pronounced as the pressure falls and the wind shifts.

WIND DIRECTIONS—A wind is named for the direction from which it comes: A wind coming from the west is a west wind; a "nor'easter" is a wind blowing from the northeast.

If you know the lay of the land where you are, you should have little trouble determining your wind directions. If you are not familiar with the locale, use a compass to determine the wind direction. Face the wind. Hold the compass in front of you. Turn the compass until the compass needle lies over the orienting arrow on the inside bottom housing. Read the compass direction on the far side, the away-from-you outside rim of the compass housing.

¶ *Tip*—For a more exact determination of the wind direction, wet your index finger in your mouth. Hold the wetted finger upright in front of you. The side from which the wind comes will feel cooler from evaporation. Face the direction indicated in this way and take a compass bearing.

Wind directions are not always dependable. Local conditions play a great part in determining how the wind will blow. Along shores, land breezes and sea breezes will tell their own story. In mountain areas, the direction of canyon winds may run counter to normal local wind directions.

For more than two-thirds of continental United States, the following holds true:

> *Good weather* comes with northwest, west, and southwest winds.
> *Bad weather* comes with northeast, east, and southeast winds.

Starting with the compass pointing north and boxing the compass —that is, moving around it clockwise—you'll find the following general effects if the wind blows steadily from a certain direction:

> N—summer: cool; winter: cold.
> NE—summer: cool, with rain; winter: snow.
> E—rain, from Atlantic to Rockies.
> SE—heavy rain.
> S—warm, with showers.
> SW—fair and warm.
> W—fair (except western Florida and Pacific area).
> NW—fair and cool.

Winds in forecasting—As far as forecasting is concerned, only a wind that is *shifting* from one direction to another tells what is ahead, according to the old saying:

> A veering wind: fair weather.
> A backing wind: foul weather.

During a rainy spell, when the wind starts "veering"—that is, shifting with the sun in a clockwise direction—from E ro SE to S toward W, it is a sign of the skies clearing, with fair weather ahead.

During a fair spell, when the wind starts "backing"—that is shifting against the sun in a counterclockwise direction—from W to S, SE, then toward E and NE, bad weather is on top of you.

OTHER WEATHER SIGNS—Morning Fog—A morning fog portends a good day ahead. It is almost certain to "burn off" before noon.

Morning rain—The same is the case with a morning rain:

> Rain before seven,
> Lift before eleven.

Rainbows—When the clouds break during a rain and the sun shines through and creates a rainbow, clearing is ahead. Rainbows at other times have a different meaning:

> Rainbow to windward [west], foul falls the day.
> Rainbow to leeward [east], damp runs away.

Dew and frost—Dew or frost—depending on the temperature—forms on clear nights because of the cooling of vegetation, but does not form in overcast weather. Hence the rhyme:

> When the dew is on the grass,
> Rain will never come to pass.
> When grass is dry at morning light
> Look for rain before the night.

LONG-TERM SIGNS—Long-term weather proverbs are meaningless. Forget them! That goes whether they refer to the groundhog and his shadow, the woolly bear caterpillar and the band of brown around its body, or the squirrel and its supply of nuts. That goes also for the supposed effect of the moon and other heavenly bodies. And it goes for the month that "comes in like the lamb and goes out like the lion" and for similar references.

Weather Logging

You may enjoy checking the weather occasionally against the weather signs described in the preceding pages, but it is only by a systematic logging of the weather over a reasonable length of time—a month or more—that you will become a good "weather-eye" prognosticator. The work of developing and keeping a satisfactory weather log consists in making regular observations, recording them carefully, deducing what they mean, and checking your deductions against what actually occurred.

Daily observations—Make your observations daily at specific intervals. If you do so twice a day, make morning observations immediately after breakfast, and evening observations immediately after supper. Or aim for three daily observations to coincide with the Weather Bureau's national reports: at 7:30 A.M., 1:30 P.M., and 7:30 P.M.

Jot down your observations in a logbook if you like, but also include them on a chart. Such a chart will give you a chance to study the records at a glance and compare them for a period of a week or longer.

The notes should cover the date and hour when the observations were made, the sky conditions and cloud types, the wind direction, precipitation, and other signs you may have observed. (If you use instruments, also include temperature, barometric pressure, wind velocity, amount of rainfall in the preceding twenty-four hours.)

Forecasting—On the basis of all your observations, arrive at a forecast of the weather for the rest of the day and for the following day. Write down your predictions in fair detail.

Checking—At the end of the prediction period, make a short report of the weather that actually occurred, matching it against your forecast. If this report confirms your deductions, you will know that the weather signs you used are reliable for your locality. If the report contradicts your forecast, you will want to check the points at which the report and your forecast failed to coincide. This should make it possible for you to determine which weather signs to accept and which to reject, and what modifications to make in the interpretation of certain weather signs to fit your local conditions. With such changes arrived at, you should be able to come up with more exact predictions in the future.

YOUR HOME WEATHER STATION

Instead of trying to develop a dependable "weather eye," you may decide to take a more scientific approach and go in for a more complete study of the weather. For this, beyond checking the weather maps of your local newspaper, you will probably want to subscribe to and peruse the U.S. Weather Bureau's Weather Maps. You will also want to establish a home weather station consisting of a few traditional weather instruments. For this kind of setup, you can get along with just four instruments: barometer and wind vane, thermometer and hygrometer.

BOOKS—B. C. Haynes, *Techniques of Observing the Weather*. New York, John Wiley & Sons.

P. E. Lehr, R. W. Burnett, and H. S. Zim, *Weather*. New York, Golden Press.

Weather Forecasting. Catalog No. C30.2:f76/3. Twenty-five cents. From Superintendent of Documents, U.S. Government Printing Office, Washington, D.C. 20402.

WEATHER MAPS—Weather maps are published and distributed

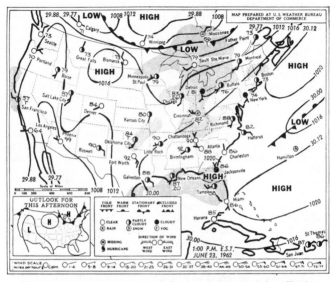

Study weather map in your daily newspaper or subscribe to weather map from U.S. Weather Bureau for more details.

daily by the Weather Bureau of the Environmental Science Services Administrations of the U.S. Department of Commerce. It contains the information gathered daily from more than four hundred stations throughout the United States, decoded, digested, and superimposed in graphical form on a map of the country.

To start with, the study of the daily weather maps may seem rather complicated since you have to learn the meaning of the "highs" and "lows," of four different "fronts"—cold, warm, occluded, and stationary—of isobars, and of a variety of symbols. But soon all of these features will become familiar to you, and the maps, from day to day, will be like panels of a comic strip telling you the story of weather across the country.

WEATHER MAPS—Daily Weather Maps. Catalog No. C30.12. $2.40 for 3 months, $9.60 for a year. From Superintendent of Documents, U.S. Government Printing Office, Washington, D.C. 20402.

BAROMETERS—The barometer—literally "weight measurer"—is used to measure the weight of the atmospheric pressure that covers a certain area.

Mercurial barometer—In the mercurial barometer, the weight of the air is indicated by the height in inches (English system) or millimeters or millibars (metric system) of mercury in a glass tube, closed at the top and suspended, at the bottom, in a small cup of mercury. The air pressure, and therefore the mercury height, fluctuates. At high atmospheric pressures, the mercury rises to perhaps 30.20 inches or more; at low pressure it may fall to 29.80 or below.

The mercurial barometer is the most exact instrument for determining air pressure. But because of its yard-long, vulnerable glass tube, its liquid mercury and special wall support, it is a cumbersome instrument used chiefly by expert meteorologists.

Aneroid barometer—Instead of using the mercurial barometer, an amateur is served better by another instrument, based on another principle: the aneroid barometer. This barometer—from the Greek *aneros*, nonliquid—consists of a corrugated metal box that is sealed after being emptied of most of the air. To the top of the box is attached a mechanism with a pointer that indicates on a dial the pressure exerted on the box by the air above it. This dial is graduated to correspond to the range of inches of mercury in the glass tube of the mercurial barometer.

Aneroid barometers are available in a variety of decorative cases at many different prices. Pick one that fits your pocketbook and fancy.

MOUNTING THE BAROMETER—The aneroid barometer is hung vertically on a wall, indoors or outdoors, whichever you prefer—the pressure is the same. Place it at a convenient height for easy reading. Select a spot where the instrument is not subject to jarring. Keep it in the shade away from direct drafts to prevent it from being exposed to rapid changes in temperature.

Before using it, you must adjust the barometer so that it gives the correct reading for your locality's height above sea level. Follow the instructions that come with the barometer.

READING THE BAROMETER—If the face of your barometer is marked with "Rain—Change—Fair," pay little attention to this legend. It is not where the needle points at any given time that counts; it is how it is moving. If the needle shows a rapid and relatively large pressure drop—0.05 to 0.10 or more in three hours—it signals the approach of a low-pressure system. This, with a shift in the wind, usually means bad weather ahead (see table, page 327). Conversely, a rapid and great rise in atmospheric pressure indicates the approach of a high-pressure system. This, with the right wind, usually brings fair weather (see table).

WIND VANE—The simplest way of determining a wind direction is to take a look at a wind vane that is properly mounted. Such a vane consists of a broad fin and a narrow pointer, arranged to move freely about a vertical axis. The wind catches the fin and swings it ahead of it, thus turning the vane in such a way that the pointer points directly into the wind.

Many different wind vanes are on the market, with from simple to very elaborate designs. If you prefer to make your own, see page 329.

MOUNTING THE WIND VANE—Although a common place for mounting a wind vane is the point of the gable of a roof, a better location is a mast or pole in an open area where the vane is not exposed to up-or-down drafts or eddy currents.

The general rule is that the vane should be at least 12 feet above any obstruction within 100 feet, and at least as high as any obstruction between 100 and 200 feet of the vane.

READING THE WIND VANE—The direction of the wind is found by checking the direction toward which the pointer of the vane is pointing against four horizontal rods below it, correctly oriented and marked for the four cardinal points of the compass: N, E, S, and W.

Wind direction and atmospheric pressure together help forecast the weather, as suggested in the table, page 327.

¶ *Tip*—If you care to spend the money, you can purchase and mount an electric wind indicator. This consists of a wind vane electrically connected to an indoor wall box with eight directional lamps representing eight compass directions. One lamp or two adjoining lamps light up to indicate the wind direction.

THERMOMETERS—A thermometer—from the Greek *therme*, heat—indicates the heat in degrees Fahrenheit (English system) or centigrade (continental system) or both.

Common wall thermometer—The common wall thermometer consists of a glass bulb attached to a thin tube of glass containing a sealed-in liquid (mercury or colored alcohol). The liquid rises and falls with changes in the temperature of the air. The temperature is read on a numbered scale placed alongside the glass tube.

Any number of thermometers are available commercially. The cost of the thermometer you pick depends on the degree of accuracy you demand of it.

MOUNTING THE THERMOMETER—Place the thermometer in a shelter outdoors, for instance on a porch with northern exposure. There must be free circulation of air around it, but it must be protected against rain, direct sunlight, and radiation.

READING THE THERMOMETER—When reading the thermometer, be certain that your eye is exactly level with the top of the mercury column in the glass tube. If you read from below or above, you will get an error—known as the "parallax error"—caused by the fact that the mercury column and the degree scale are separated by the thickness of the glass tube. Such errors are not possible in the use of the more expensive thermometers that have the scale etched in the glass.

When taking a reading, stand as far away from the thermometer as feasible and read it quickly to prevent the thermometer from being influenced by the warmth of your breath and your body heat.

A sudden well-marked drop in temperature, especially in winter, usually indicates the passage of a cold front. A rapid rise in the temperature, with an accompanying rise in humidity, suggests probability of rain and fog.

Maximum-minimum thermometers—If you are interested in knowing the lowest temperature of the night, the highest temperature

Aneroid barometer for determining atmospheric pressure.

Wind vane indicates direction from which wind is blowing.

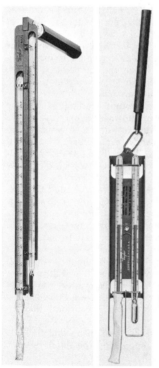

All instruments: Taylor Instrument Company

Sling psychronometers (regular, pocket-size) tell humidity.

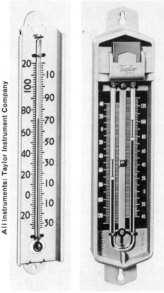

Thermometers (wall, maximum–minimum) tell the temperature.

of the day, and the temperature at the time of reading, you will want a maximum-minimum thermometer. Instead of a single column of liquid, the thermometer has a double column in a U-shaped tube. The liquid pushes a tiny float—called an index—into position to register the highest and lowest temperature of the day. When you have noted the temperatures, you reset the index with a small magnet.

HYGROMETERS—The humidity of the air is determined by reading the setting of a hygrometer. Two different types are used in weather studies, based on two different principles.

Hair hygrometer—Certain filaments—including human hair—are hygroscopic, that is, they absorb moisture. In so doing, they usually lengthen. Given this characteristic, it is possible to stretch a hair, with the natural oil removed, over a framework, and to attach a weight or spring to it to keep it taut and a pointer that will indicate the change in length.

MOUNTING THE HAIR HYGROMETER—The hair hygrometer must be placed in a spot that is shaded and protected against the rain, yet provided with free air circulation from all sides.

READING THE HAIR HYGROMETER—The hair hygrometer can never be very accurate. It takes a while for the hair to respond to increasing or decreasing humidity, particularly when the temperature drops. Because of this slow response, the hair hygrometer is not able to show rapid variations in relative humidity.

Sling psychrometer—For a correct, instant reading of relative humidity, you will need a hygrometer known as a psychrometer— from the Greek *psychros*, to cool. This intrument consists of two ordinary thermometers attached, next to each other, to a metal backing provided with a swivel handle. The bulb of one thermometer is kept dry; the bulb of the other is covered with a wick of loosely woven muslin.

USING THE PSYCHROMETER—Wet the muslin wick around the wet-thermometer bulb thoroughly with water, preferably rainwater or distilled water, then take the psychrometer outdoors to a shady spot. Grasp the handle and whirl—"sling"—the thermometers. In so doing, face the wind to prevent the heat of your body from reaching and influencing the thermometers.

READING THE SLING PSYCHROMETER—During the slinging, stop from time to time and read the wet-bulb thermometer. It will drop below that of the dry-bulb thermometer because of the evaporation of the water in the wick. Continue slinging until the wet-bulb reading reaches its lowest point. Then jot down the readings of both thermometers.

Determine the difference in degrees between them, and find the relative humidity from the table accompanying the instrument or contained in publications of the Weather Bureau.

REFERENCE—*Psychometric Tables*. Catalog No. C30.2: P95/941. Thirty cents. From Superintendent of Documents, U.S. Government Printing Office, Washington, D.C. 20402.

WIND-BAROMETER TABLE

WIND DIRECTION	BAROMETER (REDUCED TO SEA LEVEL)	CHARACTER OF WEATHER INDICATED
E to N	29.80 or below— barometer falling rapidly	Severe northeast gale and heavy rain. In winter, heavy snow, followed by cold wave.
E to NE	30.10 and above— falling slowly	Summer, with light winds: Rain may not fall for several days. Winter: Rain within 24 hours.
E to NE	30.10 and above— falling rapidly	Summer: Rain probable within 12 to 24 hours. Winter: Rain or snow, with increasing winds.
SE to NE	30.10 to 30.20— falling slowly	Rain in 12 to 18 hours.
SE to NE	30.10 to 30.20— falling rapidly	Increasing wind, with rain within 12 hours.
SE to NE	30.00 or below— falling slowly	Rain will continue one to two days.
SE to NE	30.00 or below— falling rapidly	Rain with high wind, followed within 36 hours by clearing, and in winter, by colder weather.
S to E	29.80 or below— falling rapidly	Severe storm imminent, followed within 24 hours by clearing, and in winter, by colder weather.
S to SE	30.10 to 30.20— falling slowly	Rain within 24 hours.
S to SE	30.10 to 30.20— falling rapidly	Increasing wind, with rain within 12 to 24 hours.
Going to W	29.80 or below— rising rapidly	Clearing and colder.
S to SW	30.00 or below— rising slowly	Clearing within a few hours, then fair for several days.
SW to NW	30.10 to 30.20— barometer steady	Fair, with slight temperature changes for one to two days.
SW to NW	30.10 to 30.20— rising rapidly	Fair, followed within two days by rain.
SW to NW	30.20 and above— barometer steady	Continued fair, with no definite temperature change.
SW to NW	30.20 and above— falling slowly	Fair for two days, with slowly rising temperature.

Weather Study Devices

Rather than purchasing commercial instruments, you may get a special kick out of designing and making your own. These devices will not, of course, provide the information that precision instruments do. But they will teach the principles of all the various phases of meteorology and may prove particularly helpful in getting young people—schoolchildren or campers—interested in the subject.

BOOKS—A. F. Spilhaus, *Weathercraft*. New York, Viking Press.

R. F. Yates, *The Weather for a Hobby*. New York, Dodd, Mead & Company.

Herman Schneider, *Everyday Weather and How It Works*. New York, McGraw-Hill Book Company.

WIND VANES—Wind vanes can be made to all descriptions and sizes, from the elaborate golden "weathercock" seen on ancient church spires to the simple wooden vanes and whirligigs of old New England. Two important points must be considered as you design and make your own: It must move freely and easily on its axis, with the front part pointing into the wind, and the vane part must be in balance.

REFERENCE—Ken Fitzgerald, *Weathervanes and Whirligigs*. New York, Clarkson N. Potter.

Homemade wind vanes—For a simple wind vane, cut a piece of wood, $\frac{1}{4}$ inch thick, into the shape of an arrow, a flying bird, or some other form, making certain that the vane part has more surface than the front end. Find the center of balance and carefully drill a hole through the vane. Mount the vane by slipping it over a headless nail or a piece of clothes-hanger wire inserted into a hole in the top of a post. Provide the post with pointers made of wire or wood to indicate the four cardinal compass points: N, E, S, and W.

¶ *Tip*—To cut down the friction of a small wind vane, place a copper washer or a large glass bead over the axis before placing the vane. For a larger vane, use a ball bearing.

You can also make a wind vane from a 2-foot length of 1-inch-square wood, provided with a plywood or sheet-metal arrow and vane. Or use metal tubing and cut outs of sheet metal.

A No. 10 tin can makes possible still another kind of wind vane. Remove the top and bottom edges, cut along the seam, and spread the can out flat. Cut to the design shown in the diagram (page 329) and double over the various parts, forward or backward, as indicated. Make the two holes for the axis with a nail.

WIND-SPEED GAUGES—Before the anemometer was invented for measuring the speed of the wind, British Admiral Sir Francis Beaufort, in 1806, developed a scale of wind force based on the observations and descriptions in use among sailors. This scale, with approximate speeds of the wind in miles, may be all you will need to satisfy your curiosity on this subject. If you want to be more exact, you may decide to purchase an anemometer or make one of your own.

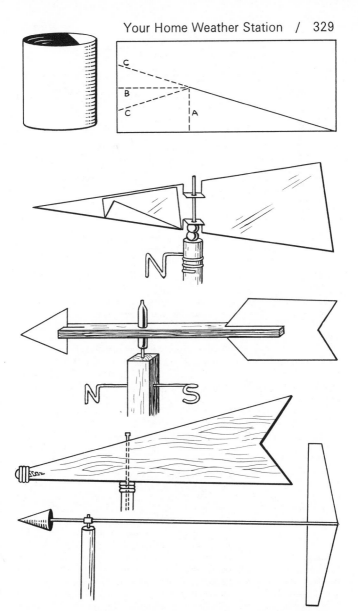

Various wind vanes. From top: made of tin can, wood, and plywood. Bottom: airfoil vane of aluminum and brass.

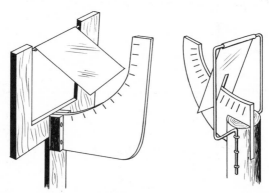

Pressure-plate anemometer can be made from sheet metal, wire, plywood. Calibrate by holding out of car window.

REFERENCE—Books listed on page 321 contain tables of the Beaufort scale.

Pressure-plate anemometer—The pressure plate of an improvised pressure-plate anemometer can be made from sheet metal, from a tin can, or from wood. The framework can be made from clothes-hanger wire or wood, the scale from wood or cardboard. The illustrations on page 330 show some of these possibilities.

To calibrate the scale, hold the anemometer at arm's length out of the right-hand window of a car, on a windless day, while the driver is driving (on the far right side of the highway for safety's sake) at various speeds: 5, 10, 15, 20, up to 40 miles an hour.

When this type of anemometer is used, it must be faced directly into the wind.

¶ *Tip*—By combining the pressure-plate anemometer with a wind vane, you can arrange for the vane to keep the anemometer correctly directed at all times.

Cup anemometer—In the cup anemometer, three or four hemispherical or cone-shaped cups are arranged on horizontal arms in such a way that they turn around a vertical axis. The opening of the cups catches the wind, and the wind forces the cups to revolve. The number of revolutions per minute gives you the wind speed.

For the cups for a cup anemometer, use your imagination. Your choice runs the whole way from paper cups and rubber-ball halves, through coffee measuring spoons (tablespoon size) and funnels, to halves of toilet tank floats and hollow cones made by soldering together the two straight edges of a semicircle of sheet metal. For the support and axis, use wood or metal parts.

When you have assembled it, paint one of the cups in any color you like so that you will know when the cups have made a complete revolution.

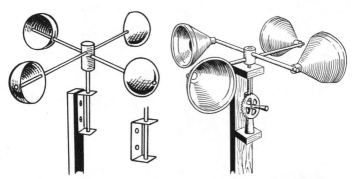

Cup anemometer consists of a number of hemispherical or cone-shaped cups arranged on arms that turn horizontally.

For calibration get the help of a driver friend to drive you along at various speeds as for the pressure-plate anemometer. But in this case you need to time the number of revolutions. So bring along a stopwatch or a watch with a sweep second hand. Count and note the revolutions in thirty seconds at the various speeds.

Mount the anemometer in a suitable position. In contrast to the pressure-plate anemometer, the cup anemometer does not have to be faced into the wind.

¶ *Tip*—At high-wind velocity, the cup anemometer may rotate so fast that it may be hard to count the number of revolutions. To overcome this problem, you can attach your anemometer to the gear part of an inexpensive household eggbeater—the type that has two beater sections. Remove the beater ends and stem of the "idling" side. Mount the remaining part vertically and attach the anemometer shaft with arms and cups (see illustration, page 331). Calibrate as above, counting the revolutions of the eggbeater handle at various speeds.

BAROMETER—Weather glass—The old-fashioned weather glass uses water to indicate barometric pressure. It consists of a glass bubble, closed at top and bottom, with a long side spout open at the top. At high air pressure, the water column is forced back in the spout. At low pressure, water drips from the open end. It is fairly reliable—but only if it is kept at a constant temperature.

You can improvise a weather glass by using a soda bottle, a cork, and a piece of plastic tubing. Fill the bottle with water, insert the cork, bend the tubing into a U, turn the bottle upside down, and hang it up cradled in strings.

Homemade barometer—For a more reliable homemade barometer, use a thermos bottle. Because of its insulated double walls it is influenced little by changes in outside temperature.

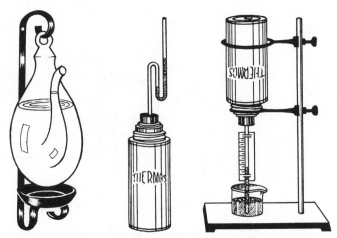

**Old-fashioned weather glass overflows at low atmospheric
pressure. Homemade barometers provide a crude estimate.**

Make a hole in the middle of a well-fitting cork large enough to
insert a glass tube or a drinking straw. Put the cork in the thermos
bottle. Turn the bottle upside down and attach it to a wooden or
metal stand. Slip a small cup—such as a ketchup bottle cap—in
under the glass tube. Pour colored water into the cup. Press on the
stopper to force out a few bubbles of air. Place a scale on the tube.
Rising pressure will push the water up into the tube; falling pressure
lets it return to the cup.

RAIN GAUGE—For measuring precipitation, the Weather Bureau
uses an 8-inch-diameter funnel on top of an overflow can, a measuring
tube with a cross-section area one-tenth the cross-section area of the
funnel, and a measuring stick. The measuring tube makes measuring
accurate: When 1 inch of rain falls into the funnel, it fills the measuring tube to a depth of ten times as much.

Homemade rain gauge—You can follow this same procedure in a
very simple fashion. Use a No. 10 tin can and a tall jar with straight
sides, such as an olive or caper jar. Fasten a strip of masking tape
to the outside of the jar. Pour water into the can until it measures
1 inch, then pour it from the can into the jar. Mark the height on
the tape for 1 inch of rain, then divide the tape into tenths. If the jar
is high enough, calibrate also for 2 or more inches of water in the can.

To use it, put the measuring can in the bottom of a pail (to reduce
turbulence and eddies around the can) and place it 2 to 3 feet above
the ground in an exposed location. After a rainfall, measure the
amount of rain by pouring the contents of the can into measuring jar.

THERMOMETER—It is not feasible to attempt a homemade

thermometer. Whatever you come up with would have to be calibrated with a regular thermometer. So why not simply get an inexpensive thermometer?

¶ *Tip*—When buying a cheap thermometer, look over all the thermometers in the shop and compare their readings. If there is a difference of several degrees between highs and lows, pick the thermometer that shows the average.

HYGROMETERS—Psychrometer—For a cheap, homemade psychrometer, obtain two inexpensive thermometers that read the same. Screw them onto a piece of plywood. Bore a hole in the plywood near the top. Tie one end of a piece of sashcord to the plywood, the other to some kind of handle. Slip the end of a 6-inch wick, cut from a clean, white shoelace, well over the bulb of one of the thermometers. Then use as described on page 326.

Chemical hygrometer—A chemical hygrometer is not very reliable, but it's fun to make. The chemical cobalt chloride ($CoCl_2$) changes color according to the amount of moisture it contains. When perfectly dry, it is blue; when moist, it is pink. Probably you have seen artificial flowers or weather cards with sails of ships or little-girl dresses that turn color with the weather.

To make your own chemical hygrometer, dissolve 3 ounces (10 g) of cobalt chloride in 3 fluid ounces (100 ml) of water. Saturate pieces of white cloth or filter paper in the solution. Remove them and allow them to dry. Cut them up in whatever shape you like and use them as you prefer, turning the pieces into flowers, or gluing them to cardboard.

NEPHOSCOPE—The nephoscope (from the Greek *nephos*, cloud) is used to determine the direction in which a cloud is moving and

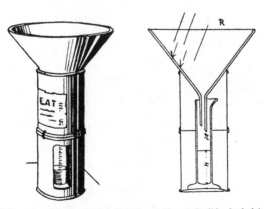

In this rain gauge, precipitation = H × r ÷ R (H: height of water in glass; r: radius of glass; R: radius of funnel).

also, by professional meteorologists using other equipment, to measure its speed.

Mirror nephoscope—The mirror nephoscope uses a black mirror. This is made in a very simple fashion: Get a sheet of glass, a piece of black paper, and a piece of ¼-inch plywood (or heavy cardboard), all of the same size: 12 inches square. On the black paper, draw, with white pencil or ink, a 10-inch-diameter circle and eight straight lines crossing in the center. Mark the ends of the lines for sixteen points of the compass: N, NNE, NE, ENE, E, and so on. Place the paper on the plywood, cover it with the glass, and bind all three things together with masking tape.

Next, make a sighting rod by pushing a 5-inch length of ¼-inch dowel into a hole bored in a small block of wood.

To use the mirror nephoscope, place the mirror flat on some kind of level support, at about waist height. Orient it with a compass but reverse all directions, that is, turn it so that the north marking points south. Decide on the cloud overhead whose direction of travel you want to determine. Walk around the mirror while looking down onto it until the cloud appears in the center of the mirror and seems to move directly along one of the compass lines. Set the sighting rod at the edge of the mirror at this point. Sight over its top and follow the reflected image of the cloud until it passes out of the mirror. The compass marking where the cloud disappeared indicates the direction from which it was moving.

Comb nephoscope—The comb nephoscope is a direct-vision instrument rather than a reflected-vision type. It looks somewhat like a garden rake standing on end, with the tines straight up. The Besson model consists of a 9-foot vertical rod with a horizontal crosspiece 3½ feet long fixed to its top. This crosspiece carries seven vertical spikes placed at equal distances apart. The vertical rod is mounted in such a fashion that it can be turned. At the bottom it has a pointer that shows on a disk marked with the compass directions in which direction the crosspiece is pointing.

Professional comb nephoscopes are made of metal. If you have the facilities, you can construct one from metal tubing. Otherwise, use a 1-inch dowel for the vertical rod and crosspiece, a ½-inch dowel for the spikes. Use 2-by-2-inch wood for the support. To allow the vertical rod to turn, provide it with a round turning disk or simply wind a rope once around it and turn it by pulling the rope ends.

To use it, walk around below the comb until the cloud you want to observe lies in a straight line with the tip of the center spike of the crossbar. Then turn the vertical rod until the spikes of the crossbar are lined up with the direction in which the cloud is moving. Then read off the direction on the direction disk.

WEATHER PHOTOGRAPHY

Any wide-view photograph is, practically speaking, a weather photograph as well. A properly exposed mountain scene or seascape

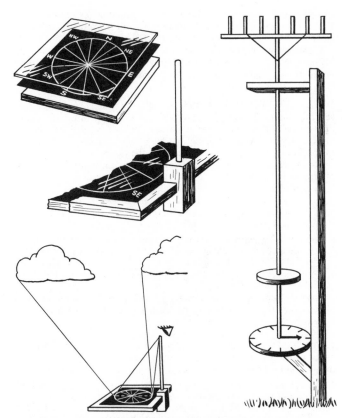

Homemade instruments for determining cloud movements: mirror nephoscope (left) and comb nephoscope.

would be quite uninteresting without clouds. Snow shots are weather shots. So are rainy-day shots. But if you really want to specialize in weather photographs, you will want to concentrate mostly on the sky, using only foreground features to emphasize what is happening overhead.

EQUIPMENT—Camera and lenses—Because weather photographs are mainly shot with the camera set at infinity, practically any camera with its standard lens will do.

Filters—Filters are a must. For black-and-white photography, a medium-yellow filter (No. 8–K2) or a deep-yellow filter (No. 16–G) will darken the blue sky into various shades of dark gray and make clouds appear whiter and crisper. A red filter (No. 25–A) will make the effect even more dramatic by turning the blue sky almost black. For color photography a polarizing filter will deepen the color of a clear blue sky, making even the wispiest cloud show up.

Light meter—With clouds varying in light reflection from the most brilliant white to the most dismal gray, a light meter is an absolute necessity for coming up with black-and-white negatives or color slides of fairly consistent exposure.

WHAT TO PHOTOGRAPH—Clouds—In the beginning, take several shots of each cloud or cloud formation—one at regular light-meter setting, another half a stop below, a third half a stop above. Decide on the exposure that best suits your taste and use that in the future, taking into consideration the filter you are using.

Don't settle for shots of only cumulus or cumulonimbus as most photographers do. Aim for a complete set of all ten types of clouds. You don't have to go far afield to take such a set. During the course of a year you will probably be able to get all ten from a window of your home. Such a set will be of even greater interest if all shots show a small amount of the same foreground features.

REFERENCE—To learn what is possible in cloud photography and to provide a special challenge, send for the cloud chart *Be Your Own Weather Prophet* mentioned on page 315. Cloud chart is the result of a hobby started from a hospital bed by a partly paralyzed amateur photographer.

Sunset—Sunsets are unsatisfactory taken with black-and-white film, but with color film—Ah-h! Your sunset shots will be among your most spectacular slides.

Use a light meter to determine the exposure. But watch out if the sun itself is in the picture. Keep the sun out of the cell and aim the meter upward at the clouds; otherwise the comparative brilliance of the sun will take over and give you a badly underexposed shot.

¶ *Tip*—If you don't have a light meter, try this: If you can look directly at the sunset without eyestrain, you can get a good result with $1/_{50}$ or $1/_{60}$ at f/5.6 using Kodachrome II or similar film (ASA 25). As the sun drops below the horizon, change first to f/3.5, then to f/2.

But remember that there is no exact exposure for sunset shots. Slight under- or overexposure will give you excellent results.

¶ *Tip*—By some quirk the human eye "sees" the sun when it is sinking as being much larger than when it is high in the sky. Therefore, sunset pictures actually showing the sun are usually disappointing. To produce a larger sun, use a telephoto lens. Because the foreground will also be enlarged, you need to move far back to get it in proper proportion.

Rainbow—A rainbow must be caught the moment you see it. Take a shot, using the same exposure as for the regular landscape shot under the same light conditions. Then wait for a few minutes—just in case the rainbow should turn brighter and make another shot worthwhile.

Cloud photography in black-and-white.

Without filter, sky and clouds show very little contrast. The picture becomes flat and uninteresting.

Yellow filter brings out a modicum of contrast between sky and well-defined clouds.

Red filter shows clouds against a sky turned almost black. It also sharpens all landscape features.

Catching the whole rainbow may require a wide-angle lens. If you do not have this, aim for a pleasing composition showing the sweep of the rainbow from the spot on the ground where the proverbial "pot of gold" is located, up and out the side of your picture.

Rain—Falling rain photographs poorly. Photograph its effects instead: raindrops on a windowpane, water rushing through a gully, people with umbrellas leaning against the rainstorm, and so on.

Snow—Snow falling close in front of a camera lens will look peculiar: The flakes appear as big blobs of cotton. Photograph them from a distance of several feet, through an open window or from a deep doorway, or outdoors by placing the camera on a tripod and holding a cloth stretched out in front of the lens. To keep the feeling of motion, shoot at slow speed, certainly not faster than $1/50$ second, with the diaphragm at whatever stop the light calls for.

For snow landscapes, wait for the sun to come out. Frontlighted snow shots are flat, so try to shoot with the sun shining from the side or almost to the front of the camera.

Snowflakes—Six-pointed snow crystals are some of the most exquisite creations of nature. You will be able to photograph them if you have access to a low-power microscope and have a camera with a removable lens so that you can couple it onto the microscope; the lenses used are those of the microscope.

Bring all equipment outdoors on a snowy day when the temperature is below freezing. Set up the equipment on a protected spot, such as a front porch. Leave everything outdoors for at least one hour to chill well before work begins.

Catch the snowflakes on a piece of black velvet or flannel. Transfer a selected flake to a chilled glass slide with the point of a toothpick or by simply turning the cloth over. Place it under the microscope object lens and shoot.

To get the right exposure, you may have to take a number of test shots. Once the correct exposure has been established, shooting can proceed quickly. You can photograph all day—and all winter long, for that matter—without ever getting a duplicate design.

REFERENCE—W. A. Bentley and W. J. Humphreys, *Snow Crystals*. New York, Dover Publications.

¶ *Tip*—By using a method developed by Dr. Vincent J. Schaefer, you can not only photograph snow crystals but also preserve them for permanent collection. In this method, the snowflake is placed on the glass slide in a drop of 1 percent solution of the plastic resin polyvinyl formal (trade name: Formvar 15–95, Shawinigan Products Corporation, Springfield, Massachusetts) in ethylene dichloride. The method is described in Publication No. 41, Atmospheric Science Research Center, State University of New York, Albany, New York.

Frost—The fernlike traceries of frost on a windowpane are easily photographed. But experiment with backgrounds before shooting: Have someone stand outside and hold up a black or a white cardboard, or a metallic reflector, or, for color photography, a piece of cardboard of any color you prefer.

¶ *Tip*—The design of window frost can be kept permanently by spraying with aerosol plastic spray or with the solution used by Dr. Schaefer. In the latter case, the thin film can be stripped off in a single sheet for easy storage.

Lightning—Photographs of lightning require time exposure. You can't synchronize yourself with a lightning flash. This means that you must set up your camera on a tripod, aim it toward the part of the sky where the lightning occurs, set the distance for infinity and open the shutter, wait for the lightning bolt, and close the shutter.

Lightning pictures are particularly exciting when taken over water. The flash will produce a light track over the water.

WARNING—Play safe. Photograph lightning from a protected shelter only, never from a spot where you may be exposed to danger.

DAYTIME—A daytime shot of lightning is a gamble. Use the smallest possible diaphragm opening. Take a meter reading of the sky. Since the overcast makes the day dark, the meter may call for an exposure of a couple of seconds. Open the shutter, hope for a lightning bolt, and close the shutter after twice the length of time the meter called for. Repeat if you didn't get a lightning flash. If you overexpose too severely, the lightning streak may be just barely visible.

NIGHTTIME—You will have a better chance if the lightning occurs in the night. In this case, open the diaphragm to its largest opening. Keep the shutter open for one or more lightning flashes, then close it. Several streaks of lightning on the same negative or slide make the storm look particularly impressive.

Storms—Daring photographers have taken dramatic shots of tornado funnels whipping across the landscape and of devastating hurricane winds uprooting trees and whipping waves into a fury. You may have neither the occasion nor the inclination to go in for this kind of photography, but you may be interested in photographing afterward the destruction caused by a hurricane or a snowstorm, the floods resulting from a rainstorm.

Movies

Regular movie shots of weather phenomena will look much like stills of the same subjects. In a good movie you want the actors to move. In a good weather movie you want the clouds to move, the sunset to blaze and fade away. That means time-lapse photography.

TIME-LAPSE PHOTOGRAPHY—Time-lapse photography is the opposite of slow-motion photography. In slow motion, the film is shot at high speed (say, 64 frames per second) and shown at regular home-projection speed (16 frames per second). The result is the appearance of greatly slowed-down action (in this case, 64 divided by 16, or one-fourth the speed of the actual action). In time-lapse, the film is shot at slow speed (say, 1 frame every 2 seconds) and projected at regular speed (16 frames per second). The action will appear greatly accelerated (in this case, 2 multiplied by 16, or 32 times as fast as the original action).

Three things are necessary for successful time-lapse photography of clouds: (1) a camera with single-frame action; (2) a solid tripod that will keep the camera in the exact position throughout the filming; (3) a suitable filter to accentuate the effect: medium-yellow or dark-yellow for black-and-white, polarizing screen for color.

WHAT TO PHOTOGRAPH—Clouds—Clouds have a double action: They move across the sky, and their outlines change constantly. So before aiming your camera, determine the direction in which the clouds are moving. Then, aim your camera so that, within the length of time you intend to shoot, the clouds enter from one side, move across the viewfinder, and exit on the other side. Most of your footage will probably be of the most photogenic clouds in the sky: cumulus. Give them room on your movie frames to expand vertically in case the day seems to indicate that they may develop into cumulonimbus.

Now take a light reading, set your diaphragm, and start shooting.

¶ *Tip*—Be sure to check your movie camera's instructions for single-frame exposures. In some cameras, the use of the single-frame button lets twice as much light enter. If that's the case with your camera, reduce the diaphragm opening by one stop.

One exposure every two seconds should give you a satisfactory scene. For these two-second intervals, use a watch with a sweep second hand, or say as fast as you comfortably can: "Everything's ready; now I must shoot!" (Press button.) "Everything's ready; now I must shoot!" (Press.) And so on.

Sunsets—A speeded-up sunset—from the first rosy tinge in the skies to a murky twilight—makes a stunning spectacle. Here you do not have to worry about the horizontal motion of the clouds. Face your camera into the sunset. Take the exposure with due consideration of the hints for taking sunset stills (page 336). Then, shoot one exposure every two seconds. If the light is fading very quickly, you may have to reset the diaphragm from time to time. Do this with the utmost care so as not to shake the camera.

Sequences and series—A single scene does not make a weather movie; you need quite a number of them.

You can make up an interesting *sequence* by splicing together your shots of the various phases of a storm: cumulus turning into cumulonimbus, clouds scudding across a more and more threatening sky, the first raindrops, people scurrying for shelter, rain pouring from gutters and over the ground, then clouds opening up, the sun breaking through, a rainbow and the end of the storm.

A *series* of sunsets would be spectacular, especially against a great number of backgrounds of land or sea—and sensational if you should be able to include the peculiar blue-green flash as the sun disappears that is sometimes seen over the Caribbean Sea from Barbados and some of the other Caribbean islands.

CHAPTER 12

The Heavens

STEP out of your door on a bright day or a clear night, and all the wonders of the universe surround you. There hangs the sun as it has hung for eons upon eons and will hang for eons to come. There shine the stars in the tremendous bowl of space. And as you watch through the day or the night, the heavenly bodies pass in review.

In ancient days, when man considered himself the center of the universe, he knew within his heart and by the evidence as he interpreted it that his Earth stood still and the stars moved around him. It is only in recent moments of human history that we have come to learn of our insignificance: that the Earth is just a speck of dust in the immensity of space, turning around its own axis and swinging around the sun, chained by special forces to the sun's scorching mass.

When you take up the study of the heavens, you enter upon the oldest of all sciences. For thousands of years man had looked toward the stars without paying them much heed, except perhaps as an eternal "comic strip," reminding him by the figures they formed, of the heroes he loved and the monsters he feared. It was only as early watchers of the stars realized that the changing shadows cast by the sun could tell them of the passing of time and the rising of certain stars could inform them of the advent of the seasons that the heavenly bodies took on deeper significance. Now, for the first time, people could plan for the future, knowing what lay ahead. And so those who knew the secrets of the heavens became their first priests and scientists. And out of astronomy came the sciences of geometry and arithmetic, the science of telling time in terms of hours and weeks and months and years, the science of navigation for traveling by land or by sea, and eventually by air and by rocket power, and numerous other sciences.

There are many doors by which a person can enter into the study of the heavens. Some people want to know about the stars "because they are there." Others may become intrigued by the ancient myths and will want to locate the characters in the sky. Some will feel that knowing the stars is a part of an educated person's equipment. Others may become deeply engrossed in the complex mathematics involved in predicting astronomical phenomena. A photographer can get interested in shooting the heavens, a handyman in making his own instruments for star study.

It will make little difference how you enter upon the study of the heavens.

Whether you enter because of a simple interest in finding out a bit about the stars through easy *stargazing*, or because of a desire to penetrate into the subject through more serious *sky observing*, you will find astronomy an exciting activity with all the thrills of boundless exploration.

BOOKS ON GENERAL ASTRONOMY—H. J. Bernhard, D. A. Bennett, and H. S. Rice, *New Handbook of the Heavens*. New York, McGraw-Hill Book Company.

Robert H. Baker, *Astronomy*. New York, D. Van Nostrand Company.

W. T. Skilling and R. S. Richardson, *A Brief Text in Astronomy*. New York, Rinehart & Winston.

David Bergamini, *The Universe*. Chicago, Time-Life Books.

Working with Others

Astronomy is a field in which you will be particularly happy to have a guide to help you find your way into its intricacies. Fortunately, it is a rather simple matter to find such a guide. In practically every city and town you will find amateur astronomers who meet together in small local clubs, some of them independent, others part of national organizations. In most cases, your local library or a local science teacher should be able to tell you about such groups. If not, write to one of the national astronomical societies mentioned below.

State universities and natural history museums have astronomy departments, many of them with their own observatories equipped with telescopes and other astronomical instruments. A number of them have a regular program of lectures, classes, field trips, observations. In addition, many major cities have planetariums, buildings containing intricate instruments that project the stars on large indoor domes. These planetariums put on performances to show the travels of the planets, eclipses of the sun and the moon, and other astronomical phemomena.

SOCIETIES—American Astronomical Society. Headquarters: Department of Astronomy, University of Illinois, Urbana, Illinois 61801. Periodical: *Astronomical Journal*.

Astronomical League. Headquarters: Science Service Building, 1719 N Street, NW, Washington, D.C. 20036.

Amateur Astronomers Association. Headquarters: 212 West Seventy-ninth Street, New York, New York 10024. Periodicals: *Sky and Telescope*, *Skylines*.

Astronomical Society of the Pacific. Headquarters: California Academy of Sciences, Golden Gate Park, San Francisco, California 94118. Periodicals: *Leaflet* and *Publications*.

STARGAZING

For easy stargazing, you need no expensive astronomical equipment—only an inquiring mind and good eyes. Whereas in most other nature pursuits you can get along with fair to middling eyesight, for stargazing good to excellent eyesight is imperative. If you want to go in for serious stargazing, have your eyesight tested and have it corrected with suitable glasses, if necessary.

¶ *Tip*—Test your eyes against the second star in the "handle" of the Big Dipper. Your eyesight is fine if you see this as a double star and thereby meet the old Indian eyesight test of locating "the little papoose" on "the big squaw's" back. Or test yourself against the Pleiades, or Seven Sisters. If you can make out six stars in this cluster, your eyesight is excellent.

Equipment for Stargazing

CLOTHING—Dress warmly, whether summer or winter. Even on a warm summer night you may get chilled, standing still for any length of time gazing at the stars.

STAR MAPS—In the same way that you need a good route map for finding your way across country, you need a good map for finding your way among the stars.

Planisphere—The simplest star map to use is a planisphere. This is a circular map of the constellations, centered in the North Star. It is usually printed on stiff cardboard and enclosed in a frame with a window that can be set to show the visible constellations for any day and hour of the year.

Most planispheres show the ecliptic, the path followed by the planets. A few have the stars printed in luminous paint.

Star books—Several excellent books are available with clear star maps. They show the constellations on separate monthly charts. Most of these books also contain individual charts of the major constellations and describe special features to look for.

Planisphere is easiest map to use for locating the constellations. It has a frame and a circular map that can be rotated to show the sky for any day and hour.

BOOKS FOR FIELD IDENTIFICATION—POCKET-SIZED—Donald H. Menzel, *Field Guide to the Stars and Planets*. Boston, Houghton Mifflin Company.
William T. Olcott and R. Newton and Margaret W. Mayall, *Field Book of the Skies*. New York, G. P. Putnam's Sons.
Herbert S. Zim and Robert H. Baker, *Stars*. New York, Golden Press.

BOOKS FOR IDENTIFICATION—LARGE-SIZE—Samuel G. Barton and William H. Barton, *A Guide to the Constellations*. New York, McGraw-Hill Book Company.
Kelvin McKready, *A Beginner's Star Book*. New York, G. P. Putnam's Sons.
H. A. Rey, *The Stars—A New Way to See Them*. Boston, Houghton Mifflin Company.

Other star map sources—Instead of using books for locating stars, you can cut out and use the star charts published each month in many newspapers, generally in the weather report section. Or you can subscribe to a monthly magazine dedicated to astronomy and use its monthly page of the constellations and the visible planets among them.

PERIODICALS—*Sky and Telescope*. Sky Publishing Corporation, 49–50–51 Bay State Road, Cambridge, Massachusetts 02138.
Review of Popular Astronomy. Bimonthly, Sky Map Publications, Inc., P.O. Box 231, St. Louis, Missouri 63105.
The Griffith Observer. Griffith Observatory, Los Angeles, California.

Flashlight—You will need a flashlight to illuminate the map as you look for the constellations on it. A pencil light will do the job.

¶ *Tip*—Cover the lens of the flashlight with red cellophane or plastic. Or paint it with red nailpolish. Otherwise, you will have trouble adjusting your eyes back and forth between the dark night sky and the illuminated book page.

¶ *Tip*—A flashlight makes an excellent tool for pointing out the constellations to a friend or a group of people. For this, use a flashlight with a narrow beam—preferably a five-battery flashlight. Keep it directed upward and turn it off after each pointing.

Binoculars—If your main interest in stargazing is to be able to identify the constellations, binoculars will prove of little help. With the sky measured in 90 degrees from the horizon to zenith (a point directly overhead), the angle of the sky occupied by most constellations amounts to 20 or more degrees. The angle of the usual 7 × ,50 binoculars is only around 6 degrees, the angle of good wide-angle binoculars (6–700 feet at 1,000 yards) only around 12 degrees, covering less than half of most constellations.

However, you may want a pair of good binoculars for viewing the moon and the planets and for studying special features of the different constellations.

Tripod and tripod mount—For steady viewing, you need to fasten your binoculars to a steady tripod with the help of a suitable mount.

A tilt-top head on the tripod will make it possible for you to aim the binoculars in any direction. Even better is a tripod with a pan head. Various types of binocular mounts are on the market. If you are handy, you should be able to figure out the kind of mount you need and make it yourself.

Field Observations

For your stargazing, pick nights that are as clear as possible—free from haze or fog, cloudless, or with only a few scattered clouds. Get as far away as you can from the glow of city lights; go into the darkened countryside. Pick a viewing spot that is unobstructed by trees or buildings, with no direct lights of lamp posts or neon signs in sight.

The Constellations

Today, when we speak of constellations—from the Latin *con*, together, and *stella*, star—we refer not only to the imaginary star figures themselves but also to the parts of the sky dominated by the eighty-eight major constellations. Of these, about half are visible from the northern hemisphere.

Around two thousand years ago the Greek astronomer Hipparchus divided the stars he could see in the Greek sky into six magnitude classes. He gave the brightest stars the designation of 1st magnitude and the weakest that could be seen with excellent eyesight the designation of 6th magnitude. The bodies of the major constellations are made up mostly of stars of the first four magnitudes. It is only rarely that a star of 5th magnitude is included.

¶ *Tip*—For a measure for comparing star magnitudes, take a look at the "bowl" of the LITTLE DIPPER. It contains four stars—one each of 2nd, 3rd, 4th, and 5th magnitude. For 1st magnitude, refer to *Aldebaran* in the constellation TAURUS or to *Altair* in AQUILA.

WHERE?—Begin your stargazing by locating the BIG DIPPER. Draw an imaginary line between the two stars in the bowl farthest from handle: the "Pointers." Continue this line for a distance of about five times its length until you hit a star of 2nd magnitude at the tip of the tail of the Little Dipper. This is *Polaris*, the North Star or Polestar.

¶ *Tip*—While facing straight north to locate Polaris, use the occasion to learn to orient yourself quickly and easily in regard to the directions in the field: south to your rear, west to your left, east to your right.

Now add to the two dippers the other "circumpolar" constellations that swing counterclockwise around Polaris and are always visible from the latitudes of the United States: W-shaped CASSIOPEIA, house-shaped CEPHEUS, snake-shaped DRACO (Dragon), indistinct CAMELOPARDALIS (Giraffe).

Once you have oriented yourself, use Polaris for orienting your star chart, and the Big Dipper and Cassiopeia as your "bases of operation" for finding your way across the heaven.

WHEN?—Time of year—The picture of the skies varies with the seasons. Because of the twenty-three-hour–fifty-six-minute rotation of the earth on its axis, the stars (beyond the circumpolar constellations) seem to rise from the east, move up into the sky, and set toward the west. This rising and setting happens nearly four minutes earlier on each succeeding night, or two hours earlier in a month, or six hours earlier in a season—until after the twelve months of a year, the picture looks the same at a certain hour of the night.

The result is that by watching the sky each night or each week at the same time, you will in the course of the year see all the constellations that are visible in your latitude.

¶ *Tip*—Try a "Star Vigil," alone or with a group. During such a vigil, extending for six hours—from 9:00 P.M. to 3:00 A.M., for instance—the constellations of a whole season will pass before your eyes.

Time of night—The stars can, of course, be seen throughout the night when the sky is clear. But there is a special thrill in beginning to study them soon after sunset. First the stars of 1st, 2nd, and 3rd magnitude make their appearance and start to form the patterns of the constellations. Within half an hour or so, the stars of 4th and 5th magnitude complete the patterns.

¶ *Tip*—Many astronomers suggest that beginners start their study of the stars on a cloudless night when the waxing moon is between crescent and first quarter. The moonlight during this period blots out from the sky the thousands of confusing stars of 5th magnitude and below; this makes the constellations show up clearly.

HOW?—With the naked eye—In the beginning, concentrate on learning the constellations and locating the major stars that definitely identify them. In many instances, these bright stars will help you further orient yourself in the heavens by the special patterns they form: the prominent triangles made up of Sirius-Procyon-Betelgeuse and Spica-Arcturus-Denebola, and the "Heavenly G" of the winter sky formed by the nine bright stars Aldebaran-Capella-Castor-Pollux-Procyon-Sirius-Rigel-Bellatrix-Betelgeuse, seven of them stars of 1st magnitude.

With binoculars—After mastering the constellations, locate special features within the constellations and turn your binoculars on them—such as the V-shaped *Hyades* in Taurus, the globular star cluster of Hercules, the *Northern* "*Coal sack*" of Cygnus, the nebula of Orion, the galaxy of Andromeda, and many others. With binoculars, you are able to see stars of 7th, 8th, 9th magnitudes.

The Planets

The ancient observers of the night sky noticed five stars that did not behave "right." Instead of twinkling, they glowed with a steady

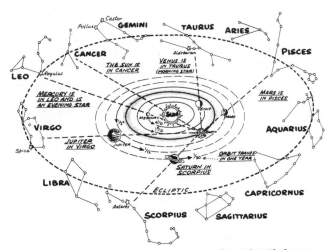

Edmund Scientific Company

This diagram indicates what is meant when it is stated that a certain planet is "in" a certain sign of the Zodiac.

radiance. Instead of staying in fixed positions, they moved among the stars. The early observers called them by the Greek name *planetes* or "wanderers."

Today we know of nine planets, including the Earth. The five seen by the ancients—Mercury, Venus, Mars, Jupiter, Saturn—are still visible with naked eyes. Uranus may be seen in good field glasses, Neptune and Pluto only in strong telescopes.

WHERE?—The ancients noticed that the planets moved among certain constellations that represented different creatures. They called their path the Zodiac, from *zoion*—living things. Today we define the Zodiac as an imaginary band, extending 8 degrees on each side of the "ecliptic"—the path of the sun across the sky. This band is divided into twelve equal parts, each part dominated by a constellation:

> The Ram, the Bull, the Heavenly Twins
> (ARIES) (TAURUS) (GEMINI)
> And next the Crab, the Lion shines,
>   (CANCER) (LEO)
> The Virgin and the Scales.
> (VIRGO) (LIBRA)
> The Scorpion, Archer, and the Goat
> (SCORPIO) (SAGITTARIUS) (CAPRICORNUS)
> The man who holds the watering pot
> (the Water Carrier: AQUARIUS)
> And Fish with glittering tails.
> (PISCES)

The planets are always found in the Zodiac. The planets are not, of course, actually "in" among the stars of the constellation. The planets are close to Earth, the stars inconceivably far away. When we say, for instance, that "Saturn is in Aquarius," we mean that the planet is in that Zodiacal sign. Two thousand years ago, when this concept was introduced, this literally meant that the constellation Aquarius formed the background for it—but not anymore. Since then, each sign in the Zodiac has moved backward 30 degrees into the constellation west of it. So now, when you read that "Saturn is in (the sign of) Aquarius," you must look for it against (the constellation of) Capricorn.

WHEN?—Look for the planets in the evening just after sunset, before the stars of the constellations brighten. Then you can easily locate the visible planets because of their brilliance, and you can follow them throughout the night.

If you want to know in advance which planets are visible, you will find the astronomical calculations for the rising and setting of each of them for each day of the year, as well as their positions, in various astronomical periodicals (see page 344), in almanacs, and in astronomical yearbooks.

REFERENCES—*World Almanac, Information Please Almanac, Reader's Digest Almanac, New York Times Encyclopedic Almanac, Old Farmer's Almanac*, and other current almanacs.

American Ephemeris and Nautical Almanac.

The Observer's Handbook.

Patrick Moore, *Yearbook of Astronomy.* New York, W. W. Norton & Company.

THE INFERIOR PLANETS—The "inferior" or "inner" planets —those with their orbits around the sun inside the Earth's—move with the greatest irregularity. Their movements must be checked regularly against published calculations.

Mercury is at its best at its "greatest elongation"—that is, when it is farthest away from the sun as seen from the Earth. This happens six times a year. At its "greatest western elongation" in the fall, it rises in the morning shortly before the sun, then fades as the light of the sun blots it out. At its "greatest eastern elongation" in the spring, it slowly emerges in the evening sky at sunset time and sets soon after the sun does—perhaps before. Few stargazers get to see Mercury —Copernicus is said to have died without having seen it.

Venus is the brightest object in the sky after the sun and the moon. It emerges, when visible, either as an "evening star" in the evening twilight near the western horizon, or as a "morning star" in the morning twilight toward the east. It appears not earlier than three hours before the sun rises and stays no longer than three hours after the sun sets.

THE SUPERIOR PLANETS—The "superior" or "outer" planets —those with their orbits outside the Earth's—are at their best when they are at "opposition"—that is, in a position opposite to the sun as seen from the Earth. On these occasions, they rise in the east at sunset, remain in the sky throughout the night, and set in the west at sunrise.

Mars is bright one year, reaching three times the brightness of Sirius, and dim the next, down to 2nd magnitude. It is brightest when it shines in the southern sky at midnight, especially if its opposition happens in August or September. It uses about fifty-seven days to pass over one constellation of the Zodiac.

Jupiter is distinguished easily among the stars because of its brilliance, exceeding all in brightness except Venus. Because of the duration of its orbit (about twelve years), it stays within the same Zodiacal constellation for about a year. Therefore, when you have once located it, you will know where to look for it each succeeding week or month.

Saturn is brighter than the average 1st magnitude star. Its time of revolution around the sun (twenty-nine and a half years) causes it to stay within the same Zodiac sign for almost two and a half years.

HOW?—With the naked eye—Seen with the unaided eye, the visible planets look like dots—brighter than the stars, but much like them. The main satisfaction you get from locating them is that of knowing they are there and being able to follow them in their wanderings.

With binoculars—Seen through binoculars, the planets look like tiny disks instead of points. Under good viewing conditions, you may be able to see the phases of Venus, four of Jupiter's twelve moons, perhaps even the rings of Saturn. To do this, you will need to have your binoculars steadied on a tripod. Uranus may be located through especially high-powered binoculars if you know exactly where to look for it.

The Moon

With the success of the space program, and the landing of astronauts on the moon, the attention of people around the world has been turned toward the moon more than ever before. And yet, most people notice the moon only when it shines brightly in the night sky, its full face reflecting the sun's light. It is then that they may look for the figures of the man in the moon, the girl and her lover, the rabbit of Indian legend.

The real fascination in watching the moon comes when you begin to follow it in its journey and study more carefully its behavior.

WHERE?—The moon—like the planets and the sun—"wanders" across the sky in the Zodiac, at the rate of about one Zodiacal constellation in two days.

As you know, the moon's phases are caused by the sun half-lighting it as it circles the Earth, showing varying amounts of the lighted half. By keeping this in mind, you should have no trouble figuring out its position in relation to the sun:

Face north at midnight. At that time the sun is in the north, below the horizon. If this were the time of the full moon, the moon would be right behind you, in the south, opposite to the sun. A waxing moon in the first quarter would be to your left, in the west. A waning moon in the last quarter would be to your right, in the east. Use this same general idea to determine other positions of the moon in its various phases as you face the setting or the rising sun.

WHEN?—To familiarize yourself with the timing of the moon, follow its wanderings for a month, beginning with the beginning.

Find out from the almanac when the new moon occurs. On that particular date the moon is in the sky during the day, backlighted by the sun and therefore invisible. A couple of days later, you will see the moon, at sunset time, as a thin crescent that sinks soon after the sun. In another couple of days the moon has "waxed" into first quarter, rising at noon, reaching its highest point almost due south at sunset, setting at midnight. Next comes the "gibbous" phase— that is, with a hump—of the waxing moon, rising in the afternoon, and setting in an early morning hour. At $14\frac{3}{4}$ days after new moon, the moon is full, rising toward the east as the sun sets toward the west, crossing the southern sky, setting in the west at sunrise.

Immediately after, the moon starts losing light. It gets into the gibbous phase of the "waning" moon, then into the last quarter, rising near midnight, setting at noon. The moon becomes crescent again, with the "horns" pointing in the opposite direction from their direction during waxing, rising in the eastern horizon before the sun. Finally, after twenty-nine and a half days, the moon is back to "new".

Moon eclipses—It sometimes happens that the moon, at full, gets caught up in the shadow the Earth throws into space. The result is a moon eclipse.

A total moon eclipse is a spectacular show that may last as long as three hours and forty minutes.

¶ *Tip*—For the dates of forthcoming moon eclipses, consult a current almanac.

HOW?—With the naked eye—In addition to simply watching the moon, there are certain simple studies you can undertake.

Timing the moon—Time the moon on the occasions when you see it rising on the horizon. You will find that it rises later from night to night. The shortest delay, of only twenty minutes each night, occurs near the autumnal equinox (about September 23) when the "harvest moon" provides extra welcome hours of light. Sometimes the moon will be as much as an hour and a half later than the night before. The average for the year is fifty-two minutes.

Altitudes of the moon—At a specific time every night, when the moon is in the sky, say, at 9 P.M. or 10 P.M., determine its altitude— that is, its height above the horizon expressed in number of degrees.

You can do this with a simple *quadrant*: Buy a cheap protractor. Fasten a piece of soda straw, with strips of tape, across the pro-

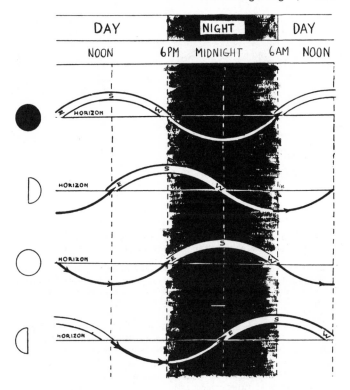

Chart showing the rising and setting of the moon at its different phases tells you when and where to look for it.

tractor from the 90-degree point of the semicircle to the opposite side. Tie a thread around the soda straw at the 0–180-degree line, and attach a weight (a stone or a washer or a bolt) to this thread to form a plumb line. To use it, hold the protractor vertically, sight through the straw to the lower edge of the moon, with the plumb line hanging free. When you have taken the sight, press the thread against the protractor with the thumb and read off the altitude in degrees.

¶ *Tip*—For a rough estimate of degrees in the sky, use your hand and your fingers, by holding them out in front of your eyes at arm's length. Test your personal measurements against degrees in the sky: 5 degrees between the Pointers of the Big Dipper, 10 degrees between the two stars at the top edge of the Big Dipper's bowl,

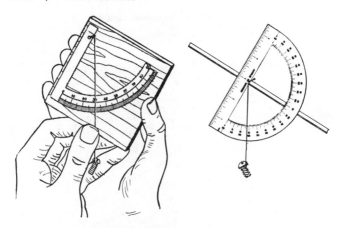

A simple quadrant constructed from a protractor makes it possible to determine the altitude of the moon or a star.

20 degrees from the middle star in the handle to the farthest star of the bowl, 28½ degrees from Pointers to Polaris, 3 degrees across Orion's belt. You may find that your hand will cover 8 degrees, your middle finger 2 degrees, the outspread of your fingers 20 degrees.

If you take these altitude readings at different times of the year, you will find that the moon rides low in summer (when the sun is high in the sky) and high in the winter (when the sun is low).

HOW?—With binoculars—When you look at the moon through binoculars, your old friend the man in the moon disappears as you see the moon's actual face, with its brighter areas made up of mountain ranges and craters, its darker areas consisting of relatively smooth plains, known as *mares*—seas, although the moon has no water.

For best results, study the moon at phases other than full at which time the moon is frontlighted and all its features are flat. Particularly good is the period when the moon is waxing from crescent to gibbous. At that time, the moon is sidelighted, with long shadows that exaggerate the mountain ranges.

BOOK—Ernest H. Cherrington, *Exploring the Moon Through Binoculars*. New York, McGraw-Hill Book Company.

The Sun

The sun is the nearest star to the Earth. It is so easy for us to take the sun for granted: It has been in the sky for millions of years and will remain there for millions of years to come. But each of us should know a bit more about it than we do.

WHERE?—The idea that the sun rises in the east and sets in the west

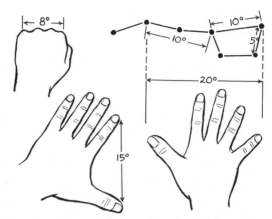

For rough estimate of degrees, use your hands and fingers, holding them out in front of your eyes at arm's length.

is an old fallacy. Only twice a year is this saying true: on the two days that day and night are of equal lengths—at the vernal equinox, about March 21, and at the autumnal equinox, about September 23. The rest of the year it is more correct to say simply that the sun rises toward the east and sets toward the west.

In the summer the sun actually rises toward the northeast, reaches its highest point in the sky at the summer solstice, about June 22, and sets toward the northwest. In the winter, the sun rises toward the southeast, reaches its lowest height in the sky at the winter solstice, about December 22, and sets toward the southwest.

WHEN?—For the exact hour of sunrise and sunset for each day of the year, consult a current calendar and your daily newspaper.

Sun eclipses—In its travel through space, the new moon occasionally cuts across the direct line between the Earth and the sun. The result is a sun eclipse.

Although sun eclipses are more frequent than eclipses of the moon, fewer people have a chance to see them. A total moon eclipse can be seen by the people of half of the Earth—those on the side where it is night at the time. A total sun eclipse, on the other hand, can be seen only for a maximum time of $7\frac{1}{2}$ minutes within the path of a quickly moving circle at most 167 miles in diameter, and a partial eclipse by people along the path of a circle about 4,000 miles in diameter.

If you desperately desire to see a total sun eclipse, you will have to travel to the part of the world where one occurs, according to the forecast in your astronomical almanac. If you live around New York, you'll have a chance to see the next scheduled total solar eclipse for that area if you hang around long enough—on October 26, 2144.

HOW?—With the naked eye—Of course, when the sun is out, you can see it with unaided eyes. But never look at it directly with unprotected eyes. The intensity of its light may do permanent damage and may possibly even blind you.

To study the sun, protect your eyes with a smoked glass or a dense photographic negative, or watch its projected image.

Direct viewing—Smoked glass—Get a piece of windowpane. Light a candle. Hold the glass horizontally and move it slowly back and forth through the candle flame until the bottom surface is densely coated with an even layer of soot. Look through this coating at the sun, but for only short periods at a time. Handle the glass with care so you don't rub off the soot.

Photographic negative—Expose a piece of sheet film to direct light. Develop, fix, and dry it in the usual way. You will have a dense and completely black negative through which you may look safely at the sun, but only for a couple of seconds at the time.

¶ *Tip*—In your photographic file, you may have a badly overexposed or overdeveloped negative. This may do the job, provided you take care to look only through an area that is completely black.

Projected viewing—"Camera obscura"—You have probably seen "sunspots" on the forest floor while walking through the woods on a summer day. Although the openings among the leaves are of all kinds of shapes, the sunspots are circular; they are all projected images of the sun. The ancient astronomers made use of this phenomenon. They darkened a room and permitted the light of the sun to enter only through a small hole in the wall. On the opposite wall would form a bright circular spot—an image of the sun. Johannes Fabricius used such a darkened room—*camera obscura*—in 1611 when he observed sunspots for the first time.

Darken a room facing east, south, or west, by taping wrapping paper or pieces of cardboard over the windowpanes. Make a hole in the paper a couple of inches in diameter. Over this hole, tape a piece of cardboard in which you have punched a clean-edged hole, $\frac{1}{8}$ inch or slightly larger in diameter. At a time when the sun shines through this hole, hold a piece of white cardboard in the rays. Move it closer or farther away from the window until the circular spot on it appears as sharp as you can get it. If it is correctly focused, you should be able to see the spots on the surface of the sun. Since no correcting lens is used, the image will be upside down.

HOW?—With binoculars—The warning "NEVER look directly at the sun" is even more emphatic when it comes to using binoculars. Instead, use the binoculars to project an image of the sun.

Projected viewing—Binoculars—Cut a hole in a large piece of cardboard just big enough to fit around one of the eyepieces. Aim the binoculars toward the sun in such a way that the sunlight shines through it. Hold a piece of white cardboard in the rays emerging from the binoculars. Rack out the eyepiece and move it back and forth until the sun image is in sharp focus.

Comets

At rare intervals, a comet hangs in the sky at night, apparently motionless. In spite of the fact that a couple of new comets are discovered every year, many people live through a lifetime without seeing one. Although they are often of tremendous size, most comets are invisible to the naked eye.

BOOK—Robert S. Richardson, *Getting Acquainted with Comets*. New York, McGraw-Hill Book Company.

WHERE? and WHEN?—Except for a few periodically returning comets, there is no way of predicting where or when a comet will appear. When an old comet is due or a new comet has been discovered, every astronomical journal will bring you the details of Where? and When?

Check the position of a returning comet or of a newly discovered comet in the pages of an astronomical journal. Get out a star map or atlas and mark its position on it. Determine which major stars in its vicinity may most easily guide you to it. Then get out under the stars. Locate the guide stars, then study the area until you locate the comet.

HOW?—With the naked eye—If you are alive in 1986, you will have a chance to see the most famous of all comets: Halley's—named for the English astronomer Edmund Halley who plotted its course and predicted its reappearance every seventy-six years. It was last seen in 1910 when it was the astronomical sensation of the day.

With binoculars—Except for seeing Halley's comet, you will need binoculars for looking for comets. Best for the purpose are wide-field binoculars, mounted with an attachment to a firm camera tripod. The 12-degree field makes it possible to view most comets in their entirety. Also, the wide field makes it easier to locate comparison stars for determining the comet's magnitude.

Meteors

Space is full of debris, much of it from existing or dead comets. Generally this debris is invisible, but when particles of it get caught by the Earth's gravity and fall through the atmosphere, the friction created causes them to glow. When these pieces of debris cross the sky in a bright streak, we often call them shooting stars. The correct term is meteors.

From time to time, as the Earth passes through a swarm of such particles, meteors fall through the sky in great numbers, in a regular meteor shower.

WHERE?—Practically every night, as you look around the sky, you will see the streak of an occasional meteor. But for greater success, you should know the places in the sky where most meteors are seen.

The major meteor showers seem to radiate out of certain constellations. They are therefore called by the names of these constellations: the Leonid for the constellation Leo (the Lion), the Orionid for Orion.

WHEN?—Time of year—Meteor showers appear with great regularity throughout the year. The following table of the principal annual showers will tell you on what dates you will see them in greatest numbers (the dates given are for the night when the maximum is due, even though the shower may appear after midnight). But start looking several nights before and continue looking several nights after.

Name of shower	Radiant constellation	Date for maximum	Time of night	Type of trail
QUADRANTID	asterism in Draco	January 3	Late night, after 10 P.M.	Slow, long trails
LYRID	Lyra	April 21	All night, best 1–4 A.M.	Very bright, swift
AQUARID-ETA	Aquarius	May 4	Early morning	Swift streaks
AQUARID-DELTA	Aquarius	July 28	Early morning	Swift streaks
PERSEID	Perseus	August 11	Best after midnight	Swift streaks
DRACONID	Draco	October 9	Late night, after 10 P.M.	Swift streaks
ORIONID	Orion	October 19	Best after midnight	Swift streaks
LEONID	Leo	November 16	Early morning	Very swift streaks
GEMINID	Gemini	December 12	All night, best 1–4 A.M.	Swift, short paths

For the average year the Perseid is the most abundant shower. After that come the Geminid and the Orionid.

Time of night—In the same length of time, you will see twice as many meteors *after* midnight as you will see before. The reason is simple: In the morning we are on the advancing side of the Earth and meet the meteors head on. In the evening we are on the rear of the Earth and the meteors have to catch up with us.

HOW?—For seeing meteors that shoot out of the sky with unpredictable suddenness and disappear within a few seconds, you need the wide-angle view of your unaided eyes. Binoculars are of little use; by the time you get them aimed the meteor has burned out.

Casual observation—If you are just curious about knowing how meteors look, get out under the open night sky for an hour or more at the date for the maximum of one of the principal showers. Dress warmly against the cold of the night. Bring a reclining beach chair for comfort, if you like. Face the constellation from which the shower will radiate and watch the heavenly fireworks. Sate your curiosity, then turn in.

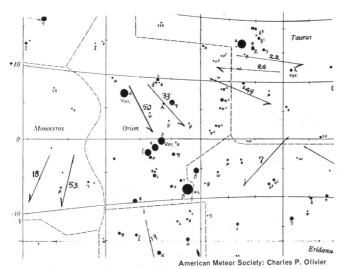

American Meteor Society: Charles P. Olivier

Meteors of the Orionid shower fan out in different directions and are recorded on star map of constellation Orion.

Regular observation—Many amateur astronomers become intensely interested in meteors and do a valuable work in observing and reporting on their observations.

The work of a meteor observer involves watching the skies regularly for two- to four-hour periods on clear nights and making a record of each meteor seen, on a star map of the section of the sky under observation, drawing the paths of the meteors, and numbering the paths in the order seen.

If you are interested in undertaking serious study in the field of meteors, then by all means become a member of the American Meteor Society and join in its activities.

SOCIETY—American Meteor Society. Headquarters: C. P. Olivier, 521 North Wynnewood Avenue, Narbeth, Pennsylvania 19072.

SKY OBSERVING

If stargazing gets you under its spell, the time will come when you will want to do a more thorough job of observing the sky and penetrating deeper into its wonders. For this purpose the unaided eye or your favorite binoculars will no longer suffice. You will need to go to the trouble of choosing and the expense of buying or building a telescope to fit your requirements and of obtaining the necessary accessories.

TELESCOPES—A large number of stores sell telescopes and usually make a great point of advertising the telescope's power of magnification. While these telescopes may satisfy a rank beginner, they will soon disappoint the serious amateur astronomer. You will want better equipment than that. But for this you must be prepared to pay what it is worth. High-quality telescopes are expensive and should be chosen with great care.

¶ *Tip*—Before purchasing a telescope, find out what amateur astronomers live in your neighborhood. Ask for a chance to see their equipment and get their advice.

In choosing a telescope, check carefully for good workmanship and consider each of these points:

Light grasp—The light-gathering power, often referred to as the light grasp, depends on the size of the objective, which may be a lens or a mirror. An objective one inch in diameter gathers as much light as nine human eyes. The power increases by this amount (9) multiplied by the square of the diameter of the objective. A 3-inch objective ($9 \times 3 \times 3 = 81$) would be more than twice as light-gathering as a 2-inch ($9 \times 2 \times 2 = 36$), a 6-inch objective ($9 \times 6 \times 6 = 324$) four times as light-gathering as a 3-inch.

Stars are mathematical points in the sky: You can't increase their size even with the largest telescope, but you can increase their apparent brightness.

The light-gathering power, therefore, rather than the magnification, is what determines the effectiveness of a telescope. As a trained astronomer would say, "To find a lost object in a dark room, you need a light rather than a magnifying glass."

Magnifying power—The objective of the telescope gathers the light and converges the rays into a focal plane image. The eyepiece picks up the light rays of this image, bends them, and sends them into your eye in such a way that you see a much larger image than you would see without the eyepiece. The longer the objective's focal length—the distance between the objective and the plane at which the light rays are focused—and the shorter the focal length of the eyepiece the larger the magnification or power.

This is the formula:

$$\text{Magnification} = \frac{\text{Focal length of objective}}{\text{Focal length of eyepiece}}$$

If your objective (lens or reflecting mirror) has a focal length of 50 inches and you use it with a $\frac{1}{4}$-inch eyepiece, you will get $50 \div \frac{1}{4} = 200$ power ($200 \times$). With a $\frac{1}{2}$-inch eyepiece the same objective would give you $50 \div \frac{1}{2} = 100 \times$ magnification.

Don't aim for too high a magnification. With high magnification you magnify not only the image but also the vibration of your telescope and other disturbing factors, while at the same time decreasing the image brightness. Experts on telescopes agree that the maximum useful magnification is about $50 \times$ per inch of objective

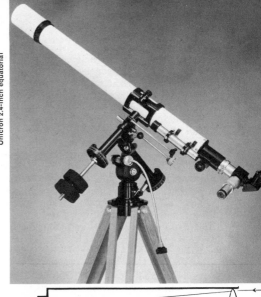

Refracting telescope consists of a closed tube with an objective lens at the top and an eyepiece at bottom.

Unicron 2.4-inch equatorial

Diagrams show principles of the two major kinds of telescopes: refracting (top), and reflecting (bottom). Light enters from right.

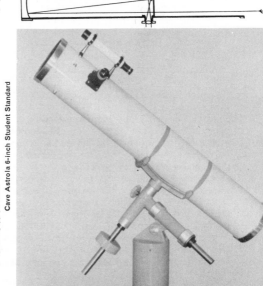

Cave Astrola 6-inch Student Standard

Reflecting telescope has an open tube with a concave mirror at bottom, a smaller mirror at center, and an eyepiece on the side.

diameter. This means a maximum of 150× for a 3-inch telescope, 300× for a 6-inch telescope.

Resolving power—The resolving power of a telescope is its power to bring out sharp details of the heavenly bodies at which it is pointed—the craters of the moon or the markings on Jupiter or Mars—and to separate objects that are close together, such as double stars and the stars of a cluster.

The resolving power depends on the size and quality of the objective. The larger the diameter, the greater the power. But here again, there is a certain limit known as "Dawes' limit." This limit, expressed in seconds ($1/3600$ of a degree of arc), is found by dividing the number 4.5 by the diameter of the objective in inches. Within this limit, a 3-inch lens should show, as two separate stars, a double with its components 1.5 seconds apart.

Refracting telescopes—The refracting telescope consists of a closed tube with an objective lens at the top and an eyepiece at the bottom. The lens gathers the light, refracts (bends) the rays into a focal plane image, which is then magnified by the eyepiece. The resulting image is inverted—upside down and "left-handed." In good telescopes, the lens is "achromatic," that is, it refracts light in such a way that the image is practically free from extraneous colors.

Advantages: The closed tube eliminates disturbing air currents; the optical elements stay in perfect alignment indefinitely and require no special care.

Disadvantages: The tube of a refractor needs to be long and therefore requires a heavy mounting; the color fringes—"chromatic aberration"—cannot be completely eliminated; its cost is high because the manufacture of the objective lens calls for high-grade glass and expert craftsmanship, and its assembly requires high precision.

For serious study, the objective lens should have a minimum diameter of 3 inches. Because of cost and portability, a 4-inch refractor is probably the maximum that most amateur astronomers will want to buy.

Reflecting telescopes—The reflecting telescope consists of an open tube, in the bottom of which is placed a glass disk turned into a concave mirror by an aluminum coating, a small mirror set at a diagonal in the center of the tube, and an eyepiece near the front end of the tube. The light from the stars is reflected from the concave mirror into the diagonal mirror and focused into an image which is then enlarged by the eyepiece.

Advantages: The cost is low as compared with the cost of a refractor of the same objective size—about one-third. The reflector is entirely free of color errors because the light is reflected, not refracted. It is easier to align than the refractor. For these reasons, the reflector is the most popular choice among amateur astronomers.

Disadvantages: These all result from its open tube. Air currents within the tube may fuzz the image, and moisture and dust on the mirror will necessitate occasional realuminization of the mirror.

OTHER EQUIPMENT—Finder scopes—The telescope itself has a very small field of view. Therefore it should be provided with a finder scope of a wider field of view that will help in aiming the telescope toward a specific part of the sky. Finder scopes usually have a magnification of 4× to 7×.

Eyepieces—You need several removable eyepieces of varying focal lengths for getting the desired magnification. Most commonly used eyepieces are of ¼-inch, ½-inch, and 1-inch focal lengths. For a refractor telescope, you will want a *prism star diagonal* for ease in observing.

¶ *Tip*—You may want to include a Barlow lens in your equipment. This lens, placed in the tube behind the eyepiece, will double or triple the magnification.

Mounts—A portable telescope is mounted on a sturdy tripod for viewing. A semiportable telescope—one in which the instrument can be removed from the mount—may be used on a mount set permanently into the ground or onto a roof. An extra heavy telescope would be attached to a permanent mounting set on the floor of an observatory building. Mountings of two types are used for telescopes: altazimuth and equatorial.

ALTAZIMUTH MOUNT—The altazimuth mount permits the telescope to be swung up and down for altitude, from side to side for azimuth. It has the disadvantage that it needs to be reset continually, as the stars move out of the viewing field.

EQUATORIAL MOUNT—The equatorial mount is the mount used by all serious amateur astronomers. It has two axes at right angles to each other: polar and declination. After the polar axis is fixed to the celestial pole, the telescope can be moved about the declination axis to find a star and to keep it constantly in view as the Earth rotates. Some of these mounts come with *setting circles* for the quick location of an object in the sky.

¶ *Tip*—A *clock drive* attached to the equatorial mount will do the tracking for you. This attachment is imperative for long-exposure photography.

Specialized accessories—For special studies, you will need special accessories: solar filter and projection screen for studying the sun, lunar filter and lunar lens for viewing the moon, and color filters for the planets.

SUPPLIES—REFRACTOR TELESCOPES—Unicron Instrument Company, 66 Needham Street, Newton Highlands, Massachusetts 02161.

REFLECTOR TELESCOPES—Astronomics Inc., 1 Industrial Road, Woodridge, New Jersey 07075.

Cave Optical Company, 4137 East Anaheim Street, Long Beach, California 90804.

Criterion Manufacturing Company, 331 Church Street, Hartford, Connecticut 06101.

Optical Craftsmen, Inc., 20962 Itasca Street, Chatsworth, California 91311.

Sight Instruments, 2620 East Pacific Highway, Long Beach, California 90804.

REFRACTORS AND REFLECTORS—Edmund Scientific Company, 100 Edscorp Building, Barrington, New Jersey 08007.

Telescope Making

To get special satisfaction and to save money, numerous amateur astronomers make their own large-objective telescopes. Some of them buy the parts and assemble their telescopes themselves. Others go a step further: They grind their own optics and build their telescopes and mounts from various pieces of pipes and joints.

It is well-nigh impossible for an amateur to make a satisfactory refracting telescope. The lens is the major obstacle, but the precision needed for assembly is hard to achieve.

It is a different matter with the reflector. The mirror can be ground quite easily from a glass blank by a person with sufficient determination, endurance, and muscle power, and the assembly is not too difficult. To simplify matters: There are several excellent books on the subject; several optical companies make kits available with full instructions; and certain universities, observatories, natural history museums, and planetariums have classes in mirror grinding and telescope making.

BOOKS ON TELESCOPE MAKING—Albert C. Ingalls, *Amateur Telescope Making.* Book I (Elementary), Book II (Advanced), Book III (Specialized). Scientific American Inc., 415 Madison Avenue, New York 10016.

Allyn J. Thompson, *Making Your Own Telescope.* Sky Publishing Corporation, Cambridge, Massachusetts 02138.

Jean Texereau, *How to Make a Telescope.* New York, John Wiley & Sons.

Sam Brown, *All About Telescopes.* Edmund Scientific Company. (For address, see below.)

Henry E. Paul, *Telescopes for Skygazing.* Philadelphia, Chilton Book Company.

Neale E. Howard, *Standard Handbook for Telescope Making.* New York, Thomas Y. Crowell.

KITS FOR TELESCOPE MAKING—Edmund Scientific Company, 100 Edscorp Building, Barrington, New Jersey 08007.

A. Jaegers, 691 Merrick Road, Lynbrook, New York 11563.

Using the Telescope

When you first obtain a telescope, you will want to go hunting with it for the "showpieces" of the universe. You will probably aim it first at the moon to see with your own eyes what you have so far seen only in photographs: craters and clefts, walls and rays. Next come the planets. You will study the belts of Jupiter, you will see the rings of Saturn, and you may succeed in locating Uranus and

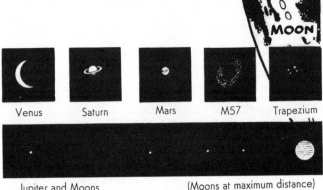

Venus   Saturn   Mars   M57   Trapezium

Jupiter and Moons   (Moons at maximum distance)

**Look at sketches with one eye from distance of ten inches
to get the same size obtained with a telescope at 100×.**

Neptune. Then comes the turn of special features among the constellations: the gaseous Great Nebula of Orion, and the hazy smoke Ring Nebula of Lyra, the globular cluster of Hercules, perhaps Mizar in Ursa Major, the first double star discovered.

With those out of your system, you will start looking for numerous other objects in the sky. For this, you will need star maps and atlases, special charts, and list of the spectacular "M" objects, enumerated by the French astronomer Charles Messier.

BOOKS—R. N. Mayall, M. Mayall, and J. Wyckoff, *The Sky Observer's Guide*. New York, Golden Press.

T. W. Webb, *Celestial Objects for Common Telescopes* (two volumes). New York, Dover Publications.

Menzel's *Field Guide* and Olcott's *Field Book* suggest many objects for telescope study.

ATLASES—A. P. Norton and J. G. Inglis, *Norton's Star Atlas*. Sky Publishing Corporation. (For address, see page 362.)

ANNUALS — *The American Ephemeris and Nautical Calendar*. Catalog No. D213.8 (current year). $6.00. From Superintendent of Documents, U.S. Government Printing Office, Washington, D.C. 20402.

Observer's Handbook (current year). Royal Astronomical Society of Canada, 252 College Street, Toronto 28, Ontario, Canada.

Keeping records—For all serious study, you will want to keep records of your work. When observing, have a small table near at hand for atlas, red flashlight (see page 344), notebook, and pencils.

Make notes of the date and time, the viewing conditions and magnifications used, the objects studied, special features observed.

If you want to go one step further and are willing to undertake specialized astronomical work, you will find that there are two areas in which amateur astronomers are particularly qualified to make major scientific contributions: in the study of variable stars and in planetary observations.

Variable Stars

Thousands of amateur astronomers around the world are joined in an association for observing variable stars. Their work consists in comparing a certain variable star's magnitude at regular intervals with the magnitude of neighboring stars, and in submitting their findings monthly on special report blanks. Such reports have made it possible for professional astronomers to compute the periods of numerous variables and to predict the time of maximum and minimum brightness. They have also added to a further understanding of the structure of the universe.

SOCIETY—American Association of Variable Star Observers. Headquarters: 187 Concord Avenue, Boston, Massachusetts 02138.

BOOK—Margaret W. Mayall, *Manual for Observing Variable Stars*. $1. From AAVSO headquarters.

Planetary Observations

If you possess a 3-inch or better telescope and have just the least bit of drawing ability, you can participate in a valuable scientific pursuit by joining with many other amateur astronomers who concentrate on the study of the planets. The task consists in observing the planets and then sketching inside previously drawn circles at least 2 inches in diameter (or on blank disks provided by ALPO to its members), the markings you have observed: the polar caps and "canals" of Mars, the belts and zones and "red spot" of Jupiter, the rings of Saturn, the slanting bands of Uranus. Upon completion, send your sketches, with complete data and notes, to ALPO headquarters.

Carefully made drawings of these planets have provided data about their changing appearances and their rotation speeds and may,

Blank (left) as used by members of Association of Lunar and Planetary Observers for sketching Jupiter (right).

eventually, clear up some of the mysteries still connected with these distant bodies.

The magnification most frequently used in planetary work ranges around 30× or 40× per inch of objective.

SOCIETY—Association of Lunar and Planetary Observers. Headquarters: Box AZ, University Park, Las Cruces, New Mexico 88001. Periodical: *The Strolling Astronomer*.

ASTRONOMICAL PHOTOGRAPHY

The scope you set for photographing the heavenly bodies depends on your ambition and your pocketbook. For simple photographs of the stars in their courses, you may use whatever camera you have. For true astrophotography intended for astronomical investigation, you need special cameras attached to telescopes that can follow the object for hours, if necessary.

Simple Photography

EQUIPMENT—**Camera and lenses**—For photographing star trails and single constellations, any camera will do as long as it can take a time exposure. To be sure to get a whole constellation onto your negative, you may have to use a wide-angle lens. For photographing the moon, you will need a telephoto lens.

Tripod—Since most astronomical photography requires time exposure and is done with the camera at odd angles, all shots will require a sturdy tripod provided with a tilt-top head.

Cardboard square—In some cameras, opening and closing the shutter—even with a cable release—is accompanied by a slight jarring of the camera. Such a movement may result in a "pigtail" on your negative. To prevent this, use a piece of black cardboard in front of the lens for controlling the exposures.

Films—For photographing star trails and constellations, pick a high-speed black-and-white panchromatic film of good contrast or a high-speed color film.

WHAT TO PHOTOGRAPH—Photographing the stars in their apparent motion across the sky will result in some spectacular shots.

Circumpolar star trails—Pick a moonless night with a clear, black sky. Adjust your camera on its tripod in such a way that it is aimed at the northern sky with Polaris in the center. Set the distance for infinity, the lens at the widest opening, the shutter for time. Hold the cardboard in front of the lens, open the shutter, wait five seconds for possible camera movement to stop. Remove the cardboard. Keep the shutter open for at least three hours. Again cover the lens with the cardboard, and close the shutter. The result is a circular sweep of the stars, as of a giant carousel.

Other star trails—On other nights, face east, west, and south, and take other star-trail photos. East and west shots will show almost straight slanting lines. The south shot will have long rather flat arcs.

Constellations—Black-and-white—While the ordinary film in the ordinary camera will make it possible for you to photograph star trails, it takes an extremely high-speed film and a special camera to photograph individual constellations. Such a film is the Polaroid 3000. And such a camera is the Polaroid Land camera of a model that permits time exposure.

Set up the camera for taking a star trails photo, but aim it at the constellation you desire to photograph. Use the black cardboard in front of the lens while opening the shutter, as described above. Expose for 30 seconds. Replace cardboard and close the shutter. Then, for extra contrast, develop two to four times the length of the usual development time—that is, 30 to 60 seconds instead of 15 at 70° F, 2 minutes or more at 35° F, and so on.

Constellations—Color—Shots of the constellations taken with highest-speed color film can be very spectacular in showing the different colors of various stars: red Betelgeuse, bluish-white Vega, yellow Capella, golden Albireo. Because of the comparatively slow speed of color films, these shots have to be taken in the form of star trails, at 10- to 20-minute time exposures.

¶ *Tip*—To make the constellations more prominent when projected, make a fine needle-prick in the slide at the end of each star trail.

Moon—The moon, covering only $\frac{1}{2}$ degree of the sky, is unsatisfactory unless shot with a telephoto lens. When shooting the moon in black-and-white, use a medium-fast film and increase the contrast with a yellow filter over your lens. When using color, do not shoot beyond 1 second; at slower speeds the moon will have moved so much that a blurred picture results.

For a sequence of the phases of the moon, start by taking several shots of the full moon to determine the proper exposure. Then, after the next new moon, shoot the other phases, increasing the exposure ten times for the crescent moon, five times for first quarter, two times for the gibbous phase.

Astrophotography

Photographing the craters of the moon, the planets, the nebulae, the galaxies, and other astro objects requires the use of a telescope on an equatorial mount provided with a clock drive. Depending on the telescope you have, you may be able to use your favorite camera. If you want to go in seriously for astrophotography, it will pay you to provide your telescope with the kind of camera arrangement most suited for it.

For this kind of photography, you need special handbooks, with tables of angular and linear fields, image size, equivalent exposure for various f/ values, etc.

REFERENCES—Sam Brown, *Photography with Your Telescope*. Edmund Scientific Company. (For address, see page 362.)

George T. Keene, *Star Gazing with Telescope and Camera*. Philadelphia, Chilton Books.

opposite edge of the table. Turn the umbrella slowly in a counter-clockwise motion to show the rising and setting of some of the stars and to show that the circumpolar stars never dip below the horizon.

Canetarium—A planetarium is an expensive gadget; a canetarium isn't. As the word suggests, a canetarium is a primitive planetarium made from tin cans.

Collect a number of empty tin cans of the same size—frozen-juice cans, soup cans, vegetable cans, or even gallon cans. Remove the tops completely from the cans. Spray or brush insides and outsides of the cans with flat black paint or dull black enamel. Dry. From one of your star books, copy the main constellations on thin tracing paper, in a size to fit one end of each tin can. Paste each drawing face-down onto the bottom of a tin can. Using a hammer and nails of different sizes, make a hole for each star. Vary the size of the holes in accord with the star's magnitude.

Line up the cans along a windowsill and look into them against the light.

Constellation projector—Prepare the cans as for the canetarium, but do not blacken the inside.

Put on a show in a darkened room. Light a flashlight. Hold it inside each can in turn, shining the light at a slant against the inside of the can to project the resulting constellation image onto the white ceiling.

SOLAR SYSTEM PROJECTS—Comparative planet sizes—To demonstrate the comparative sizes of the planets, make a display of a number of globular items of varying diameters: ball bearings, marbles, Christmas balls; peas, nuts, citrus fruits; ping-pong, tennis, basketballs. Or roll the balls from modeling clay. Line up the balls with a label next to each item giving the name and actual size in miles, as given in your almanac. A 1-inch Earth would require that you keep your ambition within bounds.

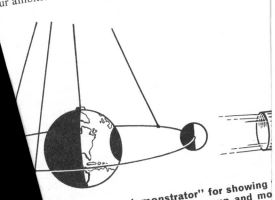

a simple "lunar demonstrator" for showing the moon and eclipses of the sun and moon

Circumpolar stars make a circular trail when camera is pointed toward northern sky and left open eight hours.

Color slide of Orion (left) with main stars accentuated by needle pricks. Black-and-white Polaroid of Orion (right).

STAR STUDY DEVICES

"Go, and catch a falling star," said the poet. Wish it were possible, but it isn't. You cannot catch a star and put it on a pin for display as you can an insect. You cannot press a constellation between sheets of blotting paper the way you can a flower. But you can make representations in miniature of the heavenly bodies and models of their apparent motion that will give you—and others to whom you show them—an idea of the wonders of the heavens. And you can develop certain devices that will give you and others a better insight into astronomy.

STAR PROJECTS—Polaris sighting sticks—Cut two straight sticks, 2 and 4 feet long respectively. On a starry night, push the taller stick upright into the ground. Get down on all fours. Move the shorter stick until you have its tip lined up with the tip of the longer stick and the two tips with Polaris. Push the shorter stick into the ground.

The line between the longer stick and the shorter stick is a true north–south line. Mark it by stretching a string between the sticks.

The degrees of the angle between a line connecting the tips of the sighting sticks and a horizontal line is your local latitude.

Star map—Get a circular star map. Depending on the use you want to make of it, pick a map centered on Polaris (to emphasize circumpolar stars), a map showing the summer sky, or one showing the winter sky. Copy the map onto tracing paper. Crisscross it with horizontal and vertical lines at even distances apart. Paste pieces of paper together into a sheet 4 feet square and draw on it a 4-foot circle. Mark off the sheet into as many squares as you have on the small map. Enlarge the constellations, by the square method, onto the large sheet.

Cut out a 4-foot circle from wallboard or plywood, and paint it

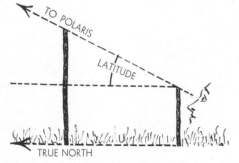

At night, set up two sticks and sight them toward Polaris, to find north direction and the local latitude.

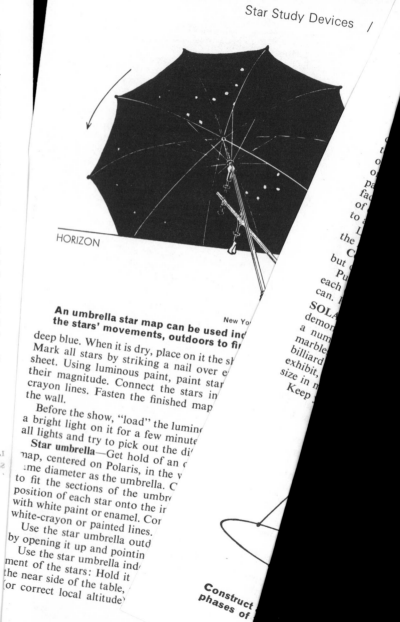

HORIZON

An umbrella star map can be used ind New Yo **the stars' movements, outdoors to fi**

deep blue. When it is dry, place on it the s
Mark all stars by striking a nail over e
sheet. Using luminous paint, paint star
their magnitude. Connect the stars in
crayon lines. Fasten the finished map
the wall.

Before the show, "load" the lumin
a bright light on it for a few minute
all lights and try to pick out the di'

Star umbrella—Get hold of an
map, centered on Polaris, in the v
me diameter as the umbrella. C
to fit the sections of the umbr
position of each star onto the ir
with white paint or enamel. Cor
white-crayon or painted lines.

Use the star umbrella outd
by opening it up and pointin
Use the star umbrella ind
ment of the stars: Hold it
the near side of the table,
or correct local altitude

**Construct
phases of**

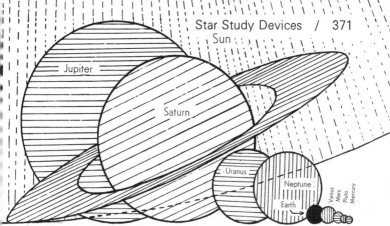

By using globular items of various sizes, you can arrange a display showing the comparative sizes of the nine planets.

a 1-foot Jupiter and a 9-foot sun. A diameter of $\frac{1}{4}$ inch for the Earth may be more appropriate (in the proportion of $\frac{1}{32}$ inch equals 1,000 miles). In this case, you might use the following items (or other items of same size): Mercury, tiny pea ($\frac{3}{32}$ inch); Venus and Earth, peas ($\frac{1}{4}$ inch); Mars, small pea ($\frac{1}{8}$ inch); Jupiter, orange ($2\frac{3}{4}$ inches); Saturn, tangerine ($2\frac{1}{4}$ inches); Uranus and Neptune, walnuts (1 inch); Pluto, small pea ($\frac{1}{8}$ inch); sun, beach ball (27 inches). Use thin cardboard to make the ring for Saturn, with $2\frac{1}{4}$-inch-inside and 4-inch-outside diameters.

¶ *Tip*—To remember the order of the planets from the sun, use this sentence: *Me*n *V*ery *E*arly *Ma*de *J*ars *S*erve *U*seful *N*eeds. (*P*eriod)

Comparative planet orbits—Don't attempt to make an indoor exhibit showing the comparative size of the planet orbits using your planet models. At whatever dimension you made it, the comparable size of the planets would be that of grains of sand. Instead, turn this into a dramatic outdoor demonstration for the group you are working with.

Take the planet models, in the $\frac{1}{32}$-inch equals 1,000 miles size used above, onto a football field. Place the model of the sun on one goal line. Give a "planet" to each of your helpers. Send the person with the tiny pea representing Mercury 31 yards down the field (to a point 1 yard beyond the 30-yard line). Send the pea for Venus 58 yards down the field (8 yards beyond the center line), the pea for Earth 80 yards (the opposite 20-yard line), the tiny pea for Mars 123 yards (a point 23 yards beyond the opposite goalposts). This is probably where you would want to stop because Jupiter should be $\frac{1}{4}$ mile away from your starting point; Saturn, $\frac{1}{2}$ mile; Uranus, 1 mile; Neptune, $1\frac{1}{2}$ miles; Pluto, 2 miles.

Lunar demonstrator—You can demonstrate the phases of the moon, and the eclipses of the sun and the moon, with an easily made "lunar demonstrator."

Bend a 10-foot length of heavy wire, 16 gauge or better, into a ring about 3 feet in diameter. Get a white ball a couple of inches in diameter (styrofoam, rubber, ping-pong). Make a hole through the ball to fit the diameter of the wire and push the ball onto the wire. Solder or tape the wire ends together. Tie four strings to the ring. Suspend the ring horizontally at eye level from a hook in the ceiling or in a wide doorway. Darken the room. Illuminate the ball with a flashlight, an unshaded bulb, or, even better, a slide projector or a photographic spotlight.

MOON-PHASE DEMONSTRATION—Place the light source outside the ring, slightly higher than the ring. Step inside the ring and bring your eyes up to the level of the ring. Move the ring around slowly. When the ball is between your eyes and the light (the sun), it will be black: new moon. Ball to your left will show first quarter; ball to your right, last quarter; ball behind you, full moon.

SUN-ECLIPSE DEMONSTRATION—Place the light source outside the ring, at the height of the ring. Hang a large ball (to represent the Earth) or, better, a globe, in the middle of the ring, at the same height. Take a position near the light source, outside the ring. Swing the ring around so that the ball on it (the moon) is between the sun and the Earth and casts a shadow on the Earth. Inhabitants of the Earth within the darkened part will see an eclipse of the sun, covering only a part of the Earth.

MOON-ECLIPSE DEMONSTRATION—Same setup as for sun eclipse. Swing the ball representing the moon to the opposite side into the shadow of the Earth. The result is a moon eclipse, completely swallowing up the moon in the Earth's shadow, visible to all inhabitants of the dark side of the Earth.

SUN PROJECTS—Direction finding—Sun-and-watch method—Hold your watch in a horizontal position. Place a short piece of straw upright against the edge of the watch at the point of the hour hand.

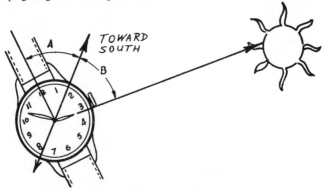

Use wristwatch to check directions. Point hour hand to sun. Line halfway between hand and 12 points toward south.

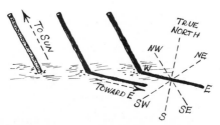

Push a stick into the ground, pointing it directly at the sun. Wait for a shadow to form. Shadow will point east.

Turn the watch until the shadow of the straw falls exactly along the hour hand, that is, until the hour hand points toward the sun. A line from the center of the watch, dividing in half the angle between the hour hand and the numeral 12, will give you an approximate direction toward true south, provided the watch shows standard time.

Shadowless shadow-stick method—Push a short straight stick, about 10 inches long, into the ground in such a way that it casts no shadow, that is, so that it points directly at the sun. Wait until the stick makes a shadow about 6 inches long. This shadow forms a fairly accurate west–east line, with west at the stick and east at the shadow tip.

Shadow-stick method—Push a straight staff, about 5 feet long,

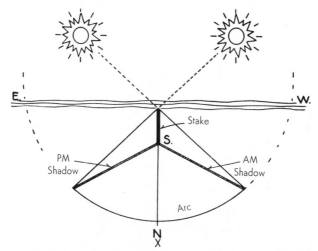

To find true north, set up shadow stick and divide distance between tips of morning and evening shadows in half.

upright into the ground on a level, cleared spot. In the morning, scratch an arc of a circle on the ground, with the staff as center and the length of the staff's shadow as radius. To do this, tie one end of a string loosely around the staff with a loop (bowline), and tie the other end onto the short pointed stick you use for the scratching. Push a peg into the ground at the point where the tip of the staff's shadow touched the arc of the circle — then wait. As the sun climbs in the sky, the staff's shadow gets shorter, then lengthens again in the afternoon.

When the tip of the staff's afternoon shadow touches the circle, place another peg at the touching point. Draw a line from this peg to the peg you placed in the morning. Find the halfway point of this line. Draw a line from this point to the staff. This is a meridian line. This is the line along which the sun casts the shadow at its highest point in the sky for the day. It is a true north—south line, with south toward the staff.

SUNDIALS—If the Earth rotated with even speed within a twenty-four-hour period, the shadow stick would be a perfect timepiece: Just divide the movement of its shadow into 15-degree segments, and each would represent one hour. Unfortunately, as the ancients found out, that is not the way it works out. But also, as the ancients discovered, by pointing the shadow stick toward the celestial pole, toward Polaris, the problem could be overcome except for a difference of a few minutes. And so they developed the sundial in the form we still have it today: a dial surface marked with the hours of the day and provided with a shadow-casting pointer, or *gnomon*.

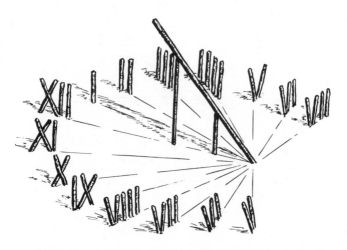

For a rustic sundial, setup the gnomon over the tips of two Polaris sighting sticks. Show hours in Roman numerals.

**Vertical sundial is designed
for hanging on a wall facing
exactly toward the south.**

**Equatorial sundial uses half
a ring or a complete ring
instead of flat dial.**

All photos courtesy:
Sundials, New Ipswich, N.H.

**Horizontal sundial is placed with its dial level on a column
or post and its gnomon pointing directly toward Polaris.**

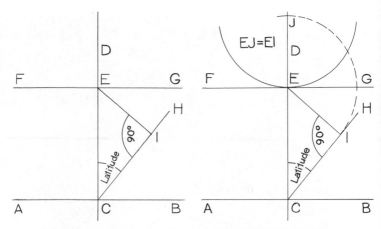

The construction of a sundial is a geometrical project. It is quite easy if you follow the steps described on page 377.

This pointer can be an actual pointing rod, pointing toward Polaris. Or it can be the hypotenuse of a right-angled triangle aimed at Polaris. The latter is the method used in the usual commercially available garden sundial in which the triangular gnomon is made of metal or some other permanent material. The former is the method you would use for putting up a rustic sundial in camp.

Sundial in camp—To make a simple sundial for camp, start by setting up on some starlit night, on a cleared spot, the Polaris sighting sticks described on page 368. With this task done, rest a long, straight, pointed stick on top of the two sighting sticks, with its point touching the ground. Now, keeping the stick at the angle at which it is resting, hammer its pointed end firmly into the ground, and you have established the gnomon of your sundial.

The north-pointing line underneath the gnomon stick is the 12 noon line of your sundial. A line at right angles to this first line, at the point where the stick enters the ground, gives you the 6 A.M. line toward the west, the 6 P.M. line toward the east. Divide the right angle toward the west into six equal angles to establish the lines for 7, 8, 9, 10, 11 A.M. Divide the right angle toward the east similarly to establish the lines for 1, 2, 3, 4, 5 P.M. Mark these lines by scratching the numerals in the ground or by pushing short sticks into the ground in the shape of the Roman numerals.

On sunny days, the shadow of this primitive gnomon will give you a fair idea of the passing of the hours.

Horizontal sundial — To lay out the dial surface of a more exact sundial, you must go in for a bit of geometry:

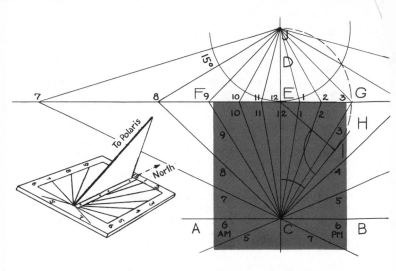

The shaded portion of the finished design is the actual dial. Set up sundial and gnomon as shown in sketch to the left.

On a large sheet of paper (a cut-up large grocery bag will give you a sheet about 18 by 35 inches) draw a horizontal line AB. This will be the 6 A.M. to 6 P.M. line of your dial.

At the middle of line AB, mark point C and draw a vertical line through it: CD. On this line, about 10 inches above C, mark point E. Through this point, draw a horizontal line FEG.

To the right of the line CD, from point C, draw a line CH in such a way that the angle DCH is equal to your latitude. From E, draw a line to cross line CH at a right angle; mark the crossing point I. On line CD, lay off EJ equal to distance EI. With J as the center and using a protractor, lay out 15-degree angles to line FEG. Mark those to the right of E for the afternoon hours of 1, 2, 3, 4, and 5; those to the left of E for the morning hours of 11, 10, 9, 8, and 7.

From C, draw lines to these ten markings. Draw the 5-A.M. line as continuation of the 5-P.M. line, and the 7-P.M. line as continuation of the 7-A.M. line.

Your geometrical constrution is now completed. Develop the part below the line FEG into whatever shape of dial you prefer: square, rectangular, or circular. Then transfer the design to your material— wood or metal — and paint in the hour markings.

Note—If the gnomon you intend to use is wider than a piece of sheet metal, cut the pattern along line CD and separate the two parts by the thickness of the gnomon.

Place the dial horizontally and fasten onto it a gnomon made to the triangular design of CEH, with its EC edge on the dial's EC line. Turn the finished dial in such a way that the CH edge of the gnomon points directly to Polaris.

Vertical sundial—Instead of a horizontal sundial, you may prefer a vertical one, placed on a wall facing due south. For this, follow the same geometrical procedure as above, with this difference: The angle DCH must be equal to 90 degrees minus your latitude.

The completed vertical sundial is hung on the wall with the 6-A.M.—6-P.M. line horizontal and the 12-noon line at the bottom.

Sundial time—Sundials kept marvelous time in ancient days — when all the people of the community lived by the sundial on the church tower or the manor house. Nowadays they don't—what with sidereal time, mean time, standard time, daylight-saving time, time zones.

Sundials are on clock time around solstice times—June and December—but up to sixteen minutes off in February and October. For the number of minutes to be added or substracted for each day of the year, to arrive at mean solar time, refer to your copy of *American Ephemeris* (see page 363) or to the following table.

Jan.			Apr.			Aug.			Nov.		
	2	+ 4 min.		2	+ 4 min.		12	+ 5 min.		10	—16 min.
	5	+ 5		5	+ 3		17	+ 4		17	—15
	7	+ 6		8	+ 2		22	+ 3		22	—14
	9	+ 7		12	+ 1		26	+ 2		25	—13
	12	+ 8		15	+ 0		29	+ 1		29	—12
	14	+ 9		20	— 1	Sept.	1	+ 0	Dec.	1	—11
	17	+10		28	— 2		5	— 1		4	—10
	20	+11	May	2	— 3		8	— 2		6	— 9
	24	+12		15	— 4		11	— 3		9	— 8
	28	+13		28	— 3		13	— 4		11	— 7
Feb.	4	+14	June	4	— 2		16	— 5		13	— 6
	20	+14		10	— 1		19	— 6		15	— 5
	27	+13		15	— 0		22	— 7		17	— 4
Mar.	4	+12		20	+ 1		25	— 8		19	— 3
	8	+11		24	+ 2		27	— 9		21	— 2
	12	+10		29	+ 3	Oct.	1	—10		23	— 1
	16	+ 9	July	4	+ 4		4	—11		24	— 0
	19	+ 8		10	+ 5		7	—12		27	+ 1
	23	+ 7		19	+ 6		11	—13		29	+ 2
	26	+ 6					15	—14		31	+ 3
	29	+ 5					20	—15			
							28	—16			

Sundial mottos — Somehow, a sundial without a motto seems incomplete. Here are a few traditional ones. Pick whichever you like or write one of your own:

I show only the sunny hours.   Time waits for no man.
It is later than you think.   Tempus fugit.
The hour passed cannot be recalled.   Our time is all today.
Tomorrow is another day.

ACKNOWLEDGMENTS

A BOOK of this type is not one man's job. A hundred years of living would not suffice to carry through its many suggestions. The activities described in it have come into being through the work of a great many scientists throughout the years. In gathering them together in a single volume, I have received the help of numerous people—in person and through their writings. The books that are listed throughout this volume have been valuable sources of information and inspiration. I owe to each of their authors a great debt of gratitude. Many of the methods described are standard procedures—originated, tested, and improved by countless nameless scientists; others are the ideas of individuals whose names are known. Wherever possible, I have traced the source of an idea and have given the originator due credit. In the cases where I may have failed, I offer my apologies. Credit would certainly have been given if I had known to whom it belonged.

For the checking of the manuscript, I have received the willing and generous help of a large number of people. Part I was checked by Raymond L. Taylor, American Association for the Advancement of Science; Harry E. Radcliffe, American Nature Association; Richard L. Weaver, American Nature Study Society. The chapters of Part II were checked as follows: Birds—Carl W. Buchheister, National Audubon Society; Herbert Friedman, Smithsonian Institution. Mammals—A. L. Nelson and William H. Stickel, Patuxent Research Refuge, Fish and Wildlife Service, U.S. Department of the Interior; Donald F. Hoffmeister, American Society of Mammalogists. Reptiles—Roger Conant, Philadelphia Zoological Garcen; M. Graham Netting, American Society of Ichthyologists and Herpetologists; Chapman Grant, Herpetologists League. Insects—Cyril F. dos Passos, American Museum of Natural History; Avery S. Hoyt, Bureau of Entomology and Plant Quarantine, U.S. Department of Agriculture. Flowers—Reed C. Rollins, Gray Herbarium, Harvard University; P. L. Ricker, The Wild Flower Preservation Society; Edna A. Clark, The Garden Club of America. Trees—J. P. McWilliams, American Forestry Association; Charles E. Randall, Forest Service, U.S. Department of Agriculture.

Of the 300 drawings and diagrams that illustrate the book, more than 90 per cent were made by the late artist, Francis J. Rigney. Credits for the remaining drawings are given directly below them.

With the exception of a number of photographs taken by the author, the photographic illustrations were provided by various organizations, manufacturers, biological supply houses, and individual naturalists. Their names are indicated in credit lines next to their contributions. A special vote of thanks goes to Ward's Natural Science Establishment, of Rochester, New York. Not only did this establishment, through Mr. Henry L. Gresham, make available a number of original photographs, it also made it possible for me to take a number of photographs on its premises, with the able assistance of several of its staff members.

—WILLIAM HILLCOURT

PROJECT INDEX

While this *Field Book of Nature Activities and Hobbies* contains close to 1,000 suggestions for nature activities and hobbies, the following 500 projects are particularly suitable for group work—school, camp, club, Scout patrol or troop, Cub Scout and Brownie group—along the lines indicated on page 40.

You may also want to accept some of them as personal challenges. They are graded as follows:

- ● Simple projects for beginners, requiring little or no equipment.
- ● ● Projects involving elementary knowledge, sustained effort, and some equipment.
- ● ● ● Projects requiring advanced knowledge, extra effort, and specialized equipment.

3. BIRDS

4. ANIMALS

5. SNAKES, LIZARDS, AND TURTLES

6. INSECTS

7. WATER LIFE

9. TREES

11. WEATHER

12. THE HEAVENS

Subject Index